# THE
# FRENCH BETRAYAL
## OF
# AMERICA

ALSO BY KENNETH R. TIMMERMAN

# THE
# FRENCH BETRAYAL
## OF
# AMERICA

KENNETH R. TIMMERMAN

CROWN
FORUM
NEW YORK

Published by Crown Forum, New York, New York.
Member of the Crown Publishing Group, a division of Random House, Inc.
www.randomhouse.com

CROWN FORUM and the Crown Forum colophon are trademarks of Random House, Inc.

Printed in the United States of America

*Design by Barbara Sturman*

Library of Congress Cataloging-in-Publication Data is available upon request.

ISBN 1-4000-5366-8

10  9  8  7  6  5  4  3  2  1

First Edition

To Jim White,
whose memories of landing on the beaches of Normandy in June 1944
stayed with him and his children all of his life;
And for all his comrades,
who died for our freedom

# CONTENTS

# THE
# FRENCH BETRAYAL
## OF
# AMERICA

# INTRODUCTION

## What's Wrong with France?

---

Going to war without France is like going deer hunting without an accordion. You just leave a lot of useless noisy baggage behind.

—JED BABBIN, former deputy undersecretary of defense, 1989–1992, January 30, 2003, on MSNBC's *Hardball*

As the United States and France faced off in the United Nations in late 2002 and early 2003, France's betrayal of America seemingly had no end. Americans watched with revulsion as Foreign Minister Dominique de Villepin leapt from capital to capital like an overwound ballet dancer in his effort to convince members of the UN Security Council to vote against any resolution that would authorize the use of force against Saddam Hussein's regime. Villepin was not content to disagree with the United States, as did a certain number of our allies; he actively sought to rally world leaders and public opinion to treat the United States—not Saddam Hussein—as the enemy.

The enormous difference between those two positions—legitimate dissent and active subversion of America's right to self-defense—was not lost on President George W. Bush and his top advisers, who renamed the French toast served on Air Force One "Freedom toast."

In France, anti-American propaganda spread to the general population in ways that had never been seen before. "The Yankees are having a nervous breakdown," read a typical entry on the popular Weblog of the left-wing French daily *Libération*. "Good God, please let Dubya swallow another pretzel the wrong way! And make sure it stays stuck this time!"

If you were in France, as I was during the first few weeks of the war, you were immersed in a very different reality from what Americans heard and watched and read about—even in the Bush-hating press.

The French called Basra, Iraq's largest city in the south, the "martyred city"—not because Saddam had murdered so many of its Shiite inhabitants, but because U.S. and British troops had laid a careful siege to minimize the suffering of civilians.

By the end of the first week of the war, French media pundits had concluded that the Anglo-American "aggressors" were mired in a "quagmire." Civilians were being massacred by trigger-happy U.S. troops, who were guilty of "war crimes." The French gave prominent coverage to antiwar protests around the world to show how "isolated" America was, and to protesters in America itself (including one presidential candidate, Massachusetts Democrat Senator John Kerry) who were calling for "regime change"—in the United States, not Iraq.

The average Frenchman listening to state-run France Inter radio or France 2 television during the first week of the war in Iraq saw the United States spiraling toward a humiliating defeat and George W. Bush, the "cowboy" president, headed for ignominy, if not impeachment. In tones that mixed elation and awe, French newsmen and pundits began speculating on how the Middle East would look the day after the United States *lost the war* against Saddam. Wouldn't this dramatic display of U.S. vulnerability encourage other nations and terrorist groups to challenge U.S. military might?

Most striking in the French coverage was the total absence of any criticism of government policy or of President Jacques Chirac. This is a president who attracted just 19.8 percent of the voters in the first round of the April 2002 elections, squeaking past neofascist leader Jean-Marie Le Pen, who came in second with 16.8 percent. In normal times, the opposition Socialist Party would have been all over Chirac and France's lively opinion journals would have skewered his policies from all sides.

French war coverage was not merely one-sided: it was willfully inaccurate and openly anti-American. One example of the kind of hate journalism that became prevalent was a pop culture radio show that aired just two days before the war began. The disk jockey played a pastiche of speeches by President Bush—in the president's own voice—assembled to convey precisely the opposite of their original meaning. The United States, Bush said, "is about to launch attacks against Great Britain and forty other countries. We are attacking freedom. The name of today's operation is called Enduring Fear. The people of Iraq will suffer." As the president spoke, a driving chant in the background of *Allahu Akbar* (God is Great!) gradually overpowered his words. You might have thought that this crude attempt at arousing anti-American hate was the product of one of the many Arab-owned radio stations in France, but it wasn't. It aired on French state-run radio, nationwide. It was an outrageous appeal to France's huge Muslim population to identify Americans as the enemies of God.

My favorite was a quote from a freelance "military analyst" who ranted about punch-drunk twenty-year-old U.S. soldier-cowboys who were shooting civilians at will. "They face no sanction when a soldier kills civilians," he said. "They even shoot cows!" That was on the front page of the gray lady of French journalism, the Paris daily *Le Monde*.

Given this climate, it came as no surprise when a French public opinion survey came out showing that 25 percent of those polled said they hoped Saddam Hussein would win the war. It got so bad that French prime minister Jean-Pierre Raffarin issued an alarmed statement, warning his fellow citizens that despite French rejection of the U.S.-led war, Saddam Hussein was the enemy, not America.

What's wrong with France, a nation and a people that have sided with America repeatedly over our two-hundred-year shared history? Secretary of Defense Donald Rumsfeld was said to relish repeating a comment, attributed to former undersecretary of defense Jed Babbin, whenever asked whether he regretted the French refusal to join the U.S.-led coalition: "Going to war without France is like going deer hunting without an accordion. You just leave a lot of useless noisy baggage behind."

French-U.S. ties go way back. When Lord Charles Cornwallis realized he had been beaten at Yorktown, Virginia, by upstart American colonials on October 19, 1781, he ordered his second in command to deliver his sword to the Comte de Rochambeau, the French general whose forces had provided the muscle for the crushing British defeat.

In our schoolbooks, American children learn how the French came to our assistance in our time of need, just as French children learn how America returned the favor twice in the last century. As he stepped onto French soil at the head of the American Expeditionary Force in 1917, General John Pershing famously uttered, "Lafayette, we are here!" Again, in World War II, America paid the price of friendship with the blood of her children.

Yet since the end of World War II, America and France have enjoyed a love-hate relationship, just like old lovers or ex-husbands and wives. In 1966, when General Charles de Gaulle pulled France out of the NATO unified military command and ordered the United States to depart from bases in the Paris suburb of Saint-Germain-en-Laye, President Lyndon Johnson reportedly asked him if he also wanted us to take the graveyards full of the American dead who had fallen at Omaha Beach.

De Gaulle didn't want that, of course; nor do the French of today. But the venom and the grudges go deep.

*The French Betrayal of America* examines the U.S.-French divorce as it gradually has developed over the past ten years, while reminding readers of the long-standing ties between the two countries and their strategic cooperation during the cold war.

As a reporter who was based in France for eighteen years (1975–1993), I was a firsthand witness to many of the scenes that will be described in this book. Some of my sources I have known for more than twenty years, following their careers as they were promoted upward in the French civil service and the military to positions of ultimate authority. Along the way, they shared insights and information normally beyond the reach of reporters, especially if you were not French. Having written and published in French, with a career as a foreign policy commentator on French radio and numerous appearances on French television, I was always something of a transatlantic hybrid, almost French in so many ways, and yet, when it came to the basics of freedom and my unshaken belief in the sovereign right of nations and individuals to self-defense, fundamentally American.

During the cold war, France repeatedly came to America's aid, at times when just the opposite course seemed to be the most obvious. Ironically, at no time in our recent history was Franco-American strategic cooperation stronger than during the early 1980s, when the Socialist François Mitterrand and the conservative Ronald Reagan forged a solid and effective partnership, based on the shared goal of defeating the Soviet Union.

*The French Betrayal of America* will describe some of the lesser-known episodes of this relationship, from the surprising peaks in the 1980s to the apparent divorce of 2003, from the perspective of a reporter who was an eyewitness to many of the events he describes. But it also will focus relentlessly on the nearly three-decade-long French dalliance with Saddam Hussein, an affection that over time would seemingly replace the 225-year marriage between France and the United States.

# 1

# Le Divorce

---

When I first met him, many years ago, the butt end of his .357 Magnum peeped out whenever he unbuttoned his coat. Today, he has given up the Magnum in favor of around-the-clock bodyguards. At the time of the September 11 attacks on America, French counterterrorism judge Jean-Louis Bruguière arguably knew more about Osama bin Laden and his al-Qaeda network than any man alive. I bumped into him in the staircase of a secluded wing of the Palais de Justice in Paris in early October 2001 just ahead of a scheduled interview and remarked the almost boyish gleam in his eye. He had just come back from interrogating a detainee and looked like a cat that had swallowed a canary.

"You've heard about Moussaoui?" he said, unable to suppress a wide grin. Zacarias Moussaoui was the alleged twentieth hijacker who had been arrested on August 17, 2001, by Immigration and Naturalization Service (INS) agents because of suspicious activity while attending the Pan Am International Flight Academy in Minneapolis, Minnesota. The case against Moussaoui being worked up by lead U.S. prosecutor Rob Spencer in Alexandria, Virginia, was in trouble. Evidence tying Moussaoui to al-Qaeda was circumstantial, as were his ties to the 9/11 hijackers. Indeed, the initial grand jury indictment against Moussaoui was a boilerplate document for the overall conspiracy that mentioned him by name only a handful of times.[1] But Moussaoui had left a long trail behind him in France. If anyone had the goods on him, that would be Bruguière.

"There are new developments that are going to be of great interest to our friends in Virginia," he said with a toss of his head up toward his office. With Bruguière, that meant a file a foot high crammed with seized documents, flowcharts of conspiratorial telephone calls, interrogation transcripts, and reports from French intelligence on Moussaoui's travels, his friends, and his bank accounts. Bruguière liked to call al-Qaeda and its followers a global "spider's web." Since 1995, with method and determination, he had been pulling it apart thread by thread.

The French judge has received letters of commendation from former FBI Director Louis Freeh and from Attorney General John Ashcroft, thanking him for his help in convicting al-Qaeda terrorists in the United States, in particular "Millennium bomber" Ahmad Ressam, who plotted to blow up Los Angeles International Airport on New Year's Eve 1999. At Bruguière urging, French intelligence gathered on-the-ground intelligence on bin Laden's rat line into Afghanistan and his support network in Pakistan, which he personally provided to the United States in a still-classified March 1995 report. The information was so detailed it included the names of top al-Qaeda recruitment officers, detailed rosters of foreign cells, and photographs of safehouses and "welcome centers" in Islamabad, Peshawar, and elsewhere. Even more significantly: it traced the rat line back to recruiting centers in Europe, Asia, and North America. Bruguière had twice tried to warn the Clinton administration of imminent terrorist threats from al-Qaeda networks operating inside the United States, but was waved off. When by luck an alert U.S. Customs officer in Port Angeles, Washington, caught Ressam as he got off the ferry from Vancouver, British Columbia, with a truck filled with explosives, Bruguière not only turned over his files to the U.S. prosecutors; he gave detailed testimony at the trial that helped put the would-be Millennium bomber in jail for life, as I first revealed in a *Reader's Digest* exclusive.[2] Now that cooperation was about to come to an end, just when America needed it the most.

Shortly after our meeting on October 8, 2001, the French Ministry of Justice put the kibosh on Bruguière's effort to assist the Moussaoui prosecutors by providing documents that could be introduced at trial. The French claimed they had a "moral" objection to providing the documents because Moussaoui, a French citizen of Moroccan descent, could face the death penalty for his crimes. French officials, of course, tried to paint a less dire portrait. "We gave the United States all the intelligence we had on this and indeed all other terrorist cases," a senior French official knowledgeable of the intelligence exchanges on al-Qaeda later told me in Paris, insisting that nothing had gone awry. "But French law prevents us from turning over any evidence to a U.S. prosecutor if it could help convict a French citizen to death."[3]

The formal U.S. request for documentary assistance was known as an international rogatory letter. It had to be presented through the Ministry of Justice, which turned down the U.S. request. Bruguière complained and ultimately met with the visiting U.S. prosecutor that fall, against the will of Socialist justice minister Elisabeth Guigou. "Even if I couldn't give him documents, I agreed to walk him verbally through all we had," Bruguière said.[4] That included the dates of Moussaoui's trips to Afghanistan, his contacts with bin Laden trainers, his precise role in the "spider's web," and lots more. Yet despite Bruguière's willingness to help, the U.S. prosecutors returned home empty-handed, because the French government wouldn't allow the judge to turn over the documents they desperately needed.

Attorney General John Ashcroft told the French during meetings in Paris in May 2003 that the lack of cooperation meant that the Justice Department probably would be forced to abandon its case against Moussaoui and hand him over to the Pentagon for trial before a military court instead.[5] The depth of Ashcroft's deception at the lack of cooperation on the Moussaoui case must be measured by the extent of Bruguière's knowledge and his potential to help. Just one week after Moussaoui's arrest in August 2001, Bruguière had sent a fax to the FBI. "I told them Moussaoui was dangerous, that he'd been trained in Afghanistan. I told them he was capable of carrying out a terrorist attack. I told them to look at his laptop, because that was where he stored all of his contact information and plans. But by the time they got around to it, well after September 11, he had succeeded in erasing everything of interest from the hard drive."[6]

Why did the French government show such solicitude for a self-avowed Islamic extremist, who dismissed his defense attorneys in a courtroom temper tantrum, claiming they were "Jewish zealots," "pigs," and "bloodsuckers"?[7] Until 1973, France used to put criminals to death by lopping their heads off on the guillotine. They executed political prisoners as recently as

1963, when the last of four members of the Organisation de l'Armée Se-crète that had organized a military putsch to overthrow de Gaulle was exe-cuted by a firing squad. But in the early 1980s, French president Mitterrand abolished the death penalty. Now, it seemed, his successor was bent on making sure the United States could not execute criminals in our own coun-try, even if they were proven guilty of conspiring to mass murder. It was just one more example of a growing French effort to offer their values and political culture as a self-righteous "moral alternative" to America's.

For Secretary of State Colin Powell, the U.S.-French divorce began on Janu-ary 20, 2003, when French foreign minister Dominique de Villepin blind-sided him during a press conference outside the UN. After a special session of the Security Council devoted to the war on terror, held at Villepin's per-sonal request, Powell had driven over to the French UN ambassador's official Park Avenue residence, where Villepin was to host him to an exclusive lunch along with UN secretary-general Kofi Annan and the thirteen other foreign ministers who had attended the morning's formal meeting.

Instead, Villepin stayed behind at the UN and announced to the world that France would never support a U.S.-led military intervention against Saddam Hussein. As Powell saw the man he thought was his friend appear on the video monitors in the French ambassador's residence, his jaw dropped, says his deputy and confidant, Richard Armitage. "He was very unamused," Armitage recalls. "When he's unamused, he gets pretty cold. He puts the eyes on you and there is no doubt when his jaws are jacked. It's not a pretty sight."[8]

What Powell watched broadcast live by CNN went far beyond the self-righteous platitudes Villepin had uttered that morning inside the formal council chamber. Villepin had worked hard to set up the special ministerial meeting. Indeed, French and U.S. diplomats told me in interviews, he badgered the foreign ministers of other Security Council members for ten days straight in early January, twisting arms to get them to agree to come. To overcome U.S. reticence, Villepin insisted that the meeting would not be about Iraq, recognizing that would be too divisive. Instead, it would be devoted to generating international support for the war on terror. "The French can be persistent to a painful degree, so Villepin got his meeting," a U.S. participant said. "We thought from the beginning it was going to be a setup, and so did the White House."

During the session, Villepin "preened and postured and got applause from the gallery for what were really just self-righteous platitudes," recalled a deputy to U.S. ambassador John Negroponte.[9] After a tepid homage to the victims of 9/11, Villepin urged the United Nations to take over the global fight against terror by sending international bureaucrats to third world nations that were harboring or sponsoring terrorist groups. He wanted the World Bank and the International Monetary Fund to get involved, although both organizations have been strongly criticized by anticorruption advocates—and even their own staffs!—for having supported hopelessly corrupt governments in Indonesia, Brazil, Zaire, and countless other developing nations. He proposed a new international arms control treaty to track the commercial use and shipment of radioactive materials, surely a move that would prove as useful in preventing nuclear terrorism as the Nuclear Nonproliferation Treaty, which France signed belatedly in 1992, has been in preventing nations such as Israel, Pakistan, India, and North Korea from going nuclear. "Let us look at things with lucidity," he said finally, his voice quivering with compassion. "Terrorism feeds on injustice. So an equitable model of development is therefore necessary to definitely eradicate terrorism."[10]

It was not exactly what you'd call an earthshattering speech. No sense of urgency drove it, and Villepin had no real proposals to make. In fact, he seemed more intent on how his hair looked in the closed-circuit TV cameras than on what he was saying. Said one diplomat who knew Villepin well, "I've always thought it was a real mistake when they put the TV cameras in the Security Council chamber. It encourages people like Dominique to indulge in their natural tendency toward grandstanding. And he *loves* to grandstand."[11] The Americans were very happy once the meeting was over. "Colin Powell didn't want to be there in the first place," a member of the U.S. delegation told me. "He had other commitments. After all, it was Martin Luther King Day—and don't forget, Powell's middle name is Luther. But he came as a special favor to his friend Dominique."

It wasn't until Powell saw "Dominique's" familiar face on CNN that it dawned on him what it was all about.

"We thought from the beginning that this special session was going to be a setup," the UN aide said. "But State, in their general naiveté—where it's more important to use the right fork than to lose a country—said it was fine. In fact, the whole thing was a platform from which Villepin clearly intended to ambush the United States and the secretary of state. That was their plan for many weeks, if not months. They created a forum that was supposed to be discussing terrorism, but that was never their intent. Villepin used the thirteen other countries as props for him to stand up and shake his finger at the United States and the secretary of state."[12]

After briefly summarizing his proposals on terrorism, Villepin told the news cameras that he now wanted to say "a few words" about Iraq. That caught Powell's ear. Just the evening before, over a private dinner at the Waldorf-Astoria, where Villepin was staying, the two men had discussed possible wording the French government could accept in a new UN resolution (the eighteenth, in fact) that would authorize the use of force against Iraq. Powell would say later that he had thought they were close to an agreement. Diplomats at the UN were actually laying bets—at 100-to-1 odds—that the United States would get the votes for the resolution. None of them was prepared for what the Frenchman said next.

"If war is the only means of resolving the problem, then we have reached a dead end. . . . A unilateral military intervention will be the victory of might makes right, an attack on the primacy of international law and morality." The UN should wait until the UN inspectors made their next report, scheduled for January 27, before deciding on any further action, he said. At that point, "Iraq must understand that it is time for it to cooperate actively."

To Powell and his advisers, it was clear that Villepin was trying to run out the clock, so Saddam could finish hiding his weapons and prepare for war. "Since we can disarm Iraq through peaceful means," the Frenchman went on improbably, "we should not risk the lives of innocent civilians or soldiers, endangering the stability of the region, widening the gap between peoples and cultures, between our peoples and our cultures, [since it will only] feed terrorism." The French forgot to show such solicitude when sending their own troops to back unpopular dictators in Africa.

Later, in the reconstruction of the day's events he and other top French officials gave to reporters, Villepin denied he had tried to ambush Powell or that he had disguised an intention to use the ministerial session of the UN Security Council on terrorism as a platform to attack the United States on Iraq. "There was no ambush," he told the *Financial Times.* "I did not mention the word *Iraq* once in my speech. It was only at a press conference afterwards that I discussed Iraq in reply to a very aggressive question." I read that account to a U.S. official who knew Villepin and had watched the tape of that press conference many times. "That's just a lie," he said. Indeed, the written record of Villepin's press conference, provided to me by the French foreign minister, shows on the contrary that it was Villepin who shifted directly to Iraq in prepared remarks at the very beginning of his press conference and went on and on in his condemnation of the United States well before the questions began. "We will not associate ourselves with military intervention that is not supported by the international community," he said finally. "Military intervention would be the worst solution." Even *The Washington Post*, which highlighted international opposition to the Bush administration's position on Iraq, called Villepin's performance "theatrical."[13]

When Villepin finally showed up for the lunch, it got worse. German foreign minister Joschka Fischer berated Powell and President Bush for having decided to move forward with military action and claimed that Iraq "has complied fully with all relevant resolutions and cooperated very closely with the UN team on the ground," certainly an Alice-in-Wonderland version of the facts even as they were presented by the well-heeled UN chief inspector, Hans Blix.[14] Villepin painted a disaster scenario of region-wide instability resulting from war in Iraq that would have far worse consequences than putting up with a tinpot dictator who was safely ensconced in his box and wasn't threatening anybody. Finally Powell had heard enough. "He got an edge to his voice—something Powell prides himself on not doing—and said, 'You said the same thing before Panama and we went in, and three days later, everyone forgot.' " The scales fell from Powell's eyes that day, an aide said. "He suddenly realized this was a game of hardball politics and that he had let himself be used and abused."

From that moment on, the relationship between the two men turned to ice. No more letters from Villepin addressed "Cher Colin." No more cozy lunches. Communications became stiff and formal, while the top leaders traded broadsides across the Atlantic.

Standing side by side with German chancellor Gerhard Schroeder in Paris on January 22, President Chirac hurled another cannonball. "War is always an admission of defeat," he said, "the worst of solutions. Hence everything must be done to avoid it." Some French sources claim that Chirac had been "set up" by Schroeder, whose harsh criticism of the United States at that event went way beyond the prepared speech he had given

Chirac's advisers beforehand. In fact, many senior members of Chirac's own ruling party still believed that Chirac intended to join the U.S. and British–led war effort at the last minute, after squeezing from the United States a maximum of commercial concessions in postwar Iraq in exchange.[15] But Chirac and Villepin didn't realize that Bush was not in a mood to "deal." Nor did they appreciate the tremendous impact of the September 11 attacks on the collective will of the American people.

The next morning, writing in *The New York Times,* National Security Adviser Condoleezza Rice chastised the French and other critics who wanted to give Iraq more time to cooperate with UN weapons inspectors. "Has Saddam Hussein finally decided to voluntarily disarm?" she asked. "Unfortunately, the answer is a clear and resounding no. There is no mystery to voluntary disarmament. Countries that decide to disarm lead inspectors to weapons and production sites, answer questions before they are asked, state publicly and often the intention to disarm, and urge their citizens to cooperate. The world knows from examples set by South Africa, Ukraine, and Kazakhstan what it looks like when a government decides that it will cooperatively give up its weapons of mass destruction." Iraq's behavior certainly did not fit the bill. "By both its actions and its inactions," she concluded, "Iraq is proving not that it is a nation bent on disarmament, but that it is a nation with something to hide."[16]

Deputy Secretary of Defense Paul Wolfowitz gave a more detailed presentation on the same theme to the Council on Foreign Relations in New York. "It is not the job of inspectors to disarm Iraq; it is Iraq's job to disarm itself," he said. "Think about it for a moment. When an auditor discovers discrepancies in the books, it is not the auditor's obligation to prove where the embezzler has stashed his money. It is up to the person or institution being audited to explain the discrepancy. It is quite unreasonable to expect a few hundred inspectors to search every potential hiding place in a country the size of France, even if nothing were being moved."

For twelve years, Iraq had been playing a game of "rope-a-dope in the desert" with the UN inspectors. That game was about to end, because of a renegade Saudi named Osama bin Laden. "As terrible as the attacks of September 11 were, however, we now know that the terrorists are plotting still more and greater catastrophes," Wolfowitz said. "We know they are seeking more terrible weapons—chemical, biological, and even nuclear weapons." Because of this, he argued, disarming Iraq had become a vital part of the war on terror. "The threat posed by the connection between terrorist networks and states that possess these weapons of mass terror presents us with the danger of a catastrophe that could be orders of magnitude worse than September 11. Iraq's weapons of mass terror and the terror networks to which the Iraqi regime are linked are not two separate themes—not two separate threats. They are part of the same threat."[17]

French officials say they never bought the U.S. argument of a "convergence" between Iraq, weapons of mass destruction (WMD), and terrorism. "The U.S. argument was highly speculative," a senior adviser to Villepin told me in Paris. "If there was going to be convergence between terrorists and WMD, it would happen with renegade scientists from Biopreparat in Russia, who decide to go to work for al-Qaeda. It would happen in Pakistan, but not in Iraq. Saddam Hussein's regime was not known for spontaneous behavior. He had no objection to using terrorism, but he would never give weapons to groups that were not thoroughly under his control, who could act autonomously in ways that could pose a threat to his regime."[18] But of course, that was precisely what the United States contended when it cited Saddam's use of al-Qaeda offshoot al-Ansar al-Islam, which was operating with the support and protection of Saddam's intelligence arm, the dreaded Mukhabarat. The United States presented evidence that al-Ansar was training with biological and chemical weapons, but the French remained unconvinced.

On October 27, 2003, Undersecretary of Defense Douglas Feith sent a classified memo to the Senate Select Intelligence Committee detailing no fewer than fifty separate credible intelligence reports on contacts between top al-Qaeda members and Iraqi intelligence.[19] It's simply inconceivable that the French, for all their close ties to Saddam, had seen none of it.

Powell and Villepin continued to duke it out in Davos, Switzerland, during the World Economic Forum that weekend. Villepin again warned that France would veto any U.S.-backed resolution at the UN to authorize the use of force and said his European colleagues agreed with him that the UN inspections should be extended by "several weeks or for several months."

Powell reminded the Frenchman of the bonds of blood tying America to France and the sacrifices Americans had made to free Europe from tyranny. "We've put wonderful young men and women at risk, many of whom have lost their lives," he said. "We've asked for nothing but enough land to bury them in." Now, things appeared to have changed. "One or two of our friends, we have been in marriage counseling for 225 years non-stop," he said, indicating France. He didn't utter the word *divorce,* but it was clear that the marriage counseling had reached an impasse.[20]

The French never fully appreciated the dramatic changes in American thinking that followed 9/11, a top Villepin adviser admitted. They found it inconceivable that the United States could feel threatened by the possibility of a nuclear-armed Saddam Hussein or by Iraqi collusion with terrorists. But when I asked how French national security would have been threatened by acquiescing to U.S. war plans—what was so important to French vital interests to require them to actively oppose the United States?—Villepin's adviser sank into a stunned silence that lasted nearly a minute. In the end, he uttered a mush about the possibility of civil war in Iraq and hurting the feelings of the Arabs. "Nations don't always act from self-interest, but also from conviction," he said finally. "We believed someone had to speak up to express the objections of a large majority of the international community who disagreed with the American policy and who had no spokesman. We were like the Roman tribune."[21]

In fact, there was "very little debate" within the Foreign Ministry or elsewhere about opposing America during the crisis, another top official told me in Paris. "The policy was driven by Villepin and by Chirac person-ally. Only five or six senior advisers dared to raise questions about how Villepin was handling himself." That small group of dissidents thought Villepin had made "a huge blunder" by sandbagging Powell on January 20 at the UN. "That press conference was a radical departure from the type of consultations we had had before. All of a sudden, France was saying it would not *under any circumstances* support UN action on Iraq." The naysay-ers were in a distinct minority at the Quai d'Orsay and nonexistent at the presidential palace; indeed, they keep a low profile these days. "There was never any misunderstanding between us and the Americans," this official said. "Both sides knew each other's positions very well. It was a fundamen-tal difference in viewpoints. We simply didn't share the U.S. perception of the threat and actively tried to block the United States from preventive mil-itary action it considered to be an act of legitimate self-defense."[22] A U.S. diplomat involved in the exchanges agreed. "The French knew exactly what our thinking was—up to a point. But until January 20, we had thought they were totally with us."[23]

There was good reason for the Bush administration's confidence, as I can reveal here for the first time. Until January 20, I learned in interviews with a half-dozen administration officials directly involved in the negotiations, the French had gone out of their way to privately assure the president, the secretary of state, and U.S. diplomats working the issue that they backed the United States in the showdown with Saddam, even if it included the use of force. When the Iraqis stonewalled United Nations arms inspectors in late October 2002, Chirac picked up the phone and called President Bush in the Oval Office to reiterate French support for a strong United Nations resolution that would include the option of using force. In early December, he sent a top French military official to Centcom headquarters in Tampa, Florida, to negotiate the specifics of the French participation in the war. "Chirac personally told the president he would be with us," one senior administration official told me. "We didn't know until the ambush that France would go to war with us. We thought they might complain, or abstain, or not vote—but not that they would actually veto." Added another, who was privy to the Oval Office conversation, "Chirac's assurances are what gave the president the confidence to keep sending Colin Powell back to the UN. They also explain why the administration has been going after the French so aggressively ever since. They lied."

Back in Washington that Sunday, Pentagon adviser Richard Perle said publicly some of the things Powell was too polite to utter even in private. A former undersecretary of defense in the Reagan administration, Perle now headed the Pentagon's Defense Policy Board and was close friends with Secretary of Defense Donald Rumsfeld, Deputy Defense Secretary Paul Wolfowitz, and Powell's deputy, Richard Armitage. Far from being an automatic France basher, Perle was a dedicated francophile who owned a vacation home in France and for two decades had maintained close personal ties to many top figures in the French defense and security establishment. The French government, he told *FOX News Sunday,* was acting not on principle, as it claimed, but on behalf of its commercial interests. "It's ironic that people accuse the United States of being interested in oil," he said. "If you want to see who's interested in oil, look at French policy. It is entirely self-concerned, and it has to do with oil contracts and very little else."[24]

*FOX News* did a little digging and found further evidence of French commercial interests in Iraq, which it claimed were driving French policy.

"These French companies do substantial business in Iraq," reported correspondent Major Garrett. "Automakers Peugeot and Renault, the oil company TotalFinaElf, and telecommunications giant Alcatel."[25] As we shall see, that was just the beginning.

Behind the scenes, Powell was working contacts of his own. On January 30, *The Wall Street Journal Europe* and *The Times* (London) simultaneously published a letter cosigned by eight European leaders—the prime ministers of Spain, Portugal, Italy, the United Kingdom, Hungary, Poland, and Denmark and the president of the Czech Republic, Václav Havel—that urged the European Union (EU) to back the United States in the face-off with Iraq. "The real bond between the U.S. and Europe is the values we share: democracy, individual freedom, human rights and the rule of law," they wrote. "These values crossed the Atlantic with those who sailed from Europe to help create the United States of America. Today they are under greater threat than ever." Recalling that America had come to Europe's defense in two world wars in the twentieth century, they argued that Chirac and Schroeder had gone way beyond a dispute over policy and were now threatening the very fabric of the NATO alliance. "The transatlantic relationship must not become a casualty of the current Iraqi regime's persistent attempts to threaten world security," they wrote.[26] Villepin was furious when the letter was published, and when the two next met in New York, shortly before Powell's Security Council presentation of Iraqi weapons violations on February 5, he blasted Powell for having gone behind his back. "Villepin went literally nuts. What he was saying was, 'I can play the game of trying to isolate you, but it is unacceptable for you to play it on me,' " a U.S. diplomat said.[27]

Richard Perle became a stalking horse for Secretary of Defense Rumsfeld and for the "hawks" in the Bush administration. At a conference on Iraq in Washington, D.C., the day before Powell's presentation, he suggested that France by its behavior was demonstrating that it had parted company with the United States.

"France is no longer the ally it once was," he said. "I think it is reasonable to ask whether this country should now or on any other occasion subordinate its most fundamental national security interests to a show of hands that happens to include governments whose interests are different from our own. Deep in the soul of Jacques Chirac, he believes that Saddam

Hussein is preferable to the alternative that is likely to emerge when Iraq is liberated."[28] I will examine Chirac's close personal ties to Saddam in great detail throughout this book.

All that night, a team of officials from the CIA, the National Security Council (NSC), and Powell's own staff argued over intelligence information Powell could safely reveal in his February 5, 2003, presentation to the UN Security Council. There were heated discussions of whether Powell should play the actual tape of an intercepted conversation from an Iraqi colonel, who was instructing a subordinate to eliminate all references to the term *nerve gas* in his official communications, in case UN inspectors came looking for evidence. Making the tape public, National Security Agency (NSA) analysts argued, would reveal the extent of their electronic eavesdropping capabilities in Iraq and perhaps give the Iraqis key tips on how to avoid surveillance in the future.

All those present agreed enthusiastically to include one particular piece of evidence, however. When Powell turned to it the next day, he studiously avoided the angry glare of his former friend Dominique Galouzeau de Villepin. It was video footage showing a French-built Iraqi Mirage F1 fighter-bomber, flying just over the rooftops of a medium-size town, emitting a "white cloudlike spray." In describing this test flight of a new system to disperse biological agents, Powell said tersely: "Note the spray coming from beneath the Mirage. That is two thousand liters of simulated anthrax that a jet is spraying." It absolutely infuriated the French foreign minister.[29]

In the end, no Security Council member changed its position as a result of Powell's speech. Villepin read a canned statement that skirted the new evidence and made clear that his government simply did not view Iraq as a threat. Instead of military action, he suggested, why not "double or even triple the number of inspectors and open new regional offices. Let's go even further: Couldn't we establish a specialized corps, whose mission would be to maintain constant surveillance of sites and zones already subject to controls?"[30] The next thing the French would be offering would be the resumption of nuclear cooperation with Iraq, just as former International Atomic Energy Agency (IAEA) chief nuclear inspector Maurizio Zifferero had suggested to me in an interview in Vienna in September 1992.[31] To these partisans of a world elite, it mattered little that dictators like Saddam murdered his own people, as long as he paid his bills.

In the United States, Powell's speech had a tremendous impact, convincing even dedicated liberals such as *New York Times* commentator Maureen Dowd, who had never supported a Bush administration policy before, to declare that Powell "finally has the goods" on Saddam. Thomas Friedman, writing four days later, suggested that France be replaced as a permanent member of the Security Council by India, "the world's biggest democracy."[32]

A captive French press had taken to lionizing Chirac and Villepin. The conservative daily *Le Figaro* announced improbably that the French proposal of reinforcing the UN inspection regime had won over a "majority" of the Security Council and called the French effort a "war against war."[33]

The transatlantic rift was not contained to the UN. As part of the military preparations for eventual hostilities in Iraq, the Pentagon sought to deploy the Fourth Infantry Division through Turkey to open a northern front. In addition to increasing the possibility of a quick victory on the ground, the goal was to allow the U.S.-led alliance to avoid an ecological disaster, by securing the oil fields near Kirkuk before Saddam's sappers could blow the wellheads as they did during the first Gulf War in 1991. But Turkey needed a strong show of NATO support to quell domestic opposition to the war. Once again, France leapt into the breach.

French hostility toward Turkey was legendary. Using its veto power at the European Council, France had for well over a decade single-handedly blocked Turkey's bid to join the European Union. Some would argue that France was just repaying Turkey for the sins of the Ottoman Empire, which had mercilessly persecuted the Christians of the East. On February 10, France joined Germany and Belgium in formally objecting to a U.S. proposal at NATO headquarters in Brussels to send defensive equipment to Turkey.

Turkey then appealed to NATO for AWACS radar planes and Patriot missile batteries, as well as biological and chemical weapons detectors, under Article 4 of the 1949 North Atlantic Treaty, the mutual defense clause that bound NATO members as an alliance. It was the first time in the history of NATO that a member nation had formally requested military assistance from the alliance against an external threat. The eventuality of such a request was the very reason NATO was first established. What tied the United States to Europe was the rock-solid assurance that an attack on one NATO member would be considered an attack on all. During the cold war, this strategy helped deter the Soviet Union from nibbling away at Western Europe. But once again France, Germany, and Belgium said no, in essence voting to put an end to two generations of NATO solidarity.

President Chirac explained France's reasoning, after meeting in Paris with Russian president Vladimir Putin: "Nothing today justifies war. Russia, Germany, and France are determined to ensure that everything possible is done to disarm Iraq peacefully." He added, "I have no evidence that these weapons exist in Iraq," a breathtaking assertion from the president of a country that had supplied some of the UN's most capable weapons inspectors, men and women who had briefed him personally on the extent of Saddam Hussein's nuclear, chemical, biological, and missile programs. Nicholas Burns, U.S. ambassador to NATO, said the French were "gambling with NATO's future."[34]

In a lead editorial the next morning, *The Washington Post* accused France and Germany of "standing with Saddam" and of weakening both NATO and the United Nations. The *Post* noted ironically that Saddam Hussein had started taking his cue from the French, calibrating his response to the demands of the UN inspectors to what he perceived to be the furthest reaches of French support. "That [French] slogans are being mimicked by Baghdad's thugs ought to trouble French President Jacques Chirac and German Chancellor Gerhard Schroeder," the *Post* said.[35] But neither the French nor the Germans seemed to care.

During a stormy February 11, 2003, congressional hearing, Democratic senator Ernest F. Hollings of South Carolina accused the Bush administration of wrecking the fifty-four-year-old transatlantic alliance. "Who is breaking up the alliance?" Powell replied. "Not the United States. The alliance is breaking itself up because it will not meet its responsibilities."[36] Commenting on the NATO decisions in Brussels, a U.S. diplomat quipped that the only nations that were opposing the U.S. effort to muster an international coalition to disarm Saddam were "France and Germany, backed by mighty Luxembourg, and Belgium, whose contribution to foreign affairs is the waffle. Sixteen other European nations were supporting us."[37]

On February 18, ten former Soviet-bloc nations released a letter endorsing a European Union warning to Iraq that it risked war if it failed to cooperate with UN disarmament inspectors. The letter from the so-called Vilnius 10 infuriated Chirac when it became public. Speaking in Brussels, the French president said the aspiring EU members should have consulted the big boys in Berlin and in Paris before issuing their statement. "They missed a great opportunity to shut up," he added. When it came time to vote on EU membership for the Vilnius 10, he vowed that France would re-member their stand on Iraq.[38]

While some dismissed Chirac's "emotional outburst" as just one more sign of French arrogance, it infuriated the East Europeans, who bitterly re-called decades of similar bullying by their former Soviet occupiers. Czech foreign minister Cyril Svoboda responded, "We are not joining the EU so we can sit and shut up."[39] Romanian president Ion Iliescu wondered whom Chirac and Schroeder had consulted before they issued their own declara-tion against the war the month before. But the French remained unrepen-tant about Chirac's outburst. Many months later, a top French diplomat explained, "We ask the so-called new Europe to express their views in a way that is not humiliating to France and Germany, for Chirac and Schroeder. We can't allow them to insult us!"[40]

The French press continued to paint a picture of the diplomatic tug-of-war that showed the United States as isolated and France as the voice of reason, whose proposals to prolong the UN inspection regime "have been particularly well received." The arms inspectors had just reported that "the verification of Iraq's disarmament is now within reach," *Le Figaro* gushed in a modern-day version of the infamous "peace in our time" com-ment by British prime minister Neville Chamberlain after he and his French counterpart had ceded Czechoslovakia to Hitler in Munich in 1938. Foreign Minister Villepin was an international celebrity, "whose speech [at the UN] received a standing ovation from the gallery reserved for the public and the press."[41]

Others were less flattering and referred to Villepin as the "Energizer Bunny of diplomacy" or took to calling him "Zorro," *The New York Times* reported. "If Villepin has a vision, it is to revive the greatness of France—a romantic view he articulated in his book *The Hundred Days* [*Les Cent-Jours*], the first published volume of a biography of Napoleon that tells the story of the emperor's return from exile, his triumphant march across France, and his final defeat at Waterloo one hundred days later. Describing Napoleon's philosophy as 'victory or death, but glory whatever happens,'" Villepin said he felt an "imperious need" to keep Napoleon's example con-stantly before him to "advance further in the name of a French ambi-tion."[42] I will examine Villepin's veneration of Napoleon in the last chapter of this book.

What so infuriated Americans about France's behavior was not the fact that the government disagreed with us about the threat posed by Saddam Hussein or what to do about it; so did Russia, China, Syria, and Saudi Arabia. It was the sense of being betrayed by an old ally. As Vice President Dick Cheney would say later, for Bush not to have acted against Saddam in the wake of 9/11 would have been "irresponsible in the extreme."[43]

When it appeared that the United States, Britain, and Spain were close to forcing a vote on a new UN Security Council resolution to approve the use of force, Villepin rushed off on a tour of African countries (Angola, Zaire), offering them economic and diplomatic incentives if they voted against the United States. And when President Bush ultimately decided to abandon the UN, issuing an ultimatum to Saddam Hussein on March 17, 2003, to leave the country within forty-eight hours or face an allied military assault, Chirac called the U.S.-led war effort "illegal" and a "violation of international law" and stated repeatedly that Europe should serve as a "counterweight" to American military power. "A relationship that can be described by the term *counterweight* is not a relationship of alliance," Richard Perle pointedly observed at a gathering at New York's Regency Hotel.[44] In moments of candor, Chirac and other top French officials called America a "hegemon." Ironically, such terms—from a French president who claimed to be a conservative—had more in common with the worldview of leaders in Communist China, Cuba, the Islamic Republic of Iran, and Libya than they did with anything resembling the Western values of democracy and freedom Chirac claimed to defend.

So what was going on?

In a groundbreaking essay published by the Hoover Institution the summer before the Iraq crisis erupted, neoconservative foreign policy guru Robert Kagan made a compelling case that the end of the cold war had unleashed a host of fundamental conflicts that had come to divide the United States from Europe, especially France and Germany. Those conflicts ultimately fed the bitter public divorce over Iraq. "On major strategic and international questions today, Americans are from Mars and Europeans are from Venus," Kagan argued. "They agree on little and understand one another less and less."

The United States had become the world's preeminent military power, with virtually sole responsibility for policing the world, while Europe was living in a postmodern society where even the thought of spending on defense—let alone war—had become anathema. "When it comes to setting national priorities, determining threats, defining challenges, and fashioning and implementing foreign and defense policies, the United States and Europe have parted ways."[45]

Kagan's essay "has been made the basis for seminars and widespread discussion throughout European Union officialdom," writes City University of New York professor Bernard E. Brown, "and has become a factor in hastening the political divorce between the United States and Europe that he purports merely to describe."[46]

Kagan argues that Europe's current attitude toward the use of force is "quite new" and "represents an evolution away from the very different strategic culture that dominated Europe for hundreds of years and at least until World War I." Europe played power politics for as long as it was powerful; now that it is weak, it has adopted a different approach. Similarly, America's current willingness to project power is a recent development. "When the United States was weak, it practiced the strategies of indirection, the strategies of weakness; now that the United States is powerful, it behaves as powerful nations do." In other words, over the past two centuries "Americans and Europeans have traded places" on the world stage.

Although World War II "destroyed European nations as global powers," Europe remained key to the Western alliance as a bulwark against Soviet expansion. "Europe lost this strategic centrality after the cold war ended, but it took a few more years for the lingering mirage of European global power to fade." Europe's inability to end the Balkan crisis in the early 1990s revealed the new Europe in all its nakedness. It took American military muscle and diplomatic perseverance to end the fighting. "As some Europeans put it, the real division of labor consisted of the United States 'making the dinner' and the Europeans 'doing the dishes,' " Kagan wrote.

> Today's transatlantic problem, in short, is not a George Bush problem. It is a power problem. American military strength has produced a propensity to use that strength. Europe's military weakness has produced a perfectly understandable aversion to the exercise of military power. Indeed, it has produced a powerful European interest in inhabiting a world where strength doesn't matter, where international law and international institutions predominate, where unilateral action by powerful nations is forbidden, where

all nations regardless of their strength have equal rights and are equally protected by commonly agreed-upon international rules of behavior.

As a result, the Europeans, led by France and Germany, have sought "to constrain American power without wielding power themselves. . . . Europeans oppose unilateralism in part because they have no capacity for unilateralism," Kagan writes.

This power disparity also has brought with it diverging perceptions of what constitutes a tolerable threat.

> The psychology of weakness is easy enough to understand. A man armed only with a knife may decide that a bear prowling the forest is a tolerable danger, inasmuch as the alternative—hunting the bear armed only with a knife—is actually riskier than lying low and hoping the bear never attacks. The same man armed with a rifle, however, will likely make a different calculation of what constitutes a tolerable risk. Why should he risk being mauled to death if he doesn't need to? This perfectly normal human psychology is helping to drive a wedge between the United States and Europe today. Europeans have concluded, reasonably enough, that the threat posed by Saddam Hussein is more tolerable for them than the risk of removing him.

Some Europeans acknowledge that their nations have been getting a free ride since the end of the cold war, with defense spending plunging to all-time lows of around 2 percent of gross domestic product at best. Indeed, as one French active-duty general admitted to *Le Figaro* once the war in Iraq had been won, "Our matériel is insufficient. We have nothing that moves satisfactorily. And whatever you say, I know we didn't go to Iraq because of that fact."[47]

The Europeans sneeringly refer to Americans as "cowboys." If there is some truth in this, then Europe "is more like a saloonkeeper," Kagan writes. "Outlaws shoot sheriffs, not saloonkeepers. In fact, from the saloonkeeper's point of view, the sheriff trying to impose order by force can sometimes be more threatening than the outlaws who, at least for the time being, may just want a drink." In the end, as Europe focuses on trade and on balancing the books of an increasingly expensive social welfare system, "Europe does not see a mission for itself that requires power. Its mission is to oppose power."

Kagan calls Europe's belief that force has become a relic of the past century a "geopolitical fantasy." Others call it appeasement. "America's

power, and its willingness to exercise that power—unilaterally if necessary—represents a threat to Europe's new sense of mission." These differences are profound, long-lasting, and irreconcilable, Kagan believes. The
ultimate irony is that Europe has "neither the will nor the ability to guard
its own paradise and keep it from being overrun, spiritually as well as physically, by a world that has yet to accept the rule of 'moral consciousness.' "
Because of this, Europe "has become dependent on America's willingness
to use its military might to deter or defeat those around the world who still
believe in power politics."

B ut Kagan's thesis didn't explain why Britain, Italy, Spain, and Poland
sided with the United States in the war with Iraq while France and Germany did not. Nor did it explain why Chirac was wedded to "a vision of a
multipolar world, in which Europe would become a counterweight to the
military and political power of the United States," in the words of Chirac
political ally and confidant Pierre Lellouche.[48] Indeed, much more was involved than just weakness, national pride, or delusions of Napoleonic
grandeur, although these were all important parts of the mix.

Former undersecretary of state William Schneider now heads the
Defense Science Board for Secretary of Defense Rumsfeld and has been
dealing with the French government at the highest levels for the past
twenty years. "The problem with Germany is Schroeder," he says. "The
problem with France is France. The French refused to honor the U.S. belief
that we were defending our vital interests in going into Iraq, and that is
pretty much unprecedented." President Chirac believed that support for
the U.S.-led war against Saddam would have permanently marginalized
France and Europe as players on the world scene. "The French diplomatic
interests that Chirac expressed led him over the precipice," Schneider
believes.[49]

At the most bitter moments of the U.S.-French divorce, once the fighting began in Iraq, you would never have known that our two countries
were bound by a shared heritage and ties of blood. Protesters in Paris
burned effigies of President Bush and stormed McDonald's fast-food
restaurants. After the owner of a well-known wine bar in the eleventh ar-
rondissement of Paris expressed support for the war, someone threw a
rock through the plate-glass window of his restaurant.[50] French pundits
and newsmen kept up a steady drumbeat of paranoid conspiracies that al-

ways seemed to end with the refrain that America was fighting a "war for oil." Rumsfeld ridiculed the charge in an interview with *Le Figaro*. "To suggest that the Americans are seeking to control Iraq's oil resources is totally absurd. Countries that have oil sell their oil, and it really doesn't matter to whom they sell it. If they say no to one customer, that customer will simply go to another supplier."[51] Rumsfeld's mini-lesson in market economics was lost on the conspiracy-minded.

Two weeks into the war, National Front leader Jean-Marie Le Pen predicted that Baghdad would become America's Stalingrad and mocked the Pentagon for having underestimated the courage and will to fight off the Iraqi army. "Gentlemen, long live Iraq!" he belted out to a crowded audience on March 31. He demanded that U.S. leaders be brought before "international tribunals" for having prepared the war in secret for more than a year. "This crime has no excuse because, in fact, it was carried out with premeditation."[52] Eight days later, Baghdad fell.

At the other spectrum of French politics, Jean-Pierre Chevènement, a deeply anti-American former defense minister, said the conflict was a U.S.-led "war of recolonialization." Writing in *Le Monde*, he claimed the war had been "dreamed up by the Pentagon strategists as a war of world domination through the occupation of Iraq and the control of the Middle East. . . . We need to help the United States to profoundly revise their relations with 'the rest of the world.' "[53] A Socialist, he had only praise for Chirac and his anti-American policies.

An opinion poll published on April 1, 2003, in the daily *Le Monde* showed that Frenchmen by a slim majority (53 percent) nevertheless hoped for a coalition victory in Iraq. (The question did not use the word *coalition*, but rather a victory of "Anglo-American forces.") Of much greater concern was the second half of the poll. Fully 25 percent of Frenchmen polled said they hoped Saddam would win the war.

Sensing that the demagoguery had gone too far, French prime minister Jean-Pierre Raffarin told an audience in Clermont-Ferrand that they needed to return to reason. "We think this war is not a good alternative," he said, reminding listeners of the reasons his government refused to endorse the coalition effort. "But this is not a reason to mistake the enemy. The Americans are not the enemies. Our camp is the camp of democracy." For the French prime minister to feel that he needed to remind the media and the public that America is not the enemy showed the extent of the damage Chirac and Villepin had done to U.S.-French relations, let alone to rational public discourse in France. Not since the Vietnam War had a visceral anti-Americanism trickled down to the popular level with such force.

And trickle down it did—right from the top. When the Élysée Palace issued a statement similar to Raffarin's appeal to reason, it paraphrased Chirac without actually quoting him. Indeed, Chirac never backed off, never appealed to the press to cease its vicious anti-American coverage, and has never admitted that his behavior might have caused his country harm. "The president has always denounced the dictatorial regime in Baghdad and has reaffirmed that we are allies of the United States," spokeswoman Catherine Colonna said, apparently with a straight face. To thus describe the positions of a politician who for more than a quarter century has boasted that Saddam Hussein was a "personal friend" was yet another example of the Alice-in-Wonderland mood that had gripped France.

I n America, similar animosities also came out.
    At a dinner party at the home of Indian consul Skand Ranjan-Tayal in Houston, House majority leader Tom DeLay ripped into a French diplomat who was criticizing the U.S. position on Iraq. "It was obvious we were not going to agree," DeLay said, so he asked the Frenchman if he spoke German. "And he looked at me kind of funny and said, 'No, I don't speak German.' And I said, 'You're welcome,' turned around, and walked off."[54]

A spontaneous consumer boycott of French products mushroomed in March after a public appeal on *The O'Reilly Factor* by Dave Bossie of the conservative public action group Citizens United and relentless broadsides by the popular Newsmax.com Web site. By some accounts, it led to a plunge of nearly 15 percent in French exports to the United States. (The French dismissed the U.S. anger as "a campaign led by right-wing pressure groups" without any popular support.)[55] Even in cosmopolitan Manhattan, French restaurants that had been in business for decades were forced to lay off most of their staff because they had no customers. Once the fighting in Iraq began, American tourists began avoiding France like the plague. As the American cyclist Lance Armstrong pedaled his way to his fifth straight victory in the Tour de France in July 2003, the left-of-center daily *Libération* ironized that this year the cycling competition should be called the "Detour of France," because that's what American tourists were doing. According to César Balderacchi, president of the Syndicat National des Agents de Voyages (National Union of Travel Agencies), the plunge in American tourism in France was breathtaking: down 80 percent during the first quarter of 2003 compared to the year before. The French Tourism Ministry acknowledged a drop of 30 percent for the first five months of 2003.[56] In France, tourism was the number one foreign currency earner and employed several million people.

On Internet discussion boards, jokes went to the heart of French honor. "Why are French streets tree-lined?" went one. Answer: "So the Germans can march in the shade." And: "How many Frenchmen does it take to defend Paris?" Answer: "No one knows. It's never been tried."

Former CIA director R. James Woolsey argued in a *Wall Street Journal* op-ed that such jokes miss the point of the real, stubborn differences that divide us and "should not only be beneath us but are quite false." He pointed to the Battle of the Marne in September 1914, when Parisian taxi drivers were mobilized to rush reinforcements to the front to save the city, a moment of French history "as famous in France as Washington's crossing the Delaware is to Americans."*

Similar jokes about Germany fail to acknowledge the courageous opposition to Hitler during the Third Reich, when diplomats such as Ulrich von Hassell plotted to remove Hitler and paid for it with their lives. "We diminish ourselves and our arguments by denying the noble side of these nations' history and slandering their national honor," said Woolsey.

And Woolsey is right. As a reporter who has spent eighteen years in France, I have deployed overseas with French marines and spent time as a hostage in a Beirut cellar with a French Foreign Legionnaire, where we ate dirt, sweated fear, and prayed together. I have dined with the commanding officer of the French Foreign Legion, who voiced admiration for America and criticized the lack of resolve of his political masters back in Paris. And I have long befriended pro-American voices in France—some of whom

---

*The most famous anecdote French schoolchildren are taught about the Battle of the Marne is slightly more nuanced than Woolsey's account. When several hundred taxis had assembled at the Esplanade des Invalides in Paris, one of the drivers turned to the French army officer in command and asked, "What about the fare?" After a bit of haggling it was agreed to pay the drivers 27 percent of the meter reading for the harrowing sixty-mile round trip to Nanteuil-le-Haudouin. But thanks to their heroism, the German advance on Paris was stopped.

will appear in the pages of this book—who believed they were engaged in an epic battle within their own country against the forces of appeasement and compromise.

As they continue to remind me even today, it wasn't always this way.

I have two stories to tell in this book, neither of which is well-known to American readers. The first involves the impressive, and often secret, military and strategic cooperation between France and America during the cold war. The second, less glorious but at times Rocambolesque, involves the long love affair of the French elite with former Iraqi dictator Saddam Hussein.

# 2

# Second Marriage

No country without an atom bomb could properly
consider itself independent.
—GENERAL CHARLES DE GAULLE[1]

Michel Jobert, France's foreign minister under President Georges Pompidou, rushed to the western White House in San Clemente, California, as soon as he learned what President Nixon had just done.

Jobert was a small man with a very large ego. A perennial presidential candidate, Jobert headed a political movement he insisted be named for him as if he were a major city. (Parisians came from Paris. Followers of Jobert were known as "Jobertistes.") Michel Jobert was the Henry Wallace or the Ralph Nader of France, a "third force" of French politics many mainstream politicians considered to be little more than a pest. Eschewing the Left, but not finding his home in the center-right parties that were dominated by men of better-honed political skills with egos matching his own, Jobert was a political loner. Idiosyncratic to the point of quirkiness, he was always the contrarian. Even to his friends, he was frequently cranky. As a journalist, however, I always found him a terrific interview. Up until his death at the age of eighty in May 2002, he continued to gaze back fondly to the golden age when France was a major player on the international scene. He was referring, of course, to the two years of his brief stewardship of the Quai d'Orsay, home of the French Foreign Ministry.

Jobert was alarmed when he first learned that President Richard Nixon and Secretary of State Henry Kissinger were planning to sign a new Agreement on the Prevention of Nuclear War with the Soviet Union. Although the United States considered the agreement largely ceremonial, the French were suspicious. They were concerned that it masked a secret U.S.-Soviet effort to enact a comprehensive nuclear test ban that would mean the end of their independent nuclear deterrent. Unknown to the French public, who believed that France was already a major nuclear power, the French nuclear forces were in their infancy in the early 1970s and France was scrambling to catch up with Britain, the United States, and the Soviet Union. At the time, the bulk of the French strategic nuclear force consisted of thirty-six crude gravity bombs that had to be delivered directly over their targets by manned Mirage IV-A bombers.[2] A nuclear war would mean suicide for the French pilots, and they knew it. If they managed to penetrate Soviet air defenses and bomb Moscow, they would run out of fuel before they could make it back to NATO-controlled airspace. France did not detonate its first H-bomb until 1968—eleven years after Britain— and was still struggling with the technology of fitting twin nuclear charges into a single thermonuclear warhead. Its first ballistic missile submarine, *Le Redoutable*, left port with much fanfare for active-duty sea patrol on January 28, 1972, but its missiles carried just a handful of warheads. The ground-based portion of the French nuclear triad was equally fragile. While silo construction at the missile fields of the Plateau d'Albion just north of Marseilles had been completed by late 1969 and the missile base declared operational in 1971, the missiles themselves were still being perfected and their survivability was already in doubt.[3] The French needed dozens more tests before they could be confident they possessed an effective nuclear deterrent force.

Fearing the worst, Jobert rushed to San Clemente for two days of talks with Kissinger and Nixon almost as soon as the ink from Soviet premier Leonid Brezhnev's signature had dried on June 22, 1973. The real subject of their discussions remained a closely guarded secret for more than a decade and a half.

Jobert was carrying a detailed shopping list of nuclear weapons assistance the French were hoping to convince Nixon and Kissinger to supply, much as the United States had been helping Britain to build its nuclear forces since the 1950s. Until now, however, the United States had rebuffed these French requests, and for good reason.

In the early postwar years, the French agency in charge of nuclear weapons development, the Commissariat à l'Energie Atomique (Atomic Energy Commission), or CEA, was dominated by pro-Soviet leftists. Indeed, the first head of the CEA, a member of the French Communist Party, was fired in 1950 after he announced at a Party rally that "the French people do not [want] and never shall make war against the Soviet Union."[4] The United States continued to be suspicious of security procedures at the CEA and feared that any transfer of U.S. nuclear weapons secrets would be leaked to the Soviet Union.[5]

In addition, Presidents Kennedy and Johnson had never liked the haughty general Charles de Gaulle, who kept on insisting that Paris should become a full nuclear partner within the NATO alliance and be given independent authority over U.S. nuclear weapons stationed on French territory. The United States feared de Gaulle would launch weapons against the Soviets without first informing Washington, triggering a massive Soviet retaliatory attack against the U.S. mainland. For his part, de Gaulle justified the extraordinary expense of developing an independent nuclear deterrent for France on grounds that it was unreasonable to expect the United States to "risk their survival to defend Europe," even in the case of a Soviet attack.[6]

When Johnson rebuffed de Gaulle's demands for command authority over NATO nuclear weapons, the Frenchman pulled France out of NATO and ordered the seventy thousand U.S. and NATO troops then stationed in France under the North Atlantic Treaty to pack their bags and leave. Announcing his decision on March 10, 1966, de Gaulle gave the United States one year to get out of France. This forced the U.S. European Command into overdrive, initiating "Operation FRELOC (Fast RELOCation), with the daunting mission of relocating some 70,000 personnel and 400 military facilities, including 30 major Air Force, Army, and Navy Installations,"[7] as well as the NATO headquarters in the Paris suburbs. This is when President Johnson famously asked de Gaulle if he also wanted the United States to bring back the bodies of American soldiers who had given their lives to liberate France twice from German occupiers. The first divorce between Paris and Washington was quick but bitter.

Henry Kissinger recalls his first meeting with de Gaulle during a trip to Paris in March 1969 with President Nixon. The French president was hosting the Americans to a reception in the Élysée Palace. When he spied Kissinger on the other side of the room, de Gaulle sent an aide to tell him the president wanted to speak to him. "Somewhat awestruck, I approached the towering figure," Kissinger writes. "Upon seeing me, he dismissed the group around him and, without a word of greeting or other social courtesy, welcomed me with this query: 'Why don't you get out of Vietnam?' "[8]

But with de Gaulle's abrupt resignation in 1969, things changed, and for a variety of reasons the United States was quietly considering retying the knot with France. Jobert appears not to have been aware of the change of heart and walked like an unsuspecting bride into an engagement party in San Clemente that had already been laid out in advance. Kissinger not only sought to allay French concerns regarding the new agreement with the Soviets, but popped the question that would change the course of history, according to Princeton University scholar Richard H. Ullman.

> The United States had noticed, Kissinger is said to have commented, that the French program to develop multiple warheads for SLBMs [submarine-launched ballistic missiles] had run into difficulties because of an inability to stabilize the spin of the missiles themselves. Would the French like to know how American engineers had solved the problem? Jobert replied affirmatively and indicated that France would welcome American help in solving other problems as well.[9]

Well aware that open technical assistance for the French nuclear weapons program was prohibited under the Atomic Energy Act of 1954, as amended, Kissinger proposed a system of "negative guidance," which came to be known as the "twenty questions," to avoid any direct transfer of restricted data. French experts would sit down with their U.S. counterparts from the national nuclear labs and "describe what they were thinking of doing, and then their American interlocutors would let them know, in general terms, whether they were on the right track."[10] While such a system of winks and nods might appear cursory, given the extraordinary complexity of designing ICBMs and miniaturizing nuclear warheads, in fact it was invaluable and saved the French years of development time and billions of dollars. Just three years after the U.S.-French nuclear cooperation began, France managed to resolve all the technical difficulties of a new generation of warheads and missiles that would vastly increase its ability to inflict damage on the Soviet Union.[11]

Jobert dutifully reported back to President Pompidou, who dispatched his defense minister, Robert Galley, to set up a working relationship with his American counterparts during an extended trip to the United States in September 1973. But when he returned, Galley "reported that the American offer had no substance" and that the Pentagon officials he had met "knew nothing about Jobert's conversations."[12] Jobert, whose relationship with Kissinger "was one of mutual affection tempered by mutual distaste," concluded that the secretary of state had tricked him into revealing France's true sentiments. But he was wrong, and he left office shortly thereafter apparently without ever learning the truth. It had simply taken more time to work out the technical arrangements.

Blinded by his inflated opinion of himself, Jobert later thought that it was his brilliant exposition of the benefits of U.S.-French strategic cooperation that had won over Kissinger and Nixon. Again, he was wrong. Kissinger and Nixon had deliberately chosen to initiate the nuclear cooperation with France as part of a larger strategy to "enhance (qualitatively) the nuclear capabilities extant in Western Europe" in the wake of the 1972 Strategic Arms Limitation Talks, which established U.S.-Soviet nuclear parity.[13] A more robust, and much larger, French nuclear force added an element of uncertainty to Soviet nuclear planning. Since French forces were no longer integrated into NATO, the Soviets could never know for sure whether the French would join a NATO second strike in the event of a Soviet attack on the United States or on NATO forces in Europe; and in the doomsday calculus of nuclear strategy, that uncertainty was a precious asset for the United States.

On the technical side, Kissinger knew precisely what the French needed to improve their forces, thanks to a highly classified report from the Stanford Research Institute (SRI) that described the shortcomings of the French program. The August 1972 report stated:

> France has become acutely aware of the duplication in time and effort in developing its nuclear forces without cooperation from the United States. On several occasions in the past it has sought to win approval in Washington for access to American nuclear technology or for purchasing U.S. auxiliary equipment and materials that would support its nuclear program. American policymakers generally adopted a negative position—a position which French leaders, in light of U.S. willingness to share much of its nuclear technology with Britain, bitterly resented.[14]

The SRI report went on to describe the difficulties the French were encountering in designing warheads with effective penetration aids that could defeat the rudimentary ballistic missile defense shield around Moscow and suggested providing "moderate" support for the French program to include "technology for nuclear safety devices, technology for longer range missile engines, and unrestricted access to U.S. computers and computer technology." If the administration felt it could safely seek approval from Congress for more extensive (and more open) assistance, the report suggested that it "offer France support with its nuclear rocketry" and, eventually, in "perfecting France's nuclear-powered submarines and their associated missiles."[15] Unknown to the general public in either country until now, the highly classified 1972 report laid the framework for nuclear cooperation between them for three decades to come.

As often happens in France with second marriages, there were no elaborate nuptials or even a church wedding. The two partners fell into the new living arrangements as if the divorce under de Gaulle had never occurred. But the French, even more than the Americans, were intent on keeping it a secret liaison. For one thing, the French nuclear barons did not want to reawaken the Gaullist ghost and risk being severed from the U.S. nuclear weapons labs. They were already winning expanded budgets and prestige by their claims of having developed the French strategic nuclear forces with no foreign assistance, so there was no point in telling their political masters the whole truth. "It was the French who wanted to keep it very secret, and we obliged them as a matter of prestige," says Fred Charles Ikle, undersecretary of defense for policy during the Reagan administration and one of the key players in the nuclear exchanges as they evolved during the 1980s.[16] Keeping the alliance secret allowed France to preserve a large measure of political independence from the United States.

On the U.S. side, the SRI report argued that lingering resentment over the French pullout from NATO in 1966, France's refusal to sign the 1963 Partial Test Ban Treaty, its continued atmospheric tests, and suspicions that the CEA was heavily penetrated by Soviet moles were likely to persuade the U.S. Senate to withhold its approval were the administration to submit a formal nuclear cooperation agreement.[17] As the anti-French feelings dissipated, the Carter administration again raised the idea of formalizing the relationship, arguing that they would be able to provide more significant assistance if they had U.S. Senate approval. The French "evidenced a disinterest" in a formal agreement, according to a previously classified 1978 Department of Energy report obtained by Natural Resources Defense Council (NRDC) researcher Robert S. Norris.[18] This did not stop the Carter administration from quietly agreeing to sell the CEA state-of-the-art Cray supercomputers to help the French perform the calculations needed to enhance their warhead designs.[19]

Only a few officials on either side of the Atlantic were aware of the military nuclear cooperation. When the program of exchanges began, outside of the French ambassador to Washington, Jacques Kosciusko-Morizet, a personal confidant of Pompidou, "no one else in the embassy knew the purpose of the visits of the specialists from Paris, who were usually led either by André Giraud, then chairman of the CEA and more recently minister of defense, or by Jean-Laurens Delpech, who was head of the Délégation Générale pour l'Armement [DGA], the government agency that controls arms production."[20] Both men and their respective agencies would remain central to strategic cooperation between the United States and France for many years to come. Indeed, in the case of Delpech, his banner would be taken up by his daughter-in-law, Thérèse Delpech, who in the 1990s became a strategic affairs adviser to President Jacques Chirac and, later, one of the few senior French officials who continued to plead in favor of close ties to Washington.

For the most part, Ullman found, the U.S.-French exchanges "have steered away from the actual design of nuclear weapons—the physics packages—so as not to run afoul of U.S. legislation." Yet both Ullman and Norris concluded that they should have been covered by a special Nuclear Cooperation Agreement, as called for under Section 91c of the Atomic Energy Act, as amended.

Randy Rydell, who was a senior staff member of the Senate Governmental Affairs Committee at the time these exchanges were taking place, pointed out that no provision of the Nuclear Nonproliferation Treaty prohibited military cooperation among nuclear weapons states, but that political considerations prevented successful U.S. administrations from notifying Congress of the cooperation until 1985. "They got around the law through the Socratic method, using questions to shut off blind alleys" in critical areas of weapons design. "Technically, that may not qualify as an illegal transfer of information," he told me. "It was all about helping an ally to save investments, save resources, prevent wild goose chases so they could have a more efficient program."[21]

But the Socratic method could get mightily specific. Ullman found through his interviews with U.S. and French scientists involved in the exchanges that "the French sought and received advice on miniaturizing their warheads and on shielding them from electromagnetic radiation generated by nearby nuclear explosions," a phenomenon known as "fratricide" and one of the most difficult technical problems for weapons designers to resolve. "Accordingly," said Ullman, "French scientists were allowed secretly to expose their own materials and components to radiation from underground explosions at the U.S. test site in Nevada."[22] At one point, the United States offered to allow the French to actually test complete weapons in Nevada, but the French refused, apparently fearing that testing on U.S. soil "seemed too great a symbolic diminution of French independence, and also because the French were reluctant to provide the detailed design information the United States would have required (and which the British routinely provide) in order to properly configure the test facilities."[23] In other words, the French were happy to receive technical assistance and top-secret nuclear weapons information from the United States, but they still had secrets of their own they wanted to preserve.

As General Pierre-Marie Gallois, one of the architects of the French strategic nuclear deterrent, explained to me in Paris in the mid-1980s, one faction within the French nuclear establishment—to which he belonged—actually believed in the slogan de Gaulle had invented to describe the delicate balancing act he believed France needed to play between the Soviet Union and the United States. The French strategic nuclear forces, he said, had been designed to deter attacks on France "de tous azimuths"—from all directions, including from the United States.[24]

But that wasn't how it was perceived in Washington, D.C., or at the three national nuclear labs (Lawrence Livermore, Los Alamos, and Sandia), where U.S. nuclear scientists happily received their French colleagues in their homes and jawboned the arcana of nuclear weapons design far from any security minders. From my own discussions with U.S. and French physicists still engaged in these exchanges, it was clear that over the years they had formed deep personal friendships. "Scientists by their nature love to share," a former top Department of Energy official involved in protecting the labs from foreign espionage said. "The universe of nuclear weapons designers is very finite, so when they get together they find it only natural to share the excitement of their latest discoveries. Even if the French dropped a nuke on us, I bet you'd still find people at the labs who would argue that we can learn something from it," he added.[25]

It would be inaccurate to describe U.S.-French nuclear cooperation as a one-way street, solely in favor of the French. In one sense, what the United States received in exchange was far more important than what it gave to France, because it was something we didn't have and eagerly sought. And it would have made de Gaulle turn over in his grave.

# 3

# Dangerous Liaisons

---

I t was a magnificent early autumn afternoon when the green-and-white Boeing 707 touched down at Orly Airport in Paris, decked out with the eagle of Saladin, Iraq's martial national symbol. The date was Friday, September 5, 1975. Jacques Chirac, then the youngest prime minister of France, was on hand to greet his visitor the instant his foot touched French soil. A long red carpet led into the VIP lounge, where champagne and French cocktail sandwiches awaited the Iraqi guests. "I welcome you as my personal friend," Prime Minister Chirac told his visitor. "I assure you of my esteem, my consideration, and my affection." Chirac's "personal friend" was Saddam Hussein. Although officially he was still just Iraq's vice president, he had already become the acknowledged strongman of the Baathist regime.

Saddam returned Chirac's courtesies with just a hint of the megalomania for which he would become famous later on. "We hope that the relations France maintains with [other] Arab countries will benefit from the same warmth and cordiality as today. The relations between our two countries can only improve as a result of my visit, which, I hope, will be beneficial for world peace in general."[1]

The Iraqi vice president had come to France to seal a strategic pact he had been negotiating with Chirac for the better part of a year. Their "friendship" would soon translate into massive French arms sales and the transfer of critical nuclear technologies to Iraq, dramatically accelerating the Middle East arms race and marking the start of Saddam's ambitious nuclear weapons program.

The French accorded the thirty-eight-year-old Saddam all the honors of a head of state. They lodged him at the sumptuous Marigny Palace in Paris, where visiting kings and state presidents had resided before him. They threw a gala reception in his honor at the Château of Versailles. President Valéry Giscard d'Estaing invited him for state lunches at the Élysée. Prime Minister Chirac stuck to him like glue. The five-day trip was a long succession of photo ops and champagne panegyrics. The French wanted Saddam as desperately as Saddam wanted them, for the Iraqi had something they needed to keep their economy afloat: oil. French media pundits, taking a tip from the spin doctors at the Élysée, called it "a marriage of reason." Today, it has become a cliché to speak of arms-for-oil deals, but this is where it all started, as a love affair between France and Iraq.

That weekend, Chirac tapped an old Gaullist party hand who controlled one of the most superb medieval sites in France, to assist him in the wooing of oil-rich (and arms-hungry) Saddam. Raymond Thuillier was one of France's best-known chefs. He had served as the mayor of Baux-de-Provence for more than twenty years and had hosted the mighty at his hostelrie many times before. His exclusive weekend resort went by the quaint provençal name L'Oustau de Baumanière and was one of the most extravagant hideaways frequented by the French political elite. Nestled along an isolated ravine not far from the Mediterranean coast, it offered a dramatic view of an abandoned medieval fortress perched among the tumbled crags of Provence like a Wild West version of the Hanging Gardens of Babylon.

Although he was almost ninety years old when I traveled to Baux in the spring of 1988 and got him to recall the scene, Thuillier's mind was as lively as ever. He described the menu in detail and dug up photographs of Chirac sitting side by side with the new master of Babylon, drinking coffee after their meal in the sheltered gardens of L'Oustau. "Chirac never left him for a second," Thuillier recalled. "They were like bride and bridegroom." In the photographs Thuillier showed me, Saddam Hussein is wearing a white-and-black checkerboard suit with a colored shirt and mismatching tie. "He glowed like a peacock," Thuillier said, laughing. Not long after this trip, Saddam invited a French tailor to take up residence at his court in Baghdad, so he would never be embarrassed by the poor quality of his Arab suits again. (It was said that the tailor, who was of Lebanese descent, provided key assistance to the French and even opened doors for several French arms contractors.)

After lunch, Chirac had prepared a surprise for his guest: a bullfight through the streets of the ancient necropolis up on the cliffs. Thuillier, who had personally supervised the restoration of the medieval ruins, handled all the arrangements. The site was sealed off from tourists, bleachers were set up, and a large, well-protected bullpen was erected among the crumbling buildings. The village boys had trained for days in preparation for the event. Unlike Spanish bullfights, the provençal *jeu de taurillons* involved no bloodshed. But it was still a high-spirited sport that exposed the boys to the angry bulls as they scampered through the ring, trying to get close enough to pluck the bright flower that had been pinned behind the ear of the bull.

"Saddam caught on almost immediately," Thuillier recalled. "After the first bull, he was jumping up and down and shouting, encouraging the boys. Then one of his retainers came up to me and said he was offering one million francs [around $200,000] to the boy who could beat the next bull. You can imagine what happened after that! Every boy in town tried to get into the ring."

Three times, Thuillier said, Saddam bet on the bulls, and each time he promised a one million-franc prize. "After it was all over, the kids who won came up to me and asked if I thought he was serious. 'Of course he is,' I said. 'Just you wait and see.' "

A few weeks later, Thuillier said, an emissary from the Iraqi embassy in Paris showed up at his office with three checks, each for one million francs. Saddam had come through for the local boys. Soon he would come through for the big boys as well. Over the next fifteen years, he would spend a good $20 billion on French arms. For Saddam Hussein, it was the price of independence from the Soviets. For the French, it was manna from heaven.

Saddam had solid reasons for turning to France. Over the previous two decades, Iraq had become a Soviet client state. Successive Soviet governments had delighted in supplying Iraq with MiG fighters, tanks, artillery, SCUD missiles, and warships as a counter to the growing U.S. presence in neighboring Iran. By the time Saddam turned to France, Soviet advisers were virtually running his country. Soviet oil experts were building pipelines and exploring new oil fields; Soviet hydraulic engineers were building new dams; Soviet military advisers were training Iraqi tankists and air force pilots how to use the weapons the Socialist sister nation had so graciously supplied.

But to Saddam, the Soviets were cumbersome allies. They counted on him to tow the line on major foreign policy issues and UN votes. Worse, they interfered in his bloody war against his political rivals inside Iraq, insisting he ally himself with the local Communist Party, which he hated. When Saddam launched an assault in 1974 against his own Kurdish population, another favorite of Moscow, the Soviet Politburo decided to teach the aspiring Iraqi dictator a lesson and stopped deliveries of ammunition and spare parts. Saddam later said that the Iraqi army was on the verge of defeat by the Kurds because of the Soviet arms embargo and that his air force had "just one bomb left." The bitter experience convinced him to find other weapons suppliers. By turning to France, he was hoping to break the Soviet stranglehold on his growing ambitions.

The French also had good reasons for wooing Saddam. In addition to a guaranteed supply of cheap oil—critically important after the quadrupling of world oil prices in 1973–1974—they needed to discover new export markets for French weapons. The French defense budget was simply not big enough to finance the massive costs of developing new combat aircraft, ballistic missiles, and nuclear weapons for French use alone. They needed economies of scale to defray development costs, and Iraq was a natural fit.

The French gambit with Saddam fit the strategy of Secretary of State Henry Kissinger, who had viewed the signing of a ten-year Treaty of Friendship and Cooperation between the Baathist regime and the Soviet Union in 1972 with concern. "At the time, Iraq was considered by the Americans as a 'yellow light' country, one that should be treated with caution, but to whom the door should certainly not be shut," notes French foreign policy analyst Alexandre Adler. "By audaciously engaging Iraq, France thus served as an opening for the whole Western camp."[2] It was the type of team playing that had been notably absent under de Gaulle and was part of the new climate between the two countries generated by Kissinger and Nixon as a result of the secret nuclear cooperation.

Speaking to the French press after a three-day trip to Baghdad on De-

cember 2, 1974, Chirac gushed that Saddam was offering France a "verita-
ble bonanza" of new contracts. Among them was a seemingly innocent
pact, signed between the Iraqi and French ministers of agriculture, to establish a bacteriological laboratory under the tutelage of France's prestigious Institut Mérieux. United Nations arms inspectors concluded years
later that the ad-Daura plant could have been used "with some modifica-
tion to produce large amounts of pathogenic material" as part of Iraq's
clandestine program to build biological weapons.[3]

To the French public, Chirac and his advisers described their willingness to sell arms and technology to Iraq in grandiloquent terms as part of a
"philosophy" of technology transfer to empower the third world. Chirac
claimed that France could offer a "third way" to nations such as Iraq that
allowed them to buy security with no political strings attached. A future
Socialist defense official agreed, writing that French arms export policy was
correctly oriented "toward helping those countries desiring to throw off
the yoke of a super power."[4]

It was an argument that struck home with the independent-minded
Saddam Hussein, who liked to refer to himself as an Arab Charles de Gaulle
fighting a foreign "occupation" of his region. The only way to chase the Jews
and "imperialist" powers from the Arab Middle East, he believed, was for
Iraq to become a major military power equipped with nuclear arms.

C hirac also had a personal reason for wooing Saddam. Although he had
taken office only one year earlier, he was already at odds with Giscard, a
center-right technocrat he had helped to elect in March 1974 by withdraw-
ing his support at the last minute from the Gaullist front-runner, Jacques
Chaban-Delmas. Chirac suspected that his days as premier were numbered
(they were) and was hoping that the "affection" of the Iraqi leader would
save him from long years in the political wilderness, deprived of important
sources of financial support in a country that had no legal system to regu-
late the flow of money to politics. Thanks to his "personal friendship" with
Saddam, which he spoke of repeatedly,[5] Jacques Chirac came to be recognized by businessmen and politicians alike as the head of the unofficial
"Iraq lobby" in France. Just one year after his forced resignation as prime
minister in August 1976, he was able to launch a well-funded political
movement, the Rassemblement pour la République (RPR), which consistently championed French relations with Iraq and Saddam's friends in the

Arab world, while promoting a certain distance from the United States, even at the height of the cold war. It was never clear, even then, where the money came from.

Chirac was a former president of the Gaullist goon squad known as the Service d'Action Civique, whose members raised money for the Party through strong-arm tactics, and carried out operations of physical and psychological intimidation against their political opponents. It was an affiliation not well-known outside of France (and one that does not figure on his official résumé). Over the years, he cemented ties with the parallel intelligence networks operating in Africa and the Middle East under the stewardship of former de Gaulle aide Jacques Foccart. Giscard fired Foccart soon after entering the Élysée in 1974 as part of an effort to crack down on the Gaullist networks, but Chirac rehired him just weeks later once he was appointed prime minister. According to U.S. intelligence analyst Douglas Porch, whose 1995 work, *The French Secret Services,* describes Chirac's close ties to the parallel networks, Foccart was put in charge of "channeling funds from Gabon and Iraq into Gaullist party coffers."[6] Both countries had privileged oil supply contracts with France, with large margins that could accommodate political payoffs.

Who made those payments and where they ended up is likely to remain a mystery. But according to Sarkis Soghanalian, a Lebanese arms merchant of Armenian extraction who helped the French make some of their biggest deals in Iraq, there was "no doubt" that Saddam made payments intended to help Jacques Chirac. "Saddam was friends with Chirac, and he was generous. He had unlimited access to cash money. I carried cash several times to make payments myself."

Under special arrangements worked out ahead of time between Baghdad and their French suppliers, Soghanalian said he was given a torn dollar bill as an identification signal. "I would go to the UBS bank in Switzerland along with an employee and someone from the Iraqi embassy, with instructions from Baghdad to make cash withdrawals. Each package had something like a Marlboro cigarette wrapper around it, but a little bit wider. Each package contained $440,000 in crisp $100 bills." At a prearranged rendezvous, always in Switzerland (but never in France), he would hand over the package to an emissary who showed the other half of the torn dollar bill. "The politicians had front people. You'd never ask their name, they'd never ask you your name. You have half of the dollar, and he has half of the dollar. You match the serial numbers and make the exchange. That was how it worked."[7]

On their way down to the bullfights at Les Baux, Saddam's French hosts took him through the Cadarache nuclear research center, one of the largest and most advanced in Europe. This small provençal town just north of Marseilles was where the French Atomic Energy Commission, the CEA, had set up its first experimental fast-breeder reactor. They called it "Rapsodie." It certainly enchanted Saddam. In the official photograph of their visit, Chirac and Saddam are wearing white lab coats and are caught gazing upward, almost in apprehension, as if someone had just told them that some very large object was about to fall on top of them.[8]

The French were interested in breeder reactors because they produced bomb-grade plutonium as a by-product of electrical generation, thus "breeding" more nuclear material than they actually consumed. At the time, this technology was considered a promising means of increasing France's stockpile of nuclear weapons material rapidly and at a relatively low cost. But it was inherently proliferating. Selling it to Saddam virtually guaranteed that he would be able rapidly to acquire large amounts of weapons-grade fuel.

The Iraqis said they wanted to develop a nuclear power industry. For a nation sitting on top of the world's second-largest oil reserves, that should have been a tip-off to Iraq's true intentions. They inquired into the possibility of purchasing a five-hundred-megawatt natural uranium/gas-graphite reactor, a French design more remarkable for the amount of plutonium it produced than for efficient electrical production. By the time Saddam toured Cadarache on September 6, 1975, the gas-graphite design had already been dropped for electric power production by Électricité de France in favor of more efficient light-water reactors, which the French manufactured under license from Westinghouse. The French government continued to operate a few gas-graphite plants, however. All served as plutonium breeders for the French nuclear weapons program.

As an alternative to the gas-graphite reactor, the French suggested that Saddam consider a forty-megawatt Osiris research reactor, which could breed smaller quantities of bomb-grade material. Saddam agreed, on one condition: that France deliver an extra four-year supply of reactor fuel at start-up. The Osiris reactor was designed to run on weapons-grade uranium, enriched to 93 percent, CEA officials acknowledged when I toured the original plant in Saclay in October 1990. If they wanted to, the Iraqis could simply take the reactor fuel and use it directly to make bombs. A four-year supply of fuel came to seventy-two kilograms. It was enough for at least two bombs the size of those used on Hiroshima.

The Iraqis called the reactor Osirak but changed the name after the French press referred to it derisively as "O'Chirac" in honor of the prime minister. The pilot plant and the research reactor became known as Tammuz I and Tammuz II after the Sumerian corn god, lover of Ishtar, who was brought back to life from the netherworld to symbolize the eternity of the harvest. Tammuz was also the name of the month when Saddam's Baath Party seized power in 1968.

CEA director André Giraud was contemplating far more than just selling Iraq a nuclear bomb plant, a top CEA official told me later. "Giraud discussed inviting Iraq into Eurodif," a French-led consortium that supplied enriched uranium to the European nuclear power industry. "He wanted to give them gaseous diffusion enrichment technology, and the Chemex (chemical enrichment) process. The idea, he told us, was to give Iraq enrichment independence, which would have made it impossible to control how much weapons-grade fuel they were producing. It was quite alarming, actually. We finally managed to put a stop to the whole thing in 1980 or 1981."[9] Based in part on information obtained officially from the French government, United Nations arms inspectors told me more than a decade later that they believed Iraq had succeeded in acquiring this technology.

After visiting Cadarache, Saddam gave an interview to a Lebanese weekly, *al-Usbu al-Arabi*, which was published the same day he ended his official visit to France. "The agreement with France," Saddam declared, "is the first concrete step toward the production of the Arab atomic weapon." His statement rang like an alarm bell—in the United States and Israel. But it was virtually ignored in France.

After the weekend of play with the provençal bulls, Saddam and Chirac returned to serious business. On Monday morning, September 8, 1975, Chirac accompanied Saddam and his personal secretary, Adnan Hamdani, on the spectacular fifteen-mile drive through the *garigue* to the French air force testing ground at Istre, just northwest of Marseilles. They were joined by Saddam's military adviser, General Saadoun Ghaidan, and a horde of

French officials. Chief among them was the elegant, bespectacled Hugues de l'Estoile, one of the principal architects of the massive French arms sales to Iraq.

At the time of the first major contracts with Iraq, de l'Estoile was in charge of arms exports at the French Ministry of Defense. His talents as a salesman were so appreciated that when he decided to head through the revolving door into private industry, he could write his own ticket. He chose to become the right-hand man of aerospace magnate Marcel Dassault and would personally oversee the sale of 133 Mirage jet fighters in ever sophisticated versions to Iraq. His job description remained the same; he merely changed hats.

The Istre base was a must for all important foreign visitors. It was dotted with sumptuous chalets run by the major French aerospace contractors, where they could entertain foreign dignitaries while showing off helicopters, jet fighters, trainers, cluster bombs, runway-busting bombs, air-to-air missiles, and air defense systems—the latest inventions of France's innovative aerospace industry.

Initially Saddam Hussein had told Chirac that he wanted to buy the same Mirage fighters that Israel had used with such success against Egypt and Syria during the 1973 war. But when Dassault and French military engine manufacturer Snecma sent a technical team to Baghdad, they offered him one better. The French air force was just completing flight tests of a new-generation fighter, the Mirage F1, that was far superior to the Mirage III the Israelis had received, they said. The new plane was equal to the American F-16, which had just narrowly beaten out the Mirage in the "contract of the century" to reequip half a dozen NATO air forces. The French arms salesmen showed films of the new fighter in action and gave an extensive technical briefing of the weaponry it could deliver. They reported back home that Saddam's men were overjoyed.[10]

As he watched the acrobatics of the latest Mirage from the terrace of the Dassault chalet at Istre, Saddam turned to his air force expert, General Ghaidan. "This is the plane that nearly beat the F-16?" When Ghaidan nodded his assent, Saddam appeared to make up his mind. "When can we get it?"

Hamdani asked the French about delivery lead times, while Ghaidan discussed the type of avionics the French were offering. Iraq would settle for nothing short of the best, Saddam insisted. He wanted the same equipment that Dassault had promised to the French air force: the same radar, the same electronic countermeasures (ECM), the same weapons system. He wanted a front-line NATO fighter, and in the end he got it. Dassault designated the Iraqi jets the "EQ" planes, in keeping with the code-letter system the company used to designate export aircraft by country of purchase. Successive versions were numbered EQ2, EQ3, EQ4, EQ5, and EQ6, to distinguish their weapons fit.

When they returned to Paris from the south of France, Saddam decided to prepare a surprise for his "personal friend" Jacques Chirac. He wanted to seal their pact on a personal note. Much to the consternation of the maître d'hôtel at the French government palace where he was staying, Saddam ordered his personal cook to fly back to Baghdad on the presidential plane to retrieve a load of victuals. At the top of the list was 1.5 tons of an Iraqi river fish called *masgouf,* which Chirac had enjoyed while in Baghdad the year before. As Iraqi security guards patrolled the kitchens of the Marigny with their machine pistols, Saddam's cooks roasted the huge greasy carp over open fires. Even Chirac thought it was a bit much. "The whole place smelled of charred flesh. It was amusing, but a mess," he told Raymond Thuillier later.

By the end of Saddam's trip to France, the Quai d'Orsay was briefing the press on the "objective, historical reasons" for strengthening ties with Baghdad. As *Le Monde* wrote, Iraq saw France "as the most natural ally on the geopolitical scene today to help it escape the hegemony of the superpowers. . . . If Paris is seeking to convert its political capital into economic gains, Baghdad hopes to turn its economic strength into political gains."[11] It was a nice formula that elevated France's mercantile interests to the realm of a grand geopolitical vision.

Chirac waxed eloquent as he bade his guest farewell. French policy, he declared, "is not merely dictated by interest, but also by the heart. . . . France deems it necessary to establish relationships between producers and consumers on terms that best conform to the interests of both parties." Beyond Iraqi oil and the Mirage deal, those interests included petrochemical plants, desalinization plants, gas liquefaction complexes, housing projects, telecommunications systems, broadcasting and jamming equipment, fertilizer plants, defense electronics factories, car assembly plants, a new airport, a subway system, and a navy yard, not to mention Exocet, Milan, HOT, Magic, Martel, and Armat missiles; Alouette III, Gazelle, and

Super Puma helicopters; 155mm-GCT howitzers; Tiger-G radar; and, of course, a nuclear reactor capable of making fuel for the bomb. It was a multibillion-dollar relationship, and it was based on the kind of "balance" that appealed to Saddam Hussein: a balance of terror.

Just two months later, French president Valéry Giscard d'Estaing dispatched one of his most trusted political allies to Baghdad. In his briefcase was the final text of the Franco-Iraqi nuclear cooperation treaty. When Minister of Industry and Research Michel d'Ordano initialed the treaty in Baghdad on November 18, 1975, it was billed by the French press as a simple export sale. Worth 1.45 billion French francs (around $300 million at then current exchange rates), the agreement covered the sale of Osiris/Tammuz I, the 40 MW research reactor, and Isis/Tammuz II, an experimental scale model. Tammuz II was an important addition, since it allowed Iraqi nuclear scientists to experiment with different reactor loads without shutting down the Tammuz I bomb plant. "France will be training large numbers of Iraqi personnel," said d'Ordano. "Paris hopes that our cooperation in this area will be exemplary."

The full text of the Franco-Iraqi nuclear cooperation treaty was made public only eight months later in an obscure notice in the French public register, dated June 18, 1976. The Iraqis insisted that "all persons of the Jewish race or the Mosaic religion" be excluded from participating in the program, either in Iraq or in France.[12] Saddam's visceral hatred of Jews didn't bother the French, who agreed to this condition without batting an eye.

The French were committed to training six hundred Iraqi nuclear technicians, more than enough to launch a bomb program. "Some of them attended French universities," a high-level CEA official told me. Others received training at CEA research facilities, where they gleaned nuclear weapons secrets from their French colleagues. "We also trained Iraqi chemists," the official said.[13] This laconic admission is of capital importance, because complex chemical processes were required to extract military plutonium from spent reactor fuel.

One final irony involved the fuel. The French had to make special arrangements to be able to provide the large quantities of highly enriched uranium (HEU) Saddam was seeking. For years, the French had been importing the 93 percent–enriched uranium fuel they used to power up their own Osiris reactor from the U.S. Department of Energy, since every gram of HEU made in France was manufactured exclusively for French military programs. The last thing they wanted was to have the U.S. government start poking its nose into French nuclear exports. So a secret deal was struck, and by special order, the Tammuz reactor fuel was manufactured at a French bomb plant.[14] In Saddam's hands, of course, the bomb-grade fuel would be used only for "peaceful" purposes.

C hirac had important allies in putting together a powerful pro-Iraq lobby in France. Chief among them was aviation wizard Marcel Dassault, a French Jew who had been deported by the Vichy authorities during the Nazi occupation, survived the death camps, and built an industrial empire out of the ruins of Europe.* He had supplied the French air force with every fighter they had ever owned, including a few the generals claimed they never wanted. Dassault, who converted to Christianity after the war, argued that arms sales to Iraq would create jobs, improve the balance of payments, and reduce development costs on new weapons programs.

Marcel Dassault was a French institution. Besides heading the most prestigious industrial empire in postwar France, he also sat in the French National Assembly. While he rarely attended parliamentary debates, his presence alone among the elected made a powerful statement about the marriage between the defense industry lobby and the French government. No one complained about a conflict of interest; not even Dassault's political enemies called on him to resign as head of his industrial empire if he wanted to remain in Parliament. This was one particularity of the French political system that would have major impact on arms sales policy over the next fifteen years: industry and government were virtually one. There was not even a fig leaf of parliamentary oversight.

A tiny man with often impractical ideas, Marcel Dassault was much revered, perhaps because he had succeeded in the nearly impossible task of bridging the social and political chasm that divided the French Left from the French Right. His political philosophy placed him on the Right, from whose ranks he was elected to Parliament, while the labor policies he pioneered at his aircraft and electronics factories had earned him the fidelity of the powerful Communist Party trade union, the Confédération Générale

---

*For more on Chirac's relationship to Marcel Dassault, see chapter 11.

du Travail (CGT). When the government tried to reduce air force orders, Dassault's Communist workers would lead the protest to prevent defense cuts. When he proposed selling fighter-bombers to Israel, the CGT cheered. When de Gaulle imposed an arms embargo on Israel in 1968, Dassault flipped his vest and sold the same planes to Libya, Iraq, South Africa, and Chile's General Augusto Pinochet, and the CGT cheered again. Dassault's foreign sales were in the national interest, whether they helped democrats or dictators. French arms sales meant jobs.

After Dassault, Saddam's most outspoken advocate in the defense industry was General Jacques Mitterrand, president of the French National Company of Aerospace Industries, Société Nationale Industrielle Aérospatiale, later known more simply as Aérospatiale. As the older brother of opposition leader François Mitterrand, the general served as a discreet bridge between the Gaullist conservatives and his brother's leftist coalition. In these early days of the arms bonanza in the Gulf, Aérospatiale cashed in by selling Iraq thousands of antitank missiles and dozens of combat helicopters. Once the Mirage deal went through, the company offered Saddam its most advanced weapons system: the sea-skimming Exocet, which Iraq used subsequently to attack the USS *Stark* in 1987, killing thirty-seven U.S. sailors.

Dassault and General Mitterrand received critical help in authorizing these sales from the all-powerful Délégation Générale pour l'Armement, which bore responsibility for French weapons programs, procurements, and foreign sales. DGA boss Henri Martre believed that a "marriage of reason" with Iraq could improve the Defense Ministry's endemic cash flow problems, which were the direct result of French nuclear doctrine. Even with U.S. assistance, building and deploying a sizable nuclear weapons arsenal was expensive and consumed nearly half of the entire research and development budget of the Defense Ministry. This meant that many worthy conventional weapons programs went begging for funds. Iraq offered a neat solution to this problem. Martre's deputy, Hugues de l'Estoile, told me later that by weaning Iraq away from the Soviets, France was contributing to the Western alliance. "Our main competitor was almost always the Soviets," he said, "not the Americans." Intelligence chief Count Alexandre de Marenches was also on board, although he argued unsuccessfully that no U.S. technology should be transferred to Iraq, since Soviet agents at Iraqi military bases were sure to steal it. The other key pillar of the French alliance with Saddam was CEA boss André Giraud, who believed that the proliferation of nuclear weapons was in the strategic interest of middle-rate powers such as France, since it helped to weaken the superpower condominium. A well-respected technocrat, Giraud went on to become minister of industry under Giscard and, later, minister of defense.

As the strategic relationship with Saddam expanded in the late 1970s and early 1980s, arms sales to Iraq accounted for an astronomical portion of overall French arms sales. Nearly one thousand French defense contractors cashed in, from the giants—Dassault, Aérospatiale, Thomson-CSF, Matra, and GIAT (Groupement des Industries d'Armement Terrestre)—on down to manufacturers of electronic circuit boards, fiberglass boats, parachutes, and camouflage nets. The real question was not who belonged to the pro-Iraq lobby, but who would dare to oppose it.

Figures I compiled in 1990 from official Defense Ministry sources and from French defense companies have never been disputed. At the peak of the relationship, in 1983, Saddam alone bought 51.5 percent of all French arms exports.[15] This ever increasing economic dependence on Iraq had profound and far-reaching consequences. Given that the next largest market for French weapons was Saudi Arabia, it motivated successive French governments to modify their foreign policies to accommodate their best clients. "Traditionally, the Quai d'Orsay experts take their desires for realities whenever they pretend to speak in the name of an 'Arab world' they claim to be fundamentally anti-American," says French philosopher and political writer André Glucksmann.[16] By the time of the 2002–2003 Iraq crisis, those pro-Arab views had become indissociable from the anti-Americanism.

At Tuwaitha, in the desert just fifteen miles south of Baghdad, work on Iraq's nuclear research center was progressing rapidly. So were the protests, which came ringing in from Israel, the United Kingdom, Saudi Arabia, Syria, and elsewhere. All expressed concern to the French that the Osirak reactor was really intended as a nuclear bomb plant.

To head off the criticism, French president Valéry Giscard d'Estaing ordered the CEA in 1979 to develop a "clean" fuel for the Osirak reactor, so France could honor its lucrative nuclear contract without adding to proliferation fears. The CEA began to experiment with a new fuel pack they called "Caramel." It was made of uranium enriched to just 7 percent, sufficient to drive the Osirak reactor but unsuitable for nuclear weapons without additional enrichment. The French urged Saddam to accept the new fuel, but Saddam coldly refused. While publicly he lavished praise on his French "partners," privately he threatened to cancel juicy nonmilitary contracts if the French didn't deliver his bomb-grade uranium.[17]

Once the twin Osirak reactor cores had been completed, the CEA hauled them down to the port of La Seyne sur Mer near Toulon, to await the arrival of an Iraqi container ship. Security procedures were elaborate: the CEA had done everything to avoid publicity. The precious cargo arrived in the dead of night in a convoy of armored cars. The plan was to load the reactor cores onto the Iraqi ship before dawn on the morning of April 9, 1979, before the day shift ever arrived.

At Tuwaitha, just south of Baghdad, everything was ready to receive the reactor cores. The huge reinforced concrete reactor pool, dug deep into the rocky earth, had been completed on time by French contractors. The large crane used to hoist the reactors into place and to manipulate spent fuel rods had been tested and greased to perfection. Test equipment was coming in from all over the world. The head of the Tuwaitha project, Dr. Ja'afar Dhia Ja'afar, told his European friends that a great day was about to dawn.

But he had spoken too soon. On April 4, three young men stepped off the commuter flight from Paris at the tiny Toulon-Hyères Airport. Without a word to one another, they hailed separate cabs and headed off to different hotels. All three were carrying European passports. On April 6, four other "tourists" arrived in Toulon. Without arousing suspicion, the seven young men met that evening near the waterfront to observe the habits of the nightwatchman guarding the warehouse where the reactor cores had been stored. Once they were sure the watchman had gone on his break, they climbed over the security fence and headed silently for the warehouse, which they opened with an exact replica of the key the watchman had used only a few hours earlier to close it down for the night.

Inside the hangar, their attention was drawn by eight large crates, which contained the honeycomb structure of the reactor cores. This is where Dr. Ja'afar and his colleagues would place the zirconium-clad fuel rods a few months later when they were scheduled to start up the Osirak bomb plant for the first time. Working quickly but carefully, the intruders packed specially designed high-explosive charges around the reactor cores. The explosives were powerful enough to penetrate armor plate.

At approximately three-fifteen on the morning of April 7, an enormous blast rocked the warehouse, totally destroying the reactor cores but causing little other damage. No one was hurt. To this day, the French police have found no trace of the bombers, and these details would never have come to light if it hadn't been for the publicized "confession" of one member of the seven-man commando in the German press a year later.

All seven members of the commando were Israeli. Mossad had struck. The attack at La Seyne was code-named Operation Big Lift.

When Saddam learned of the bombing at La Seyne sur Mer, he was furious. The French, of course, would have to replace the reactors, since they were responsible for security while the reactors remained on French soil. But the French would have to do more besides. Three weeks after the explosion, Saddam dispatched one of his cousins, Defense Minister Adnan Khairallah, to Paris to demand the replacement of the destroyed reactor cores and to deliver Iraq's final refusal to accept anything but bomb-grade fuel.

To soften the hard line on the nuclear deal, Khairallah met with his French counterpart, Defense Minister Yvon Bourges, on May 4. Top on the agenda was a detailed briefing on Dassault's latest plane, the Mirage 2000, then in an advanced stage of development. Iraq was prepared to leap directly from the Mirage F1, which it had not yet received, to the Mirage 2000, Khairallah told Bourges. But there was a hitch: Saddam wanted Dassault to build an assembly line in Iraq and train thousands of Iraqi workers.

To Bourges and to his top arms salesman, Hugues de l'Estoile, the assembly-line idea was out. They feared Iraq would dump its planes on third world markets at a later date, undercutting by a wide margin the exorbitant prices Dassault could maintain through its monopoly. What they told Khairallah, however, was different. The Mirage 2000 was several years from deployment, and Iraq needed a front-line fighter-bomber now. Instead of banking on the new plane, Iraq would do better to buy more F1s, especially since Thomson-CSF was just then putting the finishing touches on a new radar, the Cyrano IV, that would enable the Iraqi planes to fly for hundreds of miles at sand-dune level without being detected by enemy air defenses.

With the new radar and low-level navigation package, the Iraqi air force would have the ability to strike Israel. The deal sounded like music to

Saddam's ears. He summoned Giscard's latest prime minister, a former university professor named Raymond Barre, to Baghdad on July 7 to accept the French proposal. Negotiations were over, Saddam told an enthralled Barre. The time of the payoff had come.

"We will never forget your positive attitude and your comprehension at the most difficult moments of our history," Saddam said. "You were the only Western power to recognize the legitimacy of our decision, a few years back, when we nationalized the oil companies. You were the only ones not to provide support to the Kurdish rebellion, not to intrigue against the central government in Baghdad." Iraq and France had become strategic partners, Saddam said. And to prove it, he pledged to step up oil deliveries to France by half.

Saddam's oil offer was received graciously by Raymond Barre, whose natural bonhomie and roly-poly features were spoiled only by an overbearing pomposity he brought with him from academia. France had suffered more than most from the break in Iranian oil deliveries that Ayatollah Khomeini's chaotic revolution had provoked earlier that year. Iraq now supplied France with roughly 25 percent of its oil, and France had become Iraq's third trading partner, after West Germany and Japan.

The rewards for so much French "comprehension" were on their way. By the end of Barre's July 1979 trip to Baghdad, Le Monde announced that French suppliers were being considered for naval purchases worth between $1.4 billion and $2.3 billion. By October, French nonmilitary exports to Iraq were up 53 percent. In December 1979, a contract for twenty-four additional Mirage fighter-bombers was signed. It was billed as a way of "better preparing the purchase of the Mirage 2000 when the new combat aircraft from Dassault becomes operational."

For Dassault, Thomson-CSF, Matra, and Aérospatiale, Iraq was the best game in town.

When Saddam ascended to the presidency in July 1979, finally assuming absolute power in Iraq, he executed one-third of the ruling Revolutionary Command Council in a sweeping purge of high-ranking Baath Party officials he accused of dual loyalties. Among his victims was Adnan Hamdani, the man who had worked out the financial arrangements for Saddam's arms purchases from France.

French defense contractors working in Iraq at the time had heard rumors of Hamdani's forthcoming demise, and in the weeks before his execution in August 1979, they rigorously avoided him. "By the time you heard that this or that official was on the take," one arms salesman recalled, "it was already too late. Within weeks—months at the most—he disappeared."[18]

Saddam discovered that Hamdani had cut a deal with a Palestinian middleman, Ramzi Daloul, who represented the largest French companies in Iraq. Together they were taking 10 percent off the top of every arms deal Iraq signed with France. Half of that amount went to Hamdani, a kickback the French considered a fair price for his help in gaining exclusive access to Saddam. The French rolled the "surcharge" into their costs, which were paid by the Iraqi government.

What so incensed Saddam, besides the fact that neither he nor his family had gotten their cut, was the thought that a foreign government might have succeeded in gaining access to Iraqi state secrets. This was because Hamdani was one of three people in Iraq who knew all about Saddam's long-range strategic plans to acquire weapons of mass destruction.[19] He had personally negotiated many of the arms deals and knew in detail about Saddam's attempts to purchase chemical weapons and nuclear technologies from Western countries, China, and Brazil. After forcing Hamdani to confess, Saddam summoned Daloul to Baghdad in a fury and demanded his money back. The terrified Palestinian forked up $8 million in cash and may have made other "contributions" to a secret Baath Party fund held in a Swiss bank, one of his French partners told me. Saddam then went to the French and angrily informed them that he was refusing to pay the commissions and would be chopping 10 percent off the top of every payment outstanding. The French swallowed hard and finally agreed to charge no more commissions. Instead, they negotiated a secret deal with Daloul for future services, which continued all through the 1980s. It was hard to stop paying kickbacks once you got into the habit.

By 1979, the nuclear cooperation begun by Presidents Nixon and Pompidou had blossomed into a renewed military and strategic alliance between France and America. Quietly, without any public announcement, French chiefs of staff began meeting with their American counterparts at Supreme Allied Command Europe "to assure that even though France was not a member of [NATO's] integrated military organization, its forces could effectively participate in the defense of the West."[20] French military commanders prepared detailed plans with their American counterparts to ensure the ability of the United States to resupply the alliance in the event of a Soviet thrust into central Europe. The French agreed to give the United States "access to French seaports, airports, pipelines, railways, and highways, rather than be confined to more vulnerable lines of communications in West Germany. Daily guaranteed tonnage levels [were] set."[21] Because the secret arrangements with the French were not part of official NATO planning, they expanded the options available to U.S. political and military leaders and gave them more flexibility in their response to Soviet aggression at a time when East-West tensions were escalating dramatically.

The alliance with France was more than just a tacit understanding. President Carter's deputy national security adviser, David Aaron, "would go regularly to Paris, sit down with [Jacques] Wahl [the secretary-general of the Élysée], and go over all the things we needed to do together. I'm certain we would not have been able to do that had we not had this other relationship," said a Washington insider. "It was not just philosophical or personal, but also an enormous lever which Giscard had over the Gaullists in his security establishment."[22] These were the same Gaullists—Chirac, Henri Martre, and André Giraud, among others—who were hyping the relationship with Saddam Hussein.

The consultations became personal at the very top. Presidents Jimmy Carter and Valéry Giscard d'Estaing developed a close relationship based on trust and mutual respect, to the extent that Carter would stop off in Paris to confer with Giscard after meeting with other foreign leaders in Europe and the Middle East. The most famous instance of this occurred after Carter's state visit to Iran on January 1, 1978, where he declared the ailing shah's regime an "island of stability" in a troubled region. According to one Carter aide, who was knowledgeable of the growing U.S.-French strategic cooperation, "We had the best relationship with France in my memory. I think it was based to a large extent on the mutual confidence and intimacy that grew up as a result of our willingness to engage in this program" of nuclear exchanges.[23]

When the Soviets deployed SS-20 intermediate-range nuclear missiles in Europe, Giscard phoned Carter at the White House, strongly urging that they hold a crisis summit. They could disguise the urgency and the subject of the meetings by conducting them under the guise of the annual eco-

nomic summit of the G-7 powers. But Giscard insisted that they meet without Japan—which as a non-European and a pacifist power was not directly
affected by the Euromissile crisis—and without the "lesser" partners of
the group, Italy and Canada. This was all about the security of Europe and
about NATO and should be kept among the "Big Four," he argued.

Carter agreed. At 11:50 A.M. on the morning of January 4, 1979, he departed with National Security Adviser Zbigniew Brzezinski on Air Force
One from Andrews Air Force Base for Pointe-à-Pitre, the main city on the
French Caribbean island of Guadeloupe. He was welcomed at the airport
by frequent White House visitor Jacques Wahl. An hour later, Giscard
came to his hotel.[24]

To give the unprecedented five-day summit the air of a midwinter
Caribbean holiday, Carter took along his wife and daughter, Amy, and
showed himself frequently in their company, taking leisurely strolls
around the old port and the beach. For sure, the January 4–9, 1979, talks
included scuba diving, half-day fishing trips, leisurely courtesy calls to
local officials, jogging, and lengthy meals. But the closed-door sessions
with Giscard, British prime minister James Callahan, and German chancellor Helmut Schmidt were deadly serious. At the top of the agenda was
their effort to develop a joint NATO strategy to combat the dramatic escalation of East-West tensions that had been caused by the introduction of
deadly new Soviet missiles thrust deep into the European heartland. The
main decision adopted at the seaside Ajoupa meeting hall was the so-called
two-track policy: pushing ahead with development of Pershing II and
nuclear-tipped cruise missiles but putting off deployment, in hopes that
strategic arms negotiators could get the Soviets to withdraw their SS-20s
before NATO was ready to deploy.

Many years later, Giscard told a radio interviewer in Los Angeles that
another key decision was also made in Guadeloupe involving a far different
part of the world: Iran. Carter had become convinced that "the moment
had come to have a political change" in Iran, and the four leaders agreed to
work together in developing an alternative to the ailing shah. Giscard
claimed he was "surprised" by Carter's position, "since we were under the
impression that the United States was supporting the Iranian regime."[25]
Giscard's comment may have been self-serving, since his government had
welcomed Ayatollah Khomeini to exile in the Paris suburb of Neauphle-le-
Château in October 1978, apparently thinking the ayatollah would be eter-

nally grateful (he wasn't). But Giscard was right about Carter's ambiguity toward the shah. "I fully expect the shah to maintain power in Iran and for the present problems in Iran to be resolved," Carter told a White House press conference just two weeks before Guadeloupe. "The predictions of doom and disaster that came from some sources have certainly not been realized at all."[26] Carter made these remarks even though he had already dispatched air force general Robert Huyser, deputy to the commander of U.S. forces, Europe, on a secret mission to Iran to encourage loyalist officers to seize power.

The French arguably had better insight into events then taking place inside Iran, since their foreign intelligence service had not developed the incestuous relationship with the shah's SAVAK that clouded the judgment of the CIA and the U.S. State Department. Indeed, a former French intelligence officer posted to Iran in the late 1970s told me that he had warned the shah twice about the growing opposition. "We told him, you must react or else it'll be all over," he said. "It was enough to poke your nose out in the street to understand what was going on."[27] That was the type of intelligence gathering the CIA appeared to have overlooked.

On November 4, 1979, Iranian "students" who called themselves Followers of the Line of the Imam (Khomeini) stormed the U.S. embassy in Tehran and took U.S. diplomats hostage. Giscard and his intelligence chief, Alexandre de Marenches, offered Carter a broad range of quiet assistance in obtaining their release. French lawyer Christian Bourguet was soon traveling back and forth between Paris and Tehran carrying offers and counterproposals aimed at convincing Khomeini to release the U.S. hostages. When that effort failed, Carter ordered a rescue attempt in April 1980 that also failed, this time costing the lives of American servicemen when their helicopter collided with a C-130 transport plane at Desert One, the rendezvous point near the southeastern Iranian town of Tabas.

The Iranians responded by dispersing the hostages in small groups to secure locations throughout the country. Carter and his advisers were frantic to locate them. So Marenches agreed to help the CIA with a plan to send a private U.S. businessman to Tehran to gather intelligence.

I learned about this little-known aspect of secret U.S.-French intelligence cooperation years later from the businessman, who eventually agreed to tell me his story, and from former French intelligence officers, who corroborated key elements of his account. Marenches's service provided the CIA with commercial cover and a fresh European passport for the emissary, who traveled to Tehran after the failed April 1980 rescue mission on the pretext of pursuing commercial contracts between European companies and the new revolutionary regime in Iran. During his discussions, he eventually learned that the Iranians had brought all the hostages back to Tehran in the belief that the Carter White House would not risk a second rescue attempt. Marenches relates what happened next.

> We noticed that the Ayatollah went frequently to his own home in the holy city of Qom. He lived in a fairly quiet neighborhood, not far from an open field where helicopters could land. It occurred to us that we could seize His Eminence and take him, politely but firmly, to a navy ship waiting off the coast of Oman in the Indian Ocean. We worked it out to the last detail, and eventually the plan was put to President Carter. . . . While he found it original and fascinating, he said, 'You can't do that to a bishop, especially not a man of his age!' End of quote."[28]

During the first week of July 1980, on a mission to explore yet another approach, National Security Adviser Zbigniew Brzezinski headed for Amman to meet with Jordan's King Hussein, who was Saddam's closest confidant in the Arab world. On the table were detailed plans by Saddam to attack Khomeini's Iran that aimed at putting a violent and immediate end to radical Islamic fundamentalism in the region, with the by-product of liberating the U.S. hostages. Saddam's plan was to launch the invasion in response to an appeal from loyalist Iranian officers, who were plotting an uprising. The officers had been organized by the shah's last prime minister, Shahpur Bakhtiar, a former resistance fighter who had been awarded French citizenship for his valor in defending France against the Nazis. After Khomeini seized power on February 12, 1979, Bakhtiar fled to France, where he rallied royalist officers to join him. By the time Brzezinski was meeting with King Hussein in July 1980, the coup plotters were operating from Baghdad and from a training camp in the Kurdish town of Sulimaniyah with Saddam's full blessing and support. They had assured Saddam that everything was proceeding according to plan.

In fact, as I learned later from Abolhassan Bani-Sadr, who was then Iran's president, Khomeini's government had been tipped off about the impending coup by Soviet agents working in France and in Latin America. Just days after Brzezinski's meetings in Jordan, Bani-Sadr gave the orders to round up six hundred pro-Bakhtiar officers who were attending a planning session at the Nogeh air base outside the city of Hamadan, midway between Tehran and the Iraqi border. Without a word leaking out, he successfully put an end to the coup.[29]

Undeterred, Saddam decided to invade anyway and unleashed his armies against Iran on September 22, 1980, along a 1,200-kilometer-long front. The very next day his deputy, Tariq Aziz, was in Paris, demanding that the French make good on their commitment to deliver the Mirages. Giscard publicly fretted that the war changed everything and feared that Iran would attack Iraq's oil export terminals, thereby reducing critical oil supplies to France. It took several more visits by Aziz to Paris and a mixture of bribery and strong-arming—including an Iraqi threat to suspend oil deliveries to France, which by then was importing nearly 25 percent of its oil from Iraq—before the French delivered. But by Christmas, the pro-Iraq lobby in France won the day. Saddam got his Mirage fighter jets and much more, including the first shipment of 12.5 kilograms of high-enriched uranium fuel for Osirak.

Given the proper weapons design, it was enough to build a single nuclear device.

# 4

# Communists in the Cabinet

At Giscard's urging, Dassault delayed the delivery of the first Mirage fighter-bombers to Iraq until the U.S. hostages in Tehran had been released, the very minute Ronald Reagan took the oath of office on January 21, 1981. Just ten days later, the planes were ferried by French air force pilots to Larnaca, Cyprus, where Iraqi crews took over and flew them for the last leg of the journey to Baghdad. From then on, the French delivered the planes at the rate of two per month, while hundreds of Iraqi Mirage pilots and mechanics were sent for training at special centers in Brittany and Bordeaux. Those who passed the course successfully returned to Iraq, where former French air force pilots perfected their tactical skills.

"When the war with Iran started," a senior French defense executive who was in Iraq at the time told me, "we did everything we could to get their pilots up to speed. We sat behind them on training missions. We helped them plan tactics. We taught them how to use new missiles. Sometimes our guys even leaned on the stick, to help them maneuver into a better firing position. We did everything except pull the trigger."[1] The French-Iraqi relationship was as close to a strategic alliance as you could get, short of the actual deployment of French combat troops in Iraq, and all of it was a closely held secret.

I was one of the first reporters to document the extent of Franco-Iraqi cooperation from Baghdad in a series of articles that appeared initially in *Le Monde* and, subsequently, in French and international defense magazines.[2] The Iraqis were not pleased when the first piece came out and banned me from the country for more than a year. I learned later that the reason for Iraq's anger was not that I had revealed their cooperation with France, which made them proud, but that I had suggested their pilots lacked the necessary skills and doctrine to fully exploit the capability of the sophisticated French systems they were using, in particular the Exocet anti-shipping missile. Unbeknownst to me, they were locked in a commercial dispute with the French, claiming that the missiles were defective, and were seeking reimbursement of hundreds of millions of dollars. The French, of course, rejected the Iraqi claims and told me grisly stories of how Iraqi pilots would shoot missiles into the water when no target was in sight, because to come home still armed could have put an end to their career. I compared the number of "maritime targets" the Iraqis claimed to have destroyed using Exocet missiles against the number of ships Lloyd's of London reported had been hit and found that the Iraqis scored hits roughly 20 percent of the time. Apparently, that was news to Saddam.

Within weeks of the first Mirage delivery, the Franco-German Euromissile consortium announced that Iraq had agreed to purchase Roland 2 air defense missile batteries in a $2.9 billion package deal. The French had developed the Roland to rival the U.S.-built Hawk, which had been delivered in large quantities to the shah of Iran in the 1970s. Besides 113 Roland 2 fire units, the March 1981 KARI deal included new missiles for the Mirage fighters, Panhard armored cars, HOT antitank missiles, and much more, French defense contractors told me. KARI was "Iraq" spelled backward in French and was the code name for a series of air defense contracts that ultimately led to the integrated air defense network the U.S. Central Command (CENTCOM) had to neutralize before launching Desert Storm in 1991.

Despite the purchase of these new high-tech weapons, Iraqi troops were being mauled on the battlefield by the large numbers of M-109 self-propelled howitzers the shah had purchased from the United States. These were sophisticated guns that could "shoot and scoot." They outdistanced and outshot everything in Iraqi inventory, and the Iraqis felt the disadvantage keenly. Thus, early in 1981, the Iraqi Ministry of Defense alerted military attachés serving in Iraqi embassies overseas to urgently search for an equivalent system. One of the first places they looked was France.

The French army was just then completing trials on a new long-range field howitzer it had mounted on its AMX-30 tank. Called the 155 mm GCT ( *grand cadence de tir,* or "rapid fire"), they advertised it on the world arms market as the fastest and most accurate gun in the world. Development work was partially funded by Saudi Arabia, since the French Ministry of Defense was still spending most of its R&D money on nuclear weapons, not conventional armor. Built by GIAT, it was marketed by two specialized export sales agencies: SOFRESA, which handled Saudi Arabia and the lower Gulf countries; and SOFMA, which was in charge of Iraq, Morocco, and South America. I spoke frequently to officials from both companies during the 1980s, in Iraq and elsewhere, and interviewed French artillery officers who had been detailed to Iraq on training missions on their behalf. Once Iraq had beaten Iran in July 1988, they felt comfortable telling the dodgier parts of the story they had personally witnessed.

When selling arms to the Middle East, there was always an intermediary, even in such a tightly controlled place as Saddam Hussein's Iraq. The intermediary was in charge not just of bringing buyer and seller together, but also of handling more sensitive arrangements, such as making special payments into offshore accounts to officials in both countries. SOFMA turned to Lebanese arms dealer Sarkis Soghanalian, who had become Saddam's trusted agent. Soghanalian took one look at the new gun and saw instant money. It was exactly what the Iraqis had said they wanted.

Everything about Sarkis was big. Weighing well over 300 pounds, his appetites were gargantuan. In March 1981, Soghanalian flew a group of top SOFMA officials to Baghdad on board his private jet, the *Spirit of Free Enterprise,* serving them French champagne during the six-hour flight from Paris. Among his guests were General Daniel Huet, President of SOFMA, Michel Beillan, SOFMA's Managing Director, Colonel Jacques Masson-Regnault, a retired artillery officer who was in charge of the project, and his assistant, Michel Obilinski. "When we saw that he was cleared to land at al-Muthana air base, not the international airport, we knew he was all that he said he was," one of the French participants told me. The al-Muthana base was used by Iraqi officials and special guests so they could avoid unwanted publicity and customs formalities. When the Frenchmen went to Baghdad on their own, they invariably landed at the main airport, then known as Saddam International.

To present the new GIAT gun to Iraqi procurement officers under realistic battlefield conditions, General Huet "borrowed" a battery of six guns from his competitors at SOFRESA, who had just completed a demonstration to the Saudi army. The huge vehicles were loaded onto tank transporters and hauled across the Saudi desert to Basra in southern Iraq. Meanwhile, French artillery crews flew down to Basra with Soghanalian on Iraqi army helicopters for firing and mobility trials out in the desert, within earshot of the Iranian army.

The Iraqis loved the new gun. Mounted on a treaded tank chassis, it could go anywhere, fire a rapid barrage at distant targets, then duck for cover before enemy artillery spotters could locate it. It was so efficient that a competent crew could "shoot and scoot," then fire from a new location in just a matter of minutes. The Iraqis set up targets of wrecked Iranian tanks and told the French reservists to go to work. Then they took the SOFMA salesmen to watch the show from an observation bunker protected with little more than cinder blocks and sand that was within binocular range of the target area. The guns were so far away that no one really heard the firing begin, but all of a sudden a circle of explosions erupted just hundreds of meters from where they were standing, filling the desert with a deafening roar. Even though the guns were firing at their maximum range of twenty-four kilometers, they scored hit after hit, smashing into the Iranian tanks thanks to a sophisticated electronic fire control computer. "It would have been a bit embarrassing if they had missed," one of the participants joked years later. "In truth, we were all in a sweat." When it was all over, the Iraqis applauded. It was the most impressive display of precision firepower they had seen. And their French guests, too, had passed the test.

In the end, the Iraqis purchased eighty-three guns, ammunition, training, and support, for a whopping $1.6 billion. Like other contracts in Iraq, this one received its own special code name: Vulcan, after the god of the underworld, which is where the Iraqis were hoping to dispatch their desert enemies. The French were overjoyed. "Normally, the Iraqis paid a 20 percent deposit, another 20 percent in six months, and left the rest until later. This time they paid us $800 million cash up front. So you can see why we were so happy," one of the French arms salesmen told me. For Soghanalian, the Iraqi willingness to meet the French commercial demands was driven by necessity. "The French were the only ones who had what we needed," Soghanalian told me simply.[3]

The Vulcan deal meant business for dozens of French defense contractors. Munitions makers had to double their production. GIAT had to build a new factory to meet the Iraqi order in time. So much good fortune had a down side, however, once the Iraqi orders slacked off and the new plants and facilities ran idle. But the French weren't looking that far ahead. These were the golden years, when the Iraqi bonanza had something for everyone.

A t home, Giscard had become increasingly unpopular. An aloof technocrat, more patrician than politician, he prided himself on his superiority over the ordinary Frenchman. A series of scandals that broke near the end of his seven-year presidency had eroded his credibility and, worse, his dignity.

The May 1981 elections pitted him in a rematch against Socialist candidate François Mitterrand, who this time had managed to hold together his on-again, off-again alliance with the powerful French Communist Party (PCF). The PCF was one of the last Stalinist parties in Europe. In 1979, as European Communist Party leaders in Spain and Italy broke openly with the Soviet Union and declared their independence from Mother Russia, PCF leader Georges Marchais boasted that the record of fifty years of Soviet communism—despite the purges, the famine, and the mass murders during Stalin's reign—was "globally positive." It was not a chance phrase or a mistake. Marchais repeated the formula like a schoolboy proud of having memorized his lesson at every possible occasion, even after the Soviet invasion of Afghanistan. The opinion polls showed that Marchais and his Stalinist party were poised dangerously close to seizing power with their Socialist allies. At the peak of the cold war, France was drifting dangerously to the Left.

In the months before the first round of voting, the French satiric weekly *Le Canard Enchaîné* hammered Giscard with allegations that he had taken gifts of diamonds from Central African dictator Jean-Bedel Bokassa, a French-backed despot best known for serving guests at his palace succulent stews made from the children of his political enemies. Whenever Giscard appeared on the campaign trail or in televised debates, he was asked if there was any truth to the allegations about "Bokassa's diamonds." Despite his denials, the rumors of bribery may have swayed just enough voters to push Mitterrand over the top and into the Élysée, which he won on May 10, 1981, with 52 percent of the vote.

France virtually shut down for a week as the French Left celebrated what it considered a historic resumption of the "progressive" policies of France's last "great" left-wing alliance, the Popular Front, led by Socialist premier Léon Blum in the 1930s, which laid the foundations of Europe's social welfare system. (Few of Mitterrand's allies wanted to remember the new president's own previous stint in government in the early 1950s, when a Socialist-led government made the costly decision to pursue nuclear weapons and committed troops to Indochina and Algeria in unsuccessful attempts to preserve what remained of France's Colonial empire.)

From virtually his first day in office as French commander in chief, Mitterrand was assailed with unforeseen challenges. The most public of them involved the consequences of his predecessor's policies toward Saddam Hussein's Iraq.

Just south of Baghdad, hundreds of Iraqi nuclear weapons scientists and French engineers were feverishly carrying out last-minute preparations to start the French-built nuclear reactor. Osirak was set to go critical on July 1, 1981. By early 1981, Giscard's government had delivered the first load of 93 percent–enriched uranium to the site, and the ghostly blue cooling channel was ready to be filled with water. Once the Frenchmen declared the site operational, their contract was up and they were supposed to leave the country. Under Saddam Hussein's personal orders, Iraqi weapons scientists led by Ja'afar Dhia Ja'afar were immediately to begin producing plutonium by gradually irradiating hundreds of tons of uranium yellowcake they had been purchasing secretly from Niger, Brazil, and Portugal. Saddam's goal was to transform Iraq into a nuclear weapons power within just two years.*

---

*In one of history's great ironies, key elements of the Iraqi bomb program at Tuwaitha were sold by an Italian named Maurizio Zifferero, who went on to become the top official at the Vienna-based International Atomic Energy Agency in charge of *dismantling* Iraq's bomb program after the first Gulf War in 1991. ("Of course, I was specially qualified for dismantling the Iraqi nuclear program, since I had been involved in nuclear cooperation with Iraq in the 1970s," he told me with a straight face.) While serving as a consultant to the Iraqi Atomic Energy Organization in the late 1970s, Zifferero had supervised the sale and installation at Tuwaitha of a series of hot cells from the Italian nuclear firm Snia Techint that were specially designed to extract plutonium from targets irradiated in Osirak. He also helped Iraq acquire fuel-manufacturing laboratories from other Italian firms. Zifferero acknowledged his earlier role in arming Saddam in a series of long discussions we held in 1991 and 1992 in his spacious office on the twenty-eighth floor of the IAEA towers, overlooking the Danube and the Vienna woods.

In the spring of 1981, just before Mitterrand took office, the IAEA completed its regular six-month inspection of Iraq's nuclear research center at Tuwaitha. As during previous visits, the nuclear "watchdog" agency found nothing out of the ordinary. But IAEA chief Hans Blix went even further, reassuring the IAEA board of governors in his cover letter to the report that Iraq showed no signs of violating its commitments under the Nuclear Nonproliferation Treaty. Blix was rewarded by the UN for his willful blindness toward Iraq's nuclear weapons program by being put in charge of not one, but *two* separate UN efforts to verify Iraq's disarmament. In both cases, he failed again to find anything out of the ordinary.

Privately, however, some IAEA officials were worried. Robert Richter, one of the inspectors who had visited Iraq, broke ranks and went public with their fears. Richter revealed to a U.S. Senate committee in 1981 that Iraq had built secret facilities at Tuwaitha that were off-limits to IAEA inspectors, just hundreds of feet away from the reactor and the labs the UN agency was allowed to inspect. The IAEA refused to challenge the Iraqis about the hidden laboratories, which he believed contained reprocessing facilities, because they had never been declared as nuclear facilities and placed under safeguards. Richter and other IAEA officials calculated that Iraq could manufacture its first bomb by 1983 and by 1985 could be making five bombs per year. IAEA director Hans Blix promptly fired Richter, an American citizen, for his candor.[4]

Richter was not alone in decrying the dangers posed by Iraq's nuclear program. In France, three physicists who had worked on developing the original Osiris reactor and knew its capabilities completed a report, submitted to President Mitterrand just days after he took office, that showed the Iraqi "research" reactor was designed to make the bomb.[5]

Someone else was worried about the Osirak reactor. It was Israeli prime minister Menachem Begin. In April 1981, Begin concluded that Israel would have to destroy the Iraqi nuclear plant if it wanted to avoid a catastrophe later on. The only time to do it was now, before the nuclear fuel was loaded into the reactor. He instructed air force chief of staff General David Ivry to begin planning Operation Babylon.

A Polish Jew who had survived the Holocaust, Begin needed no help in understanding Saddam's intent, which was to complete the Holocaust by destroying the Jewish homeland in the Middle East. He was determined to thwart the Iraqi bomb no matter the cost. Overriding the objections of his intelligence community, which downplayed the Iraqi threat, he had Ivry build a full-scale model of the Iraqi nuclear plant so air force pilots could practice bombing it. The pilots remarked how closely Osirak resembled Israel's own bomb plant at Dimona, which also had been supplied by the French.[6]

On Sunday morning, June 7, 1981, the Israelis struck. On the daring five-hundred-mile flight to Baghdad, the Israeli pilots were never out of enemy territory for more than three minutes. General Ivry had chosen his team of pilots for their linguistic as well as their combat skills. When they were crossing Jordanian airspace, they conversed with one another in Saudi-accented Arabic and told Jordanian air controllers they were a Saudi patrol that had gone astray. When they entered Saudi airspace, they switched accents in Arabic and pretended they were Jordanians. When they finally reached Tuwaitha, they approached from the east so the air defense gunners defending the site would be blinded by the morning sun. Eyewitnesses later reported that a first wave of Israeli F-16s punched a hole through the very center of the reactor dome of Tammuz I with precision-guided missiles. Through that hole, a second wave of fighters dropped two-thousand-pound "dumb" bombs with such accuracy that they destroyed the reactor core, its containing walls, and the gantry crane.[7] The damage was so great that Osirak was declared dead. With it died Saddam Hussein's crash program to get the bomb.

One of the first world leaders to protest the daring Israeli raid was the new French president, François Mitterrand, whose election had been greeted with jubilation in Israel. The first Socialist to win the French presidency since World War II, Mitterrand was a strong supporter of Israel who had no soft spot for the Arab world, as did Giscard. As interior minister in 1954–1955, he had played a premier role in the French attempt to crush the Algerian rebellion and became a key member of the French government of Prime Minister Guy Mollet that approved the contract with Israel in 1957 to build the Dimona bomb plant in the Negev desert.[8] Menachem Begin delayed the execution of Operation Babylon until Mitterrand was firmly in command and informed the new French president of his intentions before the raid, Israeli and French intelligence officials told me. Indeed, despite the fact that hundreds of French workers were still present at Tuwaitha at the time of the Israeli raid, they received the unusual order to hold mass that Sunday morning at a building far away from the reactor dome (Sunday was an ordinary working day in Iraq). According to a former French intelligence official who was a top aide to Mitterrand, only one Frenchman died in the raid, and he was an intelligence officer, whose job it was to plant a homing beacon on the reactor core so the Israelis would know precisely where to strike. He died because of a last-minute delay.[9]

Mitterrand's protest was expected, and limited. He called for no sanctions against Israel and made only the vaguest of promises to Iraq to rebuild the Osirak reactor, although officials at St. Gobain Nucléaire, a front for French nuclear exports, pushed hard to convince him otherwise. More forceful was the protest from the United States, which President Reagan delivered personally. Twenty years later, Vice President Dick Cheney would finally thank Israel publicly for having destroyed the Iraqi bomb plant, an action he acknowledged had set back Saddam's nuclear designs by a full decade.[10]

Mitterrand's election worried Saddam Hussein. The Iraqi leader had long been suspicious of the French Socialists because of what he perceived to be their pro-Israeli sentiments. Just one week after the Osirak raid, another event gave the Iraqi leader further reason to fear that Mitterrand was about to change French policy to Iraq's detriment. It was customary for the French president, accompanied by his defense minister and the head of the French Aerospace Association, Groupement des Industries Françaises Aéronautiques et Spatiales (GIFAS), to tour the Paris air show on opening day. As luck would have it, the acting president of GIFAS in June 1981 was General Jacques Mitterrand, the older brother of the president (intimates called the general "Jacko"). A fraternal relationship with the head of state should have been a glorious event for French arms exporters. It was not.

The new president ordered his brother to have every weapon removed from the premises before the presidential tour began. All night long the arms exporters toiled, removing bombs, missiles, and rockets from beneath the scores of aircraft on display on the tarmac of Le Bourget Airport and from hundreds of stands in the covered exhibition halls. (Some were still at work by the time the Mitterrand brothers arrived. The presidential cortege neatly avoided the offenders.) The new Socialist government would no longer export weapons blindly to dictators all over the globe, Mitterrand told the press. Moral considerations would now dictate where France would export her finest.

I heard the story of what happened next from a senior French aerospace official who toured the air show in the presidential entourage. As they walked along, "Jacko explained to his brother that illustrious foreign guests had traveled to France just to see the latest in French weaponry. It would be unwise to disappoint them," he argued. Among the visitors was General Abdul Neguib Jenaab Thanoon, the Iraqi chief of staff. General Jenaab was a good client and would not understand the president's gesture if the weapons were not immediately put back on display. After all, Iraq had standing orders with French exporters and had made substantial down payments for military equipment that was flying off the assembly lines of French factories as they spoke. Did the president want to make these clients believe that he was going to cancel their contracts? That would be tantamount to betraying France's credibility as an international trading partner.

The general won. As soon as the presidential cortege left the air show, he ordered the bombs and the missiles and the rockets returned to the display areas. For French arms contractors, it was going to be business as usual.

S addam Hussein was not the only foreign leader who was worried about the dramatic changes the new French government would bring. In Washington, top officials in the Reagan administration were monitoring events in Paris with growing alarm.

When the French get huffy about America, they dismiss us as an "upstart" country, with scarcely two hundred years of history. But since 1789—the very year of the French Revolution—America has known but one form of government. Our constitutional republic has held together without major institutional changes through civil war, economic depression, and challenges from abroad, standing the test of time. The current form of French democracy, by contrast, dates from just 1958, when the Fifth Republic was established by General de Gaulle. When the French embarked on political change, they often trashed their entire system of government along with their leaders.

Shortly after he won the runoff on May 10, 1981, Mitterrand dissolved the National Assembly and called for snap parliamentary elections, betting that the momentum of his presidential victory would also bring him a majority in Parliament. Controlling Parliament was important in the Fifth Republic, since the prime minister, although appointed by the president, had to win a vote of confidence from the legislature.

Communist Party leader Georges Marchais was also eager for new elections. He was hoping to translate the stunning 15.3 percent he had won in the first round of the presidential election into real power. In the pre-election bargain known as the Union de la Gauche (Union of the Left), the Socialists and Communists had agreed to support each other's candidates in the runoffs whenever the left-wing candidate was pitted against a challenger or incumbent from the Right. Nationwide, this electoral horse-trading was a boon for the PCF and enhanced Marchais's role as kingmaker. Although Mitterrand's Socialist Party won 258 seats in the parliamentary elections—an absolute majority—Marchais could still claim that he was responsible for that success and that without his support Mitterrand would be unable to govern. Now it was payback time. Marchais wanted half a dozen ministerial positions in the new government. It was the first time in cold war Europe that a Communist Party was poised to enter government since the Communists were ejected from governing coalitions in Italy and France in 1947.

Mitterrand rejected Marchais's outlandish demand, but he knew that he couldn't keep the Communists out of government entirely. Eventually he offered Marchais four cabinet positions, including the Ministry of Transportation. In the centrally controlled system the French loved, the Transportation Ministry had absolute control over the entire national transportation grid—highways, railroads, seaports, airports—as well as over the strategic oil pipelines linking France's Atlantic seaports to the NATO supply network. NATO military planners were now counting on these assets to resupply NATO forces in Europe in the event of a Soviet attack, as a result of the secret strategic cooperation between Paris and Washington. If the pro-Soviet French Communists got the Transportation Ministry, they would gain access without espionage to a critical part of NATO's strategic war plan.

In Washington, the news that Communists were about to enter the French cabinet—especially with such a sensitive portfolio—was received with alarm. The French Communist Party had proven immune to the wave of reform known as "Eurocommunism" that had moved Communists in Spain and Italy to distance themselves from Moscow. The PCF Central Committee was packed with committed Stalinists, starting with Marchais himself, who marched in lockstep with the Communist Party of the Soviet Union. The State Department issued a dramatic public warning in June when the deal with the PCF was formalized: "The tone and the substance of our relations as allies will be affected by the arrival of Communists in this government, as in any government of our West European allies." Vice President George Bush reinforced the warning in a personal audience with Mitterrand at the Élysée Palace that same day. A NATO ally, even a prickly ally such as France, seemed in danger of slipping out of the Western orbit.

Behind the scenes, the Reagan administration was considering all options, including moves to undermine the new French government. "There was a great deal of uncertainty, because the news about Mitterrand's past was not good, especially his courting of the Communists," recalls Fred Charles Ikle, undersecretary of defense for policy at the time.[11] Indeed, this was not the first election where they had formed a governing pact. An earlier, failed version, known as the Programme Commun, included a pledge to unilaterally disband the French nuclear deterrent and close down its nuclear weapons labs, transforming France into a pro-Soviet "neutral" state such as Finland. Further igniting U.S. suspicions, Mitterrand brought into the Élysée as strategic adviser a well-known admirer of Fidel Castro named Régis Debray, who boasted of having been thrown in jail in Bolivia in 1973 as a companion of Castro's legendary revolutionary sidekick, Che Guevara. (Mitterrand, already a friend, had gotten him out of jail.)

But Mitterrand was a skilled political operator and recognized the dangers of alienating Washington. After the Élysée Palace meeting with Bush, he had Defense Minister Charles Hernu quietly dispatch to Washington his top adviser, François Heisbourg, with a clear message. "Heisbourg went out of his way to reassure us that the security apparatus was in good hands," recalls Richard Perle, an assistant secretary of defense who met with Heisbourg at the Pentagon. "He insisted that there were no Communists in sensitive positions—no Communists at Defense, the Ministry of Foreign Affairs, or in the intelligence services."[12]

Behind the scenes, and without Mitterrand's knowledge, another French emissary visited Washington. His name was Henri Conze. He was not a politician, but a senior official in the Délégation Générale pour l'Armement (DGA), the French armaments board, who was well-known to Washington insiders because of his pro-American views. "Conze told us that things were not as bad as they seemed," recalls Stephen Bryen, who worked at the Pentagon under Fred Ikle. Since the mid-1970s, Conze had participated in the top-secret nuclear weapons exchanges with the United States, so his word carried significant weight. As Conze remembers it, he made his trip just before Mitterrand won the runoff, because he was concerned by what he had been hearing from Washington. He told Bryen and other friends at the Pentagon that Mitterrand was indeed going to win the elections and that he would bring Communists into the cabinet, "but I bet that in two years they would be gone."[13] Still, it looked as if the United States and France were headed on a collision course.

Just as the Americans had feared, the first act of Communist transportation minister Charles Fiterman when he entered his new digs was to rush to his office safe in search of the strategic mobilization plans for the French national railroads and Air France. But as luck would have it, no one was around who happened to have the combination of the safe. Within hours, the incident was reported to the Élysée and the top-secret mobilization plan was withdrawn from the competence (and the safe) of the transportation minister, on the personal orders of Mitterrand himself. The incident remained unreported for many years.[14] As I learned later, the person who helped to convince Mitterrand to withdraw the strategic mobilization plans from the competence of the Ministry of Transportation was Henri Conze.

In July, Mitterrand's new foreign intelligence chief, Pierre Marion, flew to Washington, D.C., where he was given a cool reception by CIA director William Casey. The Americans wanted to dispatch former secretary of state Henry Kissinger to brief Mitterrand privately on the Soviet threat and to reinforce the administration's concern over the Communists in the cabinet. Marion feared that he was about to become the bearer of bad tidings but said he'd see what he could do.

Pierre Marion had come to his new job from the French national airlines, Air France, after many years overseas in the aerospace industry, where he had occasionally performed services as an "honorary correspondent" for French intelligence. He was neither close to Mitterrand personally nor an intelligence professional. Mitterrand appears to have chosen him to head up the Service de Documentation et de Contre-Espionnage (SDECE) because he was the only person Mitterrand knew on the Left who had had any positive relationship with the intelligence service. Marion's primary mission was to weed the Gaullists out of the SDECE and to reorganize it to serve the new Socialist regime.

The Kissinger visit, Marion wrote later in a memoir, "was problematic on both sides. Kissinger was reserved, and Mitterrand had a horrible memory of the cold welcome he had received from the secretary of state when he had traveled to Washington ten years earlier as a politician with no governmental position."[15] During the entire month of July, Mitterrand had no time for Marion, who communicated the American request to Mitterrand's chief of staff, Pierre Bérégovoy. Then, to Marion's surprise, Mitterrand abruptly agreed to the meeting. Stranger still, he proposed to honor the former U.S. secretary of state by inviting him to his farm in Latché, in the sandy pine forests of Les Landes not far from the Atlantic seacoast in southwest France. Only Mitterrand's close friends were invited to Latché.

Marion served as chauffeur and translator for the August 3, 1981, meeting. He went to pick up Kissinger in Deauville, where he was vacationing at the Normandy estate of beer magnate Loel Guinness. After tennis, a small private dinner, and an hour-long private conversation with Kissinger, Marion spent the night. The next morning, he escorted his guest to Deauville Airport, where they embarked on a Mystère 20 corporate jet for the hour-long flight southwest to Biarritz. "It was beautiful. Kissinger was in a good mood. We were alone on the plane and plunged into our newspapers," Marion recalls. At the airport, they were picked up by an unmarked SDECE sedan, which whisked them along country roads to the Mitterrand residence. "You're not going to hand me over to Basque separatists, I hope," Kissinger joked as they bounced along a dirt track through dense pines.

Mitterrand was standing outside to welcome them when they arrived. "He was all smiles, and the first contact went well," Marion wrote. Kissinger spent the entire day with the French president. Mitterrand's wife fixed them lunch, which they ate out on the shaded terrace along with top presidential advisers François de Grossouvre and Jacques Attali, with Marion interpreting. After lunch, Mitterrand took his guest on a walking tour of the property, an honor he reserved for favored guests. "François Mitterrand spoke little," as Kissinger embarked on a "geopolitical world tour, an exercise he obviously relished."

The former U.S. secretary of state spoke at great length about the Soviet threat, but he also revealed his belief that the Soviets had entered a period of economic decline. He spoke about the Middle East and informed Mitterrand of the threats posed to the West by Cuba and the Sandinistas in Nicaragua, regimes that "must not be encouraged." As they drove back to the airport, Mitterrand began to speak for the first time, Marion says. "He went back to Kissinger's analysis of the Soviet Union, but curiously, he didn't talk about the international aspects but about domestic French politics, and the strategy he had set in motion to weaken the Communist Party. 'See, I too am betting on a rollback of communism,' Mitterrand said with a sly smile."[16]

Marion didn't get it. He'd been led to believe in Washington that Kissinger had been dispatched to France to read Mitterrand the riot act. Instead, the American had adopted a good-natured, professorial tone and listened intently when Mitterrand told him his plans for smashing the French Communist Party. In fact, that critical information was just what Kissinger—and Reagan—had wanted to learn. It confirmed what they now believed was a whole different side to the new French president and reinforced their belief that he was about to become America's best ally in Europe.

For Kissinger and Mitterrand knew something the new French intelligence chief did not. It was a secret that was about to change the world.

Mitterrand made his international debut at the G-7 summit in Ottawa, two weeks before the cordial meeting with Kissinger. Tensions were high between Paris and Washington, and the press was expecting fireworks. Would Reagan expel the French Socialist from the Western alliance if he refused to boot the Communists from his cabinet? Were the Americans set to announce economic and security measures to isolate the new French government? The press on both sides of the Atlantic was rife with speculation and fully expected the meeting to include a testy confrontation.

Instead, after a private meeting between the two men, Reagan completely changed his attitude toward Mitterrand. "Was the American president simply blown away by the justice of France's political choice?" wrote French journalist Thierry Wolton. "Had the French president, a lawyer by training, pleaded the cause of Socialist France with such brio that he succeeded in seducing the man who held him in the highest contempt? Not at all. In fact, the two presidents remained ensconced in their positions."[17]

What happened instead "was an event of such magnitude that it changed Washington's tone on the spot," Wolton wrote. "It instantly dispelled the American concerns and brought a spectacular improvement in French-U.S. relations, despite the persistent political differences."

What happened was one small word: Farewell.

Dr. Stephen Bryen was in charge of technology security at the Pentagon and, in particular, Soviet efforts to steal Western military secrets. The new U.S. administration was determined to shut down Soviet access to Western high technology, which the Pentagon believed was helping the Soviets to build more accurate strategic missiles, better bombers, and in some cases direct copies of NATO weapons systems. "When they sat down together in Ottawa, Reagan sought to impress upon Mitterrand the seriousness of the Russian threat," Bryen says. "I know the gist of what he said because I wrote the briefing paper he used for the meeting. It was my first official paper at DoD [the Department of Defense]." When Reagan had finished describing hostile Soviet activities, Mitterrand just smiled. " 'Oh, it's much worse than that. The Soviet Union has this huge operation against you, and against us. But we have information.' "[18]

The French president then went on to describe the broad outlines of one of the most extraordinary intelligence coups in the history of modern espionage.

France had recently developed a source in the highest echelons of Soviet intelligence, he told Reagan. His access was so total that he was able to provide documents that had been annotated by Yuri Andropov, then head of the KGB, and initialed by General Secretary Leonid Brezhnev. The French had given him the code name Farewell. He worked at the top of the T Directorate, the section of the KGB's First Chief Directorate responsible for carrying out scientific and technological espionage against the West. Thanks to Farewell, the French were able to read the same information that the KGB was providing to the Soviet Politburo.

Mitterrand proposed sharing the entire take with Reagan because he wanted to defeat the Soviet assault on Western military secrets. "Mitterrand said he was just as worried about the Soviet effort against French technology as against our own," Bryen recalls. He proposed sending a personal emissary to Washington within two weeks to provide more details. Before leaving, he gave Reagan a sample document that had been supplied by Farewell. It was stamped "Soverchenno Sekretno"—a Soviet version of "Top Secret" held so closely that each copy was numbered. As the Americans would learn over the next eighteen months, virtually all the documents provided by Farewell bore the number 1, indicating that they had been produced for the head of the T Directorate.[19]

In the rarefied intelligence world, Farewell's access was considered "cosmic."

Colonel Vladimir Ippolitovitch Vetrov was a fifty-three-year-old engineer assigned to evaluate the intelligence collected by the T Directorate, "an ideal position for a defector in place," says Gus W. Weiss, the CIA analyst put in charge of handling the Farewell dossier later that summer.[20] Vetrov volunteered to spy for the French in March 1981 out of a mixture of idealism, disgust with the Soviet system, and nostalgia for an early sojourn in France. As a young intelligence officer in Paris in 1965, he had an accident while driving an official embassy car, an event that, if discovered, could have broken his career. Instead, he was befriended by a French businessman who worked for Thomson-CSF, who fixed the car for him before Vetrov's superiors could find out. Vetrov's gratitude was certainly justified, "even if the friendly gesture of this businessman was not entirely disinterested," says Marcel Chalet, the former head of the French counterintelligence service, the Direction de la Surveillance du Territoire (DST).

Chalet's account of Vetrov's career as Farewell provides a fascinating inside picture of one of the most productive spies of the cold war. For reasons that even today remain obscure, when Farewell made his decision to spy for the French, he contacted a friend in Moscow whom he knew was in touch with the DST, not their foreign espionage unit, the SDECE (now known as the Direction Générale de la Sécurité Extérieur, DGSE). Chalet doesn't say why Farewell made that choice, but he notes that the Russian was an intelligence professional who knew what he was doing and that he had chosen the DST on purpose, perhaps out of concern that the SDECE would not be able to keep his treason secret from the KGB. The decision to bypass Marion and the SDECE in running Farewell went all the way up to Mitterrand himself, Chalet said. The DST had never before run such a complex operation overseas.[21]

The DST had no one within its own ranks who could quickly move to Moscow to run Farewell without arousing KGB suspicions. In the end, Chalet says the DST recruited as Farewell's handler an individual "who had diplomatic immunity, in whom we had total confidence." They gave him special training in espionage techniques and instructed him to set up a series of "dead drops" in the Moscow area, where Vetrov could leave documents for the French to be copied and then returned. "We had thought of everything," Chalet says, "except the peculiar mentality of Farewell himself."

In his memoir, Chalet refers to the diplomat by the pseudonym "Maxime." When the two first met in Moscow, "[Farewell] made Maxime understand that he was a highly trained professional, who was now working on his home territory, and that he intended to establish the method of their contacts," Chalet says. Among other things, "he declared his total hostility to a system that would have reduced the personal meetings with Maxime to a minimum. . . . He needed the human contact."[22]

A heavy drinker like most of his KGB colleagues, Vetrov delighted in taking risks that made his French handlers gasp in a mixture of awe and dismay. "Farewell loved to take Maxime for long drives in his car, showing him various military-industrial installations (weapons plants, research centers, design bureaux specialized in advanced technology, etc.). One day, they were driving near what we in France would call a target of the highest sensitivity, when he told Maxime that he wanted to take him inside for a visit. It turned out to be a missile plant. He drove full speed into the courtyard, after showing his KGB pass to the security guard, then made a U-turn and drove out. You can imagine the face on Maxime!"[23]

From April 1981 until he disappeared in February 1982, Chalet says Farewell delivered 2,997 pages of documents to the French, all of them highly classified. Among the intelligence he provided were lists of Soviet agents working undercover in the West who had penetrated top-secret weapons labs and the names of traitors operating in the West who were selling military secrets to the KGB—information that blew the lid off the Soviet high-technology espionage effort in the West and exposed its critical importance to the Soviet military.[24]

Two weeks after Mitterrand first revealed the existence of Farewell to Reagan, Chalet arrived in Washington with an armful of documents from the Farewell file. The first U.S. official he met was not CIA director William

Casey—so as not to arouse the suspicions of Marion's SDECE, which handled liaison with the CIA—but Vice President George Herbert Walker Bush. The two met on August 3, 1981, on the grounds of the vice presidential mansion—just as the unsuspecting Pierre Marion was translating for Henry Kissinger with Mitterrand in Latché, 3,500 miles away. "I was not addressing the vice president of the United States so much as the U.S. official best suited to understand the technical contents of a counterespionage case such as this," Chalet said.[25] When he sensed the import of the documents, Bush asked CIA director Casey, FBI director William Webster, and NSA director Bobby Inman to join them by helicopter. Chalet recalls, "We had in front of us the heads of all the major U.S. intelligence services. They were stunned, white as a tablecloth!"[26] A special channel was quickly established that cut the SDECE out of the loop, for fear of eventual Soviet moles. The Farewell dossier confirmed and developed what Reagan and his top advisers had known all along: The Soviet system was totally corrupt, incapable of innovation, and continued to exist as a superpower solely because it was devoting the overwhelming majority of its economic assets to weapons production.

Based on Farewell's documents, in 1982 the French produced a top-secret report entitled "The Soviet Organization for the Acquisition of Western Technology," which showed that high-technology theft was not an incidental program, but in fact essential to the Soviet military. But unlike the Reagan administration, they kept the report and the information secret.[27]

At the summit of the Soviet effort to acquire Western military technology was the powerful Military Industrial Commission, the VPK (Voienno-Promychlennaia Kommissia), which reported directly to the Presidium of the Council of Ministers, headed by the general secretary of the Communist Party of the Soviet Union. Each year, at a secret meeting in the Kremlin, the VPK established collection requirements of Western military or dual-use technologies—the "targets" of Soviet intelligence operations. The target list was then distributed to Soviet embassies abroad, to the KGB and GRU *rezidentura*, and to dozens of scientific collection agencies. Farewell obtained the target lists as well as the identity of the collectors. What the United States and France eventually learned from them had far-reaching consequences not just for the intelligence world, but for every major Western manufacturer of high technology.

"Casey would send the Farewell documents for me to read along with a CIA handler, who never let them out of his sight," recalls one senior Pentagon official. "They were blue border documents. Documents with blue borders were tightly controlled. I remember one of the early Farewell reports that read almost like a Sears catalog, enumerating Soviet military programs that utilized Western technology."

Other documents provided by Farewell were accountant-like reports to the Soviet Politburo, giving the precise amount of money saved by Line X through stealing this or that piece of Western technology. "I cannot recall a single instance where the KGB revealed how much it cost them to steal the technology," another consumer of the Farewell file told me. "They used this notion of saving R and D money to justify their vast foreign espionage operation."

CIA analyst Gus Weiss says that reading the Farewell documents "caused my worst nightmares to come true. Since 1970, Line X had obtained thousands of documents and sample products, in such quantity that it appeared that the Soviet military and civil sectors were in large measure running their research on that of the West, particularly the United States. Our science was supporting their national defense. Losses were in radar, computers, machine tools, and semiconductors. Line X had fulfilled two-thirds to three-fourths of its collection requirements—an impressive performance."[28]

Suddenly, as Marcel Chalet tells it, in February 1982 Farewell failed to show up at a prearranged meeting with Maxime in Moscow. He also failed to make a fallback rendezvous or to leave prearranged signals to indicate to the French that he was in danger. He just vanished into thin air. By the time Chalet resigned as head of the DST nine months later, in November 1982, there was still no word from Farewell. All efforts by the French to locate him had failed. "By that time, I had gone well beyond the threshold of concern," Chalet says.

The French learned of Farewell's fate only three years later, when a Soviet counterespionage officer named Vitali Yurchenko defected to the United States. Some senior French officials to this day believe that Mitterrand was wrong to have identified Farewell to President Reagan and that Farewell was exposed thanks to Soviet agents within the CIA. "All we know about his end is what the Soviets wanted us to know," one former top official told me. "Who knows if that is what actually happened?"[29]

According to Yurchenko, Farewell had been drinking champagne with a mistress in his car one night when a militia member rapped on the window. Farewell jumped out of the car and stabbed the man to death. Seized with panic, his mistress fled. Farewell ran after her and stabbed her as well, then drove off. An hour later, apparently seized with remorse, he returned to the scene of the crime, where, to his surprise, his mistress was not dead, but was denouncing him to the militia. "Here he appears as a character straight out of Dostoievski," Chalet said of Farewell's demise. "A tormented man, suddenly struck down by destiny, a momentary criminal who is seized with remorse and returns to the scene of his crime."[30]

Vladimir Ippolitovitch Vetrov was sentenced to twenty years in jail for murder in November 1982. But the KGB still had no clue that he was one of the most spectacular double agents in Soviet history, Yurchenko said. Only later were their suspicions aroused, when Vetrov sent a letter from prison to his wife, in which he wrote of "something enormous" he'd been forced to stop at the time of his arrest. Finally the KGB launched an investigation, and Vetrov confessed. The KGB announced that he was executed for treason on January 23, 1984, but not before he composed a final letter explaining that his goal had been to expose the realities of the "tired old whore" of the Soviet system to the West.

Yurchenko claimed that Vetrov's text, which he had read in manuscript as the KGB considered publishing it as a warning to future traitors, was so compelling that it moved him to defect. Despite Yurchenko's own strange behavior—defecting back to the USSR just three months after arriving in the West—Chalet felt that his account of Farewell's ultimate demise was authentic. "His final text, far from being a 'confession,' must have been a stunning *'J'accuse,'* " Chalet says, a reference to the famous broadside by Émile Zola exposing the anti-Semitism of the French officer corps during the Dreyfus affair in 1895. "That's why it was never published, even in the internal bulletin of the KGB."[31]

D espite the ambiguity surrounding Farewell's disappearance and ultimate demise, there was never any dispute as to the authenticity of the documents he provided or of the damage he had done to the Soviet Union. At the urging of Pentagon official Stephen Bryen and others, the CIA ultimately distilled the Farewell documents into a "white paper" in 1985 that laid out for the first time in public the extent of Soviet high-tech theft and explained the structure of the VPK. In so doing, the white paper exposed dozens of previously secret Soviet intelligence collectors, including seemingly innocuous international organizations devoted to scientific exchanges.[32]

Indeed, thanks to Farewell, the Reagan administration was able to convince previously reluctant allies in Europe to reinvigorate efforts to control the sale of dual-use technologies to the Soviet bloc through an old cold war mechanism in Paris known as CoCom, the Coordinating Committee for Multilateral Export Controls. Starting in 1982, with active French help, CoCom shut down large segments of the high-technology pipeline to the Soviet bloc, triggering panic in the higher echelons of the Kremlin and seriously hampering Soviet efforts to keep up with Western advances in military technology.

"There was a before and an after Farewell," Chalet said.[33] Everyone I have spoken to on both sides of the Atlantic who had access to the Farewell documents agrees. All through the 1980s and into the 1990s, France's petty sins were overlooked, and her greater sins were discussed but never punished—because there was Farewell. It is impossible to underestimate the importance of Mitterrand's decision in July 1981 to share the Farewell file with Reagan, or his personal contribution to strengthening the strategic relationship between the United States and France at what soon became the turning point of the cold war.

Given a choice between freedom and tyranny, Mitterrand didn't hesitate an instant. Despite his leftist philosophy and political affinities—and an ingrained suspicion of America that surfaced again and again—he chose America as his ally. It is by this standard that Jacques Chirac and Dominique de Villepin must be judged today.

# 5

# Honeymoon

---

I n Paris, the star of Henri Conze was rising.

Born in 1939, Conze joined the Commissariat à l'Energie Atomique as a young man under de Gaulle to work on the French bomb program. When the Kennedy and Johnson administrations denied France access to U.S. nuclear weapons technology, Conze was part of a small team of top-flight French scientists and intelligence operatives who improvised work-arounds. When possible, Conze directed CEA procurement officers to purchase items for the French bomb program they couldn't produce themselves on the open market. When necessary, they conducted clandestine operations to acquire needed items in the United States. "I helped organize the effort under de Gaulle to break the U.S. embargo on nuclear technologies to France," Conze told me at one point. It was an elegant way of describing the marriage of patriotism and deep understanding of the United States that marked his whole career, without betraying the specifics of what he had actually done.

In 1971, Conze moved from the CEA to the Defense Ministry to work on the military requirements for nuclear warheads. As the secret nuclear cooperation between France and the United States took off, Conze naturally was tapped as a key participant. By 1975, at the age of thirty-six, he was put in charge of nuclear weapons development at the Defense Ministry's Armaments Delegation, the DGA, a position that kept him in touch with the U.S. weapons labs under the secret agreement hammered out between Nixon and Pompidou. "Sometimes politics between nations comes down to relationships between individuals," Conze said, recalling the early days of the U.S.-French strategic exchange. In the case of the nuclear agreement, it was all about Nixon. "In November 1962, Nixon had just been defeated in his race for governor of California," Conze recalled. "In the United States, everyone was saying his political career was over. But when he came to Paris a few months later, de Gaulle received him as if he were a sitting president. Nixon never forgot that. He was the one on the U.S. side who was pushing strategic cooperation with France."[1]

With de Gaulle's successor, former banker Georges Pompidou, Nixon established a close personal relationship. In 1970, the French government announced a major sale of Mirage jet fighters to Colonel Muammar al-Qaddafi in Libya on the eve of Pompidou's first state visit to the United States. The American Jewish Committee and other groups sent protestors to greet the French president at every stop of his trip. When Nixon heard that they had also convinced New York Governor Nelson Rockefeller and New York City Mayor John Lindsay to boycott a gala reception for the French president and his wife at the Waldorf-Astoria in Manhattan, he was furious and decided to fly up to New York secretly to attend the dinner. "My appearance at the dinner came as a dramatic surprise, and nothing I said in our many talks over the years on substantive matters did as much to win Pompidou's friendship and cooperation as this gesture."[2]

Those substantive talks were not limited to nuclear matters: there were lots of areas where the United States and France worked together secretly, starting in the Nixon years. Much of the work was aimed against the Soviet Union, but not all. Most of it remains secret to this day. "I knew Conze from the nuclear testing business in the late 1970s," said William Schneider, who worked on nuclear testing and weapons design issues for the U.S. Congress from 1971 to 1981 and went on to become undersecretary of state during the Reagan administration.[3] Over the next twenty-five years, Conze made more than 150 trips to the United States, hammering out the nitty-gritty of the strategic cooperation between the United States and France.

President Mitterrand's first defense minister, Charles Hernu, understood almost immediately that Conze could help reassure the Reagan administration that the new French government had no intention of abrogating the secret nuclear cooperation pact. His success in Washington convinced Hernu to put him in charge of armaments cooperation with NATO and the United States. After the failure of the Mirage F1 to win the "contract of the century" competition for the next-generation NATO combat jet in the mid-1970s, the very notion of armaments cooperation with NATO was a novel approach, to say the least. But Conze took the new assignment as an opportunity, and he ran with it.

The one successful defense cooperation program between the United States and France was the CFM56 jet engine, which was developed as the result of a fifty-fifty partnership between General Electric and Snecma in the 1970s. Certified by the Federal Aviation Administration in 1979 for commercial use, the CFM56 was adopted by Delta and other U.S. carriers to power their Boeing 707 and, later, Boeing 737 jetliners. In France, the new engine powered the first Airbus 300, Europe's competitor to Boeing, which was just then getting off the ground. Conze helped push the French military to adopt the engine for use on its fleet of U.S.-built KC-135 military jet tanker aircraft and, later, in U.S.-built AWACS aircraft. More than 13,500 of these engines are today in service with 350 customers around the world, so most Americans who fly—at one point or another—have entrusted their lives to French technology.

Under Conze's direction, transatlantic defense cooperation was expanded and transformed. For the first time ever, both French and American government officials began talking about a "two-way street" of defense sales, rather than just European purchases of U.S. weapons and equipment.

I was introduced to Conze as a young foreign correspondent in Paris by Colonel Mark Broman, who was in charge of the Office of Defense Cooperation at the U.S. embassy in Paris when I first met him in September 1982. I was doing a story on the furious debate then under way about the pending deployment of U.S. Pershing II and nuclear-tipped cruise missiles in Europe and asked how the presence of Communist Party ministers had affected the U.S.-French relationship. Broman's response surprised me, because it ran counter to everything I was reading in the so-called mainstream press.

"The Communist ministers in the French government have had no impact on our defense cooperation," he told me. "This government is more pro-NATO, more anti-Soviet, and perceives the threat from the

Soviet Union more clearly than the previous government," Broman said. "Giscard took the position that France could be an 'honest broker' between the United States and the Soviets. Mitterrand doesn't. He is solidly in our camp."[4]

When I expressed surprise at this, he went on to describe the benefits of having France maintain an independent nuclear deterrent, outside the NATO unified military command. "The French position presents the Soviets with an additional dilemma," he said. "Not only do the Soviets have to deal with NATO if they invade Western Europe, but they must also deal separately with France. Having the French outside the NATO unified command makes life infinitely more complicated for the Soviets, because of their independent deterrent." He suggested that if I wanted to learn more about French nuclear posture, he could introduce me to a close friend of his at the DGA. That would be Henri Conze.

Neither Conze's schedule nor my own allowed us to meet immediately. However, when I had returned from an extended trip to the Middle East, he graciously agreed to receive me at his office in a secluded annex of the Defense Ministry. At the time we both were heavy smokers, and the overheated winter air of his small office was thick with the stench of French black tobacco. Just over forty, dressed in a tweed jacket and mismatching trousers, his eyes encased in thick tortoise-shell glasses, he punctuated his remarks with deep drags on the ever present unfiltered Gauloises that left brown tobacco stains on his fingers. Conze did not cut an elegant figure. Awkward, eager, and no better dressed, I too was no candidate for high-society balls. But we hit it off immediately. And it was clear to me as I listened to Conze speak that he was a rare individual: brilliant, well informed, thoughtful, and undogmatic. He was a straight shooter, a species even more rare in the French bureaucracy than in the twisted corridors of Foggy Bottom or the Pentagon in Washington.[5]

He began by explaining how France had responded to President Reagan's call to the European allies to increase their defense spending to 3 percent of their gross national product (GNP), to help share the military and economic burden in facing the threat from the Soviet Union. France was now spending 4.15 percent of their GNP on defense, he said, "more than any other NATO partner besides Britain."

In addition, France had its own independent nuclear force and was intent on expanding it further. "We need to have tactical nuclear weapons to counter a Soviet conventional attack on Europe," he said. Rare was the French politician who would admit this aspect of French nuclear strategy openly, especially to a foreign reporter.

The current generation of strategic missile, the M20, allowed each French submarine to launch sixteen thermonuclear warheads against the USSR. They were huge city-busters, one megaton each. "This puts us roughly in the same class as U.S. subs," Conze pointed out. It was a discreet nod to the top-secret nuclear cooperation then under way between Paris and Washington that had helped the French finalize development on the M20 in just three years, after nearly a decade of blind alleys and technological dead ends. The next-generation missile, designated M4, was going to carry six MIRVs (multiple individually targeted re-entry vehicles), he said, without mentioning that technology needed to put multiple warheads on the missiles had also been shared with France by the United States. "The most important element of our deterrent is *not* to make France a sanctuary," he emphasized, contradicting what many Gaullists and Socialists liked to repeat when speaking to the French public.

Conze explained that while the French position was to use nuclear weapons only for the defense of French territory, France "will do all that is necessary to intervene in a crisis directly concerning West Germany, on the basis of the North Atlantic Treaty. . . . Our deterrent is for the defense of our vital interests, *and Germany is part of our vital interests.*" By refusing to allow French nuclear forces to be counted in U.S.-Soviet disarmament talks, he added, the French had complicated matters for Soviet strategic planners. "The United States has sixty-four nuclear missile submarines. France has six. It's much better when facing the Soviets as an alliance to know you have sixty-four plus six submarines than just to have seventy. It creates uncertainty in the mind of your opponent."

And by not formally rejoining the NATO unified military command, France was making a greater contribution to the defense of Western Europe and America than it could by being a formal ally. For instance, France had earmarked forty thousand troops as a "rapid deployment force" to stop Soviet expansionism. "This is something we couldn't have developed or used as part of NATO," he said. "We force the Soviets to imagine scenarios for how our forces could be used."

Conze was describing in January 1983 the general outlines of the strategic cooperation then under way between France and the United

States at the peak of the life-or-death struggle that was the cold war. It was not well-known, and he and other officials I spoke to at the Defense Ministry and the Élysée felt it was a message that was important to get out.

After Farewell, U.S. assistance to French nuclear weapons programs was "extensive and detailed," a senior Reagan administration told me twenty years later. "Because of U.S. laws prohibiting the transfer of nuclear weapons technology, we had to find creative ways to be helpful to the French; and we did. That help was not marginal, it was vital. They would not have a competent nuclear program today if it weren't for the assistance from the United States. This is not because their scientists were no good—they were first-rate—but simply because the cost of maintaining a nuclear program with safe, secure, high-quality warheads was extraordinarily high. Just the ability to know what worked and what didn't was worth billions; we gave it to them for nothing, as the gesture of one ally to another. We accepted that we were in an alliance together, that together we were facing common threats. In such a situation, that was what you did to help an ally."[6]

When I asked Conze recently his opinion of this assessment, he insisted that the French had also provided valuable insight and technology to the United States, especially as regarded warhead safety. "We were able to show the [U.S. weapons] labs things they told us they greatly appreciated. We all liked to work together. We were a team."

"So it was no accident," I said, "that France all of a sudden solved its problems in MIRVing missiles."

"That's true. It went very quickly, and it didn't cost a lot. And it's still secret—so I can't talk about it," Conze said, putting on his Cheshire cat smile.

The extraordinary meeting of the minds on strategic issues did not mean there were no disputes between Paris and Washington during the early Mitterrand and Reagan years. There were, and they were significant. They involved questions of industrial policy and, especially, of technology transfer to the Soviet bloc. At times, these disputes became quite bitter as the French openly defied U.S. pleas to restrict particular high-technology sales to the Soviet Union. The French invariably argued that they did not feel the transfers posed a strategic threat and that if their companies didn't sell the goods, somebody else would.

The earliest and most public of these clashes involved French opposition to a Reagan administration embargo on technology assistance to the gigantic pipeline the Soviets were building to link the natural gas fields of Siberia to Western Europe. President Reagan viewed the project not only as an economic lifeline for the failed Soviet regime, but also as a means for the Soviets to blackmail Europe by controlling its energy supplies. And he knew it couldn't be built without Western credits and Western technology. Under the guidance of CIA director William Casey, Secretary of Defense Caspar Weinberger, and National Security Adviser William Clark, senior officials in Washington drafted a "competitive strategies" approach for defeating the Soviet Union that sought to exploit the weaknesses of the Soviet economy while leveraging America's strengths. This idea was to force Soviet leaders "to make more and more difficult decisions on how increasingly limited resources would be allocated."[7] That approach was laid out in a still secret, eight-page national security decision memorandum, signed by President Reagan in May 1982. One element of the strategy was to reduce Soviet hard currency earnings from the sale of crude oil and natural gas. To accomplish that goal, it was imperative to block the multibillion-dollar project to build the Siberian gas pipeline.

The fight with the French that ensued was monumental. Key to ensuring that gas kept moving through the 3,300-mile pipeline were forty-one compressor stations the Soviets needed to build. In the initial contract, General Electric was to provide the gas turbine engines and specially designed rotor blades used to drive them. Reagan's first stroke was to ban U.S. companies from providing such assistance. But almost as soon as he did that, French and other European suppliers jumped in "at flank speed" to replace them, said Roger Robinson, a former National Security Council economic analyst.[8] In early 1982, despite an agreement by NATO foreign ministers not to allow European companies to undercut the U.S. ban, Mitterrand's government gave the go-ahead to Alsthom-Atlantique to supply identical equipment, which it made under license to GE. In Washington, tempers were boiling.

The French argued that the pipeline was just a commercial contract and not at all defense related. So at the G-7 economic summit in Versailles from June 4 to 6, Reagan tried a different approach. If Mitterrand and German chancellor Helmut Schmidt couldn't accept a total embargo, couldn't they limit their sales so the Soviets could build just one strand of the pipeline, not two? In exchange for easing off on the sanctions, Reagan asked them to cut off subsidized credits to Moscow and to work with the United States at CoCom to further restrict high-technology sales to the Soviets. Again, the Europeans turned him down. "Mitterrand and Schmidt left the final ceremony and told their media and publics that there would be no change in their pattern of financial or energy relations with the USSR," Robinson said.[9]

Reagan decided to turn up the heat and expanded U.S. sanctions on June 18 to include "denial orders" on the sale of U.S. high-technology goods to any foreign company that worked on the pipeline project. The goal of the new ban was to present companies such as Alsthom and Thomson-CSF with a clear choice: Respect the U.S. embargo on the pipeline or lose access to U.S. technology. In France, Minister of Industry Jean-Pierre Chevènement, a left-wing Gaullist, threatened to "requisition" the production facilities of any company that refused to honor its contracts with the USSR. At his urging, Creusot-Loire, which held the French licenses for equipment designed by Dresser Industries of the United States, began shipping sanctioned compressors on August 26, 1982.[10]

So was this a case of French "ingratitude," a slap in the face from an ally that was getting secret assistance from the United States to build better nuclear weapons? Before jumping to that conclusion, consider this. Margaret Thatcher, whom Reagan considered to be his best ally as well as a personal friend, opposed the U.S. embargo at least as vigorously as did Mitterrand or Helmut Schmidt. She told Reagan personally, "Your law doesn't apply here."[11] Indeed, America's European allies were united in rejecting U.S. efforts to impose restrictions on where their companies could export their goods. They considered such choices to be a matter of national sovereignty, national policy, and not an alliance matter. If they wanted to trade with dictators and despots, it was none of Washington's business.

It took a mixture of smooth negotiating by incoming secretary of state George P. Shultz and hardball politics to bring the French around. At stake was not just the trans-Siberian pipeline, but the entire Soviet economy. The outcome of this dispute would shape the future of the cold war.

"What was extraordinary about the French lack of cooperation at CoCom was that they knew what we knew because of Farewell," said former assistant secretary of defense Richard Perle. Limiting the flow of strategic technologies to the Soviet bloc through CoCom was one of the pillars of

Reagan's strategy for defeating communism. The French refusal to work together with the United States in this area was seen as so egregious that Perle and others at the Pentagon ultimately argued it was time to use the biggest weapon in the U.S. arsenal. "We pressured them mercilessly, and they ultimately yielded to pressure." That pressure, I can reveal here for the first time, included threats to break off the top-secret nuclear cooperation. "We said it makes no sense to cooperate in common defense when you are not cooperating in slowing the flow of technology to the common enemy," Perle said. Other former officials on both sides of the Atlantic agreed with his account.

Perle led many of the high-level U.S. delegations to the meetings in Paris once the Reagan administration revived CoCom in January 1982.[12] Established in 1949, in theory this original cold war organization could block the sale by any allied country of high-technology equipment to the Soviet bloc, but those powers had fallen into neglect during the years of détente under Presidents Nixon, Ford, and Carter. Because of Farewell, both France and the United States now understood that the Soviet Union was deriving tremendous military benefit from ostensibly civilian contracts with the West and was directly incorporating Western technology into everything from its ICBM fleet to military trucks. CoCom's importance in limiting such sales should have been absolutely evident.

But the Farewell file was still held very closely, even in France. It wasn't until the DST was convinced that Colonel Vetrov had disappeared for good, at the end of 1983, that it began distributing a top-secret analysis of the information he had provided, complete with a detailed organization chart of Soviet high-tech collection agencies. The DST report revealed that the Soviet Military Industrial Commission, the VPK, was managing an entirely separate economy for the Soviet military, with its own factories, its own cities, its own structures of procurement and distribution, all the while pretending that the large-scale purchases the Soviet Union was making in the West were intended for purely civilian purposes, by industries that in many cases simply didn't exist. Major French companies were doing business on a daily basis with VPK components, and were directly assisting the Soviet military empire.[13]

French machine tool maker Ratier-Forest (known variously as Forest-Liné, Machines Françaises Lourdes, and, later, Brissard Machines Outils) shipped machines to aircraft plants in Kiev and Leningrad to make turbine blades for jet engines, parts which required extremely precise milling machines that could cut metal from several different angles simultaneously, a capability far beyond tools then available in the USSR. The French signed these "civilian" contracts with V/O Stankopromimport, a branch of the State Committee for Science and Technology, the GNKT, which Farewell identified as a procurement arm of the VPK. In 1983, just as the United States and France were hotly debating how to revive CoCom to restrict the flow of strategic technologies to the Soviets, Forest-Liné sold eight gigantic 5-axis machines to the Leningrad navy yards, misrepresenting their specifications on export documents.[14] Such violations of the CoCom rules, which bound all members of the Atlantic alliance plus Japan, were outrageous, flagrant, and persistent. Yet despite repeated U.S. protests, the French government refused to crack the whip.

Finally, Perle and other Pentagon emissaries to Paris made it clear to the French that if they didn't tighten their export control procedures, the United States would end the nuclear assistance. "I negotiated that exchange," says former undersecretary of defense Fred Charles Ikle. "We agreed to do this, and they agreed to do that. It was not all put on the same piece of paper, necessarily, but that was how it worked."[15] Working both sides of that swap for the French was the increasingly influential Henri Conze. "Conze was a good French patriot who knew tech transfer and understood that these sales to the Soviet Union were not good for French security, either," Ikle said.

The public side of the deal, which involved the Siberian gas pipeline, was unveiled at a dramatic midnight press conference at the Quai d'Orsay, after a black-tie dinner. "We dined at a table twenty yards long that glittered in silver," former secretary of state Shultz recalled in his memoir. The state dining room itself was "so heavily adorned with gold leaf, marble, cherubs, and crystal chandeliers that I wondered whether the ceiling might collapse from the sheer weight of it all."[16] What Shultz had negotiated with his French counterpart, Claude Cheysson, was politically important for the Atlantic alliance as it confronted the Soviet Union. The deal hammered out by Fred Ikle and Richard Perle behind the scenes with Conze and others at the French Defense Ministry was essential to winning the cold war.

D r. Stephen D. Bryen worked under Fred Ikle as a deputy undersecretary of defense. He attended many of the CoCom meetings in Paris as the senior Pentagon representative and saw with his own eyes the impact of the new arrangements worked out by his boss. Nothing less than a sea change had taken place. From being one of the primary opponents of a co-ordinated Western approach toward strategic trade, the French had become a key facilitator and advocate. "The key to our success at CoCom in the 1980s was our ability to work out solutions with the French before actually going into the CoCom meetings," Bryen says. "They stopped grand-standing and rolled up their sleeves."[17] The nuclear squeeze had worked.

One example was in the area of telecommunications, a major Soviet requirement. "The French were way ahead of us," Bryen recalls. "Alcatel and Thomson manufactured the first digital switches, years ahead of U.S. companies. We had a huge battle to keep them from exporting these switches to the USSR. Eventually we cut a deal and bought ourselves four years. It wasn't easy cooperation, but it was vital cooperation. And for the French, it was a major concession." The French agreement to restrict these sales was even more remarkable because they had an existing contract with the Soviets they had to fudge. It was a potential repeat of the Siberian gas pipeline, but the outcome was now just the opposite.

Unlike Western countries, which maintained separate civilian and military communications networks, the Soviet Union had a single, integrated network. The centralization allowed the state to eavesdrop on any conversation taking place anywhere in the country, simply by turning a dial. But the Soviet system was also unreliable and inefficient. Before French telecom giant Alcatel agreed to sell digital switches to the Soviets under Giscard, the Soviet telephone system was positively third world. Brezhnev was hoping to leapfrog a generation and install state-of-the-art digital equipment across the Soviet empire, while maintaining central state control.

Alcatel had agreed to build an assembly plant at Ufa, strategically located in the Ural Mountains, to produce enough switches to equip one million new lines per year. "To put that in perspective," an Alcatel official explained, "that is about half of what we currently make here in France." Under Giscard's presidency, the French simply neglected to submit the contract to CoCom, company officials told me. Just the factory portion alone was worth one billion francs—around $230 million at prevailing exchange rates. At the Pentagon's urging, the French government slow-rolled the deal, holding up key approvals to buy time. Ufa didn't begin producing digital switches until around 1988—the "four years" Bryen referred to.[18] Those were four critical years for the history of the world that brought about the end of the cold war.

CoCom was based in a dusty U.S. embassy annex on the rue de la Boetie in Paris. An important part of adapting CoCom decisions to the pace of modern business was the installation of powerful new computers with direct data links to the seventeen CoCom capitals, so export control officials could instantaneously share information on difficult cases under discussion in Paris. But even this effort met with tough resistance from many CoCom allies, who had never liked the idea of giving other countries the power to veto their export sales. "I vividly recall a conversation with a high-level Japanese official, sent by his government to Paris for a meeting at which strengthening COCOM was on the agenda," Richard Perle wrote in the *Wall Street Journal*. "We were hoping to increase the COCOM budget, and the Japanese share of the increase would have been $45,000. With breathtaking disingenuousness, this official told me that Japan couldn't afford it. Thus lacking consensus, yet another American initiative was delayed."[19]

The Japanese were not alone, Perle explained. "Like the Japanese, the Germans have fought us every inch of the way. Always eager to expand the list of technologies [available for export to the Communist bloc], they let their assiduousness vanish when help is needed to enforce agreed controls or bring diverters to justice." This was key to enforcing export controls, since only stiff prison sentences—not slap-on-the-wrist civilian fines— could sufficiently deter the middlemen known as "techno-bandits" from pursuing their lucrative deals with the KGB.

"Other COCOM members—the Dutch, Canadians, Belgians, Italians, Norwegians, British and Danes—have, to varying degrees, resisted our efforts to obtain a level playing field in which all COCOM member countries exercise comparable diligence in implementing the embargo," Perle went on. "Virtually all of them have sought to decontrol as much technology as possible, particularly when one of their industries is directly affected. It is not uncommon at COCOM meetings to find officials of European companies whose product line is being discussed or negotiated seated behind their national delegations. The last thing in their minds is the security of the Western alliance. They are there to open market opportunities for their companies. And if the U.S. has to increase its defense budget to counter

Western technologies in Soviet military systems—well, that's not their concern."

One country was notably missing from Perle's enumeration of NATO alliance bad players. That would be France.

O n Monday, December 6, 1982, Secretary of State George Shultz left Washington, D.C., for a come-to-Jesus tour of European capitals. Shultz's mission was to convince the Europeans to go forward with the deployment of 572 American cruise and Pershing II nuclear missiles in a year's time. As he left Washington, D.C., his chances of success looked grim.

The deployment decision, initially taken at the Guadeloupe summit in 1979 and ratified by NATO defense ministers one year later, had reached crunch time. Arms negotiators in Geneva had stumbled into a dead end, the Soviets were rapidly deploying new SS-20 launchers in both Europe and Asia, and the U.S. intelligence community had begun to pick up disturbing hints that the Soviets were making active preparations to launch a nuclear war.

KGB boss Yuri Andropov had taken the reins of Soviet power from the ailing Leonid Brezhnev just the month before Shultz's trip, and already he was promising a tough new confrontation with the West. As KGB chief, Andropov had personally approved the crackdown on the Solidarity trade union led by Lech Wałęsa in Poland in the fall of 1981. He understood that President Reagan was determined to roll back communism by undermining Soviet puppet regimes in Afghanistan, Cambodia, Angola, Nicaragua, and Poland. His new defense minister, Dmitri Ustinov, launched a scare offensive in advance of Shultz's trip, accusing the United States of preparing for war. Recently declassified documents show that Ustinov was projecting Soviet war plans onto the United States.

At President Reagan's request, the National Intelligence Council (NIC) had just completed the first of several highly classified assessments of Soviet ballistic missile defenses, which it briefed to Shultz and other top administration officials. While critical gaps remained in the intelligence, the NIC concluded that the USSR was engaged in a massive, secret, and illegal effort to deploy ballistic missile defenses at a time when the United States and the USSR had committed to forgo such defenses under the 1972 Anti-Ballistic Missile (ABM) Treaty. "The consequences of Soviet acquisition of a ballistic missile defense, despite uncertainties about its effectiveness, are so serious that even a low probability of such an achievement is cause for concern," the Secret National Intelligence Estimate, dated October 13, 1982, concluded.[20]

In West Germany and Holland, antinuclear "pacifists" had launched violent street demonstrations and hung effigies of Uncle Sam from trees. In Britain, the opposition Labour Party had made "unilateral disarmament" the cornerstone of its political platform. In the United States, the "nuclear freeze" movement won the support of key Democrats in Congress, as well as that of political gadfly (and future presidential candidate) Jesse Jackson, whose Operation PUSH joined forces with the Communist Party USA and the Soviet-backed U.S. Peace Council in demanding nothing less than the unilateral dismantling of the entire U.S. military. The Communist Party's *Daily World* claimed that a June 12, 1982, rally organized jointly by Jackson and the Communists in support of this cause had attracted more than a million people.[21]

Despite the street protests, Italy and Britain appeared ready to accept their cruise missiles. The outcome in Belgium and Holland was less certain but ultimately less critical. The real test was going to be West Germany.

On October 4, 1982, the government of Socialist premier Helmut Schmidt lost a parliamentary vote of no confidence, after a key coalition partner, Hans-Dietrich Genscher, withdrew his support. Genscher, who was born in Halle, East Germany, was a fickle partner. Notorious for his "Ostpolitik" of concessions to the Soviet-dominated East, he had never been a supporter of deployment. Nevertheless, he threw his weight behind Christian Democratic Party leader Helmut Kohl so he could become foreign minister, despite Kohl's vow to make the upcoming parliamentary elections into a referendum on the Euromissile deployment.

Helmut Schmidt was replaced as head of the Social Democratic Party (SDP) by Hans-Jochen Vogel, an antinuclear, pro-Soviet pacifist. In January 1983, Vogel visited Moscow and "seemed impressed by the prospects set forth by the Soviets of benefits Germans would enjoy if they rejected the deployment of U.S. Pershing II missiles," George Shultz recalls.[22] Making matters worse, Vogel was now hinting that he supported the Soviet ploy to include French nuclear forces in any treaty limiting intermediate nuclear weapons in Europe. Into this charged domestic political dispute walked

François Mitterrand. To Vogel's utter astonishment, the French president abandoned his fellow Socialist.

In an electric speech commemorating the twentieth anniversary of the French-German friendship treaty on January 20, 1983, Mitterrand told the full German Bundestag there could be no division among the NATO allies. France and Germany belonged to the same alliance: "I repeat, the same alliance," he said. Then he presented a stinging critique of the Ostpolitik so cherished by Genscher, Vogel, and Vogel's Socialist colleagues, which Mitterrand all but called appeasement.

Nuclear weapons still remained the guarantor of peace, Mitterrand said, but there had to be parity between the two superpowers. Because of the 243 Soviet SS-20 launchers, "entire regions of Europe" had no defense against "nuclear weapons specifically aimed at them." While he wished "ardently" for the Geneva negotiations to succeed, it was essential that they proceed from a sound base. "This is why the joint determination of the members of the Atlantic Alliance and their solidarity toward each other must be clearly confirmed, in order for the negotiation to succeed." His message was absolutely clear: There could be no more waffling on the deployment decision.

Mitterrand went on to remind the Bundestag of France's direct commitment to the defense of Europe by basing the French Second Army on German soil. French forces in Germany were being significantly upgraded, he said, "to increase their mobility and firepower," and would soon receive a new generation of tactical nuclear missile, the Hades. "This is how we conceive of the defense of our territory and of our vital interests," Mitterrand said.

Turning to the Geneva arms control negotiations, Mitterrand explained why France would not allow its forces to be counted or affected by any arrangement between the superpowers.

> Between two countries who have the possibility of destroying each other several times over, which is the case of the United States of America and the Soviet Union, and countries such as my own, whose main possibility is to forbid an eventual aggressor from any hope of benefiting from war, the gap is enormous: there is a difference in kind. Let me put it more concretely: if one of the two great powers destroyed all of its medium-range missiles, it would still have thousands of rockets left, whereas France would lose a determinant element of its deterrent capability, and thus the guarantee of its

security, which would no longer exist below a certain threshold. . . . This independence [of the French nuclear deterrent] also increases uncertainty— but only the uncertainty of an eventual aggressor. By rendering deterrence more effective, it also increases the impossibility of war.[23]

Mitterrand's support for the U.S. cruise and Pershing II deployment came at a critical time for the Western alliance. Washington feared that if German voters returned the Socialists to power under Vogel, West Germany could descend into full-scale pacifism, ultimately wrecking NATO and opening the door to Soviet adventurism. By showing the Germans that a Socialist could stand strongly behind NATO, which the new SDP leader refused to do, Mitterrand helped Helmut Kohl and his Christian Democrats, who went on to win the March 1983 elections by a decisive margin. "Mitterrand was terrific," recalls Fred Ikle. "He really helped turn things around." Once again, the French president showed that when given a choice between standing up for freedom and appeasing tyrants, he would always choose freedom, even if it meant dumping a political ally.

As the countdown to the NATO deployments began that fall, the KGB launched an all-out "peace offensive" through a welter of front organizations in the United States and Europe. The French Communist Party, still in Mitterrand's cabinet but sidelined from any strategic decisions, joined the "Appeal of the 100," a petition signed by leading left-wing political and intellectual figures that called for a nuclear freeze in Europe. Of course, a nuclear "freeze" at then current force levels would have meant permanently freezing in place the Soviet advantage in troops and nuclear weapons—precisely the Kremlin's objective. But strong criticism from Mitterrand and his Socialist Party helped keep the peace movement in check. "The Euromissiles are in the East," Mitterrand remarked icily, "while the pacifists are in the West." Fewer than twenty thousand people took part in two days of "peace marches" in Paris that were organized by the Communists and their allies.[24]

"Mitterrand was not doing us a favor," insists Richard Perle. "The cruise missiles and Pershing IIs weren't being deployed in France. This was not a gesture where France made a sacrifice for us. Mitterrand was even more concerned than were some Americans that Germany was headed in a pacifist direction. It was a political judgment on the part of the French to support the deployment. It was their own interest as they saw their own interest."[25]

Richard Perle may be right as to Mitterrand's motivation. Even before he was elected president in 1981, Mitterrand had strongly criticized the Soviet Union for deploying the SS-20s, which he argued had created a dangerous strategic imbalance on the European continent.[26] Nevertheless, his support at this critical moment helped President Reagan win the cold war.

U.S.-French strategic cooperation had a robust military component that by mid-1983 was becoming an open secret, or, as the French liked to call it, *un secret de polichinelle*. I recall eating dinner at the officers mess of the Deuxième Régiment Étranger de Parachutistes in Beirut in June 1983. I was the personal guest of General Francis Coullin, the commanding general of the French Foreign Legion contingent of the multinational peacekeeping force then stationed in Lebanon. At the long deal tables in the refectory of the former French ambassador's residence near the hippodrome in West Beirut, its tall windows still bombed out from the fighting over the previous eight years, eighty-some officers stood at attention, wineglasses in hand, and sang marching songs from the 1926 campaign in the Djebel Druse, the Shouf Mountains outside of Beirut. *"Attention à la poussière . . . ,"* they belted out, making sure I raised my glass at the right moment. *"Envoyez!"* That was the signal for down the hatch. The four-course dinner was terrific, and the wine flowed generously, freshly imported from Bordeaux. General Coullin regularly invited U.S. Marine Corps officers to his table as well. None was ever known to have refused.

Manly comaraderie aside, the French were in Beirut as part of a joint NATO military operation. It wasn't described as such—it had been negotiated separately, at least in public. But without extensive French participation, the United States would have thought long and hard about sending troops back to Lebanon after the Sabra and Shatila massacres of September 1982. As it was, when Iranian-backed Hezbollah militiamen began guerrilla operations against the peacekeepers, they made no mistake about whose side the French were on. On October 23, 1983, twin Hezbollah car bombings demolished the U.S. Marines barracks at Beirut Airport and a French marine infantry barracks in the southern suburbs, in separate attacks timed just minutes apart. Altogether, some 241 marines and 58 French soldiers died that day on direct orders from Tehran.[27] Once again, our two nations were joined by a bond of blood.

In Germany, the French unit had been thoroughly integrated into NATO war plans. French and NATO planners had "worked out arrangements whereby if Paris judged war to be near, French ground forces would take up positions in central Germany and fall directly under NATO commanders there," writes Princeton University scholar Richard H. Ullman. Mitterrand continued to use the fig leaf of the twenty-year-old Franco-German Treaty to disguise French military cooperation with NATO, as he did during his Euromissile speech to the Bundestag. But the operational coordination went way beyond a mere marriage of convenience. "Although they would like to say that they are French forces supporting the NATO structure, they are going to be in the chain of command for all intents and purposes," Ullman quoted a senior NATO officer as saying.[28] I heard similar comments at the time from French and U.S. military officers.

And the cooperation wasn't just with the United States. At a British NATO base in Putlos, Germany, Brigadier Keith Crosser, commander of Britain's first brigade, called on French defense industry specialists to help with field trials of a new tank killer, which combined a French Milan wire-guided missile and a British armored car, manufactured by Alvis. When I spoke with Crosser and with the French and British technicians during field trials they had opened to the specialized press, no one expressed the slightest discomfort or surprise that a French team would be taking part in a NATO operation.[29]

The United States provided smaller, less public favors to the French as well. In July 1983, Libya's Colonel Muammar al-Qaddafi invaded northern Chad, ostensibly in support of a Chadian rebel group that was trying to overthrow the government. Chadian leader Hissène Habré had become a favorite of President Reagan's because of his willingness to stand up to Qaddafi. When Habré was in exile in Sudan in 1982, the United States had quietly provided him with military and financial aid, helping him to oust his Libyan-backed rival, Goukouni Oueddei. Qaddafi had a long history of meddling in Chad and wanted to annex the Aouzou strip along Libyan's southern border, believed to be rich in uranium and oil. Reagan saw Habré as the best bet for checking Qaddafi's expansionist dreams.

But French-speaking Chad was also firmly within France's sphere of influence in Africa, and Mitterrand was reluctant to come to Habré's aid. The Africa hands in the French intelligence service and the Quai d'Orsay hated

Habré because of his involvement in kidnapping the wife of a French schoolteacher several years earlier, known as the "Claustre Affaire." The DGSE was urging Mitterrand to teach Habré a lesson and let the situation deteriorate.

As the French hesitated, the Libyans were pouring armor and troops across the border and reinforcing their hold on the northern oasis town of Faya-Largeau. Reagan ordered the Pentagon to make an emergency appropriation of $25 million to Habré's government, to allow Habré to buy much needed equipment and ammunition. But still the French didn't move. Finally Reagan dispatched an aide to Paris with a sheaf of satellite photographs that he personally showed to Mitterrand at the Élysée. "The photographs proved beyond any doubt that the Libyans were directly involved in the fighting," a U.S. diplomat told me. "At that moment, Mitterrand had to act."[30]

Habré's fighters became legendary for destroying Libyan tanks in the desert in darting attacks from Toyota pickups, armed only with antitank rockets or machine guns. Their "Toyota war" tactics have since become standard guerrilla practice. But because Qaddafi had seized all the airstrips in the north, Habré couldn't get his troops to the battle zone quickly enough to prevent the Libyans from reinforcing their positions and moving south toward the capital, N'Djamena.

In August, Mitterrand sent in the Foreign Legion and French combat jets to help Habré retake Faya-Largeau. But neither Habré nor the French had cargo planes capable of taking off and landing from short, makeshift airstrips in the desert to bring up troops and Habré's Toyota pickups. That's when Colonel Broman, of the U.S. embassy's Office of Defense Cooperation, came up with an idea. He located a group of used C-130 Hercules transports that the Australian air force was trying to sell through an American middleman named John Ford. He invited Ford, who was then in Paris, to his spacious office at the U.S. embassy annex on the rue de la Boetie (the same building where CoCom was headquartered) and negotiated to buy one of the planes at the rock-bottom price of $2.8 million. After quickly receiving approval and the necessary licenses from the Pentagon, he arranged to pay the ferrying costs from Australia to France and on to Chad, where a French crew took over. They quickly put the plane to good use in blocking the Libyan assault. "We gave the French the Herc without their asking," Broman told me later. "It was a question of pride. The French air force didn't have a plane capable of doing what the C-130 could do. And they didn't have a requirement to purchase new aircraft. So we basically said to the French, Here, have this one."[31]

Broman agreed with Conze that a terrific way to publicly cement the secret Franco-U.S. alliance would be to pry open the hermetic world of Pentagon weapons procurement to French defense companies. It was a delicate undertaking that ran up against misunderstandings, misperceptions, and suspicion on both sides of the Atlantic. They called their effort the "two-way street," and it got lots of ink in the specialized press and, occasionally, in the major dailies as well. But because of arcane Pentagon procedures and long-standing French habits of dealing with clients who were not accountable to Congress or any public body, it was a bumpy road.

Given their experience in places like Iraq, Syria, Saudi Arabia, and the United Arab Emirates (UAE), the French believed that the decisive factor in granting major government contracts was the political will of the leadership, which could be influenced by generous payments into Swiss (or Bahamian) bank accounts. Conze knew better, of course, when it came to the United States; but it was still tough sledding to convince French defense companies to hire consultants in Washington to work Congress and to master the stunning array of Pentagon procurement regulations, set up like so many roadblocks on the narrow cart path across the Atlantic.

One success story that Conze worked jointly with Broman—whose job definition at the U.S. embassy was to facilitate both commercial and military defense cooperation between the two countries—involved a $4 billion contract to purchase a new mobile tactical communications system for the U.S. Army. Known to the Pentagon as mobile subscriber equipment (MSE), in France the system was known by the more user-friendly acronym RITA (*réseau intégré des transmissions autonome*).

By 1984, combat radios had come a long way from the John Wayne movies, where the squad leader revs up a dynamo and grabs a hard-wired telephone receiver, shouting above exploding bombs to his field commander. When at Broman's suggestion I expressed an interest in reporting on RITA's capabilities in the fall of 1984, the French Defense Ministry went out of its way to accommodate my request. So did the French manufacturer, Thomson-CSF.

It was a cold, soggy November morning when I and a handful of defense correspondents gathered at the Defense Ministry in Paris for the two-hour drive to the German border in a French army minibus. We were to rendezvous with elements of the French Second Army, the same corps that was regularly conducting joint exercises with NATO troops in Germany.

When we came to a stop in a muddy clearing in the forested hills of eastern France—the invasion route used by Hitler's Wehrmacht in 1940—a French officer emerged from a camouflaged van parked beneath the trees and offered us rubber boots. It was not merely polite, but necessary.

After a short briefing, Colonel Pierre Lemercier, the top communications officer, told us to check our watches as four camouflaged jeeps arrived in the clearing and draftee soldiers jumped out, hoisting the portable RITA antennae.

A scant ten minutes later, in the middle of the woods, Lemercier handed me a portable phone—the basic consumer end of the $4 billion RITA network. "Why don't you call Washington?" he said. I dialed my editor in Atlanta, Georgia. More than a decade before the advent of cell phones, the connection from the middle of nowhere in eastern France was made as simply and as clearly as calling from a Paris office.

A U.S. Army liaison officer embedded with the French Second Army positively glowed when he described RITA's capabilities. "RITA is years ahead of anything we've got," he said. One element of the system that particularly impressed the Pentagon procurement officers who were evaluating it was its "survivability." Whenever a transmission "node" was knocked out or otherwise disabled by jamming or equipment failure, RITA's powerful digital switches would instantaneously plot an alternate path for the call by constantly sending signals out across an electronic spiderweb. The constant signal level also increased operational security, since there were no telltale spikes in traffic during peak operations—a dead giveaway to an alert enemy. As with a civilian telephone system, each subscriber had an individual phone number, protected by strongly encrypted code. If a RITA subscriber was killed or captured, an enemy couldn't just pick up his phone and plug into the network, we were told.

The U.S. Army's purchase of RITA paved the way for the dramatic advances in battlefield communications that made for American successes in the Persian Gulf War in 1991 and many other conflicts since. But despite the state-of-the-art French technology, the Pentagon nearly balked at marching down the two-way street. Blocking the path were two strongly entrenched American competitors, AT&T and Rockwell International.

Thomson-CSF understood that it couldn't make a simple off-the-shelf sale to the Pentagon and had paired with Needham, Massachusetts, defense contractor GTE-Sylvania.[32] A Pentagon project officer I met during the demonstration explained that Thomson's American rivals were "desperately trying to get the procurement process stalled in Congress to give them enough time to develop their own system." The U.S. Army brass wanted the French system, but Congress was inclined to go along with the industry lobbyists. At the time, the French were many years ahead of their U.S. competitors.

In the end, it took the active intervention of the new U.S. ambassador to Paris, Tennessee businessman Joe Rodgers, who flew back and forth to Washington repeatedly in his private jet to plug the deal. Rodgers helped work a compromise that pleased the army, the Congress, and the French. We would buy RITA, but GTE would manufacture the equipment in the United States. The French would buy AWACS aircraft from Boeing, with Boeing also purchasing roughly an equivalent of defense equipment from French subcontractors. Each deal was worth around $4 billion, but the huge industrial and commercial offsets were at the time virtually unheard of and became a milestone in the transatlantic defense trade.[33]

Although the deal took almost two more years to close, it not only enhanced the armed forces of both countries, but increased the on-the-ground and in-the-air integration of French military forces into NATO, since the French AWACS were carefully fitted out to be "interoperable" with NATO planes. And all this with a country that on paper was not part of the NATO integrated command and kept its distance from the Atlantic alliance.

# 6

# Bonanza in the Gulf

---

A s Saddam's troops became increasingly mired in their assault on Iran, his father-in-law, Khairallah al-Tulfah, penned a propaganda pamphlet aimed at inspiring the Baath Party masses. Widely distributed inside Iraq, it boasted a chillingly explicit title: *Three God Should Not Have Made: Persians, Jews, and Flies.* Persians, wrote al-Tulfah, were "animals God created in the shape of humans." Jews were a "mixture of the dirt and leftovers of diverse peoples." As for flies, they were a trifling creation "whom we do not understand God's purpose in creating."[1] For all three, the Baath Party had a solution, which it broadcast throughout the Arab world thanks to the powerful French transmitters of Baghdad's Voice of the Masses: "There is a certain insecticide for every type of insect." It was an Iraqi attempt at humor. Like most Baath Party jokes, its punch line was death.

Despite Mitterrand's misgivings about Saddam and the arms trade in general, he quickly surrounded himself with confidants and ministers who championed his cause. Foreign Minister Claude Cheysson was well-known in France as an outspoken advocate of the third world, especially the Middle East. Unlike the United States, which Cheysson dismissed because of its "lopsided" policy in favor of Israel, France was the perfect partner for nations such as Iraq, who were seeking Western assistance for their development needs. In his initial meeting with Iraqi foreign minister Tariq Aziz, on August 18, 1981, Cheysson praised the "Iraqi experiment," an enthusiasm he shared with much of the French elite. Iraq was secular, it had water, and it had an educated population. To top it off, of course, it had oil. When Aziz asked Cheysson if France would rebuild the Osirak reactor, Cheysson gave him an unqualified yes, without referring back to his boss. Iraq's nuclear reactor, Cheysson told the French daily *Le Monde*, was a "monument to peace." (Mitterrand later withdrew Cheysson's offer, and Osirak remained in ruins.)

Mitterrand appointed other pro-Arab ministers as well. His minister of cooperation, Jean-Pierre Cot, elevated Cheysson's anti-imperialistic cant to the realm of doctrine in op-eds and books. Jean-Pierre Chevènement, who was married to an Egyptian woman, was an unabashed admirer of Saddam Hussein.[2] Although Chevènement was serving as minister of education in Mitterrand's first cabinet, he exerted a powerful influence on the ruling Socialist Party, since he controlled one of its largest factions. Another pro-Arab was Mitterrand's cranky minister of foreign trade, Michel Jobert, who resented America's dominant position in Europe and displayed an often visceral hatred for the state of Israel. Jobert traveled repeatedly to Baghdad bearing gifts with the names Mirage, Exocet, HOT, Milan, and Roland. According to French journalist Jean Montaldo, Mitterrand and his son, Gilbert, benefited indirectly from some of these sales through a personal stipend paid to them by longtime crony Roger-Patrice Pelat, ostensibly for legal services. Pelat's company, Vibrachoc, was receiving a commission from Aérospatiale on the Exocet deal with Iraq, intelligence sources said. It was just a small part of the shady underside of Mitterrand's presidency described by Montaldo, who details the Vibrachoc payments in his 1994 book, *Mitterrand and the Forty Thieves.* . . .[3]

Supporting Iraqi dictator Saddam Hussein during his eight-year war against the ayatollahs in Iran was another area of U.S.-French strategic co-operation. Frequently misrepresented in the press, it has rarely been acknowledged and even less understood. The account that follows is based on my interviews with many of the key players in Baghdad, Paris, and Washington.

By May 1982, Iran succeeded in expelling the last of Saddam's troops from Iranian territory and took the war across the border into Iraq, threatening to capture Basra, Iraq's second largest city and its only gateway to the Gulf. In desperation, Saddam sued Ayatollah Khomeini for peace. When that failed, he lit another fire in the region, hoping to divert Iranian attention to a common enemy, Israel. On June 3, a Palestinian gunman attacked Israel's ambassador to London, Shlomo Argov, mortally wounding him on the steps of London's Dorchester Hotel. The assassination, which initially appeared to be the handiwork of Yasser Arafat's Palestinian Liberation Organization (PLO), was all the government of Israeli premier Menachem Begin needed to launch its long planned military incursion into Lebanon to destroy the PLO infrastructure.

Within hours of the Israeli invasion on June 5, Saddam again appealed to Ayatollah Khomeini. Iran and Iraq should stop fighting each other, he argued, and join forces in a holy war against Israel. Again the Iranian leader declined. Later, the police investigation in London concluded that the weapon used by the gunman to assassinate the Israeli ambassador had been supplied by a military intelligence officer at the Iraqi embassy in London. Iraqi agents had planned and financed the operation, which was carried out by a hired assassin from the Abu Nidal organization, then based in Baghdad.

The United States may have known about Saddam's involvement in the Argov assassination, but by that time the Reagan administration had decided that Saddam's war on Iran served the greater purpose of limiting Ayatollah Khomeini's ability to spread Islamic fundamentalism beyond Iran. In March 1982, Iraq was taken off the State Department list of state sponsors of terrorism, preparing the way for the "tilt" in official U.S. policy that soon followed. Bogged down in their own war in Lebanon, the Israelis weren't going to draw attention to an obscure London police investigation, either, since it would suggest that they were attacking the wrong target. When I later asked the State Department's top Arab hand, Richard Murphy, about the Argov shooting, he just shrugged. "There was never any discussion at State to put Iraq back on the terrorism list. The subject simply never came up."[4]

The other subject that didn't come up—at least not in a negative sense—was the ever increasing flow of sophisticated French weapons to Saddam. "Did we object to the French arming Saddam?" retorted Fred Ikle when I asked him if the subject had ever led to friction. "We were *supporting* Iraq in the 1980s!"[5]

Part of that support was the supply of operational intelligence on the flights of Iranian air force jets as they were tracked by U.S. AWACS planes based in Saudi Arabia, U.S. diplomats posted to Baghdad in the mid-1980s told me.[6] Another was to encourage Iraq's principal Western arms supplier, France, to extend new loans to Iraq to keep fresh arms flowing through the pipeline. "The Americans pushed us to deliver to Iraq—faster, faster, they kept saying," recalls Henri Conze, who was then a top official at the International Sales Directorate of the French armaments board. "I remember a White House meeting not long after the war began. The NSC noted that the Soviets were delivering arms to Afghanistan, and to Iraq. The United States did not want Iraq to become a Soviet client state. So France served a strategic purpose."[7]

But there was much hand-wringing in public and in the press about the French arms deliveries to Iraq. In the fall of 1983, news leaked out that Iraq was seeking the loan of five Super Etendard fighter-bombers from France as a stopgap measure before the next batch of Mirage F1s arrived. As the delivery date approached, Iran threatened to blockade the Strait of Hormuz, the choke point through which more than half the world's oil continued to flow. Fearing a worldwide oil shortage, the British Foreign Office appealed publicly to France not to deliver the planes. The United States dispatched the aircraft carrier USS *Ranger* and its entire battle group from Central America to the Indian Ocean to show its determination to keep the strait open.

That October, Tariq Aziz met again privately with George Shultz, this time in New York. He asked why the delivery of five aircraft, of a type no longer produced, was creating such a fuss in a war where human losses could be counted in the hundreds of thousands. The enemies of Iraq were behind all the media attention, he said. Principal among them, of course, was Israel. Aziz feared the French would back off from delivering the aircraft if they felt the United States was opposed to the deal and was trying to allay Shultz's natural suspicions.

For the Iraqis, the Super Etendard was a strategic weapon, the first of several they would use during the war. If delivered, the French fighter-bombers would be the first aircraft in Iraqi inventory capable of delivering the powerful Exocet antishipping missile, which had just proved so deadly during the 1982 Falkland War when an Argentine Super Etendard sank the British destroyer HMS *Sheffield.* Armed with the Exocet, the Iraqis would be able for the first time to target Iran's oil exports, since all of Iran's oil was hauled to foreign markets by ship. Instead of extending the war, Aziz argued with Shultz, Iraqi attacks on Iranian shipping could shorten it. For without the money to purchase arms on the black market, Iran would soon be forced to drop out of the fighting. Shultz says nothing about this meeting with Aziz in his memoirs, but the record shows that neither he nor any other Reagan administration official did anything to impede the delivery of the French planes.

Back in Paris, other heavyweights were applying pressure on the French government to make good its promise to Iraq. Hugues de l'Estoile, who had left the Defense Ministry to become Dassault's principal arms salesman, had already done a lot of arm-twisting to convince the French navy to loan the Super Etendards, which had to be withdrawn from active duty on a French aircraft carrier. Only eighty-six of these planes had ever been produced, and most of them belonged to the French navy (Argentina got the other fifteen). De l'Estoile argued that the temporary "loan" was a small price to pay for the nearly $2 billion deal he had negotiated earlier that year, to sell Iraq an additional twenty-nine Mirage F1 fighter-bombers. The new Mirages, specially redesigned for Iraq to carry the Exocet, would not be ready until late 1984. Until then, de l'Estoile argued, Iraq needed the Super Etendards to keep Iran from winning the war; in fact, their delivery had been a condition of the Mirage sale. De l'Estoile was so successful that he even managed to enlist the help of President Mitterrand, who declared publicly in Cairo, "We do not want Iraq to lose the war. The age-old balance between the Arab and the Persian worlds absolutely must be maintained." After a rushed meeting in Baghdad with General Amir Rashid al-Ubaydi, de l'Estoile's successor at the DGA, General Pierre-René Audran, sent a handwritten fax back to Defense Minister Charles Hernu, urging him to dispatch the planes immediately.

On October 13, Saddam Hussein summoned thirty-two French journalists to Baghdad, to hear a remarkable performance. Although the journalists didn't know it, the French government had delivered the Super Etendards one week earlier, in a secret maneuver code-named "Operation Milan."[8] Saddam's performance had been rehearsed to suggest just the opposite.

"These are our weapons, and we have paid for them," he told the journalists angrily, chewing on his cigar. Why was all this fuss being made over planes "which can't even carry a nuclear weapon"? If the Super Etendards did not arrive immediately, he warned, Iraq would be forced to take drastic measures to punish the French.

Saddam's trick succeeded beyond his wildest dreams. The Iranians, thinking that the French had gone wobbly in their support of Iraq, backed off in their threats to block the Strait of Hormuz. For months, newspapers all over France carried sightings of the planes, one time in Brittany, another time in Bordeaux, when in fact France had quietly delivered the planes when no one was looking and Iraqi pilots were already training on them in the Persian Gulf. By the end of the year, Iraqi pilots began picking off tankers at Iran's only oil terminal at Kharg Island using the deadly Exocet missiles, striking at the heart of Iran's economy.

Henri Conze was in Boston for a conference on NATO strategy when the *Boston Globe* announced on the front page the delivery of the French planes weeks after the fact and warned of increased tensions in the Persian Gulf. The United States had recently established the Central Command to regroup U.S. forces for rapid deployment to the Middle East and the Persian Gulf, and France was actively cooperating with the new commander, General Robert Kingston, and his top officers.* "We had officers going to Tampa all the time," Conze said. "We tried to give the new U.S. Command everything we had learned about Africa, about Qaddafi during the Chad wars, the Middle East." The officers sent by the French Defense Ministry were no armchair generals, but operational commanders, who went to share their experience on the battlefronts of the cold war. This was yet another aspect of the U.S.-French strategic relationship.

Conze had been invited to give a speech on French cooperation with NATO, but he knew who would be grilled on the Super Etendard story. General Kingston was just finishing a presentation on his new command, illustrating the threats facing the United States and its allies with a map of the region. Conze asked him if he wouldn't mind leaving the view graph on the projector. He planned to attack the Iraq question head-on.

"I said, 'Look at the map that General Kingston has so kindly left up. You see the Russians in Afghanistan. You see Iraq fighting Iran. If only the Soviets deliver arms to Iraq, then Iraq becomes a Soviet puppet state. If

---

*CENTCOM was established on January 1, 1983, and was formerly known as the Rapid Deployment Joint Task Force. It was headquartered at MacDill Air Force Base in Tampa, Florida.

that happens, the Soviets have both Afghanistan and Iraq. What do you think happens then to Iran?' " Since the time of the czars, he went on, the Russian goal has been to reach the warm seas of the Persian Gulf and the Indian Ocean. Their goals today were no different. "But what if the Soviets decide to play it another way and drop Iraq? Then Iran wins the war and thanks Moscow, and soon you'll have the ayatollahs in Kuwait and Saudi Arabia. So either way, France is helping the Western alliance by helping Iraq." The logic of what the French were doing, Conze said, was so clear that no one asked him a single question. "We were on the same side. It was as simple as that."[9]

France and the United States shared a concern over Iraq's chemical weapons programs, especially once Iraq began using poison gas on the battlefield against Iran in late 1983. One of the messages presidential envoy Donald Rumsfeld carried to Baghdad where he met with Saddam Hussein in December 1983 was U.S. disapproval of Iraq's use of chemical weapons. This message was not always conveyed by State Department diplomats, who feared angering the Iraqis, but Rumsfeld made a forceful presentation in a two-and-a-half-hour meeting with Tariq Aziz the night before he sat down with Saddam. Rumsfeld's December 1983 mission has frequently been misrepresented in the press but newly declassified documents set the record straight.[10]

To build his poison gas plants, Saddam turned mainly to Germany, where former Nazis, corrupt middlemen, and Iraqi intelligence operatives successfully plied their trade, aided by a compliant German administration that claimed it was unable to shut down their deadly trade. Assistant Secretary of Defense Richard Perle later told a U.S. Senate hearing that the Reagan administration had protested to the Germans so many times that he lost count. "We demarched them, we demarched them, we demarched them," Perle explained, "and then it all turned into marshmallows."[11] By the mid-1980s, 150 German companies had opened offices in Baghdad. Scores of them were later cited by United Nations arms inspectors and by Iraq itself for their role in building Iraq's growing arsenal of unconventional weapons. The role of U.S. and French companies in these programs was limited.

But the French arms industry was doing a fantastic business in Iraq. They built entire new factories just to service the Iraqi account and developed new versions of their Mirage fighters and new laser-guided missiles just for Saddam. They even built a private university at Jouy-en-Josas on the outskirts of Paris, to teach Iraqi electrical engineers how to operate equipment in a new French electronics plant, built by Thomson-CSF in a village along the Tigris near Saddam's stronghold, Tikrit.* I traveled repeatedly to Baghdad during the 1980s and got to know virtually every French arms merchant and technician operating in Iraq. Often we spoke out on hotel balconies, to escape the ever present Iraqi minders and listening devices.

The French had one problem with Saddam Hussein, and that was money. By 1984, he was having difficulty in meeting his payments, and the French Finance Ministry was getting tired of advancing funds from the government export credit agency, Coface.

Dassault's chief salesman, Hugues de l'Estoile, was working hard to get around those objections. In December 1984, he spent two weeks escorting General Amir Rashid al-Ubaydi around Paris to visit with defense contractors and government officials. General Amir, who headed an obscure body called the Scientific Research Council, was better known within the closed circles of the French defense lobby as "the father of Iraq's French air force." The Iraqi general was not just an important guest, he was about *the* most important visitor Dassault, Matra, Aérospatiale, and the other big-time arms manufacturers in France could hope to welcome.

General Amir was accompanied by a team of air force technicians, who had come to evaluate a French proposal to sell Iraq its latest combat jet, the Mirage 2000, which had just gone into service with the French air force. The Mirage 2000 was so new it had yet to receive its own radar, which militarily made it little more than a Lamborghini with wings. The Iraqis had also come to discuss a new package of Mirage F1 fighters, equipped with Aérospatiale's latest missile, the AS30-L, which was guided by a laser designation pod manufactured by Thomson-CSF under license to Martin Marietta in the United States.

De l'Estoile took the Iraqi team to visit his old boss, Henri Martre, who had left the Defense Ministry to run state-owned Aérospatiale. Martre could hardly refuse an Iraqi request, since his company was reap-

---

*The village where this plant was built, ad-Dour, was where Saddam Hussein was ultimately captured by U.S. soldiers of the 4th Infantry Division on December 13, 2003.

ing exceptional profits from its business with Baghdad. Iraq was now buying roughly three out of every four Exocet missiles to come off the Aérospatiale assembly lines, company officials told me, bringing in some $250 million every year. Added to that, Iraq was buying thousands of HOT and Milan antitank missiles, Roland 2 air defense systems, and Gazelle helicopters. In fact, Iraq bought more Aérospatiale products than the French Defense Ministry. And that was part of the problem: Iraq was in effect subsidizing the French Defense Ministry, whose procurement budget had been slashed to such a point that the French were forced to make major cutbacks in their forces. The French liked to boast of the "global responsibilities" of their armed forces, deployed around the world to secure the sources of raw materials that made French industry run. But it was in part Saddam's cash that allowed the French to pursue their global ambitions.

General Amir explained that he was ready to kick in sizable funds to speed up development of the ASMP (Air-Sol Moyen Portée), a strategic air-launched cruise missile with a nuclear warhead that could be launched from the Mirage 2000. The French air force wanted the missile badly but didn't have the money to develop it. Of course, Iraq was not interested in the *nuclear* version, General Amir reassured Martre, perceiving how uncomfortable he was with the Iraqi demand. The $6 billion arms package, French arms sellers I spoke to in Baghdad readily admitted, was "a highly offensive shopping list. It has been put together not with Iran in mind, but to attack Israel."

But there was a hitch—several hitches, as it turned out. Amir Rashid al-Ubaydi had brought along a negotiating team from the Iraqi Finance Ministry to hammer out the details of a new loan from the French government to cover virtually the entire arms package. Iraq would pump most of the money back into the French economy, General Amir pledged. Nonsense, replied French finance minister Pierre Bérégovoy. Using French government loans to purchase French-made planes for Iraq was just a way of robbing Peter to pay Paul, and Bérégovoy wanted nothing of it.

Bérégovoy and his accountants argued that there was no need to rush into huge new financial commitments to Baghdad until Iraq's tie-in to the Saudi Petroline opened later that year, boosting Iraqi oil exports (and revenues) by five hundred thousand barrels per day (bpd). Even then, France could consume only so much Iraqi oil. The last big Iraqi arms purchases the French Socialists had agreed to underwrite were still being paid for with huge shipments of Iraqi oil. Better to digest the business already in the works than to bite off more than the Iraqi economy could chew, the accountants said.[12]

Hugues de l'Estoile and the pro-Iraq lobby had never liked the Socialists and came charging back. They argued that without the new sale, the French defense industry would have to lay off workers, starting at Dassault, the nation's flagship aircraft maker. Iraq was threatening not to sign the follow-on order of Mirage F1 if the French refused to sell the Mirage 2000, and without that sale Dassault would have to close its assembly line. It was a sore point that would reflect badly on the Socialists, who had nationalized Dassault not long after Mitterrand's election. The dispute went all the way to the Élysée, where it was discussed at a December 1984 meeting of President Mitterrand's inner cabinet. Defense Minister Charles Hernu took up the industry's cause and crossed swords with the finance minister. Finally Prime Minister Laurent Fabius suggested they compromise by cutting the Iraqi order by half. In three years' time, when the first planes arrived, the French government could always reconsider the rest. It was an important deal for the French Defense Ministry. "I remember a senior French official complaining to me that they had sold only a handful of Mirages that year," recalls former deputy undersecretary of defense Stephen Bryen.[13] Iraq alone accounted for 40 percent of French defense exports by 1984, and that market appeared to be drying up.

A French Defense Ministry mission to Baghdad was scheduled for early February 1985. The compromise solution was to be delivered personally by the head of the Defense Ministry's International Sales Directorate, General Pierre-René Audran. But Audran missed the plane.

The French had their own Iran arms scandal, although it never made the headlines in quite the same way as Iran-contra, nor did it pack the same political punch. At the same time French defense contractors were selling billions of dollars' worth of advanced weaponry to Iraq, the French government was trying to open a discreet channel to Tehran through private intermediaries and government officials. This backdoor policy, which paralleled the beginnings of President Reagan's Iran initiative, included officially sanctioned gray market arms sales to Iran, primarily through the French munitions manufacturer Luchaire.

It all began in June 1984 when Roland Dumas, a personal adviser to President Mitterrand, invited an Iranian government emissary for private talks at the Élysée Palace. (The emissary was a well-known arms dealer, Sadegh Tabatabai, who also happened to be a nephew of Ayatollah Khomeini.) A few months later Dumas, who had been promoted to foreign minister, made an unannounced stopover to Tehran while on a state visit to Saudi Arabia. It wasn't long before the secret was out, and the pro-Iraq lobby jumped on it. Opposition leader Jacques Chirac wrote in a November 1984 article that France should not fail in its "moral and material support of Iraq." He criticized those who were building bridges toward Iran in the hope of better days. "Instead of dreaming about the post-Khomeini era," he wrote in *Politique Internationale,* they "would do better to worry first about Khomeini." The French "initiative" toward Iran soon turned to tragedy.

General Pierre-René Audran had played such a key role in the Paris-Baghdad saga that he had earned the nickname "Mr. Iraq." But in the months that preceded his scheduled trip to Baghdad to deliver the French response on the Mirage 2000 deal, he also made three secret trips to Tehran as part of the "initiative." The subject he was ordered to discuss with Iranian leaders involved the ways and means of opening a discreet arms pipeline to Iran. In December 1984, however, the Socialist government decided to back out of the deal. When Audran's negotiating partner in Tehran, Mohsen Rafiq-Doust, learned of this decision, he was furious. As head of Iran's Revolutionary Guards, Rafiq-Doust commanded not only hundreds of thousands of soldiers on the battlefront with Iraq, but also a phalanx of terrorists spread across the globe, including those who had blown up the U.S. and French Marine barracks in Beirut in October 1983. Rafiq-Doust told Audran that he held him personally responsible for the double dealing of the French government and intended to "make him pay." On January 28, only days before he was scheduled to leave for Baghdad, Audran was gunned down outside his home in the Paris suburbs as he was leaving for work.

Henri Conze was then working as Audran's deputy and recalls well these dramatic moments. "The next day, I received a phone call from General Amir," he said. After expressing his condolences for Audran's assassination, the Iraqi asked if he could come to Paris to meet with him in two days' time. "When he came to the ministry, he brought a copy of the contract and signed it in front of me. 'This is for Audran,' he said. Yes, in those days we were very good friends."

If France and the United States saw pretty much eye to eye on Iraq, such was not the case with Libya. Although the United States helped the French with satellite photographs and logistics in 1983 to push Qaddafi back from northern Chad, differences with the United States began to appear almost immediately. President Mitterrand was more than willing to work with the United States to expand French nuclear forces as a deterrent to the Soviet Union, but by temperament he did not like having to commit French troops to actual fighting. This was true in Beirut in 1983, when French Foreign Legion general Francis Coullin complained bitterly to me that his "political masters" in Paris were preventing him from joining the Americans in defending the Christians at Souq-al-Gharb from attacks by Syrian-backed terrorists in the Shouf Mountains above Beirut. And it was true in Chad, where Mitterrand sought to withdraw French troops almost as soon as he had committed them.

Under an agreement negotiated by Foreign Minister Claude Cheysson, the 5,500 Libyan ground troops remaining in Chad were supposed to have left by November 10, 1984. That very evening, Cheysson appeared on French television and triumphantly declared his deal a success. "There are no foreign forces left in Chad," he said. On the strength of that assertion, Mitterrand met with Colonel Qaddafi on the Greek island of Crete on November 15. Among the many subjects of conversation was the resumption of French arms sales to Libya. The French had earlier sold Qaddafi Mirage III fighter jets, and Qaddafi now wanted to modernize his fleet.[14]

The United States was closely monitoring the Libyan troop withdrawals and announced publicly shortly afterward that approximately 3,000 Libyan troops remained in Chad, although the last of France's 3,200 troops had departed. The State Department showed satellite photographs of the continued Libyan presence in the north to Chadian president Hissène Habré. French Foreign Ministry officials claimed the United States had slipped them "a banana peel."

It soon became apparent that not only had the Libyans not withdrawn, but they were actually reinforcing their presence with fresh troops, and the French press jumped all over Mitterrand, claiming he had been "hoodwinked" by Qaddafi. Cheysson's earlier formula on the troop withdrawal agreement—"If they leave, we leave. If they stay, we stay"—was turned on its head by Serge July, an editorialist at the pro-Socialist daily *Libération*. "If they stay, we will leave anyway," he wrote. "France has shown she does not keep her word. . . . The Libyans taunted us in public, and we didn't react."

Cheysson offered an explanation for the complacency toward Qaddafi that prefigured several other crises between the United States and France. "We believe the leader of the Libyan revolution should not be isolated. . . . France will not act with the Libyans as the U.S. is with the Nicaraguans," he said. An aide to Cheysson, who asked not to be identified, provided me with an even more candid interpretation for what had happened. "We don't feel as if we've been had," he said. "We simply acknowledge that Qaddafi has not kept his word. It's as if you went into a shop to buy certain goods, and coming home, you opened your bag and realized you didn't get what you had bargained for. So you take it back to the shop to exchange it, hoping that all will end on an amicable note."

Cheysson was forced to resign over Chad on December 4 and was replaced by Roland Dumas, a flamboyant lawyer who had represented the Libyan military purchasing office in Paris in litigation against a French arms broker.[15] As with Iraq, there was a strong, pro-Libya faction at senior levels within the government. A top aide to Defense Minister Charles Hernu explained their thinking to me shortly after Cheysson's resignation: "We feel the U.S. vision—that Qaddafi is irremediably lost to the Western camp—is false. Libya may be receiving arms from the Soviets, may have Soviet advisers on its soil, but then so did Egypt all through the 1960s and that didn't keep [the late Egyptian president Anwar al-] Sadat from changing camps. . . . If we want to limit Soviet expansionism in Africa, we must not act as if Libya were permanently lost to our adversaries. This would be playing into Soviet hands." Similar arguments would later be used regarding Saddam Hussein.

While the French pretended to view the exercise of power with greater "sophistication" than the Americans, often the differences came down to business. The same Defense Ministry adviser noted that the Libyans were eager to replace older-generation weaponry that had been supplied by France and that turning again to France was a natural desire. "Once Libyan troops leave Chad, the situation could gradually return to normal," he said.

When I asked Henri Martre, president of missile manufacturer Aéro-spatiale, what "normal" meant, he noted that his commercial agents had never broken all ties with Libya and "could move into action" the minute the French government gave its approval to negotiate new contracts. "As a company, we have no foreign policy, only a commercial policy," he said. "All our foreign sales depend on the government."[16]

Aerospace exports were one of the top foreign currency earners for France, and through most of the 1980s, military contracts accounted for well over 60 percent of all aerospace exports.[17] While American defense contractors would often lobby congressmen by making dire predictions of massive layoffs in their district if a particular sale was refused, no major U.S. defense company depended for over 60 percent of its revenues on foreign exports, as did the French. Selling sophisticated weaponry to dictators in Iraq and Libya was vital to the health of the French defense industry. Indeed, it was a matter of life or death.

It may also have been vital to the good health of the Socialist Party and to the campaign coffers of President Mitterrand. According to a former French counterintelligence officer, Daniel Burroni, the French Socialists regularly received large payments from the Libyan government through Ahmad Qaddafidam, the second in command of Libyan intelligence, and other channels. Among those paid off were top advisers to Mitterrand himself. One adviser, who was later appointed as French ambassador to an Arab country, was said to have received $4 million.

Burroni says the French counterintelligence service, DST, first got wind of the payoffs in 1982, less than one year after Mitterrand took power, but never "exploited" the information because one scheme involved a member of the president's own family. The DST also suspected that a Libyan "mole" was working for Mitterrand at the Élysée but sought his identity in vain for nearly five years. It was this person, along with a Libyan arms procurement officer, who set up the meeting in Crete between Qaddafi and the French president, said Burroni.[18]

Libyan intelligence referred to the mole at the Élysée by the code name December Shadow. Deputy DST director Raymond Nart traveled repeatedly to London at the end of 1985, seeking additional information from British intelligence, MI6. Finally, the Brits turned over a photograph of the mole, taken by one of their own agents who had penetrated Libyan intelligence and had since been exfiltrated to safety. According to Nart's British contacts, the mole had transmitted to the Libyans documents concerning the joint U.S.-French operation in Sudan to help Hissène Habré launch his successful campaign to oust Libyan puppet Goukouni Oueddei in Chad.

The photograph showed Mitterrand's adviser in the company of his control officer, a Libyan businessman based in London and a top Libyan intelligence officer named al-Kilani. It was taken in Malta in September 1986. "The DST concluded that this had to be an extremely important meeting to justify the movement of someone as senior in Libyan intelligence as al-Kilani," Burroni told me. "And there was no way [the mole] could have been on an official mission, sent by the Élysée, because he would have brought bodyguards, and we knew that he had come alone."

Picture in hand, Nart went to François de Grossouvre, Mitterrand's adviser for intelligence affairs, who immediately recognized the mole and had him fired. To this day, however, his name has never been made public.[19] But the important matters he was discussing with his Libyan controllers in September 1986 can now be revealed. They, too, were a matter of life and death—for the regime of Muammar al-Qaddafi and for the United States.

Colonel Qaddafi had been on President Reagan's mind almost from the start of his presidency, but by 1986 Libya had become a preoccupation. General Vernon Walters, a former deputy director of the CIA, came to Paris on January 23, 1986, to ask Mitterrand to join a covert U.S. effort to destabilize Qaddafi.

Mitterrand trusted Walters more than any other U.S. official. It was not just his fluent French. Nor was it his knowledge of France. It stemmed from Walters's personal experience with virtually every French leader since he had served as translator to General Dwight D. Eisenhower during World War II whenever Ike met with the finicky French resistance leader, Charles de Gaulle. Walters's French counterpart was a young French aristocrat named Alexandre de Marenches. The careers of the two "translators" dovetailed each other for decades, until Mitterrand replaced Marenches in 1981 after eleven years as head of French intelligence. Since then, Marenches and Walters had assumed roles as confidential advisers to their presidents, outside of government but privy to many of its secrets.

The United States saw Libya as a Soviet client state, intent on advancing Soviet influence in Africa, Walters told Mitterrand. Since Saddam had expelled Abu Nidal in late 1983, Qaddafi had not only welcomed the Palestinian terrorist and his cohorts to Libya but had set up training camps for them and for other terrorist groups. We want your help in taking them out, Walters said.

Mitterrand listened intently but refused to make a commitment. One reason, former French counterintelligence officer Daniel Burroni told me, was the fact that some of the terrorist training camps the United States wanted to destroy had been built in the guise of "agricultural complexes" by a French company that was later exposed as a conduit for covert campaign contributions to Mitterrand's Socialist Party. "These particular 'agricultural complexes' included airstrips that were long enough to accommodate large military transport jets," Burroni said. Explaining to Qaddafi how France built the training camps and then joined a U.S. effort to destroy them could get embarrassing.

But Reagan didn't give up on convincing his ally. In late February, the United States asked France to join a limited campaign of air strikes against targets in Libya. Again, Mitterrand refused. But when General Walters returned to Paris on March 3, 1986, the French president went to great lengths to explain that his refusal did not mean that France opposed U.S. action against Libya.[20]

Jacques Attali's three-volume chronicle of the first decade of Mitterrand's presidency is unprecedented in French literature. Unlike memoirs written by politicians, such as Mitterrand, Michel Jobert, or Dominique de Villepin, Attali's account contains few polemics and little self-congratulation. Instead, *Verbatim* aspires to document the day-to-day affairs of France as he jotted them down in notebooks when he was Mitterrand's chief of staff. From that privileged position, Attali watched, listened, and made verbatim reports on Mitterrand's meetings with staff, visitors, other French officials, and foreign heads of state. His chronicle of the French refusal to allow U.S. military jets overflight privileges to attack Qaddafi has never been contradicted.[21]

Complicating matters were the legislative elections in France on March 16, 1986, which Mitterrand's left-wing coalition lost. The electoral defeat ushered in a totally new era in French history, known as "cohabitation." Unlike the United States, where the president still controls the executive branch even if he loses both houses of Congress, France mixes a strong executive with a parliamentary system, such that the delineating of powers is unclear.

Mitterrand quickly took stock of the situation and appointed opposition leader Jacques Chirac as prime minister on March 20, 1986. It was sweet revenge for Chirac, who had been fired as prime minister ten years earlier by Mitterrand's center-right predecessor, Giscard. Chirac won the elections on a platform of rolling back socialism in France, starting with privatizing banks and industrial conglomerates that the Socialists had nationalized in 1981. He also had promised to roll back many of the expensive social welfare programs Mitterrand and his allies had expanded. But above all, he insisted repeatedly, he wanted a seat whenever France sat at the table of world affairs. On this last area, Mitterrand put his foot down. Under the French Constitution, he argued, the president controls foreign policy and the national defense. He would consult with Chirac, but he had no intention of allowing Chirac to run France as if he were the sole legally elected power. "France speaks with one voice," he announced to the press in Tokyo at the G-7 summit that May, with Chirac sitting—fuming visibly—at his feet. The two leaders frequently undercut each other in public and in private, sometimes with comic results.

The planned U.S. attack on Libya was the first foreign crisis to confront the new government. Mitterrand informed Chirac, the new defense minister, André Giraud, and incoming foreign minister Jean-Bernard Raimond about the U.S. requests for action against Libya at the very first meeting of the cohabitation, on March 21, 1986. Mitterrand said that he had "replied [to the Americans] that above all, we mustn't give the impression of a joint action. We would do nothing in the north, but eventually we could see in the south with Hissène Habré. . . . The American action is awkward and will unify the Arab nation behind Qaddafi. At least, that's what I think." Chirac chimed in, "That's exactly what I think, too."[22]

Later that day, Secretary of State George Shultz arrived in Paris and met with Mitterrand. So close was the U.S.-French relationship at this point that he was "the first foreigner to come to France since the elections." Shultz asked Mitterrand, who was preparing the G-7 summit in Tokyo, "a polite way of asking who was now in charge of foreign policy." Mitterrand hastened to tell him that France is "open to cooperating with you on the subject of Libya."[23]

But in fact, as Attali demonstrates, Mitterrand viewed with alarm the possibility of confronting Libya militarily. With typical bluster, Qaddafi had declared a two-hundred-mile naval and air exclusion zone off Libya's coasts, vowing that any foreign aircraft or vessel that crossed the "line of death" would be destroyed. (International law recognizes a twelve-mile exclusion zone, although France, too, insists on a 200-mile "economic exclusive zone" off its Atlantic Coast—much to the annoyance of its neighbors.) On March 24, U.S. warplanes crossed Qaddafi's line in the sea and were greeted with a volley of missiles from Libya's Russian-built SA-5 air defense batteries. Meeting with Chirac, Giraud, foreign minister Jean-Bernard Raimond, and his top military aide, General Forray, Mitterrand said that the United States, "through their missteps, are going to unite the Arab nation. We should expect the worst."

Giraud, the nuclear baron who helped build Saddam Hussein, was nevertheless favorable to working with the United States against Libya. "I am thinking of going to Chad," he said, "but I don't want to give the impression that I approve of the American action." For Mitterrand, the real threat from Qaddafi was in Africa, which France considered its baronial domain. Gabon, Angola, and Sudan were rich in oil; Cameroon, the Ivory Coast, Zaire, and Congo were rich in commissions and kickbacks to French political parties, while virtually every African country was a potential client for French weaponry. "Our primary objective," Mitterrand replied, "is to prevent Libya from reaching black Africa."[24]

The next day, in retaliation for the Libyan missile launches, U.S. warplanes sank two Libyan ships, damaged two others, and destroyed a SAM-5 site. Mitterrand refused an invitation from President Reagan to visit Washington to work out operational details for a joint attack against Libya. Attali commented that on terrorism, "we are dead-set opposed to the Americans, who want us to approve their action against Libya and to put the police forces of other [G-7] member countries under their control."[25]

M itterrand set out his moral guidelines when it came to terrorism in a briefing to Chirac and his defense and foreign ministers on the situation of the French hostages then in Lebanon. "I have chosen not to have direct negotiations with the hostage takers, for two reasons: first, to not recognize their legitimacy; second, to not accept the exchange of innocents against criminals who have been legally sentenced in our courts. We have negotiated with states: Syria, Iran . . . I have always refused and will continue to refuse to exchange one man for another, but I've always said that I was ready to make a gesture toward a prisoner, [Anis] Naccache."[26] Mitterrand was referring to the Iranian-paid agent who unsuccessfully attempted to murder former Iranian prime minister Shahpur Bakhtiar in 1980 and who was eventually released from jail as part of the hostage exchange. Encouraged by what they perceived as French weakness, the Iranians sent a second hit team that succeeded in murdering Bakhtiar in 1991.

Mitterrand's lecture was intended as a slight, since Chirac had sent his own emissaries to Lebanon and Gabon in an effort to free the French hostages before the elections. But his claim that he would never negotiate with terrorists was pretentious mush. France has repeatedly negotiated with terrorists, their representatives, their proxies, and their supporters, in the vain hope of preventing further terrorist attacks on French soil or against French citizens overseas. And French governments have repeatedly turned a blind eye to notorious murderers who have come to France for safe haven or for medical treatment. Right after World War II, de Gaulle's government welcomed Haj Mohammad Amin al-Husseini, the grand mufti of Jerusalem, who had been Hitler's personal guest in Berlin until just three days before the demise of the Third Reich, when he fled to France. Al-Husseini was employed by Hitler and the SS to stir the Arab masses to slaughter Jews in Palestine and Egypt, as part of Hitler's "final solution." In January 1977, the French government invited Mohammad Daoud Odeh, commonly known by the nom de guerre Abu Daoud, to visit France to meet with top Foreign Ministry officials, according to former Fatah colleague Abu Iyad.[27] Daoud was the notorious ringleader of the PLO hit squad that had murdered eleven Israeli athletes and trainers (including one American) at the 1972 Munich Olympics, just twelve miles from Dachau. When news of the visit was leaked to the press, the Giscard government noisily "arrested" Daoud and expelled him to Algeria. On several occasions in the early 1980s, Mitterrand's government welcomed Lebanese terrorist Imad Mugniyah to France, despite his role in the 1982 car bombing of the U.S. embassy in Beirut, and the brash hijacking of TWA flight 847 from Greece to Beirut in June 1985, where he held thirty-nine Americans hostage for seventeen days. Wearing a ski mask, Mugniyah prowled the aisles of the aircraft looking for American military personnel. When he discovered U.S. Navy diver Robert Stethem, Mugniyah tortured him, shot him, then dumped his body out on the tarmac in full view of international television cameras. Later, the FBI was able to identify Mugniyah's fingerprints in the rear toilet of the aircraft and indicted him for Stethem's murder.

The CIA station chief in Paris, Charles Cogan, bore a personal grudge against Mugniyah (as did CIA director Bill Casey), because Mugniyah had kidnapped his personal friend and colleague William Buckley, the CIA station chief in Beirut. The CIA believed that Mugniyah personally tortured Buckley to extract whatever secrets he could, then murdered him. On November 11, 1985, a CIA operative photographed Mugniyah upon his arrival at Orly Airport in Paris and passed the photographs to the French in an unsuccessful effort to get them to arrest him. Three years later, a disgusted French official gave me copies of the pictures, which I reproduced in the confidential newsletter I then published in Paris.[28]

The very day that Chirac's new government came to power, Lebanese terrorists, on orders from Iran, exploded a bomb at the Point-Show shopping mall on the Champs-Élysées, killing two people and wounding twenty-eight. The new interior minister, Charles Pasqua, rushed to the scene and told reporters that the new government would "terrorize the terrorists." Instead he continued the standard practice of sending secret emissaries to negotiate with the terrorists. And the bombings continued.

On March 26, Mitterrand received yet another American envoy at the Élysée, who had come to talk about Libya and to take a closer look at how the "cohabitation" was working. Speaking of Chirac and his new government, Mitterrand told Henry Kissinger, "They control everything, except for the essential."[29]

Qaddafi's mole surely would have been monitoring Mitterrand's exchanges with the Americans. The unwillingness of Chirac to approve an attack on an Arab state, and Mitterrand's hesitations, must have encouraged Qaddafi in his belief that he could strike America with no risk of wider retaliation. Qaddafi struck on April 5—not against U.S. warships or aircraft in the Mediterranean, but against a discotheque in Berlin that was a well-known watering hole for U.S. soldiers serving in Germany. Curiously, Attali doesn't include the La Belle disco bombing, which killed one U.S. soldier and two other persons, in his day-to-day chronicle. His first reference to the attack comes five days later, when President Reagan formally requested that the French allow U.S. FB-111 fighter-bombers based in Britain to fly over French territory on their way to attack terrorist targets in Libya.

Reagan's April 12, 1986, letter to Mitterrand formalized a request that had already been placed through channels to Mitterrand's top military aide, General Forray, former Reagan administration officials and Attali agreed. Reagan asked for an immediate reply, so U.S. tactical planners could plot the best route to the targets in Libya. He also provided Mitterrand with additional information that U.S. intelligence had picked up about Libyan plans to launch other terrorist attacks against American citizens in Sudan, West Germany, Turkey, Syria, Spain, the Central African Republic, Kenya, and Latin America. He reassured Mitterrand that the U.S. air strikes would not hit civilian targets, infrastructure, or even Libyan regular army troops, but only "targets involved in an obvious way in the conduct and support of terrorist activities." The goal, Reagan wrote, was to make Qaddafi "pay a high price" for his support of international terrorism.[30]

Mitterrand ignored Reagan's letter rather than refuse the U.S. request outright. Early on Sunday morning, April 13, he told Chirac and Foreign Minister Jean-Bernard Raimond that while France could not allow Qaddafi to continue his terrorist attacks, "it is out of the question for France to hitch its wagon behind an American action." He instructed Raimond to convoke the Libyan ambassador to Paris and convey to him a two-part message: "We have no alliance with the Americans against you, but we cannot accept your threats to southern Europe."

When Vernon Walters came back to Paris later that day, he met with Chirac at the Paris City Hall (Chirac had not yet moved into the prime minister's office from his current job as Paris mayor). The next day, Walters came to the Élysée for a long session with Mitterrand. By this point, he had dropped the U.S. request for overflights so as not to force the French to make their refusal public. Asked by Mitterrand how his meeting had gone with the prime minister, Walters laughed. "The prime minister gave me a lesson on the naiveté of the United States in the Arab world. So I got mean. I said to him, 'Your experience is very impressive. Before you came to power, you had four hostages in Lebanon, and now you have nine!' " Walters went on to explain that the United States had intercepted encrypted communications between Tripoli and the Libyan embassy in East Berlin, giving instructions to bomb a U.S. target, and an after-action report following the La Belle disco bombing.

This was Walters's third meeting with Mitterrand on Libya in as many months, in addition to his meetings with Chirac. A U.S. secretary of state had come to Paris to explain the U.S. case, as had Henry Kissinger, now a private citizen. National Security Adviser Admiral John Poindexter was in almost daily contact with Attali and Mitterrand's military aide at the Élysée.

Clearly the Reagan administration was still eager to win French support for its actions against terrorism. Mitterrand explained to Walters his problem.

> We know each other well. Let me speak to you candidly. Qaddafi has become unbearable. He is feeding a climate of war. We can no longer reason with him as before, when we thought we could find a modus vivendi. But the problem is how to do it. I told Mr. Shultz: we must avoid everything that could make Qaddafi appear as a hero in the eyes of the Arab world. . . . Western actions are not sophisticated enough.

Walters protested that the United States intended to be very careful with the attacks and would not send bombers to pound sand. "You know that the Libyans nearly managed to blow up a police van in front of the U.S. embassy in Paris? That attack was prevented by your police, he said."

While noting that he and Chirac had both agreed not to allow the over-flights, Mitterrand went out of his way to make sure that Walters understood where France stood. "I do not want to be disagreeable. I don't want to stop you, I don't want to denounce your action," he said.[31] Former U.S. defense secretary Caspar Weinberger called Mitterrand's behavior "typical, but still infuriating," since he "gave us some gratuitous advice as to how to conduct the raid" all the while he refused to allow the United States to fly over French airspace. ("Don't inflict a mere pinprick," Mitterrand advised.)[32] But Mitterrand never picked up the phone to discourage another foreign leader not to cooperate with the U.S. air strikes on Libya—unlike Chirac's behavior seventeen years later as president—and responded passively when he learned belatedly that Spain had also refused a U.S. overflight request.

By all accounts, Operation El Dorado Canyon against Qaddafi's head-quarters in Tripoli and terrorist training camp in Benghazi on April 15 was far less effective than it would have been if the French had allowed the twenty-four FB-111 fighter-bombers to fly over France. The circuitous route from Britain over the Atlantic, around Gilbraltar, and into the Mediterra-nean added several hours to the bombing run, pushing U.S. pilots to the limits of their endurance and leading to mistakes. The planes had to be re-fueled five times on the 2,800-mile journey to Libya. But the U.S. attacks struck a crippling blow on Libyan air force and naval bases, in addition to Qaddafi's intelligence headquarters and the other targets, and were far more extensive than generally reported.[33]

After the French refusal was made public, Attali complained of an "anti-French campaign" in the United States, and Mitterrand ordered the French ambassador to the United Nations, Claude de Kémoularia, to defend the French position in front of the U.S. media. Chirac's foreign minister, Jean-Bernard Raimond, was "furious," Attali says. Not long afterward, leaks began to appear in French and U.S. newspapers that the U.S. aircraft had secretly flown over France en route to striking Libya after all.[34] But such was not the case.

Chirac was soon boasting on a French television talk show that he alone had taken the decision to refuse the U.S. overflight.[35] While his lie angered Mitterrand (who nevertheless kept quiet about it in public), it revealed a jingoistic side to his character that would become predominant during the Iraq crisis many years later. Jacques Chirac was discovering the secret pleasures of standing up to America. In language understood by every Frenchman, he had uttered a giant *cocorico*—as the French represented the cry of their national bird, the rooster. It was silly. It was petty. And it was pure Chirac.

I n Baghdad, Chirac's victory in the March 1986 elections was welcome news. The Iranian army had just broken through Iraq's defenses and captured the strategic Fao peninsula south of Basra, commanding Iraq's only entry to the Persian Gulf. Despite Iraq's $5 billion debt, Chirac argued that it was no time to abandon his "personal friend" Saddam Hussein. One of his first acts as prime minister was to approve a major new arms sale package for Iraq, knowing that the Iraqis would not be able to pay for it.

The new deals were relatively modest compared to what the French arms industry had become accustomed to signing with Iraq and totaled a mere $430 million. They included half a dozen Aérospatiale Dauphin helicopters, equipped with a new-generation antishipping missile, and large numbers of high-precision mortars made by Thomson-Brandt. The contracts were given colorful code names: Jacinthe and Tulip for the helicopters, Jupiter for the mortars. Chirac also promised that France would keep open its production line for the Mirage F1, despite the fact that Dassault had no more orders on its books. Iraq needed new planes to replace war losses.

Tariq Aziz could hardly restrain his enthusiasm at finding his old friend Jacques Chirac back at the Matignon Palace. When he came to Paris to sign the Jupiter project, he bubbled with praise for the returning prime minister. "There are no clouds on the horizon of Franco-Iraqi relations," he told a press conference on June 10. "My visit has been crowned with success. My objectives have all been attained." In case the message was not clear enough, he added: "You could call that concrete results. . . . Arms orders are following their normal course. All the financial problems have been resolved."

With bombs exploding on the Champs-Élysées and elsewhere in Paris, planted by Iranian-backed terrorists, Chirac gave strict orders to keep future arms contracts with Iraq under wraps. Except for the periodic pilgrimages of Tariq Aziz to Paris, the entire subject of French relations with Iraq became one of the closest-held secrets of Chirac's second premiership. Companies like Dassault, which sorely needed to announce a new export sale to restore investor confidence, were ordered to keep silent as they continued to supply weapons to Iraq.

But those supplies did continue, and on a daily basis. A former NATO airfield, built by the U.S. Army Corps of Engineers at Châteauroux in central France, was the primary loading point for urgent deliveries of French-built missiles, cluster bombs, fuses, radar equipment, and avionics. The equipment was loaded on board giant Antonov 124 jet cargo planes of the Iraqi air force, which flew to France just to load arms. By mid-1986, the delivery rate of "consumables" became so intense that commercial flights linking Paris to Baghdad were also used to haul arms. One French technician, who accompanied a shipment of mortar ammunition on one of these flights, told me that his Iraqi Airlines flight was virtually empty, but the plane was so heavy that it barely made it off the runway at Orly. Because of the extra load, the planes had to refuel in Athens or Istanbul for what was normally a nonstop flight. "If France cut off the arms pipeline to Iraq for a mere three weeks," another French arms salesman told me in Baghdad, "Iraq would collapse."

Unable to expel the Iranians from Fao, where they had dug in with as many as three hundred thousand troops, Iraq struck back hard against Iranian oil exports in the Gulf, using its French-built warplanes and Exocet missiles. The French delivered nearly 270 Exocets to Iraq in 1986, or roughly 75 percent of Aérospatiale's total production. Within the close confines of the defense community, it became common knowledge that Iraq was also the biggest customer for the accurate, but expensive, Thomson-

Brandt mortars. The mortar deal was so huge that other companies flocked to Baghdad, hoping just to pick up the crumbs. One eager young salesman showed me the model of a dune buggy his company was hoping to sell the Iraqis, to pull the mortar across the desert. Another one showed me brochures of special harnesses and parachutes that could be used to air-drop the mortar by helicopter. Yet another described a reinforced-hull Zodiac he was proposing to the Iraqis, so they could shell the Iranians from the dense cover of the Howeiza marshes.

Meanwhile, the United States was also pitching in, providing cash through the Commodity Credit Corporation and the Banca Nazionale del Lavoro (BNL) in Atlanta, Georgia, and allowing Iraq to purchase dual-use production gear for its military factories. The United States left the arms sales to France but ultimately helped Saddam to become a real danger, by facilitating the creation of an indigenous weapons-manufacturing capability. At the time, nobody—except for a handful of Pentagon officials—saw it coming.

# 7

# Techno-tensions

M ichel Lopoukhine, a fifty-year-old Frenchman of Russian descent, was the marketing manager of a large machine tool conglomerate heavily subsidized by the French state. At ten-thirty on the morning of April 18, 1988, as he was about to board the Moscow flight at Roissy–Charles de Gaulle Airport, four men in civilian clothes came up to him from behind. "Monsieur Lopoukhine?" one of them said quietly.

"That's me," he replied, almost relieved that the dreaded moment had finally arrived.

"If you'd follow us quietly, you won't have any problem."

Without a word, Michel Lopoukhine accompanied the four men from the airport waiting room to the unmarked car parked outside. As he told me later, it never even occurred to him to ask them to identify themselves, since he knew they had to be from the Direction de la Surveillance du Territoire—French counterespionage. No one stopped to pick up Lopoukhine's baggage—for the simple reason that he had brought nothing with him except an attaché case, even though he had been planning a three-day trip. "Moscow rules," he explained with a sly grin. "Everyone you ever talked to was KGB anyway, from the president right on down to the doorman. So you learned not to bring anything with you, no papers, no documents. Just a blank notepad for the meetings."[1]

Although his family had left Russia three generations earlier, at the time of the 1917 revolution, when I met him he still spoke French with a distinct Russian accent. For forty-eight hours after his arrest at Roissy–Charles de Gaulle, Lopoukhine disappeared without a trace—a standard tactic used by the DST when debriefing a potentially "juicy" catch. But Lopoukhine was not impressed. In between interrogation sessions in the small room at DST headquarters on the rue Nelaton in Paris, he simply fell asleep in his chair. His behavior only deepened the suspicions against him. "He must be KGB," he heard his interrogators whisper among themselves. "Who else would be capable of such discipline? That takes training!"

The morning after his arrest, the DST launched a dawn raid in the sleepy provincial village of Capdenac, netting three of Lopoukhine's associates. At the home of Jean-Paul Chamouton, chairman of Machines Françaises Lourdes, the holding company that then owned Forest-Liné, the DST found a handwritten note that clearly described how the company had sold strategic production equipment to the Soviet Union in violation of the CoCom high-tech embargo. The note advised company officials to take greater care to disguise such sales in the future, since the French government was beginning to take an interest in their activities. The arrest of the sixty-year-old Chamouton sent shock waves through the French security establishment. Recently retired from the French air force as a lieutenant general, Chamouton had a stellar résumé. For nearly two decades he had been a key figure in French nuclear weapons planning, serving on the personal staff of the minister of defense and as head of French nuclear testing in the Pacific. Chamouton had even commanded parts of the nuclear strike force.[2] Also arrested were Forest-Liné president Louis Tardy, sixty-three, and a salesman, Gérard Brogniet.

The severity of the charges against these four men was unprecedented in recent French history. Far from the theoretical three-year administrative sentence meted out to vulgar techno-bandits caught on customs violations, they were charged with espionage on behalf of a foreign power, which could land them in jail for twenty years. It was not the type of indictment the French handed down lightly.

The case against them stemmed from recent contracts they had signed with the Soviet Foreign Trade Organization, Stankopromimport. The first, signed on June 6, 1986, concerned two highly sophisticated machine tools specially designed for the aeronautics industry. These machines, whose export to the Soviet bloc was strictly proscribed by CoCom, were delivered to the Ministry of Aviation plant in Douvianosk, where the Soviets wanted to use them to manufacture the USSR's top frontline fighter, the MiG-29.[3] The second contract concerned a new type of aeronautical milling machine capable of machining large structural parts—aircraft wings, stabilizers, weapons pylons—in a single piece, a key technology for manufacturing the complex shapes of advanced combat aircraft, and something the Soviets lacked. A third contract, which was stopped just in time, would have given the Soviets state-of-the-art composite-laying technologies that had been developed by the U.S. Air Force. These gigantic machines were built by an American company called Goldsworthy, which had been bought out in the mid-1980s by Forest-Liné. The planned sale of the tape-laying machine to the Soviet Union by Forest-Liné had been structured as a technology transfer agreement to make it harder to detect.[4]

Given General Chamouton's background with the French nuclear weapons establishment, the DST also worried that his involvement with the KGB might go beyond these commercial contracts—hence the espionage charges. But Michel Lopoukhine called such anxieties a carefully crafted scam. "Me, a KGB agent?" he cried, laughing from behind his Ballersteros glasses, during one of our meetings at a Paris café. "I was the one who took the risk of bringing back letters from Soviet dissidents and getting them published in Western newspapers! We were merely actors in a trade war that is taking place on a worldwide scale, from the USSR to Indonesia, where French companies are pitted against unscrupulous competitors who make no bones about calling on their governments for help when they need to clinch a deal." Lopoukhine rejected the idea that the Forest-Liné arrests had anything to do with national security. "I was the whipping boy France needed to prove to the United States they were getting tough on technology transfer," he said. He and his bosses at Forest-Liné were "merely applying an existing policy of cooperation with the USSR."

In many ways, Lopoukhine was right. Despite the hue and cry in the press and the aura of espionage the French authorities attempted to create around the case, just three months later all four detainees were quietly released. Behind the scenes, the politicians were working the ropes.

I n Washington, senior Pentagon officials knew that the Forest-Liné arrests were a direct result of the strategic cooperation between the United States and France. Cracking down on technology diverters helped justify the continued nuclear cooperation with France, which by the mid- to late 1980s focused on upgrading the French nuclear submarine fleet with a new-generation missile. It was part of the quid pro quo mentioned by Undersecretary of Defense Fred Ikle. The point man for alerting the French on this and other similar cases was his deputy, Dr. Stephen Bryen.

At the time Bryen first brought up the Forest-Liné case with the French, in April 1987, members of Congress were smashing Toshiba radios with sledgehammers on the steps of the U.S. Capitol, because the Pentagon had just revealed that Toshiba machine tools equipped with computerized numerical controllers made by the Norwegian firm Kongsberg, were being used by the Soviets to make sophisticated new propellers for their ballistic missile submarines. CoCom and technology transfer were major stories. Even the French press was taking notice. After Bryen spoke discreetly with French officials about Forest-Liné, the French Foreign Ministry took the unprecedented initiative of presenting an apology in front of other CoCom delegates for the Forest-Liné sales of the late 1970s, arguing that France had been a victim, "as others before her," of détente. "This is how a few contracts, whose seriousness has yet to be proven, managed to escape our vigilances," said the French.[5]

In October 1987, the French CoCom reps told Bryen that they were working to draft new legislation that would close the loopholes in their export control laws so they could go after Forest-Liné and other technobandits, but they needed time. Be patient and you will be agreeably surprised, they said.

On January 26, 1988, Bryen returned to France to attend a high-level CoCom meeting in Versailles. The U.S. delegation was the most powerful ever assembled. In addition to Bryen, it included Assistant Secretary of State John Whitehead, Ambassador E. Allan Wendt, and Paul Freedenberg, undersecretary of commerce in charge of the Bureau of Export Controls. At a press conference the next day, the Americans revealed that the two-day meeting had been convened at "the urgent request of the United States" in the wake of the Toshiba-Kongsberg diversion case and was "a

CoCom meeting about CoCom." The U.S. goal was to secure the commitment of all CoCom members to strengthening their national export controls, in preparation for the "license-free environment of Europe in 1992." To achieve this goal, the U.S. delegation argued, it was necessary "to harmonize controls within the CoCom countries . . . so the weakest link in the chain does not become a smuggler's paradise."

In the meantime, Bryen had learned from his French friends that the pro-export ministries were fiercely opposing stiffer export control laws. So after specifically referring to the Toshiba case at the press conference, he issued a veiled warning: "Only increased cooperation [in stiffening export controls] can prevent unilateral action by the U.S. Congress. We want to convince Congress that CoCom does work." Just six weeks later, on March 5, 1988, the new French Customs code was published in the *Journal Officiel*. If penalties for CoCom violations were not quite as severe as Bryen's French contacts might have hoped (three years maximum for each violation), French Customs was given new enforcement powers. This was taken as a sign of French seriousness.

Bryen traveled back and forth between Washington, Tokyo, and Oslo in early 1988 in an effort to convince allied governments to stiffen their export control procedures and laws. He was particularly impressed by the apparent change of heart in Japan. "They have hired over one hundred licensing and case review officers," he told me at the time, "and have jacked up the police effort. They now have twenty investigations going simultaneously." But when he returned to Paris with Allan Wendt on April 13, he learned to his dismay that Forest-Liné was still exporting to the Soviet Union as before. It had now been nearly one year to the day after he had transmitted detailed information to the French on Forest-Liné's violations, and as yet no action had been taken against the company. Speaking with the French CoCom delegate, he said it would be a shame if the French press learned the details of the story before the French presidential elections in May. Jacques Chirac was using his position as prime minister as a platform to challenge Mitterrand's reelection bid. Under the rules of cohabitation, internal security and counterespionage were his government's responsibility, not Mitterrand's. A failure to act in a case where the French strategic nuclear forces could be at risk—which General Chamouton's involvement in the scheme led many to fear—would certainly not help Chirac's electoral ambitions.

After delivering this veiled threat, Bryen dined with an old friend in Paris, who had risen over the years to become a top adviser to Chirac's defense minister, André Giraud. When they reached dessert, he told his friend that Toshiba was not the only one that had helped the Soviets build quieter nuclear submarines. Thanks to their new propellers, which were initially built with Forest-Liné machines, Soviet nuclear submarines were now so quiet that they had managed to sneak into the Chesapeake Bay without detection. In the rare stories that mentioned Forest-Liné that had appeared in the French press, the French company was portrayed as a bit player in the Toshiba-Kongsberg scandal. In fact, said Bryen, Forest-Liné was a key supplier of the Soviet military and had recently signed major new contracts. Bryen's French friend hit the ceiling. "You mean we have done nothing to stop this?"

"Not a thing."

Bryen was careful at the time not to reveal to me the identity of his French friend. But I had been working the French Defense Ministry for many years and had a pretty good hunch who it must be. I called the man's secretary (he had risen to a general's rank since I had first met him) and arranged for an appointment later that week.

"So you were the one who got the DST into the act," I said when we met.

He just smiled and pulled on his Gauloises. "I guess I have been known to blow the whistle from time to time," he said. "This time, you know, we got results."

Forty-eight hours after the general dined with Bryen in Paris, the DST pounced on Lopoukhine, General Chamouton, Tardy, and Brogniet. They had acted just in time. Key parts of the composite tape layer had already been crated up and were sitting in the loading dock outside the Forest-Liné factory, en route to the USSR.

But the initial crackdown on Forest-Liné was the exception, not the rule. Other techno-bandits were not pursued, despite a clear documentary trail showing that they were purchasing strategic equipment on behalf of the Soviet Union. Such was the case of Aimé Richardt, who had set up an entire network of obscure companies in France, with initial backing from a state-owned bank, the Société Generale, to acquire U.S.-built equipment and resell it. In one noteworthy case that became a cover story for the French newsweekly L'Express, Richardt was caught shipping an entire bubble memory production line to the Soviets. At the time, this type of computer chip, which had no civilian use, was highly sought after by the Soviets for ballistic missile guidance and for the strategic communications systems linking the Kremlin to their nuclear war-fighting command posts, since it was the only type of microprocessor that could survive the massive electromagnetic pulse of a nuclear blast. While bits and pieces of Richardt's order from V/O Technopromimport were seized in Los Angeles and Luxembourg, Richardt was never prosecuted successfully in France, despite intense U.S. pressure on the French government.

Richardt sought help from well-placed political figures. Interestingly enough, it was the French Right that responded the most favorably. Roland Nungesser, a RPR member of Parliament and a Chirac confidant, personally decorated Richardt for his contribution to French exports.[6] Another RPR parliamentarian, Robert-André Vivien, championed Richardt's cause in an appeal presented before the French Supreme Court in 1986 to release export licenses blocked by the administration. After Chirac lost the election in May 1988 and a new Socialist government came to power, an aide to Socialist finance minister Pierre Bérégovoy tried to force the premature retirement of "Richardt's worst enemy" at the Quai d'Orsay, a former DSGE officer who had become France's CoCom rep. After months of coming under fire from the Finance Ministry, the official was forced from Paris to a foreign posting.[7]

While many French officials understood the threat to French security from the sale of dual-use or military technology to the Soviet Union, when the French government cracked down on strategic trade with the Soviet Union, it was not because they believed it was bad. As the Forest-Liné and Richardt cases show, they cracked down because the United States threatened to expose their betrayal, and failed to intervene when the U.S. pressure was less intense. It was the skillful application of political pressure, not shared ideology or goals, that forced the French to cooperate.

General Bernard Retat, who was in charge of export controls and arms sales at the Defense Ministry at the time, tipped his hat to the U.S. officials who had applied that pressure. "For years," he told me, "we've underestimated our own technology and overestimated that of the Soviets. As a result, we have not taken enough steps to protect it." Richard Perle and Steve Bryen were "the prophets. We needed them. They played a major role in the awakening, demanding meetings, knocking heads together. The time was ripe. We hadn't measured the extent of the disaster, of what to do and how. It was up to the United States to mobilize the allies, and they did."[8]

There was another reason the French authorities never seriously went after Richardt or others like him who were selling strategic technology to the Soviet bloc. Mitterrand's own brother Robert had been trading with the Soviet bloc since 1970, as president and CEO of Danubex S.A., an import-export company operating out of Paris that was owned and controlled by the Bulgarian government. According to a former French intelligence analyst who examined the company's activities in the mid-1980s, "The Bulgarian employees of Danubex were intelligence operatives." It was not considered a career-enhancing move to look too carefully into the business of the presidential family. Investigating Richardt was a bit like kicking a bee's hive, without knowing how many bees were inside. There was always a lingering doubt, which I heard from several French government officials involved in investigating Richardt's network, that his activities were secretly sanctioned.

Whenever he was challenged on his motives for cooperating with the United States during the cold war, or for refusing U.S. overflights on the attack against Libya, Mitterrand liked to insist that he was "defending the interests of France." He supported the deployment of U.S. cruise and Pershing II missiles because he legitimately feared a Soviet attack and the rise of pacifism on his doorstep. Similarly, he almost single-handedly defanged the French Communist Party, delegitimizing it gradually until it plummeted from 15 percent of the vote in 1981 to less than 6 percent by 1988.

But was he truly an anti-Communist, as his defenders claim? More often than not, when fighting alongside the United States during the cold war, he was also defending the interests of the Socialist Party and his own political career. When it came to the ultra-Stalinist regime in North Korea, for instance, the cold war solidarity he professed in confronting the Soviet Union simply vanished.

François de Grossouvre, who was Mitterrand's closest companion and adviser for over thirty years, traveled with the would-be president and his family to North Korea and Communist China in February 1981. Mitterrand met with North Korean dictator Kim Il Sung in Pyongyang on February 15, 1981, and according to de Grossouvre found him to be a man "with lots of good sense and realism." After Mitterrand's election on May 10, the North Koreans asked the new president to make a gesture toward their country. As de Grossouvre told journalist Jean Montaldo, the North Koreans came to see him to suggest that they "seal the friendship between our two countries by having a French company build a luxury hotel complex." By early 1983, the Compagnie Générale de Bâtiment et de Construction (CBC) was selected to build the 1.1-billion-franc Yanggakdo resort.

But the North Koreans had problems, and they had demands. They told CBC they were short of cash, so the president of the company turned to Mitterrand crony Roger-Patrice Pelat and asked for his help in getting a 450-million-franc loan from the French government. In exchange for his services, Pelat demanded a 25-million-franc commission, which CBC paid in the form of construction work at his château just south of Paris. Pelat's most frequent guest for the exclusive hunting parties he hosted there was François Mitterrand, who arrived from Paris in the presidential helicopter at a landing pad Pelat built specially for him.[9]

The kickback paid to Pelat on the North Korean hotel complex was just one of hundreds of such deals, where state policy was determined by the amount of the bribe. Many of the cases Montaldo meticulously documents were investigated in 1992–1993 by Judge Thierry Jean-Pierre of Le Mans, who found a steady stream of commissions, kickbacks, and bribes going into Socialist Party coffers before he was abruptly taken off the case by the Ministry of Justice. It was so bad that opposition deputy François d'Aubert accused Mitterrand of transforming France into a "banana republic" and launched a parliamentary investigation into the state-owned Crédit Lyonnais bank, which he alleged was being used secretly to finance Mitterrand's Socialist Party.[10]

The corruption was by no means limited to Mitterrand or his Socialist Party, as we shall see. Corruption at the top is one of the open secrets of French politics and has contributed to rendering the French cynical when it comes to politics and the motives of their political leaders. Because their leaders are corrupt and tend to get away with it, they suspect that other countries, including America, are governed in the same way.

During the two years of his second stint as prime minister, from 1986 to 1988, Jacques Chirac and his government showed their eagerness to cooperate with the United States on strategic issues. When he first assumed power, Chirac informed President Mitterrand that he wanted France to take part in President Reagan's Strategic Defense Initiative (SDI), in response to a U.S. invitation. Indeed, opening the gate to French industry to participate in SDI had been part of his campaign platform and would have brought economic and scientific benefits to both sides. But Mitterrand refused, on the pretext that missile defense would weaken France's nuclear deterrent. Instead, he worked with German chancellor Helmut Kohl to establish a European equivalent to SDI called Eureka. Despite all the publicity, Eureka went nowhere and became a dusty dumping ground for government-sponsored research programs with little or no military utility and no clear civilian benefit.

Chirac also raised the subject of having France rejoin the NATO integrated command. Again, Mitterrand refused. So Chirac changed tack and began arguing in favor of establishing a joint Franco-German brigade, a project Mitterrand supported until it dawned on him that it would be positioned in Germany along NATO front lines and thus constitute a trip wire that could engage a French nuclear response in case of attack. "Would we send it there without a nuclear umbrella?" Attali wondered after a long discussion of the project between Mitterrand and the Franco-German working group.[11]

Chirac's motives in seeking to strengthen military ties and strategic cooperation with the United States at this time were aimed less at reasserting France's membership in the Western alliance than at demonstrating to the French public his difference and independence from Mitterrand. If Mitterrand had favored expanding the French nuclear arsenal, Chirac would have supported unilateral disarmament. Similarly, if the French president had been pro-Arab and anti-Israel, Chirac would have switched his well-known Middle East preferences to become pro-Israel and anti-Arab.

In August 1987, Chirac's defense minister, André Giraud, quietly called on the United States for help in Chad, apparently without informing either Mitterrand or Chirac. Colonel Qaddafi was once again on the move, bombing French and Chadian positions in Faya-Largeau and in the Aouzou strip along the border. "We worked with Giraud quietly, providing intelligence assistance and transportation," recalls Fred Charles Ikle. "We managed to put Qaddafi back in the box. That was the turning point of Qaddafi's expansion. It was also the peak of our cooperation with France."[12]

Chadian gunners shot down two Libyan MiG-23 fighter-bombers over northern Chad, using Redeye missiles supplied as part of an American aid package. Giraud was so incensed by the Libyan bombing raids in northern Chad that he wanted to order French air force Mirage F1s to intercept the Libyan planes and shoot them down.[13] But Chirac "was very hostile of this type of intervention, because he believed we mustn't directly confront the Libyans," chronicler Jacques Attali claims. Instead, Chirac suggested that France redeploy its forces in northern Chad to get them out of harm's way.

The fighting in Chad intensified at the end of August, when the Libyan air force destroyed Chadian army positions in the uranium- and oil-rich Aouzou strip and occupied it militarily. With quiet U.S. support, Chadian president Hissène Habré launched a maneuver reminiscent of the strikes by Afghan mujahideen units into the southern republics of the Soviet Union. He ordered troops into the desert of southern Libya on camelback, where they attacked and temporarily "disabled" the Libyan air base at Maaten-es-Sara using French-supplied Milan antitank missiles. It was a brilliant tactical strike that put a halt to Qaddafi's expansion into black Africa. When Chirac heard news of the attack, he commented wryly that "the Americans are pushing Hissène Habré to do stupid things." Two days later, he called Mitterrand and asked him to send his top military aide, General Fleury, to the Chadian capital, to warn Habré that France would cut off aid if he pulled such a stunt again.[14]

French carping over U.S. assistance to Habré became significantly more muted when gunners from the French 403rd Antiaircraft Regiment shot down a Libyan bomber on an aborted bombing run over the Chadian capital, N'Djamena. French Defense Ministry sources told me that radio intercepts before the crash confirmed the presence of two Russians aboard the Libyan plane, which was shot down by a U.S.-made Hawk missile. On September 16, 1987, TASS reported that two Soviet advisers had disappeared in southern Libya while on an "official mission to maintain military equipment" and that a demarche was under way with the French government to retrieve them. President Reagan's case that Qaddafi was the leading edge of Soviet aggression in northern Africa had suddenly become crystal clear.[15] At the French Defense Ministry, Habré soon became a hero—not just because of his daring desert warfare tactics, but because he dispatched captured SA-13 air defense missiles, the most advanced the Soviets had exported, to the United States and France where they were examined by experts and provided an intelligence windfall.[16]

I ronically, the peak of what was still secret U.S.-French nuclear cooperation took place after the United States and the USSR signed the intermediate-range nuclear forces (INF) agreement to withdraw all intermediate-range nuclear missiles from Europe on December 8, 1987.

The INF treaty made France feel more threatened, not less; on this, both Mitterrand and Chirac agreed. The problem was that without the presence of U.S. nuclear missiles in Europe, France feared the United States would not respond to a Soviet conventional attack against West Germany and that without a U.S. response, Europe would simply capitulate.

General Pierre-Marie Gallois, the father of the French nuclear force, explained the logic that was shared by both Mitterrand and Chirac. "The minute a Soviet aggression against Europe began, you would immediately have five hundred thousand demonstrators besieging the Chancellery in Bonn, the Élysée Palace in Paris, and the governments in Rome and London, demanding immediate negotiations," he said just months after the INF treaty was signed. "Even if we doubled our military expenditures from what they are today, we would still count for nothing in the face of two hundred Soviet divisions. And this is true not only for France, but for all of Europe." Gallois believed that conventional defense was simply beyond the means of European countries, singly or collectively. "If we eliminate nuclear weapons, as Reagan wants, we will be contributing to elevating the Soviet Union to the rank of the world's strongest military power. This is why France cannot follow Reagan along the path of disarmament. Without nuclear weapons, we are weak."[17]

Henri Conze remembers the final act of the U.S.-French alliance almost with nostalgia. At the time, it was a closely guarded secret. It involved the first—and last—trilateral meeting to discuss joint development of a new generation of nuclear weapons. The partners were France, Britain, and the United States.

The meeting took place on March 16, 1988, in the central French city of Bourges. Conze personally sent out the invitations, as French undersecretary of defense for policy. "The idea was to show confidence in the alliance," he said. "The United States wanted to replace its existing air-launched cruise missiles with something longer-range. And we were looking to develop our own cruise missile." As for the British, "They wanted anything they could get. Remember, at that point, they still had just gravity bombs for their air force." France had developed a new form of hypersonic air-breathing engine, known as the ramjet, which was far in advance of U.S. cruise missile motors then under development. "There wasn't one big partner and two small," Conze said with pride, "but two big partners and one small." The small one would be the United Kingdom.

At one P.M. on November 18, 1988, U.S. ambassador Joe Rodgers greeted an important guest at his official residence at 42, rue du Faubourg Saint-Honoré. The event was officially pegged as a "farewell luncheon" before Rodgers returned to the United States after his three-year stint in Paris, which had seen the peak of strategic cooperation with France. His guest was Michel Rocard, the Socialist prime minister who took over the reins of government after Chirac lost the presidential election in May.

But the discussion was far from routine; at times, it was not even polite. Rocard was surrounded by a team of experts who specialized in technology transfer and export licensing. They had come to talk about CoCom, a subject the technically minded Rocard mastered perfectly. As one of his advisers told me in describing the meeting, CoCom was the "focal point of several of the prime minister's primary interests, defense, international affairs, and large export contracts." And it was a subject that had him fuming.

Rodgers had been asked to deliver a demarche by the Pentagon to complain about ongoing deliveries by Forest-Liné to the Soviet Union. The U.S. ambassador called the shipments "egregious violations" of the CoCom rules and said that the United States believed Forest-Liné was acting with French government approval. Other French companies were engaged in similar export violations, he said.

According to French and American participants at the lunch, Rocard blew up. "Your meddling is unacceptable," he announced icily well before they had reached the dessert (which he left untouched). The United States, Rocard argued, was infringing on French sovereignty. "It's up to us, and no one else, to decide whether or not this type of contract is in the best interests of France." The discussion turned into a shouting match. Rocard and his advisers refused to budge, while Rodgers and his experts continued to lay out the facts of the French CoCom violations and uttered veiled threats of exposure if the French did not start playing by the rules.

One week later, on November 24–25, French president François Mitterrand left for a two-day trip to the USSR. It was after this trip, former Reagan administration officials agree, that the French attitude toward the United States changed dramatically. "Gorbachev went to Mitterrand and asked for help. Russia was Sierra Leone with missiles. It had no civilian industry, because they couldn't get technology from the West," says Steve Bryen. "Gorbachev asked Mitterrand to help him to get rid of CoCom. That was Gorbachev's main goal."[18]

Mitterrand pulled out all the stops in his effort to woo the Soviet leader, pledging huge loans in addition to direct access to the best of French high tech. To prove he meant business, he packed the presidential Concorde with government ministers, political heavyweights, and top French industrialists and bankers.[19] Several of the companies he invited were later implicated in corruption scandals involving kickbacks to Mitterrand's Socialist Party. Once again, state policy was about to shift, and it was all about the money.

The Élysée billed the Mitterrand trip to Russia as "more than just a state visit. This was a working trip to prepare a practical calendar for technical and economic exchanges" for the months and years to come. But privately the French security establishment was appalled. "Mitterrand has just given the Soviets everything they have been trying to steal for the past ten years, right there on a silver platter, for free," one official told me.

Many of the projects the two leaders discussed were finalized when Gorbachev paid a return visit to France on July 4–6, 1989. A credit line of 12 billion francs ($2.1 billion) was opened with Crédit Lyonnais, and numerous industrial projects were signed, financed once again by the French taxpayer. One of the most interesting (and least publicized) was a watershed space agreement with the French National Space Center, Centre Nationale d'Études Spatiale (CNES), which opened France's top space research labs to Soviet scientists in return for regular flights by French astronauts aboard Soviet spacecraft. Soviet diplomats called it the "normalization of Franco-Soviet space cooperation." A friend of mine at the DST who tracked Soviet high-tech espionage called it "a bloodless victory for the T Directorate of the KGB."

"Mastery of space," says the Soviet *Dictionary of Basic Military Terms*, "is an important prerequisite for achieving victory in war."[20] Mitterrand was not duped by Gorbachev, nor was he naive. In fact, he had been explicitly warned about Soviet intentions by his own intelligence service, which put out what amounted to a burn notice on Glavkosmos, the allegedly civilian marketing agency Gorbachev established to handle parts of the Franco-Soviet space exchanges. The DGSE report pointed out that Glavkosmos "is in fact one of the Chief Directorates of the Ministry of General Machine Building, itself one of the nine ministries of the Soviet military-industrial complex run by the VPK."[21] The Ministry of General Machine Building was responsible for *all* Soviet space programs, including strategic ballistic missiles, antisatellite weapons, and space vehicles. Glavkosmos was little more than a "cover for the VPK," the DGSE report warned, "widely used to protect the heads of Soviet armament organizations during their trips to the West."

The cold war was far from over, yet Mitterrand appeared to have switched sides.

# 8

# Gulf War One

---

S addam Hussein's best friend in France, Jacques Chirac, was roundly
trounced in the May 1988 presidential elections. But if the Iraqi lobby
lost one of its most powerful supporters, it gained a new one in exchange. Jean-Pierre Chevènement was the black sheep of the French Socialist Party. Fiercely independent, he headed the left-wing CERES faction,
which combined doctrinaire Socialist economics with uncompromising
Gaullist nationalism, held together with the spit of anti-Americanism.
Chevènement had resigned as education minister in 1983 after a political
dispute with Mitterrand, but he remained influential within the party. As
he was forming his post-election government, the wily French president
preferred to have Chevènement nearby where he could keep an eye on him,
instead of outside the government where he could make mischief. In June
1988, he appointed Chevènement as defense minister, a decision Mitterrand came to regret.

Chevènement was an old friend of the butcher of Baghdad. In 1985, he
founded the Franco-Iraqi Friendship Society, along with an apologist
for the ultra-right National Front party in France. As defense minister,
Chevènement worked hard to convince the reluctant finance minister,
Pierre Bérégovoy, to approve government financing for the Tulip and

Jacinthe helicopter contracts that had been signed by Chirac—and that was only the beginning. He wanted France to sign major new arms deals with Saddam.

By the time Chevènement took over the Defense Ministry, Saddam was rolling toward victory in his eight-year war against Iran. His best general, Maher Rashid, had routed the Iranians on the Fao peninsula in April through massive use of chemical weapons combined with a brilliant armored assault. By July, Ayatollah Khomeini announced he would accept a cease-fire, which he said was as bitter as drinking "a cup of poison." In August, Saddam wheeled around against his own Kurdish population, devastating the town of Halabja with a deadly chemical cocktail that killed more than three thousand civilians. According to a report to the United Nations, Saddam used French Mirage F1 fighters specially equipped with modified agricultural sprayers to deliver chemical weapons. Despite a graphic press reporting on the massacre, and an on-scene report from staff members of the U.S. Senate Foreign Relations Committee, the United States decided to expand trade with Saddam, pushed by an increasingly influential pro-Iraq business lobby. So did France.

By early 1989, Iraq's oil production was up, French and Russian oil companies were finding new reserves, and Saddam was seeking to sign massive new arms contracts with his best suppliers. In March, Lieutenant General Amir Rashid al-Ubaydi, whom I first met in Baghdad in 1986, came to France accompanied by his deputy at the Ministry of Industry and Military Industrialization, Lieutenant General Amir Hamoodi al-Saadi. The Iraqi embassy reserved an entire floor for the two Amirs at the five-star Hotel Crillon, a former palace just across the street from the U.S. embassy at the Place de la Concorde. The Iraqis and their bagman, Fadel Jawad Khaddum, made the rounds of everyone who was powerful and influential in France: the Finance Ministry, the Chamber of Commerce, and the French employers union, le Conseil National du Patronat Français (CNPF). As one of the defense contractors they visited told me, the grand tour was intended to "send a clear message" to the French that the Iraqis appreciated all they had done for them during the war and understood how difficult it had been. "They were saying, 'Believe in us again.' "[1]

The Iraqis attended their last but most important meeting on March 21, 1989, out at Dassault's luxurious Mirage 2000 chalet in the tony suburb of Vaucresson. Minutes of the meeting, and subsequent interviews with most of the participants, show in detail just what the Iraqis meant. The protocol signed by the two sides committed them to jointly building an entire aerospace industry in Iraq over the next ten years. It was a huge deal for the French, worth $6.5 billion right up front. They called it the Fao project, after the Iraqi victory. As Hugues de l'Estoile, the main Dassault representative, told me in Baghdad the next month, the Iraqis needed to begin their apprenticeship by rebuilding what they already had. "When you have mastered that, then you can build," he said.

Under the Fao project, the Iraqis would begin by carrying out the mid-life overhaul of their entire 133-aircraft Mirage F1 fleet, starting in 1991, in new facilities that would include workshops specially tooled for the highly complex tasks of engine and airframe rebuilds. Next, the French would help them build a separate aircraft factory called Saad 25, to assemble 134 AlphaJet trainers. Once the trainer program was up and running, Dassault would help them begin local assembly of fifty-four Mirage 2000-S "strike" aircraft. This new version of the latest French fighter was to be equipped as a low-level penetration bomber, with sophisticated terrain-following radar that would allow these planes to sneak in under enemy air defenses. It was the Israel variant, repackaged.

Fadel Khaddum tried to get Dassault, Thompson-CSF, and Matra to use the BNL credit line he had negotiated in Atlanta, but the French insisted on getting paid in cash, oil, and petrochemicals, over a nine-to-fourteen-year period. It was a costly mistake.

In Iraq, Saddam Hussein's birthday was a national holiday. Schoolchildren were encouraged to sing songs for their president. Hotels baked cakes. Cars and buses were festooned with flowers. Baghdad itself became a festival of colored lights. But April 28, 1989, when Saddam turned fifty-two, was a birthday unlike all the others. This year, Saddam had decided to prepare an additional surprise for his subjects, his arms suppliers, his bankers, and his technology brokers. He called it the First Baghdad International Exhibition for Military Production. Its symbol was an Iraqi flag shaped into the form of a dove. Its slogan was "Defense equipment for peace and prosperity." It was not Saddam's idea of a joke.

One hundred forty-eight companies from twenty-eight countries paid hefty prices to rent stands and show their wares. As I visited the exhibits of French defense contractors I had known for years, they pointed out their competitors from Italy, Spain, and Britain. "The gang's all here," one of them joked. Everyone was waiting for the visit of Saddam's powerful son-in-law Hussein Kamil al-Majid, the minister of industry and military industrialization. When he arrived, wearing his green khaki Baath Party uniform, flanked by the two Amirs, they snapped to attention and went through the pre-rehearsed drill, explaining why their implements of destruction could beat those of their competitors.

In addition to the arms salesmen, dozens of machine tool companies also paid to present their products—an unusual occurrence at arms fairs. The Bulgarians, Poles, Hungarians, and Romanians were out in force, showing 1960s machine tools driven by Japanese Fanuc controllers. The Germans and the Austrians were there, proposing state-of-the-art explosive factories.

Gerald Bull was also on hand, showing a $\frac{1}{35}$ scale model of his soon-to-be-infamous super-gun to anyone who cared to look. Few paid him or his invention much heed, since the notion of a giant artillery piece capable of launching a rocket-propelled bomb (nuclear or otherwise) against a target one thousand miles away seemed like cockeyed nonsense to the hard-nosed arms dealers of Baghdad. Bull was also the proud father of two dramatic new Iraqi weapons systems on display: the Majnoon and al-Fao self-propelled howitzers. These monster trucks of the battlefield married a French gun, a Spanish chassis, and a Swedish cab.[2]

But stealing the show was Matrix Churchill, which had been rebaptized "Nasser" for the occasion by its Iraqi owners. In fact, the Iraqis just took Matrix Churchill brochures and pasted on a sticker bearing the Nasser label and handed them out with an address in Taji. They didn't even bother to change the company logo. When I peeled away the sticker, up popped the Matrix Churchill name. Iraqi officials told me openly that they had bought the company in an effort to duck Western export controls. "We are now making three axis machine tools here in Iraq," they said at the arms fair. "Soon we will be making five axis machines, with computerized numerical controls." With few exceptions, these machines all were going into weapons factories. Under existing CoCom rules, those machines still required export licenses, but by making them in Iraq, they could skirt the embargo. It was an effective scheme.[3]

The only major Iraqi supplier not officially present at the arms fair was the United States, which had withdrawn its participation a few days before the show began, apparently anxious not to arouse speculation that the U.S. government was prepared to authorize arms sales to Iraq, which in fact it never did. "There was one munitions license to Iraq, and it had my name on it," former undersecretary of state for security assistance William Schneider told me. "We sold four ceremonial pistols to the Iraqi leadership. There were no other defense products sold, despite various efforts."[4] Reams of now declassified State and Defense Departments documents support Schneider's account. Any U.S. weapons that wound up in Iraq in the 1980s—with the exception of those pistols—were sent there illegally and without the approval of the U.S. government.

Instead of a U.S. pavilion, with U.S. weaponry on show, American companies arranged for private delegations to attend the show. Some, such as General Motors, even got to meet with Hussein Kamil al-Majid. The U.S. military attaché in Baghdad received orders from Washington not to wear his uniform when he toured the show. He and other U.S. embassy officials, dressed in ordinary business suits, took photographs of every Iraqi weapon they could see. When we crossed each other's paths, we pretended not to know each other. I traded impressions with them in Baghdad later on, just as I did with my French, Spanish, Italian, and British friends at the show.

While the Baghdad arms fair was a big deal for the arms merchants, it went almost totally unnoticed in the press. Besides myself and artillery expert Christopher Foss of *Jane's Defence Weekly*, no other Western correspondent thought the event newsworthy enough to attend. I spent two hours on opening day, in a beige suit and tie in the ninety-degree heat, press credentials prominently displayed around my neck, taking pictures of every dignitary and arms merchant who ascended the steps of the VIP pavilion as if they were about to meet the God of Mammon himself. Many of the visitors I didn't recognize; a Lebanese friend in Paris, who worked as a defense consultant, spotted Saddam's younger son Qusay among the contact sheets we perused together. My favorite was a picture I snapped of French aircraft magnate Serge Dassault and his top arms salesman, the ever elegant Hugues de l'Estoile, bowing and scraping before Hussein Kamil and the two Amirs.

But the arms salesmen were starting to get worried. The Iraqis were buying less and making more themselves. Every deal now had to include a large component of technology transfer and local Iraqi production. The French hated it, but the Iraqis had made it clear that there would be no more pure purchases of off-the-shelf weapons, including combat jets; if the French couldn't give them the technology to build their own, the Brits or the Americans would. It was this transfer of production technology, more than the weapons themselves, that contributed to making Saddam Hussein the menace he soon became.

The French were in a better position than anyone to realize that Saddam was seeking his independence. Not only did the French have an extensive presence on the ground; they had certain ideological sympathies with Saddam Hussein's Baath party that made them more tolerant than others of Saddam's excesses. When I was given a tour of the Iraqi Staff College, my hosts pointed out a plaque in the entry hall that had been presented by retired French General Pierre-Marie Gallois during a lecture series he had given Iraqi Air Force officers. The French were breeding a new generation of Iraqi officer the old way, through personal contacts and shared battles. The unusual stature of General Gallois, a long-time proponent of an independent French nuclear force aimed against both the Soviets and the Americans, wasn't lost on me or my Iraqi hosts. Just as Saddam, these staff officers and weapons procurement specialists saw the relationship with France as a "third way," helping them to carve their own sanctuary between the superpowers. It was the type of relationship that bred fierce loyalties.

The Baghdad arms fair was Saddam Hussein's coming-out party. It was intended to show the world that Iraq was not a third world nation, but solidly on the road to industrialization, and that weapons production was Saddam's chosen path to power, prosperity, and modernity. General Amir al-Saadi told me that the various arms embargoes Iraq had been subjected to had reinforced Iraq's political will to develop an indigenous arms industry. "I am personally grateful to many of the no's we received from our arms suppliers. This made us insist and concentrate our efforts" on developing a local production capability. "This was the case with ballistic missiles," he added. When I sat down to interview General Amir Rashid al-Ubaydi—our third lengthy session together over the years—the pride in Iraq's accomplishments was evident. "All over the world you hear people bragging about how much they will do," he said, "and at the end of the day they have nothing. We have chosen to keep silent all these years, even as others mocked us. But today we have something to show that no one can deny."

Featured at the arms show were Iraq's own weapons and future weapons projects. They ran the gamut from the al-Hussein missiles that would rain down on Israel in January and February 1991, which French engineers helped Iraq to design, to an improvised AWACS plane, a Soviet-built IL-76 cargo jet crammed with French radar and British avionics. I cataloged these weapons and the foreign assistance the Iraqis received to build them in an earlier book, *The Death Lobby: How the West Armed Iraq.* United Nations arms inspector Rolf Ekeus called it "the Bible" and gave copies to inspection team leaders in 1991 to help them identify Iraq's dual-use industrial facilities.[5]

General Amir's pride in Iraq's accomplishments, and his new eagerness to boast now that the war with Iran was over, trickled down to his project engineers. In the Iraqi military production pavilion where they displayed the al-Hussein and al-Abbas missiles, an Iraqi ballistics expert saw me coming and came out to greet me before I reached his stand. "Mr. Timmerman," he said, shaking my hand. I returned his greeting. "Mr. Kenneth Timmerman." I said, "Yes?" Then he repeated my name again, this time including my middle name, which was not displayed anywhere on my ID badge. By this point, I was wondering what was going on. "You must believe me, sir, I have been waiting for five days here, right on this spot, just to meet you," he gushed, still holding my hand. He went on to tell me how Iraqi engineers from the Military Production Authority had solved the problem of increasing the range of the SCUD-B missile so it could hit Tehran. Besides increasing the size, they had "tinkered" with the fuel, he said. "Think cryogenic."[6]

Sometimes the inventiveness of the Iraqis shocked their oldest friends. One poignant scene I witnessed (and captured on film for posterity) took place beneath the wing of a French-built Mirage F1 fighter-bomber. General Maurice Schmitt was chairman of the French joint chiefs of staff. He had come to Baghdad as the personal representative of French defense minister Jean-Pierre Chevènement, with whom he shared an admiration for the independence and hard work the Iraqis displayed. But when he saw what the Iraqis had done with the Mirage, he could hardly contain himself.

"What the hell is that?" he shouted at Dassault's Hugues de l'Estoile, pointing to an unfamiliar missile hanging beneath the wing of the French fighter.

"Well, General, if you ask me, it looks like a Soviet-built AS-14." The AS-14 was a laser-guided missile that bore remarkable similar ties to the French AS-30L, which the Iraqis had bought in large quantities. The AS-14 presented two distinct advantages over the French missile: it had a slightly longer range, and it was much less expensive.

Schmitt looked de l'Estoile in the eye: "What have you people been up to over here, anyway?"

"Don't look at me." De l'Estoile threw up his hands in protest. On his left wrist, he wore a gold watch bearing the portrait of Saddam Hussein like a trophy of glory. It was said that his right hand—the one he signed contracts with—was worth more than $50 billion. "We had nothing to do with this," he said. "The Iraqis have been working all by themselves."

De l'Estoile then took the general in his white kepi and white summer dress uniform over to another plane sitting on the tarmac of al-Muthana Airport. It was a Soviet-built MiG-23. "See that refueling probe?" De l'Estoile pointed to the nose of the Soviet fighter. "That is one of ours."

Schmitt was not amused, even though de l'Estoile hastened to explain that the Iraqis had adapted the French refueling probe to the Soviet fighter without ever asking Dassault. In a subsequent interview following Iraq's invasion of Kuwait in August 1990, General Schmitt told me that it was here, at the Baghdad arms fair, that he first "began to wonder whether we hadn't gone a bit too far" in Iraq. "I realized we had better begin paying closer attention to what the Iraqis were developing in the way of armament."

The picture of the Mirage with the Soviet missile caused a great deal of headache for French defense electronic giant Thomson-CSF, since it showed an Atlis II laser designation pod, produced by Thomson-CSF, that the French initially sold to Iraq in 1984–1985 to accompany the AS-30L missile produced by Euromissile (Aérospatiale). As I reported in *The Death Lobby*, the technology that went into the laser designator was developed by Martin Marietta for Thomson as part of a $37 million contract signed in 1975. Transfer of that technology to a third country such as Iraq required prior U.S. government approval. Thomson never applied for such approvals.

The potential violation became an issue in 1992, when Thomson-CSF was seeking to purchase the missile division of U.S. aerospace manufacturer LTV, which worked with the CIA and the Pentagon on numerous highly classified "black" projects. The Pentagon's Defense Technology Security Administration (DTSA) already had concerns about Thomson's trustworthiness because of other foreign sales and wanted to delay Thomson's proposed purchase of LTV so it could conduct a more thorough investigation. I was not aware of Thomson's plans to buy LTV when I took the phone call from a friend at DTSA who had bought a copy of *The Death Lobby* and read my account of the laser designation pods sold to Iraq. When I mentioned the picture of General Schmitt and Hugues de l'Estoile beneath the wing of the Mirage, he jumped. "I syndicated all those pictures from the Baghdad arms fair with Sygma, a French photography syndicate," I said. "They are commercially available—for you or for anybody."

Not long after our conversation, the French Defense Ministry tried to pull my press credentials. I thought at first that their public affairs shop had made a mistake in the annual renewal of my press card. But when I showed up for an event, a gendarme looked up my name on a list, then turned me away. "Your credentials are no long valid, monsieur," he said. "You have no reason to be here."

Phone calls to the ministry confirmed that it wasn't a mistake. My contact in the minister's cabinet confided that several articles I had written recently "have not pleased people here in high places." I went to lunch not long afterward with another good friend, who worked in a different ministry. Over dessert, he told me what was going on. "We all think you're working for the CIA," he said. "That doesn't keep us from talking to you, but in this case, there are equities at stake. Perhaps it's time that you returned to the United States."[7]

It was at about this time that my DST minder began warning me over lunch not to let my wife start our car in the morning when she took the children to school. "If she must, make sure she opens the windows first," he said.

"Why's that?"

"The explosion is always worse if the windows are closed."

American readers may find it difficult to believe that a foreign reporter in France, working on sensitive subjects such as arms sales and Middle East politics, would actually be assigned a "minder" by the French counterespionage service, as if France were some third world dictatorship. But for over five years, from 1987 until my departure from France in 1993, a DST counterintelligence officer called regularly to check up on my activities.

He wanted to find out what stories I was working on, whom I was meeting. When one minder was assigned elsewhere, he introduced me to his replacement. It was all very civilized, even agreeable.

Early on, I realized there were two ways of reacting to the French approach. I could get huffy and indignant and refuse to talk to them, or I could go along with them and more likely than not learn something useful in the exchange. I chose the second approach, much to the relief of my minders, who never missed an occasion to hold our meetings over lunch at a good restaurant. When we spoke over the phone, they made sure I suggested the restaurants where we met, since they picked up the tab—in cash. They were always happy for an occasion to tap into their expense account. From time to time, when they wanted to impress me with their knowledge of my activities, they quoted verbatim transcripts from my telephone conversations with various sources. One former French intelligence analyst explained that the government had a huge listening post in the basements of the École Militaire, built initially to spy on Soviet operatives. With the end of the cold war, they faced massive layoffs and so were "looking for something to do."

It was only after I had left France that I learned that my troubles at the Defense Ministry were related to that conversation in Baghdad between General Schmitt and Hugues de l'Estoile and, especially, to the picture of the Mirage F1 with the Soviet missile slung beneath it. From my publicly available photograph, Pentagon analysts concluded there was a high probability that the French pod used in Iraq was identical to the laser designator Martin Marietta was producing for the U.S. Air Force. These were key weapons in the U.S. high-tech arsenal. If the United States had to redesign the laser designators because they had been compromised by the French, it could cost taxpayers tens of millions of dollars, if not more. Acting on those suspicions, DTSA requested that the interagency Committee on Foreign Investment in the United States (CFIUS) block the proposed Thomson-CSF purchase of LTV's missile division, pending an in-depth investigation. Thomson was understandably furious.

Three years after the sale was blocked, a friend in the Clinton administration faxed me a copy of a June 11, 1992, Thomson-CSF "white paper" company lobbyists were circulating at the Pentagon, the State Department, and on Capitol Hill.[8] Among the salient points the men from Thomson tried to impress upon U.S. officials were these:

I. The existing export control programs of Thomson-CSF and its U.S. subsidiaries ensure compliance with U.S. export laws;

II. The Thomson Group has an exemplary record of export control compliance;

Neither Thomson-CSF nor any of its U.S. subsidiaries has experienced any problem with U.S. export controls in the past ten years.

The allegations raised in Kenneth Timmerons [sic] book The Death Lobby are baseless.

In a detailed, two-page section entitled "Thomson-CSF Response to The Death Lobby," the French company's lawyers argued that every mention of their client was false.

As a general matter, the allegations set forth in The Death Lobby pertaining to Thomson-CSF involve the distortion of a few basic facts. By taking those facts and couching them in exaggeration, innuendo, speculation and related half-truths, The Death Lobby creates the impression—one grossly at odds with the historical truth—that Thomson-CSF traded profits and self-interest for enormous security risks associated with the emergence of the Iraqi war machine, producing Saddam Hussein's military capability to challenge allied forces in the Persian Gulf War.

[ . . . ] Apart from the distortion, The Death Lobby also contains some outright inaccuracies that demand correction for the record.[9] Among them:

The allegation that Thomson-CSF helped Iraq create a combat electronics industry at a plant code-named SAAD 13. . . .

When I first reported on the Saad 13 contract in a French defense magazine in April 1985, Thomson reacted with a mixture of fury and pride. In fact, I first learned details of the contract from . . . Thomson-CSF executives during a reporting trip to Baghdad earlier that year—a full year after Thomson claimed in the white paper that they had "terminated" the contract. (What they had "terminated" in 1984, in fact, was construction of the physical plant.) One of the reasons Thomson-CSF continued to do such a large business in Iraq throughout the 1980s was precisely to help the Iraqis manage production at Saad 13. My sources, who included the vice president of Thomson International, René Anastaze, whom I interviewed on the record in 1988, told me that Thomson had trained between three thousand and four thousand Iraqi technicians to operate equipment at Saad 13 at a specially built "campus" Thomson set up in the Paris suburb of Jouy-en-

Josas. Anastaze pointed out that Saad 13 had been designed to incorporate the most advanced production technology then available, making it "one of the largest and most modern electronics assembly facilities in the world." The idea was to give the Iraqis "a tool for the future," he said, starting with assembling kits so they could acquire the expertise to eventually carry out more sophisticated tasks, such as manufacturing their own battlefield radar, electronic countermeasures, and avionics for the Mirage jet fighters. Thomson renewed Saad 13 licensing arrangements in 1987 to include production in Iraq of the Tiger-G two-dimensional early warning radar, which Iraq mounted upside down inside its Adnan-1 Airborne Early Warning aircraft.[10] As for the Martin Marietta laser designation pod, the lawyers claimed that "Thomson-CSF supplied the Iraqi Air Force with a laser-guidance system based on downgraded French technology, with the full approval of the French government. It was not, as erroneously reported in *The Death Lobby*, the same system developed in the United States for Thomson-CSF by Martin Marietta and therefore was not subject to U.S. export controls."[11]

Despite all the disclaimers, CFIUS turned down the Thomson bid to buy the LTV missile division. With the failed marriage came all the bitterness of unrequited love that would play out in an intelligence war between the United States and France I will detail in a subsequent chapter.

Although the United States still refused to sell Iraq weapons, the administration of President George H. W. Bush took the wraps off commercial deals. Scores of major U.S. corporations, from General Electric to General Motors, began sending their salesmen to Iraq. The Commerce Department approved dual-use technology sales worth $1.5 billion by the time Saddam invaded Kuwait, some of which ended up in Iraqi arms factories.[12] As one French diplomat in Baghdad put it, the French were convinced that "the Americans were coming" and were about to engage in a full-scale commercial war for the Iraqi market. It didn't help that one of Saddam Hussein's most active supporters at the State Department, Assistant Secretary Richard Murphy, was now in the private sector. He traveled to Baghdad in early 1990 representing First City Bancorporation of Texas, whose chairman, Robert Abboud, headed the U.S.-Iraq Business Forum—a lobbying group representing a broad cross-section of major U.S. corporations seeking to remove the last remaining U.S. trade sanctions on Iraq. Murphy met with Hussein Kamil al-Majid to discuss "development projects," he told me later.[13]

French minister of defense Jean-Pierre Chevènement viewed the American commercial invasion of Iraq with concern. If France did not do something fast, it would lose its privileged position, so Chevènement went to Baghdad on January 25, 1990, to "raise our bilateral relations to a higher level." It was the first trip to Baghdad by a French defense minister in more than a decade.

As soon as Chevènement arrived in Baghdad, he paid fealty in a long interview with a Baath Party newspaper. "President Saddam Hussein has a clear and interesting outlook," Chevènement said, "leading his people toward peace and the construction of his country, in spite of the challenges and difficulties with which he was confronted during the war with Iran." Just to make sure he got the point across, Chevènement added: "President Saddam has the respect and esteem of French leaders."

On the menu of Chevènement's talks with Saddam and Hussein Kamil were a broad range of new military industrialization projects as well as direct arms sales. These had been made possible by a generous settlement of the Iraqi debt on September 14, 1989, which gave the Iraqis an additional six years to repay 7 billion francs of old debts, while opening up new short-term credits.[14]

The first to benefit was Thomson-CSF. Only days before the Chevènement trip, they signed their first new arms contract with Iraq in more than two years, to supply sophisticated avionics for Iraqi fighters worth $161 million (900 million francs). Unlike previous sales, however, this time the Iraqis paid cash up front. That had been Thomson's sole condition for closing the deal.

Another sale involved sophisticated side-scan aerial surveillance cameras to equip Iraqi Mirage F1 and MiG-25 spy planes. A squadron of Iraqi Mirages was now based in Jordan. Since August 1989, they had been flying reconnaissance missions over the Jordan River, looking deep into Israel to update Iraq's operational targeting maps. Ze'ev Schiff reported in the Israeli daily *Ha'aretz* that these cameras gave the Iraqis the capability of mapping targets sixty-five kilometers inside Israel, as opposed to the forty-kilometer range of Jordan's F-5E reconnaissance planes. This meant the Iraqis could now accurately identify targets all the way to the Tel Aviv suburb of Ramat Gan, where key defense manufacturing plants and a major Israeli air force base were located. It would come in handy when Iraq decided to hit those same areas with its enhanced SCUD missiles.

What the Iraqis really wanted was Chevènement's help in convincing the French government to finance the Fao project, the $6.5 billion package that was to launch their own aeronautics industry. But this time the Iraqi appetite was simply too big. "We note that an enormous share of Iraq's GNP is currently being devoted to military industrialization projects," a key adviser to Finance Minister Pierre Bérégovoy told me, commenting on Chevènement's trip. "We do not want to finance regional destabilization. Nor will we issue any more export credit guarantees until the Iraqis make good on the debt-rescheduling deal we worked out in September. If defense companies like Thomson-CSF want to sell to Iraq, they will have to take that risk on their own." The adviser went on to reveal that the Finance Ministry was still blocking the delivery of the last eight Mirage F1s left over from the fourth contract signed by Jacques Chirac in 1987. "When the Iraqis pay, they will get their planes," he said.[15] Those planes had been sitting in airtight cocoons at the Bordeaux-Merignac Airport ever since they had rolled off the Dassault assembly line, and they were costing the French aircraft manufacturer a fortune.

In July 1990, the French reached a final settlement on the Iraqi debt. After a three-year wait, Dassault received authorization to deliver the eight remaining Mirage F1 fighters. The debt protocol was scheduled to be signed in Paris on August 4, but the curtain came crashing down on the night of August 1–2, when Saddam Hussein sent one hundred thousand troops across the border into Kuwait. "If only Saddam had waited a few more days to invade Kuwait," said one French arms salesman with a sigh, "we would have been free and clear."

President Mitterrand and most of his cabinet were on vacation when Saddam struck. President Bush was in Aspen, meeting with British prime minister Margaret Thatcher. Informed at his country home in southwestern France by Foreign Minister Roland Dumas of the U.S. request to seek a United Nations Security Council vote condemning the Iraqi invasion, Mitterrand responded immediately. "Yes, we'll vote yes."[16] He also gave orders to prepare the French aircraft carrier *Clemenceau* to depart Toulon for the Gulf, just in case.

As in so many other cases during his presidency, Mitterrand's instinct told him to support the United States, albeit cautiously. But when he convened his cabinet on August 9, he found that most of his top advisers were lukewarm to military action against Saddam. "Iraq has no more interlocutor," said Interior Minister Pierre Joxe. "We must avoid becoming involved militarily." Socialist Party boss (and future prime minister) Lionel Jospin said it "makes no sense" to intervene and counseled against joining the Americans even as part of a multinational force. Defense Minister Chevènement was the most outspoken. He went into a long apology for Saddam, arguing that what was really going on was a discussion among Arabs about "the distribution of the oil wealth." He urged Mitterrand to maintain a dialogue with Saddam, despite the invasion. "The game the Americans are playing is dangerous," he warned. If Saddam's regime were to disappear, "with it would go the only obstacle to Iranian fundamentalism." He agreed with the dispatch of a "helicopter carrier," along with a few warships, but only if they were sent as a French force, aimed at "reassuring friendly countries" in the region, not as part of a multinational naval blockade. Mitterrand became increasingly irritated with his defense minister as the meeting went on and reiterated his belief that it was not prudent to counter the Americans when they felt their security was at stake.

> We are happy to have the Americans in certain circumstances. We are their allies. They are not our allies when they give unconditional support to Israel and bomb Libya. But in the present circumstances, we need to clearly show our solidarity. If we must choose, I believe we must fight against Hussein, whatever the consequences. If we don't, we'll be called fair-weather friends [*les faux frères de l'Occident*]. We must reinforce our presence in the Gulf, including airpower under our command. . . .

Chevènement again argued strongly against any linkage between French forces in the region and the Americans. "I agree to help Saudi Arabia if they are attacked. But we must preserve the autonomy of the French command by placing our aircraft in another state. Saddam Hussein is not a new Hitler, but a mixture of Kemal Atatürk, Nasser, and Mussolini." Mitterrand retorted sharply, "Nasser never massacred his own people or used chemical weapons."[17] The defense minister was on a collision course with his president, who confided to adviser Jacques Attali later that day that he was convinced France would be forced to go to war.

To show his utter disdain for the climate of crisis the government had adopted, Chevènement promptly resumed his vacation in Tuscany after the cabinet meeting and refused to return to Paris until August 17, despite a summons from Mitterrand. "They don't need me to carry out Bush's policies," he told reporters. Behind the scenes, he worked the phones to make sure the French aircraft carrier stayed in port, to Mitterrand's "growing exasperation," Attali notes.

Chevènement saw American conspiracies everywhere, an attitude shared by many in the French intelligence services and on the political fringes, both the extreme Left and the extreme Right. On August 20, 1990, Chevènement claimed that the French defense attaché in Washington, D.C., was reporting that the United States was planning air strikes against selected Iraqi targets within forty-eight hours. Mitterrand exploded. "They're saying that everywhere! That is not a secret, that's a rumor. For the past week, that's the only thing people have been talking about. At any rate, Bush has not spoken to me about it."

Chevènement retorted: "That tends to prove that our intelligence services were right when they said all of this was a trap set by the Americans" for Saddam Hussein.[18]

When the *Clemenceau* finally left port, not a single combat aircraft was on board. Instead, the flight deck was crammed with thirty Gazelle helicopters and sixty-five trucks. It was not an impressive display of French power. Chevènement had worked hard to make sure that the French presence in the Gulf, if it ever materialized, would not be seen as a threat by Saddam Hussein. By the end of August, Mitterrand was already urging his defense minister to resign. But Chevènement stubbornly refused, apparently intent on thwarting as far as possible any French engagement alongside the United States in the Gulf War.

As French forces flowed into Saudi Arabia and worked out the details of their role as the "pincer" in General Norman Schwarzkopf's plan to entrap the Iraqi Republican Guard around Nasiriyah, Chevènement made one last effort to derail the war. At a press conference in Paris on January 18, 1991—less than two full days after allied air strikes began—the French defense minister solemnly declared that under no circumstances would French forces attack beyond Kuwait. For Mitterrand, that was the last straw. "But of course the Gulf War will not be limited to Kuwait. If needed, we will fire on Iraq. And it will be needed. So why is Chevènement saying just the opposite?"[19] On January 27, he sent his top military aide, Admiral

Jacques Lanxade, onto French television to specifically rebut his defense minister. Two days later, Chevènement handed in his resignation. Mitterrand immediately announced that he was replacing him with Pierre Joxe.

Twenty-five thousand French troops took part in the ground assault, racing across the desert in their wheeled armor vehicles. In just three days, they reached the Euphrates at as-Samawah, cutting off the retreat of Saddam's Republican Guard along Highway 8 west of Nasiriyah. Although the French hesitation—and a last-minute attempt by Mitterrand to negotiate more time for Saddam—angered many Americans, the only real glitch in the French participation in the Gulf War coalition involved the air force. General Schwarzkopf requested that no French Mirage F1 fighters take part in allied air strikes, to avoid possible confusion with Iraqi planes. The French swallowed hard and sent older Jaguar fighter-bombers instead. Better that than lose pilots to friendly fire. Some sixty-six French aircraft took part in the allied attacks.

Chevènement's mischief was not limited to delaying the departure of French forces to the Gulf or packing the French aircraft carrier flight deck with trucks and helicopters. He also gave orders that no one in the French Defense Ministry or in industry was to cooperate with the Americans by providing information on the weaponry France had sold Iraq.

I learned about Chevènement's refusal from a U.S. Air Force officer at the U.S. embassy in Paris who had gotten my name from a mutual friend. He called me one afternoon in late August 1990 and asked if we could meet.

At first, I couldn't believe what he was telling me when we finally sat down together in his office. "You mean the French have not been giving everything you need to be able to counter the French weaponry in the Iraqi arsenal?" I asked.

"It's worse than that," he said. "They won't even return our phone calls."

It was clear from our conversation that the Pentagon's knowledge of what the French had actually sold Iraq was limited. They knew there were Mirage fighters and Roland air defense missiles, but that was about it. Because we were allies, they hadn't really been paying attention. What he really needed, the officer said, was information that would allow the air force to knock out those weapons and, especially, details on the electronic countermeasures the French had sold the Iraqis for their Mirage fleet. I said I would look through the promotional brochures I had gathered at various arms fairs around the world, including Baghdad and Cairo, but I doubted I had much, since that was one area the French kept pretty quiet. I suggested he call the manufacturers directly. That's when he admitted that he didn't even have a clear idea of who they were.

As I went back through my archives, I realized there was actually quite a bit of information—on a basic level, at least—that might be of help. From the promotional brochures the French themselves handed out, some of which were quite detailed, I realized it was possible to outline what the Iraqis might conceivably have received from the French and who had manufactured it. It wasn't terribly detailed, but it was a start. Other journalists might not have agreed even to this request, but I never hesitated. The United States was at war, and the lives of U.S. pilots were at stake.

After the war was over, I met with that air force officer again. He thanked me for my help and said that it had given him the basis for presenting the French with a more detailed démarche, which had been successful. From other sources, I learned that even before Chevènement resigned, orders came from the Élysée to provide the United States with everything it wanted. "There were no secrets between us," one French defense contractor, who said he had met with the U.S. Air Force liaison officer, told me. "After all, we were at war, and we were in it together." The French provided details of the KARI unified air defense network they had built for the Iraqis, right down to the command codes for launching Iraq's French-built Roland and Soviet air defense missiles, so the United States could program their own ECM pods to jam the signals. The French assistance saved the lives of many U.S. and coalition pilots. Instead of the 10 percent losses in aircraft, which coalition commanders initially feared, the allied air forces lost just thirty-eight planes—of which twenty-seven were U.S. aircraft—out of more than 2,000 fixed wing aircraft and 1,500 helicopters that took part in the battle to dominate Iraq's airspace at the beginning of the war.[20] Chevènement and others had argued that turning over that information to the Americans would make it impossible to sell French weapons systems anywhere in the Arab world again. Mitterrand came down and said, in effect, So what. Either France wanted a seat at the table once the war was over or it could stew and brood in isolation. That was the choice.

The first Gulf War clearly exposed the contradictions in French national interests. On the one hand was its alliance with the United States; on the other were the needs of its domestic arms industry and, more generally, its export-driven economy. Mitterrand hoped that by choosing the alliance, the United States would give France its share of postwar markets.

But for the major French defense contractors such as Dassault, Matra, Aérospatiale, GIAT, and Thomson-CSF, nothing could replace the Iraqi market. They had wagered so heavily on Saddam that they had little left to ante up for the postwar game after losing their shirts in Iraq. As the extent of the damage sank in after the war, it gave comfort to Chevènement and those like him who had argued that France never should have joined the U.S.-led coalition.

Dr. Stephen Bryen believes that the United States "butchered the relationship with the Europeans" because we failed to put together a defense industrial policy. The arms market was different from the rest of the economy and "can't be run as free trade," Bryen believes, "because it involves foreign policy, security policy, and the national interest. We should have said to the Europeans in 1975: You take the lead in building the next-generation tank, because you have terrific technology that in many instances is better than ours; we'll do the next-generation combat jet. But the Pentagon wanted American businesses to do everything. I would argue that the Pentagon is the last bastion of socialism in America. It is a protected industry." The French and the Europeans "have legitimate gripes."

Those gripes would harden over the next thirteen years into a hard core of refusal the next time America asked the French for help.

# 9

# Spies and Bribes

ernard Guillet was not one to bear a grudge lightly. A top adviser to hard-nosed conservative politician Charles Pasqua, who became interior minister during the 1986–1988 Chirac government, Guillet was sidelined when the Socialists returned to power. He knew who his enemies were, and he fought against them ruthlessly. And they weren't just the Socialists.

Guillet was one of several Pasqua advisers involved in negotiating with terrorist groups in Lebanon and Syria to obtain the release of French hostages just three days before the 1988 presidential elections. Although his exploits failed to get Chirac elected, Pasqua felt a debt of gratitude nonetheless and got him a diplomatic posting through the French Foreign Ministry. It wasn't much of a job, Guillet said later when I met him at the mountaintop mansion of Lebanese businessman Walid Khoraitem, near the French Riviera perfume capital, Grasse. He referred to his 1989–1993 stint as French consul to Houston, Texas, as his "exile." His job consisted of holding garden parties and hosting delegations of French high-tech executives. Once, he took a July 14 celebration across Texas and several Southern states. But that wasn't all Monsieur Guillet was doing for *La Maison France*.

One morning in early May 1991, a security guard at the sprawling home of a U.S. high-tech executive in the ritzy Houston neighborhood of River Oaks noticed something odd. Two men in well-cut business suits, one of them nearly bald, pulled up in an unmarked van and grabbed the plastic garbage bags from the trash bin in front of the house. After tossing them into the back of their van, they sped off—but not before he jotted down their license plate number.

Company executives traced the van and discovered that it was registered in the name of the French consulate. When confronted later that day, Guillet initially denied that the consulate van had been anywhere near the River Oaks area that morning. But when the guard identified him from a photograph, he changed his story and claimed that he and an assistant were collecting leaves and grass cuttings. It seemed that Guillet had been trying to build a swimming pool (*une piscine*) at his consular residence but had failed to get the necessary permit. Guillet told the FBI that he was simply trying to fill up the hole.

It was a cute story. Back in Paris, "la Piscine" was the name commonly used by the press to refer to the headquarters of the French foreign intelligence service, the DGSE. It had acquired the name years earlier after the nearby public swimming pool on the Boulevard Mortier, and it had stuck. Swimming metaphors and "deep water" became frequent clichés used by the press and former DGSE officers to describe the trials and tribulations of the French service. (Insiders referred to the DGSE as "Mortier" instead.)

Guillet appears to have been working with a DGSE unit that specialized in economic espionage against friendly nations. They were following up on leads provided by a DGSE mole in the Defense Advanced Research Projects Agency (DARPA), a Pentagon unit on the forefront of classified defense technology. According to author Peter Schweizer, the DGSE was particularly interested in DARPA-funded research into stealth technology and had sent Guillet to a company that worked on special radar-deflecting coatings.[1]

When the FBI failed to find sufficient evidence to warrant expelling Guillet from the United States, they leaked information from the case to the press, where Guillet was mocked as "Inspecteur Clouseau."[2] In a "Style" section story two years later, *The Washington Post* remarked that "FBI agents . . . believed the French were more interested in discarded company papers than in landscaping."[3] When I met him, Guillet didn't appreciate being reminded of Houston, especially since he had just returned to France, his exile now over. Chirac's center-right coalition had won the March 29, 1993, parliamentary elections, and a new period of cohabitation had begun.

Just one month after Guillet's mishap in Houston, I watched, stunned, as Defense Minister Pierre Joxe was nearly thrown to the ground by U.S. Marine guards at the Paris air show. Joxe had crossed the rope line keeping the public away from the F-117A Stealth fighter and was attempting to rub his hand across its radar-deflecting skin. The Nighthawk had been one of the stars of Desert Storm, and it was the first time the United States had put the previously top-secret aircraft on public display. One way of learning the secrets of the radar-deflecting coatings, defense industry specialists told me after the incident, was to gather minute samples by rubbing against the surface with a hand or a cloth dipped in special glue.

Former DGSE director-general Pierre Marion publicly acknowledged the increasing emphasis his former service placed on economic espionage against "allied" countries such as the United States. "I think you have to separate very clearly what are the fields which are not covered by an alliance," he said. Armaments and diplomacy were two areas where allies "normally should not try to gather intelligence" on each other. "But in all other fields . . . states are competitors." This was especially true when it came to economic espionage. "I think that even during the cold war, getting intelligence in economic, technological, and industrial matters [from] a country [with] which you are allied . . . is not incompatible with the fact of being allied."[4]

Just before the 1991 Paris air show opened its gates, the French newsmagazine *L'Express* revealed that the DGSE had planted moles in the French offices of IBM, Texas Instruments, and Corning Glass between 1987 and 1989, to steal economic and industrial secrets on behalf of French state-owned enterprises. Marion confirmed the story to NBC's *Exposé*, which broadcast his interview on September 13, 1991. But when pressed by French state-run radio, Marion denied the most spectacular allegation of the NBC documentary, that state-owned Air France regularly planted microphones in the seats of its first-class compartment, to record the conversations of U.S. businessmen.* However, he did acknowledge

---

*Marion had been president of Air France before taking over as French spy chief in 1981.

that French intelligence officers regularly "visited" the Paris hotel rooms of U.S. businessmen, to take a look at confidential papers. Indeed, several businessmen had complained that while staying at the Concorde Lafayette, operated by Air France, their rooms had been broken into and important papers and laptop computers stolen.[5]

The misdeeds of Marion's former service came to light through a bizarre accident. In early 1989, a large manila envelope was returned by the French post office to its sender because the address label had come off. The sender listed on the envelope was an employee at IBM's head office in France. IBM security officers opened the package and were stunned to find that it contained highly confidential company documents. They called in the CIA and the FBI, who after a seven-month joint investigation identified three French moles working for the company.[6] As the investigation broadened out, the CIA and the FBI discovered French moles burrowed deep at Texas Instruments, Corning Glass, and several other U.S. companies operating in France, who were rifling company secrets on virtually a daily basis. All had been planted by the DGSE as part of Operation Chameleon, a top-secret program Marion had initiated in the early 1980s.[7] When the State Department delivered an official protest in November 1989, the French initially denied any involvement with the moles but ultimately acknowledged their activities. According to Claude Silberzahn, the newly appointed DGSE director at the time, the scandal "was discussed at the highest level, by Presidents Bush and Mitterrand," and required fully "two years of difficult, confidential negotiations" with the FBI and the CIA to repair the damage. Despite the seriousness of the affair (Silberzahn openly referred to it as a "crisis"), he noted that the United States never asked the French to withdraw any DGSE officers or "honorary correspondents" working in the United States—a courtesy the French government would not always adopt, as we shall see.[8] The DGSE reportedly found jobs for all thirty undercover agents who were fired by their American employers, after they had been exposed by the FBI.[9]

The case of the French state-owned computer maker Compagnie des Machines Bull—one of the beneficiaries of the proprietary documents stolen by the DGSE moles—shows just how galling the French can sometimes be. In October 1993, Bull decided to sue its American competitor, Texas Instruments, in a U.S. court. Bull alleged that TI was illegally manufacturing a computer chip that Bull had patented in 1978 and wanted TI to send over technical drawings and production data so they could better evaluate the potential monetary damages. According to *Wall Street Journal* reporter John Fialka, Texas Instruments was about to comply when someone at the company noticed that Bull's chip was "uncannily similar" to one that had been designed by a TI scientist four years earlier. Texas Instruments lawyers summed up their findings in a legal brief to the court. "It is apparent that the French espionage agent discovered working as a TI employee in 1989 had been feeding information useful to Bull from TI's calculator division for thirty years."[10]

After the first Gulf War in 1991, the spying intensified and turned venomous. President Mitterrand increased the DGSE budget by 10 percent—at a time when other countries, including the United States, were decreasing their intelligence budgets—and ordered a dramatic reorganization of the service to expand the quality and quantity of human intelligence ("humint"). The number of case officers whose job was to identify potential spies was increased by one-third. But most important, the reorganization opened the doors to graduates of France's *grandes écoles,* the elite national universities that supplied the best and the brightest to the French civil service. Until then, most of the DGSE's foreign operatives and analysts had been military officers, little versed in economic espionage, which Mitterrand now placed at the very top of intelligence priorities. "The French have seen their market share in almost every area decline in recent years," said one American intelligence source. "They know that the cheapest and best way to keep their companies in the game is to steal information from the competition."[11] In key areas of the world, those competitors were American companies.

When President George H. W. Bush unveiled a Middle East Arms Control Initiative on May 29, 1991, that called for a CoCom-style arrangement for conventional arms sales, the French smelled a rat. U.S. companies were reaping a huge economic windfall from the first Gulf War and were squeezing the French out of major arms markets. Why all of a sudden was the Bush administration seeking an open exchange of information on international arms sales, many French defense contractors I spoke to wondered, especially since this was an area where lucrative backdoor dealings, bribes, and kickbacks to political parties had been the accepted norm for decades? At least, for the French.*

Jean-Michel Boucheron, a Socialist member of Parliament who headed the Defense Commission, saw no reason why the French Parliament should be given oversight over French arms exports just to meet U.S. norms for transparency. "All we need is a summary presentation of the government's arms export policy," Boucheron told a conference in Paris devoted to the new arms control proposals. "Once a year will do." (Imagine members of the U.S. Congress telling the White House they didn't want to be briefed on *anything*! The U.S. emphasis on transparency and accountability is one of the most significant differences between the French and U.S. political systems.) Boucheron suggested that major arms exporters should look at regional imbalances, with a view of limiting the sale of offensive weapons but nothing else. "This means the types of weapons that are needed to seize and hold territory: tanks, long-range artillery, and attack helicopters. For a country like Iraq, for instance, it would have been acceptable to acquire a force of 1,500 tanks. But purchases of 4,500 tanks shows the will to dominate the region. For this type of equipment, there could eventually be some kind of embargo."[12]

Adding to French suspicions were U.S. actions. At the same time the U.S. president was calling on other arms suppliers to exercise "restraint," his administration was asking Congress to approve the sale of forty new F-16 fighters to Egypt, a $7 billion arms package for Saudi Arabia, advanced Apache anti-tank helicopters for the United Arab Emirates, and billions more in weapons sales to other nations in the region, including Israel. In 1991 alone, Congress approved a total of $11.8 billion in new arms sales to the Middle East out of the $22 billion the administration initially sought in the annual classified proposal, known as the "Javits list," it sent to Congress. The 1992 Javits list request was even higher: $35 billion. Arms manufacturers throughout Europe cried foul, but nowhere were the protests louder than in France. "Sure, we've got arms control," said one top French executive I interviewed at the Dubai air show in November 1991. "The Americans now control the entire arms market. That's what happens when there's only one superpower. The only competitors the Americans

---

*Since 1976, U.S. companies were prohibited by the Foreign Corrupt Practices Act from engaging in bribery, which made senior corporate officials criminally liable if they got caught.

face today are themselves." François David, deputy international sales manager for Aérospatiale, called the U.S. foreign military financing program a "disguised government subsidy" and sought to convince the French government to increase export financing for French arms sales.[13]

The French lost out to American arms exporters in virtually every competition where they went head-to-head. They lost a deal to sell tanks to Saudi Arabia; they failed to convince the Kuwaitis after Desert Storm to resume buying Mirage jet fighters or combat helicopters; even in Qatar and the UAE, they were having difficulties. And the problems weren't confined to the Middle East.

The French began to suspect that the United States had an ulterior motive in mustering an allied coalition to toss Saddam Hussein out of Kuwait: destroying the French defense industry. "You want an example?" said Yves Sillard, head of the French Armaments Directorate, the DGA. "In June 1992, we launched negotiations with Taiwan to sell sixty Mirage 2000s. One month later, the Americans offered to sell the F-16, a proposal that had been on ice for eleven years. Why did they lift their own embargo at that precise moment? I have learned from a reliable source that President Bush was given a report from the U.S. aerospace industry explaining that if they failed to make the Taiwan sale, the French armaments industry would survive. And so Bush gave in."[14] That was pure nonsense, of course—the real reasons had to do with election-year politics—but Sillard's comment is indicative of the type of paranoia then current within the French elite.

One of the tools the French used to fight back was bribery. "Bribery is extremely difficult to prove," notes *Wall Street Journal* reporter John Fialka. "One possible sign is a sudden reversal in a contract that was thought to have been won." One such reversal was the $250 million competition to sell a communications satellite to the Arab Satellite Communications Organization (ARABSAT) in 1992. ARABSAT awarded the contract to Hughes Aircraft Company on September 30, 1992, but reversed its decision on April 12, 1993, giving the business instead to Aérospatiale. In a press release after that decision was announced, Hughes noted that "some manufacturers are willing to accept extreme risks to achieve market share."[15]

French industrial espionage against U.S. companies began to take on gigantic proportions. In a written response to questions submitted by the Senate Select Committee on Intelligence in 1994, the CIA cited seventy-two cases within a seventeen-month period where foreign corporations had used "questionable business practices" against U.S. competitors, which wound up costing the American companies "about $30 billion" in lost contracts and lost jobs.[16]

R. James Woolsey acknowledged during his confirmation hearings as CIA director in February 1993 that responding to economic espionage had become a major challenge for the intelligence community. In a November 1993 speech to businessmen in Chicago, he was more specific. From now on, the CIA would take steps to protect U.S. companies from foreign espionage. "No more Mr. Nice Guy," he said. The new "get tough" policy did not mean the United States intended to engage in industrial espionage on behalf of U.S. companies, however. Whenever the agency detected that "foreign bribery occurs or is about to occur," U.S. officials would pass on the information to foreign decision makers. "Most such companies never realize that they have received our assistance," Woolsey told a Senate panel, "and even state publicly that they do not need it. That is fine with us. It is the nature of the intelligence business."[17]

Even today, Woolsey won't get into specifics about the covert war between the U.S. and French intelligence services that raged just beneath the surface during his tenure as CIA director, referring reporters to his published comments, which have been vetted by the CIA.[18] In those comments, he singled out by name just two foreign firms. Both of them were French.

Things looked different, of course, from the other side of the Atlantic. Pierre Chiquet was president of the newly renamed GIAT Industries, sole manufacturer of French tanks, when the French won their first major arms export contract to the Gulf since Desert Storm in February 1993—a $4 billion contract to supply 436 AMX Leclerc main battle tanks, ammunition, training, and maintenance to the United Arab Emirates.[19] It was a major coup for the French and for Chiquet personally. For the French, it signaled a comeback after the many humiliations of the Gulf War, when the expensive, sophisticated French weapons in Iraq's arsenal were shattered by the American military like so many toys. For Chiquet, it was a victory over his personal and bureaucratic foes, who wanted GIAT to use their overseas "networks" to channel bribes and kickbacks to their friends. Against all expectations, GIAT succeeded in selling to the UAE a tank that did not exist except on paper, while promising to draw French investments to the UAE that it acknowledged it couldn't find. It was an extraordinary feat that took the Americans almost totally by surprise. All of a sudden, an ecstatic Chiquet began to see markets everywhere that previously had seemed closed. "Oman isn't yet closed; neither is Kuwait," he told me in Abu Dhabi. GIAT could sell "up to one thousand tanks" in the Gulf alone.[20]

The main competitor of the French for the UAE tank deal was General Dynamics, which was presenting the Abrams M1A2. It was so sure it had the contract in the bag that company officials had already rented a ballroom at the Intercontinental Hotel for a lavish victory celebration and had sent out embossed invitations. When the Abu Dhabi government announced on February 14, 1993, at the International Defense Equipment Exhibition (IDEX) that the French had won the contract, the party was unceremoniously canceled. General Dynamics salesmen I spoke to in Abu Dhabi the next day blamed the Clinton administration for failing to provide the political support they needed to clinch the deal. At an emergency meeting that morning at the U.S. embassy, "we were basically told not to expect any help," one official told me. "General Dynamics was told not to rock the boat, since there were higher U.S. interests involved." One of those interests, he hinted, was to allow the French their share of the post–Gulf War arms market.[21]

Marriage counselors advise their clients to try to put themselves in each other's skins, to get a better view of their own actions. It was something from which the Americans and the French could have benefited, so dramatically different were their versions of these (and so many other) events. In a memoir published four years later, Chiquet claimed that the U.S. government had tried to block the French sale from the get-go, placing GIAT's top arms salesman, Philippe Lethier, under surveillance. "The CIA followed our man from hotel to hotel in Abu Dhabi," he wrote. "Every day, Philippe had to change residence."[22]

According to Chiquet, his thirty-five-year-old assistant had mysteriously opened doors to the top decision makers in Abu Dhabi on the sole merits of being totally honest with them about the French tank: "This total frankness became our secret weapon. . . . Aware of their own weaknesses, our clients wanted to deal with us as friends. And friends tell each other everything." So Lethier decided to tell the Emiratis the truth. "He told them that the tank being developed by GIAT existed only as a prototype, but that it was undoubtedly going to be the most advanced tank in the world," Chiquet writes. And voilà, based on those frank assertions that

France was developing a beautiful paper tank, a \$4 billion contract fell into their lap.

In the real world, of course, things don't happen quite like that. Lethier's brother was a colonel in the DGSE, perhaps leading the CIA—if indeed they followed Lethier around—to believe that he also worked for French intelligence. And the Gulf oil states were notoriously awash with bribery, kickbacks, and corruption, to which the French contributed (and benefited) with all the abandon of a fallen woman delecting forbidden fruit.[23] Within French defense industry circles it was well-known that Lethier had been ordered by Chiquet to develop his own network of inter-mediaries and commission agents, much to the anger of arms export of-fices SOFMA and SOFRESA, which had built up their networks over decades.

The competition with General Dynamics went right down to the wire, with French defense minister Pierre Joxe flying in to oversee the negotia-tions from a suite in the Intercontinental Hotel. Lethier shuttled back and forth between the palace of armed forces chief of staff Sheikh Mohammad bin Zayed and Joxe's hotel suite to report each new development. Each time he returned from meeting with the Emiratis, Joxe became more and more worried.

"So, Lethier, have we lost?" Joxe said at one point.

"No, *Monsieur le Ministre,* they haven't yet made their decision."

The real discussions, Chiquet says, were "going on behind closed doors, between Sheikh Khalifa, the crown prince, and Sheikh Mohammad, his half-brother, the army chief of staff."[24]

What Chiquet doesn't report, of course, is how Lethier succeeded in influencing the final decision and what promises he made. Indeed, the French government ultimately suspended deliveries of the Leclerc in 2001 because of an apparently hidden clause in the contract that required them to retrofit at no cost all tanks previously delivered to the specifications of the latest Leclerc coming out of the factory. That small detail, which ap-pears to have been added as a last-minute sweetener, was estimated to have cost the manufacturer 1.2 billion Euros (\$1.6 billion)—fully one-third of the entire contract price. (Imagine General Motors agreeing to upgrade your 1994 Chevy Corvette every year for a decade, without you having to shell out a nickel!) *Le Monde* attributed the staggering losses to "an agree-ment poorly negotiated from the start by the previous management"—

that is, Chiquet and Lethier.[25] A French government audit found that each Leclerc tank was costing French taxpayers 100 million francs—not the 28 million francs Chiquet claimed.[26] Subsequent French press reports alleged that seventy-three separate commissions were paid on the deal, "a good number of them coming back to Chirac's orbit."[27]

Chiquet was convinced that the CIA was behind every woe that beset the French. The very night the contract was announced, "the most poisonous rumors ran the streets of Abu Dhabi: our tank didn't exist, GIAT Industries was going bankrupt, and I don't know what else." When the Arab press published many of those statements the next day—which their reporters had heard from other French defense contractors in Abu Dhabi, just as I had—Chiquet said the onslaught "bore a distinct signature: it was as if you could see the shadow of the honorable correspondents of the CIA parading on the front pages of *Al-Watan al-Arabi*," a popular Arab-language daily published in London.[28] Even today, one French arms dealer I spoke to insisted that the Americans were "sabotaging" the tanks at the factory.

"Yes, my continental European friends, we have spied on you," former CIA director Jim Woolsey wrote playfully in the *Wall Street Journal.* But it wasn't to steal technology or to benefit American manufacturers. The real reason, said Woolsey, was bribery. "That's right, my continental friends, we have spied on you because you bribe. Your companies' products are often more costly, less technically advanced, or both, than your American competitors. As a result you bribe a lot. So complicit are your governments that in several European countries bribes still are tax-deductible."

Contrary to the practice of the DGSE, which handed over the fruits of economic espionage to French state-owned companies to help them win contracts, the CIA gave its espionage product to the foreign government the Europeans were seeking to bribe, "and [we] tell its officials that we don't take kindly to such corruption." Often those countries respond by "giving the most meritorious bid (sometimes American, sometimes not) all or part of the contract. This upsets you, and sometimes creates recriminations between your bribers and the other country's bribes, and this occasionally becomes a public scandal. We love it."

The only two cases Woolsey cited by name involved Thomson-CSF, which was alleged to have bribed members of a Brazilian government selection panel in a 7-billion-franc radar and satellite contract that pitted it

against Raytheon, and Airbus, said to have offered bribes to a Saudi official. In both cases, Woolsey acknowledged that the CIA had intervened.[29]

The covert intelligence war between the United States and France roared
out into the open in April 1993, when a reporter for the Knight Ridder
newspapers, Frank Greve, received an unmarked brown envelope at his
Washington, D.C., office. Someone had hand-delivered it to the reception
desk; it bore no postage and no return address. Inside was a twenty-one-
page document, stamped "Defense Confidential," that took the wraps off
the aggressive French espionage effort against the United States. The document purported to be the U.S. section of the DGSE's annual worldwide
collection plan, formatted as a tasking memo for French intelligence station chiefs overseas from the Department of Economics, Science, and
Technology (DEST).

The spy plan "targeted 49 U.S. high-tech companies, 24 financial insti-
tutions and six U.S. government agencies with important roles in international trade," Greve wrote. The French spying effort "focused on research
breakthroughs and marketing strategies of leading edge U.S. aerospace
and defense contractors that compete directly with French firms" and
rated U.S. technical and commercial targets on a scale from 1 to 3. The
highest priority was given to companies such as Boeing, Ford Aerospace,
Hughes Aircraft Co., Lockheed, and other defense contractors that were
competing directly with French state-owned firms.

For instance, from Boeing and McDonnell Douglas, French high-tech
spies were tasked to acquire a broad range of technical data as well as commercial strategies, to help the European Airbus consortium in its epic battle to wrest market share for its civilian airliners away from the American
giants. From the Space Systems Division of General Dynamics, the French
sought technical data on the Atlas/Centaur launch vehicles "competing
with Ariane," the French-built commercial space launcher. From Lockheed,
the French placed top priority on acquiring information on the still secret
advanced tactical fighter program. Of particular interest, the tasking
memo advised, were "aerodynamic and infra-red stealth integration of pas-
sive sensors." There were dozens more examples.

In most circumstances where a reporter comes across a classified document involving extremely sensitive intelligence questions such as this, the
CIA usually refrains from comment. In this case, Greve and other reporters

who picked up on his story found that CIA spokesmen (that would be those "senior U.S. government experts" of unspecified affiliation who get quoted in such stories) were very eager to authenticate the French document and to provide some useful background. "The list dovetails with the French orientation, their interests, their defense industrial policy, and where their deficiencies are in military technology," one "U.S. government expert" told Greve. Another official in another agency "confirmed that the French intelligence unit said to have prepared the list—the Department of Economics, Science, and Technology—was known to gather covert intelligence for French companies." When Greve called the French embassy in Washington, D.C., they went nuts. After conferring with Paris on a Friday afternoon, an embassy spokesman issued a one-line statement: "There is nothing in this document to indicate it was released by French government offices."[30] Of course not: it was classified! DGSE chief Claude Silberzahn said the document was "a fake that had been cobbled together from a real document, written earlier, in which our service summarized companies around the world engaged in critical technologies, not targets of espionage."[31]

Congress had a field day with the revelations. Secrets lost to allies such as France through espionage "have cost American companies billions of dollars and have hurt U.S. competitiveness," said House judiciary chairman Jack Brooks (D-Tex.). "The French are trying to rob American industry blind," said Representative Frank Wolf (R-Va.). "I do not object to foreign competition, but let us make sure it is all above the table." He and others urged the federal government to withdraw its participation in that year's Paris air show. "We cannot afford to send employees from our government to France where they may fall victim to cat burglar tactics," he said. He also urged U.S. defense and aerospace firms to boycott the air show.

Hughes chairman C. Michael Armstrong said he had doubts already about attending the 1993 Paris air show because of the cost, but the French intelligence effort was "the last straw" in his decision to forgo the trip. However, many U.S. defense contractors I spoke to at the air show that year thought the reports were overblown and regretted the lack of Defense Department participation. Secretary of Commerce Ron Brown had tried to convince the Pentagon at the last minute to send a B2 bomber for the static display and prominently toured the show in an effort to boost morale of those U.S. companies that maintained their presence. A former top French Defense Ministry official, who now headed a major French aerospace concern, laughed off the espionage story. The United States and France "have a long history of strategic cooperation," he said, "but that doesn't preclude competition."[32] After all, what was a little spying among friends?

That wasn't what Prime Minister Édouard Balladur thought in January 1994 when he got off his plane in Riyadh, Saudi Arabia. During the flight from Paris, Balladur phoned his contacts at Airbus, ensuring he had the latest details of the final round of negotiations they had held with the Saudis for a gigantic contract to renew the entire commercial fleet of Saudi Arabia airlines. Balladur was ecstatic at the prospect of announcing a 30-billion-franc (nearly $6 billion) triumph for French export industries. The always courteous former finance minister had been chosen by the center-right coalition to head the latest round of cohabitation with Mitterrand after the legislative elections of March 1993. Although he was an ally of Jacques Chirac, he also increasingly had become his rival. Chirac had chosen to stay on the sidelines to lay the groundwork for a presidential bid in 1995, reasoning that the day-to-day task of governing France would distract him from running for president. But power is seductive, and the more Balladur tasted the premiership, the more he was convinced to run for president. Bringing home the bacon from Saudi Arabia in such a spectacular way was sure to enhance his political career.

Crown Prince Abdallah and Defense Minister Sultan bin Abdulaziz welcomed Balladur in the VIP tent at the airport. But instead of contracts ready to be initialed, the Saudis told him they were reconsidering. According to a detailed account of Balladur's trip that appeared in the French newsweekly *Le Nouvel Observateur*, the NSA had picked up Balladur's conversation "and within the hour, had sent the White House the latest European proposals." Two months later, the Saudis announced they were buying American planes. Although "the Americans would have signed the contract anyway," the French magazine conceded, "the anecdote is symptomatic: to win the economic battle and win markets, the Americans from now on are relying on their powerful secret service."[33] Balladur was furious. But instead of shooting off his mouth, as Chirac would have done, he decided to get even.

On February 22, 1995, *Le Monde* revealed that the French government had asked five suspected American spies to leave the country, for activities "incompatible with their status." Four of the five were diplomats, including the CIA deputy chief of station, Joseph Detrani. The fifth, identified in the press as Mary Ann Baumgartner, claimed to work as a public relations specialist for a Texas-based foundation that wanted to save the Amazon rain forest. In detailed leaks from the Interior Ministry that were based on the DST's counterespionage investigation, it appeared that Ms. Baumgartner had paid $400 to a young aide working for Balladur named Henri Plagnol, to write a five-page paper on "France's relations with NATO." She also took him to lunch "on four or five occasions."[34]

According to the Interior Ministry, Plagnol had informed the DST of the American woman's advances from the start and agreed to become a double agent. As his relationship with Ms. Baumgartner developed, Plagnol was taken on seven occasions to meet with a CIA officer who had come down from Brussels. The deep, dark secrets the Americans were seeking revolved around a mystery that baffled them: Why in the world were the French threatening to block a new round of international trade talks at GATT, the General Agreement on Tariffs and Trade, over agricultural subsidies and the protection of their thriving domestic television and movie industry? The Americans who "interrogated" the young Plagnol were so skilled that they failed to notice they were under surveillance. The French had great fun laying out photographs, hotel registration signatures, and credit card imprints they claimed proved that the Americans "were using false identities" and holding clandestine meetings in an attempt to recruit French officials, providing the pretext for their expulsion.

While the French position at GATT might have been hard for Americans to understand (the French feel very strongly about protecting their farmers and their cinematographers, as part of their way of life), it was hardly a secret. "This CIA operation seems a bit silly to me, carried out by amateurs," said French GATT negotiator Bernard Miyet. "What could they possibly have learned that wasn't already in the press? The Americans would have been better advised to defend their position in Europe as we do: openly."[35] Claude Silberzahn, who had recently been replaced as DGSE director, agreed: "Between allies, this type of [expulsion] request can only be based on an extremely serious affair." While claiming not to know all the details, since the counterespionage work was carried out by the DST, "still I wonder about the GATT aspect of this business. What was there really worth spying on? In this type of negotiation, there doesn't exist the text of the French position, locked deep in some safe, that our adversaries could acquire."[36]

A subsequent investigation by the CIA inspector general acknowledged that the affair had been a series of "blunders," and Woolsey's successor, John Deutch, came to Paris to mend fences. Nevertheless, U.S. officials were shocked at the publicity the French gave to what normally would have been handled through back channels. "This will not blow over in a matter of months," an unnamed U.S. official told *The Washington Post.* "It will take several years, at least, before we can talk about serious cooperation again in intelligence matters."[37]

It soon became apparent that the timing and the publicity of the spy scandal had been orchestrated by Balladur and Pasqua, his political ally in the upcoming presidential primary against Chirac, with the aim of distracting public opinion from a wiretapping scandal that was taking on disastrous proportions. (Balladur had authorized Pasqua to place an illegal wiretap on the father-in-law of a judge who was investigating shady political finances in Pasqua's district west of Paris. The French press was calling it Balladur's "Watergate.")

One person took special pleasure in helping the DST ferret out the American spies: Bernard Guillet, who was now back in Paris and working as Pasqua's "diplomatic adviser." According to French press reports, he was also the one who leaked information to the press. For the former consul general of Houston, Texas, giving the boot to five Americans in France carried with it a sweet smell he savored like a fine wine: revenge.


B ut differences over spying and major export contracts weren't all that began to drive France and America further and further apart. There was also the matter of Iraq.

As the midnight buffet was being served at the country estate of our Lebanese host outside of Grasse, Guillet sits next to a tall, trim Samir Traboulsi, who is wearing a white suit, a dark blue tie, and a deep tan. A Franco-Lebanese businessman who did work for Thomson-CSF, Traboulsi received the Légion d'Honneur from former Gaullist interior minister Charles Pasqua for unspecified services to *La Maison France.* Traboulsi is proudly escorting his eighteen-year-old daughter, whose stunning Brazilian beauty betrays her mother's Latin genes. The two of them could have stepped out of a James Bond movie straight from the casino in nearby Monte Carlo. Framed against their elegance, Bernard Guillet's strong jaw and face carved in stone make him appear more like a former parachutist than the diplomatic adviser to a French government minister.

France made a big mistake taking sides with the United States in the Gulf War, Guillet says in response to my question about whether the French had known about Iraq's clandestine nuclear weapons program. "Saddam never opposed the West. He never tried to counter American or Western interests. What do we know about his bomb? We knew that it was not aimed against us any more than it was aimed at you. France gained nothing and lost much by its support for the Americans in the Gulf War."

At my side is a well-known Lebanese businessman, who has just invited me to return to Baghdad on his private jet to meet with Deputy Prime Minister Tariq Aziz. Next to him sits a dark-skinned Arab with a long, square jaw and a slight paunch, who looks unmistakably Iraqi. My tablemate introduces him to the others in Arabic, and my heart skips a beat: it is Anees Mansour Wadi, the man who is under indictment in Ohio and Los Angeles for having served as Hussein Kamil al-Majid's agent in the United States for the procurement of nuclear and ballistic missile technologies in the late 1980s.

Guillet is perfectly at home surrounded by these middlemen and bagmen who helped arm Iraq in the 1980s. He wags his finger at me, the only American present: France should break its alliance with the United States and help Saddam again, he says, just as it had in the 1980s. "It's time for France to make an about-face, before it is too late. Iraq is our natural ally in the Gulf."

I'm sure, even today, that Guillet was just speaking his mind. After all, we were in a social setting, albeit one rich in extravagance, where teaming with the Iraqi dictator seemed far more normal than professing belief in the two-hundred-year-old U.S.-French alliance. But Guillet actually *preferred* the regime of Saddam Hussein to the United States, for whom his antipathy was physically palpable.

Events would prove that his words, spoken in August 1994, were prophetic.

# 10

# Old Lovers

---

G uillet's presence in the south of France at a social gathering that brought together some of the biggest players in the still secret French trade with Iraq was no accident. In fact, Guillet and his boss, Interior Minister Charles Pasqua, reportedly were at the center of the effort to renew French commercial relations with Iraq after the first Gulf War.[1]

After Saddam's invasion of Kuwait in August 1990, the United Nations Security Council unanimously (that is, with French support) imposed a total trade embargo on Iraq, including a worldwide ban on the sale of Iraqi oil. It also grounded Iraqi Airways from flying beyond Iraq's borders and froze all funds belonging to Iraq or Iraqi nationals. On April 3, 1991, one month after Saddam's defeat at the hands of the international coalition led by the United States, the UN Security Council passed resolution 687 declaring a cease-fire and mandating the destruction of Iraq's weapons of mass destruction within ninety days.

To lead the disarmament effort, UN secretary-general Pérez de Cuéllar tapped diplomat Rolf Ekeus, who was Sweden's envoy to the Commission on Security and Cooperation in Europe, a post–cold war disarmament body based in Vienna. "The UN wanted someone from a neutral country with knowledge of industrial processes," Ekeus told me and CBS Evening News producers Joel Bernstein and Linda Mason over lunch in New York. "I was the one left on the beach after the flood."

Ekeus said that after reading the language of the Security Council resolution, he thought the job would be a snap. "I read the paragraph in 687 about the oil embargo and said: This guy is losing $60 million per day, $1.6 billion per month. So I told my family I had better hurry to New York. If I spent two days to get my affairs in order, Iraq would lose $120 million. I thought it would take thirty days to get the full final Iraqi disclosure of their weapons programs." Seven years later, when Ekeus finally left the UN Special Commission for the Disarmament of Iraq (UNSCOM), the Baghdad regime was still turning in what he called "full final fairy tales" instead of a frank accounting of their chemical, biological, missile, and nuclear weapons programs.[2]

Ekeus expressed astonishment on many occasions over Saddam Hussein's behavior. "All he had to do to get sanctions lifted," Ekeus remarked to me once, "was to make a full accounting of his weapons programs. After Desert Storm, Iraq couldn't have had more than a few billion dollars' worth of weapons of mass destruction. And yet to preserve this, they are forgoing $20 billion a year in oil sales." That's how important the weapons were to Saddam.

While Saddam's officers signed the cease-fire at a hastily pitched tent at Safwan Air Base in southern Iraq on March 3, 1991, he continued to refer to Kuwait as the "nineteenth province" of Iraq and refused to turn over any information on the six hundred–some Kuwaitis who were still missing after the war. (Many of them were probably killed during resistance operations against the Iraqi occupation, but some were believed to be held in secret Iraqi jails.) And despite the arrival of UN arms inspectors in April 1991, he began to rebuild his weapons plants, initially staying within the restrictions imposed by Security Council resolution 687, which allowed him to continue producing conventional weapons without limitation and ballistic missiles with a range of 150 kilometers or less but prohibited the production of nuclear, chemical, and biological weapons.

President George H. W. Bush's last act in office, on January 17, 1993, was to send cruise missiles crashing into several facilities suspected of producing parts for these prohibited weapons programs. Saddam returned the favor when the former U.S. president traveled to Kuwait in April 1993 by dispatching a team of Iraqi intelligence operatives to Kuwait with orders to assassinate Bush.

France condemned the January 17, 1993, attack, claiming that the United States had acted "unilaterally" and had "gone beyond" the framework of UN Security Council resolutions. (Sound familiar?) But the French were simply wrong. The Security Council unequivocally required Saddam (1) to destroy all weapons of mass destruction; (2) to make a full accounting of his past WMD programs, including his overseas supplier networks; and (3) to submit to long-term monitoring by UNSCOM of all industrial plants in Iraq to ensure that all sensitive equipment with potential weapons applications was being used strictly for civilian purposes.[3] Instead, Saddam Hussein was in total defiance of all these United Nations demands and was playing a shell game with UN inspectors, hauling key components for his banned weapons programs on eighteen-wheel trucks around the country in advance of the UN inspection teams.

As time went on, Saddam grew more confident that the French would succeed in preventing any further U.S. attack, and he began rebuilding his military-industrial infrastructure right under the noses of the UN inspectors. In January 1992, Iraq announced that it had already repaired and retooled more than two hundred military production lines. Saddam's son-in-law Hussein Kamil returned to power that February after a brief fall from grace resulting from a commercial dispute with Saddam's eldest son, Uday, and was once again put in charge of the military industries and Iraq's reconstruction effort. As before the war, Kamil's extremely able technical assistants, Lieutenant General Amir Hamoodi al-Saadi and Lieutenant General Amir Rashid al-Ubaydi, devised programs that thoroughly integrated civilian with military production. As al-Saadi told me in Baghdad, beyond the purpose of camouflaging military production—"a lesson we learned from war"—there was a purely practical side to the commingling. "We couldn't afford to have separate facilities for military and civilian production," he said.

The Al-Rabiya industrial complex at Zaafarniyah, which the United States partially destroyed in the January 17 attack, had continued to manufacture parts for uranium enrichment calutrons despite four visits by UNSCOM inspectors and two visits by International Atomic Energy Agency teams. Although Ekeus was relentlessly pressing the Iraqis to agree to a long-term monitoring scheme, his fellow Swede at the IAEA in Vienna, Hans Blix, was pressing with as much urgency to call it quits, end the sanctions, and return to business as usual. Blix's own experts had compiled an inventory of 603 dual-use machine tools that had survived the Gulf War that were of particular concern because they were critical for manufacturing parts and special equipment for the nuclear weapons program. The data included who had sold them, which Iraqi entity had initially purchased them, where they had been found, and their technical specifications. A source in Vienna gave me the list, which I immediately entered into a database. Upon analysis, it turned out that seventy-eight of these critical machines—13 percent—had been found in Al-Rabiya by UN arms inspectors, including equipment specifically tooled to produce parts for electromagnetic isotope separation (EMIS) and ultracentrifuge enrichment devices. Despite the clear relevance of this plant complex to Saddam's clandestine nuclear weapons program, Blix ordered the IAEA not to place controls on these machines and eventually to drop Al-Rabiya from the list of inspection sites. U.S. military planners concluded that the Iraqis considered the "sanitized" plant a safe haven for illicit activity and asked the president for authority to take it out.[4] They accomplished that mission on January 17, 1993.

Speaking before the Washington Institute for Near East Policy on March 24, 1993, Ekeus publicly warned that Iraq fully intended to restore its military-industrial base. "The capabilities are there, the supply system including banks and payments is there. The day the oil embargo is lifted, Iraq will get all the cash, and that will be a great concern. . . . With the cash, the suppliers, and the skills they will be able to reestablish all the weapons programs," Ekeus said. "It may grow up like mushrooms after the rain."[5]

The rebuilding was going on despite the most rigorous international economic sanctions imposed on any nation since World War II and despite what were supposed to be intrusive inspections of Iraqi weapons facilities by UNSCOM and the IAEA. With the imposition of sanctions, Saddam had declared his crushing foreign debt null and void, so ironically he had lots of cash, with fresh money coming in from extensive black market oil sales. He could afford to give his suppliers lots of incentives to violate the embargo; and rarely did they face any penalty. The big companies never got caught, and the small black market traders ran risks only if they operated within reach of U.S. Customs. I don't know of a single case in Europe—not one—where company executives who violated the UN sanctions on Iraq went to jail.

All through 1992 and 1993, there were unconfirmed reports that major French defense companies were selling spare parts to Iraq through front companies in Amman, Jordan; South Africa; and elsewhere. The companies cited to me by different sources—including French intermediaries I met in Amman—all denied having approved such sales, as did the French government. But by late 1992, the results were already in: Iraqi air force Mirage fighter jets were up in the air once again, brazenly flying "training" missions along the borders of the southern no-fly zone. Despite the denials, the spare parts had come from somewhere.[6]

Sometimes Iraq's resupply efforts were thwarted by U.S. intelligence, which fed information to coalition naval forces monitoring commercial traffic into the Jordanian port of Aqaba, where most of Iraq's imports flowed. In June 1993, allied warships intercepted a French-operated freighter, the *Ville de Vega*, carrying hydrofluoric acid, a chemical that proliferation analysts said could be used by Iraq for its uranium enrichment program. Because of the French involvement, I was told, the affair was hushed up and the ship turned away before it could dock.[7] But not long afterward, the French pressed hard at the UN to end the allied naval blockade of Iraq.

Another sure sign to his overseas partners that he was back in business was Saddam's appointment in September 1993 of Safa Hadi Jawad al-Habobi as oil minister. Throughout the 1980s, al-Habobi had worked out of London as Saddam Hussein's top procurement officer. As head of the Technology and Development Group (TDG), he spearheaded Iraq's takeover of British machine tool manufacturer Matrix Churchill and its U.S.-based subsidiary in Ohio. When Banca Nazionale del Lavoro executives in Atlanta, Georgia, had a problem that needed solving in their $4 billion loan portfolio to Iraq, they went to see al-Habobi. As Saddam's personal representative, al-Habobi negotiated loans, purchased equipment for the clandestine uranium enrichment programs, and sent letters to U.S. suppliers demanding a 10 percent kickback on commercial contracts. It was a technique the Iraqis would exploit increasingly.[8]

I n October 1993, Tariq Aziz made what was intended to be a quiet trip to Paris to renew contacts with old friends in the French government, to clear the path for "especially big-ticket oil deals." The trip was said to have been arranged by Interior Minister Pasqua "without the knowledge of the French foreign minister," Chirac ally Alain Juppé. When the Saudi-owned daily *Al-Sharq al-Awsat* got wind of the Iraqi's presence in Paris and his meetings with oil executives, the French hastily claimed that they had waived the UN ban on travel by senior Iraqi officials on "purely humanitarian" grounds and that Aziz had come to Paris for a series of medical tests involving a possible blocked artery.[9] U.S. intelligence officials began telling reporters that Pasqua was "coaching the Iraqis" on how to pitch their case in France but provided no details of the type of advice Pasqua was giving. The fiery interior minister had a reputation for his involvement in the "parallel networks" used by the Gaullists to finance their political activities going back more than thirty years, through the Service d'Action Civique and other groups.

Aziz was just one of many Iraqi officials who came to Paris to relaunch commercial ties during the UN embargo.[10] In February 1994, while working on a story on embargo busting for *Time* magazine, I returned to Paris, where I met with former French army chief of staff General Jeannou Lacaze, a rough-and-ready veteran of the operations wing of the French intelligence service, the DGSE. General Lacaze was a long-standing public friend of Saddam's and had signed an open letter published in *Le Figaro* on January 15, 1991, urging the French government not to join the allied coalition to fight Iraq. (Also signing the letter was André Giraud, the former defense minister who had worked so closely with the United States against Libya's Qaddafi.) Listening to Lacaze, who had just returned from Baghdad, it was as if the Gulf War had never taken place. He described a hustle-bustle of arms dealers and oil traders, including American firms, all of them knocking on Saddam's door. "It would be stupid for us to be the last ones in, when everyone else is lining up to sign contracts for the reconstruction of Iraq," he said bluntly.[11]

When no one kicked up a stink about this flaunting of the embargo, Foreign Ministry undersecretary Riyadh al-Qaysi went to Paris in March 1994 for a highly publicized official meeting with his Quai d'Orsay counterpart, Denis Bauchard. Iraqi state radio proudly announced that al-Qaysi had come to Paris "at the invitation of France" to discuss a resumption of Iraqi oil deliveries to France and the award of major reconstruction contracts to French firms. Meanwhile, the radio announced, Oil Ministry undersecretary Taha Humud was "putting the finishing touches on cooperation negotiations between Iraq and the French Total and Elf Aquitaine companies to develop oil investments in Iraq." The radio went on to report that competition among French, Italian, German, British, and U.S. companies was stiff. "Officials from these companies have been frequenting Baghdad for months to win contracts with Iraq, especially in the field of food, agriculture, and pharmaceutical items not included by the embargo. They are awaiting major deals worth tens of billions of dollars, as was the case in the seventies and eighties, once the embargo is completely lifted."[12] A senior State Department official accused the Iraqis of hyping the willingness of international businessmen to work with Baghdad again. "Iraq has been lying about its success in signing new contracts with European and American companies," he told me. "The French have been aiding this disinformation effort" by spreading lies about U.S. corporate executives visiting Baghdad.[13]

Disinformation or not, the strategy was successful. The Iraqi announcement that negotiations had begun rang out like a starter's gun. Oil executives, arms dealers, middlemen, and fixers of all stripes jumped out from the wings and made a mad dash for Baghdad, on the expectation that the UN trade embargo was about to collapse under the weight of collective greed. "In 1994, it was reasonable to think that sanctions would be lifted," a senior French official told me blandly years later.[14]

The French were increasingly brazen in their efforts on behalf of Saddam, despite his lack of cooperation with the UN inspectors. In the spring of 1994, they lobbied hard in support of a new resolution that would allow Iraq to partially reopen its oil pipeline through Turkey. Under the arrangement, Iraq was allowed to "flush" the pipeline of old oil—which the Turks argued was corroding the pipe—and fill it with fresh oil. Each "flush" was to yield around twelve million barrels of oil. Even at then deflated prices, Iraq stood to gain around $70 million per flush—and the resolution made clear there could be several flushes per year. "If you ask me," said James Placke, an oil analyst with Cambridge Energy Associates, "that sounds an awful lot like pumping oil." As an added sop to Saddam, the French pressed the Security Council to drop its long-standing demand that it control the funds. "We have deliberately left vague the question of how the money is spent," said French UN ambassador Jean-François Merimée. That dangerous omission, demanded by Saddam, was aimed at giving Iraq a legitimate source of cash it could use to purchase dual-use equipment on the international market.

There were many reasons why the French were so amenable to helping Saddam, and all of them had to do with money. Behind the scenes, intense negotiations were under way that would be worth $50 billion to the French state-owned oil company Total and huge kickbacks to the French politicians who greased the skids. If the French could pull it off, the rewards for their support of Saddam would make the arms-for-oil deals of the 1980s seem like small beer.

The French signaled their intentions at May, when they announced that they were ending naval patrols in the Gulf of Aqaba, a sore point for the Iraqis. The joint U.S.-French naval blockade off the coast of the Jordanian port that had been built by Iraq in the 1980s made it difficult and costly for Iraq to engage in massive smuggling. Indeed, the Pentagon reported that since the blockade began in August 1990, 20,000 ships had been intercepted, 9,000 boarded, and 480 diverted because they were carrying forbidden cargo to Aqaba. Dismantling the naval inspections was a major Iraqi demand. The French convinced the Security Council to replace the blockade with a loosey-goosey system of random inspections at the port itself that was abandoned almost as soon as it was set up.

On June 15, 1994, Iraq carried out its side of the bargain. After more than two years of negotiations that seemed to be going nowhere, all of a sudden the Iraqi Oil Ministry agreed to a massive new contract that gave French state-owned Total SA of France rights to the future production of the vast Nahr Umar oil field in southern Iraq. In an interview in Vienna, Iraqi oil minister Safa al-Habobi, Saddam's minister of procurement, confirmed the contract and added that his ministry had also "made considerable progress with Elf," the second French oil major, in negotiating terms for the Majnoon oil fields.[15] One week later, the French employers union, the CNPF, sent a delegation of twenty-eight CEOs to Baghdad, where they met with Lieutenant General Amir Rashid al-Ubaydi, the head of the Military Industrialization Commission and architect of much of Iraq's clandestine weapons infrastructure. According to the Baghdad government daily *Jumhuriyah*, the French were "ready to set up pharmaceutical industries in Iraq as well as factories to produce cars, agricultural machinery, petrochemicals, iron, steel, and aluminum."[16]

UNSCOM chairman Rolf Ekeus viewed these developments with alarm and hastily set off on a tour of European capitals to remind government leaders of Iraq's outstanding obligations under the Security Council resolutions. Given Iraq's track record, he understood that Saddam would use apparently civilian projects as a cover for massive purchases for his forbidden weapons programs. But the French didn't care. After Ekeus met in Paris with French foreign minister Alain Juppé, the Quai d'Orsay announced that the new agreements with Iraq were "not inconsistent" with the embargo. The following week, Fadel Otham, the head of Iraq's state oil marketing organization, SOMO, was scheduled to address an oil conference in Paris.

The key to all the French solicitude was the massive new commitment by Iraq to give France what amounted to a lock on Iraq's future oil revenues. While both the French and the Iraqis publicly lauded their new arrangement, the astonishing details of this accord with Total remained secret until former assistant secretary of defense Richard Perle referred to them repeatedly in speeches and interviews in 2003. "There's no doubt the French have big economic interests. If this war had been avoided," Perle told me, "they'd already be getting big contracts, starting with this huge oil concession."[17]

Gerald Hillman, an associate of Perle's on the Defense Policy Board, obtained a copy of the 154-page draft agreement between Iraq and Total. A political economist by training, Hillman called on friends in the oil business and went over the agreement with a fine-toothed comb. Almost immediately, he noticed that several numbered pages were left blank. "Were these sections concluded later?" he wondered. It wasn't the only oddity he found.

The Total contract to develop the Nahr Umar oil fields was "very one-sided," he told me. It was not an ordinary production agreement, which typically grants the foreign partner a maximum of 50 percent of the gross proceeds of the oil produced at the field they develop. Instead, Total was given 75 percent of the total production. "This is highly unusual," he said.

Then there was the fact that the contract included no advance payments by Total (called "bonus" payments in the contract), a standard arrangement whereby the foreign partner fronts cash to the oil-producing state against future revenues. "That suggests that the bonus was paid by some other method," Hillman said, "or that no consideration was agreed at the time. Whichever the case, it is a suspicious omission."

Beyond that, Saddam's government placed very low performance targets on Total as a condition for the French company to retain its contractual rights to the huge Nahr Umar field. "That, too, is fairly unusual," Hillman said, "because in a place as rich as Iraq's southern oil fields you would want more rapid development. It's odd to have very low production targets like this; the main impact is to reduce the risk to the oil company," by lowering the amount they are required to invest. The internal rate of return for Total was around 50 percent, based on a "minimal level" of success—a stupendous profit with zero risk, since the very first piece of the contract was to complete seismic testing of the field, already well-known in Iraq and to the oil industry as one of the richest oil fields in the world. In essence, Total's job was to drill and pump where the Iraqis told them to drill and pump, and to handle all the arrangements for importing state-of-the-art drilling gear. Iraq especially wanted large quantities of neutron generators, normally used for well logging. Documents discovered by UN arms inspectors in Iraq as well as the testimonies of former Iraqi nuclear engineers showed clearly that Iraq planned to use the neutron generators as nuclear "triggers," and had integrated them into its bomb design.

Hillman and his analysts ran a rough calculation of what the Total contract was worth, based on the bare minimum production allowed under the contract factored at the conservative oil price of $20 per barrel. "Over the seven-year initial period of this contract, Total was to earn a minimum of $50 billion," he told me. And producing the oil was just the first step to making money. "They could have had a separate deal for purchasing oil at a discount, and could expect to make additional money on each barrel of oil they transported." If they followed standard industry practice, Hillman added, they would also hedge the price by selling futures, options, and puts. "Total initially denied they had ever signed a contract, but admitted they had some kind of understanding with Iraq. How do you have an 'understanding' that is 154 pages long, for God's sake? This is not a thing you spend five minutes negotiating in some smoke-filled back room. This is a piece of real work."

But most remarkable of all was the fact that the contract depended entirely on the lifting of UN sanctions on Iraq. "So what the French are saying is, 'We will help you get the sanctions lifted, and when we do that, you give us this.' This is perfidy of the highest order."[18]

The French paid a heavy price for their open support of Saddam Hussein, although to this day they have never admitted it. A senior member of the Kuwaiti royal family I went to visit in March 1994 told me that Kuwait and Saudi Arabia were "so upset" with the French dalliance with Saddam that they took immediate countermeasures. "Kuwait has told companies currently in discussions with Iraq that the Kuwaiti people might not want to do business with them in the future," he said. In Saudi Arabia, it was even worse. "Siemens recently lost a $4 billion contract in Saudi Arabia because it accepted a $600,000 contract in Iraq." Remember French prime minister Édouard Balladur's unpleasant surprise when he arrived in Riyadh, thinking he was about to sign a $6 billion contract for civilian airliners? "King Fahd told us he was so upset with the French attitude toward Iraq that he decided to purchase $6 billion worth of Boeing airliners from the United States instead of from Airbus, despite the fact Airbus was offering a much sweeter deal."[19] To this day, the French remain convinced they lost the Saudi Airbus contract because of American dirty tricks, not because of their own policy decisions.

There was a sinister, unreported side to the French "perfidy" in Iraq. Just two months before signing the contract with Total, some twelve thousand Iraqi troops launched an offensive through the Howeiza marshes in southern Iraq from April 18 to 28, 1994. Hoshyar Zebari, a Kurdish member of the opposition Iraqi National Congress who went on to become foreign minister of the Iraqi provisional government in 2003, told me that the offensive was "specifically linked" to the oil deal with France. According to Zebari, the French were refusing to send their oil engineers into an area where they could potentially be kidnapped by rebel forces. So they suggested that the Iraqis "clean up" the area ahead of time. Thousands of Iraqi "marsh Arabs" paid the ultimate price for this particular instance of French cupidity.[20] Ultimately, Saddam ordered Hussein Kamil and his armaments engineers to divert the water sources feeding the marshes, drying up thousands of square miles of marshland and ending a way of life that had enchanted Western explorers since Wilfred Thesiger. Some three hundred thousand marsh Arabs went into forced exile in Iran, their way of life gone forever.

The French effort to get the UN sanctions on Iraq lifted was undercut by Saddam himself, who once again totally misread Western public opinion and the will of Western governments in October 1994, when he moved military forces to the border with Kuwait in preparation for a second attack. Secretary of Defense William Perry immediately ordered the reinforcement of the bare-bones U.S. force in Kuwait, while Secretary of State Warren Christopher succeeded in convincing the United Nations to expand the no-fly zone then in force to also include a "no-drive" zone in southern Iraq. The French downplayed the Iraqi troop movements, disclaiming any hostile intent on Saddam's part. The inimitable Jean-Pierre Chevènement, the left-wing Gaullist who sent the French aircraft carrier *Clemenceau* steaming into the Gulf in 1991 with its flight deck packed with helicopters and trucks, rushed to Baghdad, where he told Shebab (Youth) television that France would help Iraq "find a way out of this embargo."[21] Other French supporters of Saddam soon followed in his footsteps, from the deputy chairman of Jean-Marie Le Pen's extreme right National Front, Bruno Gollnisch, to former Socialist foreign minister and third world weeper-in-chief, Claude Cheysson. On November 21, 1994, Iraq repaid the favors and announced that it planned to buy twenty Airbus jets for the still grounded national air carrier. A beaming Tariq Aziz showed up in Paris in January 1995, where his family liked to shop at Galleries Lafayette (I know because I've got their Amex receipts), and joined with French foreign minister Alain Juppé to celebrate the reopening of the Iraqi embassy in France.

The next chapter of the France-Iraq saga was subtly shaped by the corruption scandals of 1994–1995 that Interior Minister Charles Pasqua tried to obsfuscate by concocting an anti-American spy frenzy, in an attempt to deflect attention from his political ally in the presidential race, Prime Minister Édouard Balladur. An investigative magistrate in the Paris suburb of Créteil, Eric Halphen, was looking into apparent kickbacks paid on construction and maintenance contracts for the Bureau of Public Housing, Habitation à loyer modéré (HLM), in Paris and its suburbs. Ironically, Halphen's investigation would ultimately lead to Chirac's doorstep. But in the early stages, Pasqua was concerned because Halphen was examining an alleged kickback scheme in the Hauts de Seine, the regional government Pasqua headed. In December 1994, Halphen's father-in-law, Dr. Jean-Pierre Maréchal, was arrested at a Paris airport just as a Pasqua adviser "was handing over a suitcase full of cash, allegedly aimed at buying the clemency of his son-in-law." While Halphen acknowledges in his memoir the cupidity of his relative, he believed that Pasqua's team was seeking to undermine his investigation, with Balladur's approval.[22] Considered a shoe-in as the center-right candidate for president before the scandals erupted, Balladur lost the April 23, 1995, primary to Chirac by a significant margin. A good loser, he urged his troops to support Chirac in the May 7 runoff against Socialist Party leader Lionel Jospin, which Chirac won with 52 percent of the vote.

Chirac named political ally and personal confidant Alain Juppé as prime minister and brought over Juppé's chief of staff at the Foreign Ministry as chief of staff at the Élysée Palace. Chirac's new aide, Dominique de Villepin, was a forty-one-year-old diplomat who prided himself on the American-accented English he had picked up during a tour of duty as press secretary at the French embassy in Washington, D.C., and as a diplomat's son in New York. According to Chirac biographers Marie-Bénédicte Allaire and Philippe Goulliaud, the young Villepin "won the confidence of Chirac during the dark hours of the campaign [because] he was one of the few who kept insisting, no matter how bad the news, that [Chirac] would be the next president."[23] Flattering Prince Hal brought him big rewards.

In mid-October 1995, Chirac was preparing to attend what promised to be a stormy session of the United Nations General Assembly in New York. Almost as soon as he took power, the new French president announced his decision to break a three-year moratorium on nuclear tests imposed by his predecessor, François Mitterrand. The French Atomic Energy Commission and the nuclear planners at the Defense Ministry had convinced the new president that they needed one last campaign of eight nuclear tests to perfect a new-generation warhead for the M5 missile and to guarantee the reliability of the French nuclear arsenal once France signed the Comprehensive Test Ban Treaty then under discussion.[24] But someone at the CEA hadn't done his homework. The first of the planned underwater explosions at the French nuclear test site beneath the Pacific atoll of Mururoa was scheduled to take place on August 6, the fiftieth anniversary of the Hiroshima bombing, a date that galvanized the international antinuclear movement. In Japan, Chirac was called "Hirochirac." The Nobel Prize committee in Norway awarded the antinuclear Pugwash group that year's peace prize. On June 17, the French consulate in Perth, Australia, was set on fire by arsonists. On June 23, the Australian government recalled its ambassador to France for consultations. Even in Europe, Chirac was widely condemned by his European Union partners. At the United Nations, resolutions had been drafted that condemned the French (and Chinese) nuclear tests. Chirac eventually moved the first test back to September, but it didn't help.

As he was preparing to go to New York, Chirac phoned UNSCOM chairman Rolf Ekeus and asked if they could meet privately during the General Assembly. Given that the French had stiff-armed him in the past when he had come to Paris requesting information, the Swedish diplomat was skeptical but agreed. When the French president arrived at the thirty-first floor of the United Nations tower along the East River, a source close to Ekeus told me, he apologized for past French behavior and said that from now on he intended to turn the page. Ekeus pointed out that just two weeks earlier, Foreign Minister Hervé de Charette had reiterated—yet again—that France wanted the United Nations sanctions on Iraq to be lifted. "Chirac said no, that was no longer the policy. He said he was angry with Saddam Hussein for having deceived him about the buildup against Kuwait in the fall and that he supported UNSCOM 100 percent." And Chirac followed through on his pledge. "Since that meeting, we have received significant new information from the French they had been holding back for years," my source said.[25]

Ekeus and his inspectors were then evaluating half a million pages of fresh documents on the Iraqi weapons program that had been found at the chicken farm of Saddam's son-in-law Hussein Kamil after he defected to Jordan in July. Kamil fled Iraq because he feared that Saddam's eldest son, Uday, was going to kill him over commercial and personal disputes, and he met with Ekeus and his top aides in Amman in August. The biggest revelation he made was that Iraq had weaponized biological warfare (BW) agents before the first Gulf War, although he claimed that all the weapons themselves had been destroyed. Ekeus and his inspectors were in hot pursuit of the suppliers of that equipment; and that appears to be where Chirac helped the most.

It turned out that half a dozen French companies had supplied "agricultural sprayers" and other equipment for the Iraqi BW program. "To successfully deliver BW agents, you need ultrafine sprayers capable of creating an aerosol cloud, whereas to deliver ordinary pesticides, large-particle sprayers are sufficient," an Ekeus aide told me. Thanks to the new information Chirac ordered the French government to provide, UNSCOM investigators were able to question French suppliers on their deliveries to Iraq. "The size of the particles should have tipped them off, but none of the suppliers asked any questions," one UNSCOM source involved in this effort told me. Among the French suppliers Iraq eventually admitted to having turned to for equipment for its BW program were De Dietrich, SODTEC, the Institut Pasteur, Jouannet, and Cogelex.[26] A sixth company, SOTAFI, was cited in a Pentagon intelligence report declassified after the first Gulf War for having allegedly supplied forty "Mistral 2" specially designed aerosol sprayers in the spring of 1990, which UNSCOM believed Iraq had adapted to deliver BW agents from aircraft. None of these sales were in violation of existing export control laws.

But Chirac's newfound religion of cooperating with UNSCOM appeared to be more of a tactical move than a strategic decision to put an end to the backdoor trafficking with Saddam Hussein. His target was not Saddam Hussein or his regime, but his political rivals in France, who had stepped into the lucrative business with Iraq. Once again, Chirac was reasserting himself as "Mr. Iraq," shutting down the networks of his rivals so he could move back in with his own.

If Iraq was a growing source of dispute between the United States and France in the mid-1990s, it was not the only one. In relations with Israel, the Palestinian Authority, and Iran, President Chirac and his government were engaged in an unrelenting effort to undermine U.S. policies and to position France as an alternative source of power and legitimacy to the United States.

With rare exceptions since 1968, when General de Gaulle stopped French arms deliveries to Israel, France has sided openly with the Palestinians in their conflict with Israel. Yasser Arafat and his Fatah guerrillas became cult heroes to the French Left, which treated them as the vanguard of the struggle against U.S.-led "imperialism." Harder to understand was the veneration and unquestioning sympathy Arafat continued to receive from the French media, despite the lies he and his spokesmen dished out almost daily about Israel's "misdeeds." As I reported in *Preachers of Hate,* the pro-Palestinian reporting in France went well beyond left-wing media bias and was often the touchstone of a deep underlying anti-Semitism. The most notorious was the Agence France-Presse, which systematically twisted events to give them an anti-Israeli bent. American Enterprise Institute scholar Joshua Muravchik notes in an article in the *Weekly Standard* that much of the U.S. media—and especially ABC News—similarly displayed "imbalance or outright inaccuracy tilted against Israel" in its reporting of the conflict.[27]

Notorious for his pro-Arab sentiments, Chirac went well beyond the sympathy for Arafat's person displayed by his predecessors. In an October 1996 official visit to Syria, Israel, and the territories then under Arafat's jurisdiction, the French president "clearly took sides with the Palestinians," his biographers note. It was a position "for which other leaders in the region were grateful."[28] In Chirac's France, "gratefulness" was a scarcely veiled code word for kickbacks and payoffs into political party coffers.

Beginning his tour in Damascus, Chirac was received at the airport by Syrian president Hafez al-Assad. France had long, historic ties of power and blood to Syria that went well beyond the diplomatic niceties that filled the foreign pages of French newspapers. When the French wanted to retaliate against Syria for the assassination of French ambassador to Lebanon Louis Delamare, the operations wing of the DGSE hired Iraqi mercenaries who set off a car bomb in the Ezbekhieh district of Damascus, killing sixty-one innocent civilians. It was the type of action intended to carry "a clear message" to the Syrian leadership. "You do what you have to do," a high-ranking French intelligence official told me when I asked him whether the DGSE had ordered this particular attack.[29] Similarly, when the Syrians were playing ball just two years later, in 1983, the French helped them establish a chemical weapons and ballistic missile infrastructure, the Syrian Scientific Research Center, better known by its French acronym, CERS (Centre d'Études et de Recherches Scientifiques). As prime minister in October 1986, Chirac pledged to broaden French military cooperation with Syria by reopening conventional arms sales with a 3.1-billion-franc deal to sell Damascus self-propelled howitzers equipped with night vision gear, despite Syria's involvement in the terrorist attacks in Paris earlier that year. As he showed again and again when France was attacked, his response to terror was to attempt to buy off the terrorists.

As Palestinian suicide bombers were murdering Israeli civilians in increasingly large numbers, Chirac announced in Damascus in October 1996 that he sought to impose Europe as a "co-sponsor" for negotiations between Israel and the Palestinian Authority, with the goal of establishing a Palestinian state. Neither the United States nor the government of Israeli prime minister Benjamin Netanyahu was amused by Chirac's effort to suddenly insert France into the midst of a complex and deadly situation. Netanyahu believed that Chirac's "goodwill gesture" amounted to rewarding Arafat for his murderous behavior.

But Chirac reserved his real power play for the Arab streets of East Jerusalem, where he set off on an improvised walking tour on October 22, 1996, to the utter dismay of the Israeli security forces. "All we needed was to have a European president murdered on our watch and under our eyes," a senior Israeli government official told me, explaining what happened next. "Are you kidding? Do you seriously think we could have taken a chance on Chirac's own security guard, who had never set foot in Jerusalem, didn't speak Arabic, and had not a clue as to what was happening on the street?"[30]

Chirac's determination to plunge into the crowds on the twisting, narrow streets of Arab East Jerusalem on his way to the Al-Aqsa mosque was unshaken by repeated entreaties from the Israeli soldiers and security officers who accompanied him. In the end, the Israelis wound up blocking the eager Palestinians who lined the shop fronts from approaching the French president's outstretched hand, and Chirac blew up. To French journalists, he sputtered, "This is unacceptable. What is the problem now? I've about had it!" Seeing that the Israelis continued to hold off the Palestinians, he shouted out in English so everyone could hear: "This is not a method! This is a provocation! What do you want? Do you want me to take my plane and go back home to my country? Stop it now!" Again, addressing the French reporters he kept close to him, he motioned to the Israeli soldiers in disgust: "That explains everything."[31] Three hours later, Chirac linked arms with Palestinian Muslim clerics and marched defiantly across the Temple Mount toward the Al-Aqsa mosque, which he knew the Israeli soldiers would not enter.

The next day, his biographers noted, "the French president was welcomed as a hero" as he toured the Palestinian cities of Ramallah and Gaza. "The respect of democratic principles is one of the things that guarantees you broad-based international support," Chirac told the Palestinian Legislative Council in Ramallah. Democratic principles? Members of that same Palestinian Legislative Council complained to me not long afterward that they were powerless because Arafat refused to sign a draft constitution, refused any limitations on his power, and simply jailed legislators who dared to disagree with him in public. But none of that bothered Chirac. He told the legislators he planned to work with them to craft the "future status of Israel." When challenged on this later, Chirac's handlers called his words a "Freudian slip" due to "fatigue." He had really been speaking about the future status of Jerusalem.

Beyond annoying Israeli prime minister Netanyahu, sending shivers down the spines of his security chiefs, and giving Palestinian kids a good excuse to taunt the Israeli army without getting shot, Chirac's trip accomplished no positive benefit. Nor at this point—because Chirac had not yet decided to launch a serious challenge to American leadership—did it greatly impact U.S.-French relations. But his gestures were well received in the Arab world, undoubtedly the real audience to whom the French president was playing. His defiance of the Israeli security detail that had been assigned to protect him won him high praise on the front pages of newspapers from Damascus to Cairo. His old friend and alleged financial backer Rafic Hariri, a Lebanese-Saudi businessman who was prime minister of Lebanon, proclaimed that Chirac's visit had "touched the heart of all Arab countries." Beirut's French-language daily *L'Orient le Jour* called Chirac "a messenger of peace, champion of just causes—and even, for millions of Arabs, a real hero."[32] Chirac loved it. Bathing in the praise of sycophants and yes-men, he was in his true element, a French seigneur who dared defy the great from behind the safety of his castle walls.

B y the time I met Bernard Guillet at the arms bazaar soirée on the French Riviera, the French feared once again that the Americans were going to beat them to the punch in Iraq. In fact, they were convinced that U.S. insistence on maintaining the UN sanctions was a secret plot, aimed at better positioning U.S. companies to pounce the instant sanctions were lifted. They saw that the Americans were getting all the arms export contracts in Saudi Arabia and the Gulf and had cornered the market for the massive reconstruction projects in Kuwait. Given these circumstances, it made sense for the French to look toward the Islamic Republic of Iran. With sixty million people, nearly three times the population of Iraq, it was a potentially huge market for French products. Adding to the allure was the unilateral American trade embargo with Iran, announced by President Clinton on April 30, 1995, on the eve of Chirac's election.

France had a long history in Iran, which in the 1980s and 1990s had become a minefield. One of Iran's main demands was that the French repay a $1 billion loan made by the former shah to build the Eurodif uranium enrichment plant in France. For years the French had refused to pay back the 1974 loan; to help change their mind, the Iranians ordered their proxies in Lebanon to take French citizens hostage. It was a deadly, high-stakes game that appeared to end in December 1991 when the French agreed to pay back the Iranians in full—but not before several individuals involved in the secret negotiations were murdered in mysterious circumstances. One of them had become over the years a trusted source, with whom I discreetly exchanged information in face-to-face meetings in Paris and Geneva.

Jean-Jacques Griessen was a former Swiss policeman turned private investigator, who traveled frequently to Lebanon on behalf of the French and the German governments to help get their hostages released. A fastidious, always polite, mild-mannered person who never once spoke of women in all the years we were close, Griessen allegedly died of a heart attack in the arms of a prostitute in Zurich at the age of sixty. In his last phone call, which was recorded by an associate, he said he was driving from Geneva to meet a source who had new information on the clandestine arms deals to Iran.[33] May he rest in peace.

Rumors of clandestine French arms sales to Iran abounded and were the focus of intense media speculation that often took the government of Prime Minister Édouard Balladur by surprise. The French suspected that such news reports were aimed at spoiling the only export market that seemed to hold out any promise for their flagging defense industries, that of the United Arab Emirates. Fear of Iranian aggression had sparked a huge defense spending spree by the UAE, expected to top $10 billion, above and beyond the nearly $4 billion tank deal they had already signed with France. And the French wanted their piece of the cake.

A U.S. aerospace executive I spoke to in Abu Dhabi during the 1995 IDEX show said he was surprised by the extent of the UAE's fear of Iran. "We went to talk aircraft with our UAE counterpart, and all he wanted to talk about was Iran, Iran, Iran."[34]

One cause for concern, I learned, was a series of nighttime landings by Iranian Revolutionary Guards along the UAE coastline over the previous twelve months. During the week of March 12, 1995, foreign diplomats in the UAE told me, eighteen armed Iranian Revolutionary Guards attempted a midnight landing at Chicago Beach just outside of Dubai and were arrested by the local authorities after a firefight and a house-to-house search.

Iranian weapons companies had been forbidden from exhibiting at the 1995 IDEX show after UAE authorities accused them of bringing in "large quantities of weapons and large ammunition during the previous show that were not intended for display purposes."[35] Situations in the Gulf were tense, and the United States was worried as well. Heightening the concerns were recent U.S. satellite photographs that showed the Iranians had constructed a new missile plant near Isfahan, where they were assembling North Korean Nodong surface-to-surface missiles capable of striking Israel, Turkey, and U.S. air bases deep inside Saudi Arabia.

The French felt no military threat from Iran, because the new Iranian missiles could not reach Europe. But they felt acutely the commercial pressures from the United States. They became convinced that the Clinton administration was working hand in glove with Israel to concoct a "fake threat" from Iran whose goal, once again, was to destroy the French arms industry and French export markets. Fueling their suspicions was the petrodrama that played itself out on the floor of the United States Senate, where Conoco vice president J. Michael Stinson claimed at a March 16, 1995, hearing that the State Department had encouraged his company to conclude a $600 million petrochemical agreement with Iran as part of a U.S. diplomatic overture toward the mullahs' regime. Stinson's claims were borne out by cables released soon thereafter to Senate Banking Committee chairman Alfonse D'Amato (R-N.Y.), which showed that Conoco had fully briefed State Department officials in the Gulf, who had raised no objection to the deal. Fearing the confusion would become a political liability, President Clinton stepped in and short-circuited D'Amato's proposed trade legislation by imposing a total trade embargo on Iran by executive order, killing the Conoco deal on the spot.

Of course, the French didn't believe a word of it. Even after D'Amato passed a new bill in 1996 that imposed a secondary boycott against foreign companies investing more than $40 million in the Iranian oil or gas markets (the Iran-Libyan Sanctions Act, or ILSA), the French thought it was all just a trick. Total jumped into the game, seizing the $600 million contract to rebuild the Sirri gas field off Iran's Persian Gulf coast that Conoco had been forced to abandon. By May 1997, Total president Thierry Desmarest announced that he was ready to sink $2 billion into the Iran gas project. The State Department shot back that ILSA "is the law and we will apply it fully. . . . Our position on any investments in Iranian gas and oil fields is clear: Such investments make more resources available for Iran to use in supporting terrorism and pursuing missiles and nuclear weapons."[36]

Behind the scenes, Total rushed to sell its U.S. assets—leaving nothing behind for the United States to freeze—while the French government backed Total to the hilt. Foreign Ministry spokesman Jacques Rummel-hardt told reporters huffily, "It is not a matter for governments . . . it is a commercial contract between companies." But Total, of course, was a state-owned company. That led French foreign minister Hubert Védrine, a doctrinaire, anti-American Socialist, to threaten retaliatory sanctions against the United States at GATT, the predecessor of the World Trade Organization. Not wanting to engage in a full-scale trade war with France and eventually the EU, the Clinton administration backed down.

It became impossible after these Persian intrigues to make a straight case with France that the United States had cut off investment in Iran as part of a larger strategy to weaken the clerical regime or in support of the legitimate aspirations of Iranians to select their own form of government. The French believed the Clinton administration was just seeking to leverage its commercial advantage and was comforted in that belief by President Clinton's last-ditch efforts to patch up relations with the Iranian regime shortly before leaving the presidency in the fall of 2002. "Clearly this president is hoping to make an overture to Iran before he leaves office," a top Clinton donor told me shortly before the 2002 elections. "This decision has been taken. Now it's just a question of how to engage Iran with our eyes open."[37]

Had President George W. Bush chosen to confront the Islamic Republic of Iran for its clandestine nuclear weapons program, which violated its international treaty commitments, before taking the war on terror to Iraq, the French would have led the fight against him there as well (as indeed they did when the United States sought to get the IAEA to refer Iran's violations to the UN Security Council in November 2003). The policy disputes, the suspicions, and the paranoia were already there; so were the kickbacks and commissions. Only the spark was missing.

# 11

# The Lady Is a Whore

French president Jacques Chirac likes to tell every American he meets—from Ronald Reagan, whom he received at the Hôpital Cochin in December 1978, where he was recuperating after an automobile accident, to reporters—about the summers he spent in the United States as a college student. He worked as a "soda jerk" at Howard Johnson's to pay his studies. (To French audiences, for whom no such job exists, he says that he "did the dishes.") He operated a forklift at the Budweiser beer plant in St. Louis. The first time he saw his name in print on the front page of a newspaper was in the summer of 1954, when he wrote a story that was picked up by the *Times-Picayune* about the port of New Orleans.[1] Jacques Chirac did not come from a world of privilege: he even hitchhiked across France to the Normandy port of Dunkerque, where he briefly enlisted as a merchant sailor on board the *Capitaine Saint-Martin,* a small cargo ship plying the Mediterranean trade routes to French Algeria. The message from these stories was clear: Jacques Chirac was a "man of the people," from the countryside in the Corrèze (the equivalent, say, of rural West Virginia), who had to work his way up the ladder the hard way.

The truth was quite different. Jacques Chirac was born with a silver spoon in his mouth, and it had been placed there and polished by one of the wealthiest and most powerful men in France: aircraft magnate Marcel Dassault, who became his political as well as personal patron.

Born in 1932, Chirac was just a boy when he impressed Dassault, who had already made a name for himself (and a first fortune) as the father of French aviation. At the time, Dassault was known by his birth name, Marcel Bloch; he was descended through his mother from a wealthy Jewish family in Italy and would pay dearly for that ancestry during the war. Dassault himself related the encounter to Chirac's early biographer, journalist Franz-Olivier Giesbert, editor in chief of the Dassault-owned newspaper *Le Figaro:*

> At the end of the 1930s, I was in Vichy with my wife for the thermal baths, when one day while out on a walk we saw the Chiracs sitting on the terrace of a café. I watched the cars go by with the son while the adults spoke about important things. He said, "That's a Citroën; that's a Renault." And he was never wrong. So I thought I'd give him a little test. At the time, I had a large, fairly rare automobile and I was sure he couldn't tell me what it was. I took him to the car and he cried out: "Oh, sir, that's a Graham Paige!" I must admit, I was quite astonished. We went into a toy store and I bought the whole place.[2]

The young Jacques Chirac got a whole army of lead soldiers that day. In later years, his new patron would give him the real thing.

In his official biography, released by the Élysée Palace, Chirac says he was "the son of François Chirac, corporate executive." In fact, his father, born Abel Chirac, was not just any corporate executive: he was the associate and banker of Marcel Bloch-Dassault.

Dassault had a sixth sense for politics even then. In 1935, when he began his consolidation of the French aerospace industry by buying out engine manufacturer Lorraine-Dietrich, he turned over that part of his growing empire to Edmond Giscard d'Estaing, brother of the staff director of the French air minister. Edmond's son, Valéry Giscard d'Estaing, would precede Chirac as president of France by twenty-one years.[3]

Dassault and his partner, Henry Potez, so valued the financial advice of Abel Chirac (who changed his first name to François during World War II) that they named him general director of one of their companies. "Jacques's father suddenly became one of the key men in French industry," Giesbert wrote. The Bloch and Chirac families became socially close starting in 1936, when Jacques was just four years old.

But the march of history was about to catch up with Marcel Bloch. On May 12, 1940, Hitler's troops stormed across France, seizing half the country in just eight days. Marcel called Marie-Louise Chirac and offered to drive her and young Jacques to the south of France, temporarily out of the Nazis' reach, since Abel Chirac was on a business trip in Canada.[4] On October 5, 1940, Marcel Bloch was placed under house arrest. His political connections and industrial empire helped him avoid the worst until August 1944, when he was finally deported to Buchenwald. A brother, René Bloch, was not so lucky and died in 1941 in Auschwitz. Another brother, Paul, who was a French general, joined de Gaulle in Britain with remnants of the fleeing French army in June 1940 and took the pseudonym "Chardasso" (an anglicized spelling of *char d'assault,* or assault tank). After the war, Marcel adopted the name Dassault and made it famous around the world.

While in Buchenwald, Marcel Bloch became friends with prison leader Marcel Paul, a future Communist minister in postwar governments, who took him under his protection. According to General Pierre-Marie Gallois, one of Paul's confidants, Bloch promised to pay him 10 million francs if he helped him survive, and he made good on his promise later on.[5] After the war, Marcel Bloch—under his new name, Dassault—maintained good relations with the Communist trade unions when other business leaders were plagued repeatedly with strikes. At a time when France was split into two fiercely opposed ideological camps, Marcel Dassault managed to serve as a bridge between them, by spreading the spoils. It was a lesson not lost on his protégé, Jacques Chirac.

When the young Chirac returned to Paris after the war with his family, he was "the son of one of the top industrialists of his generation."[6] François Chirac remained business partners with Dassault associate Henry Potez throughout his career. And Dassault took Chirac's son under his wing. When the young Jacques flirted too openly with the Left while in college, it was Dassault who suggested to his friend and banker François Chirac that he send him to summer school at Harvard University (which Chirac's official biography lists as one of two university "diplomas"). It was during the summer of 1953, while at Harvard, that Chirac worked as a "soda jerk," but it certainly wasn't to pay for his schooling. That was taken care of by a scholarship from the French Foreign Ministry, which also paid his travel and living expenses.[7]

Chirac's career and personal life were carefully scripted from the very start by his parents and by Dassault and other powerful friends. While at the Sorbonne, Chirac met Bernadette Chodron de Courcel, the niece of General de Gaulle's aide-de-camp during his London exile; they married in 1956. After a year as a second lieutenant during the French war in Algeria, Chirac spent two years at the École Nationale d'Administration, one of the select French graduate schools used to groom the nation's political and administrative elite. In 1962, after a boring three years at the Government Accounting Office, Chirac was thinking of leaving government for private business. That was when Marcel Dassault stepped in like a genie and waved his magic wand once again. "We're going to make you into a state secretary for civil aviation," he told the thirty-year-old Chirac.[8]

It didn't happen right away, but under Dassault's tutelage, Chirac was given a job with the chief of staff of the French government, then six months later joined the staff of Prime Minister Georges Pompidou, where he was put in charge of transportation issues, "an area where his godfather, Marcel Dassault, exercises a powerful influence."[9] In 1969, he worked "hand in hand" with the treasurer of de Gaulle's Union des Démocrates pour la République, Maurice Papon, on Pompidou's successful presidential campaign. (Papon was eventually convicted for "crimes against humanity" in 1998 for his role in deporting 1,690 Jews to the Nazi death camps as a Vichy police official in Bordeaux, but only after a twenty-year public campaign against him by Nazi hunters Serge and Beate Klarsfeld.)

Chirac's intensely personal relationship with Marcel Dassault would follow him throughout his career, and he would often repay the favors Dassault had showered on him. As the youngest prime minister of France, in 1974, he pushed hard to sell Mirage jet fighters to Iraq; as prime minister in 1988, just weeks before the presidential election (which he lost), he ordered the French air force to pay development costs for Dassault's latest creation, the Rafale fighter, over the objections of his own defense minister, André Giraud. The air force didn't want the plane because it was too expensive and was already outdated before it was built. By the end of 2001, only 5 Rafales had been delivered to the French air force instead of the 137 initially planned, at a cost to French taxpayers of 7 billion Euros.[10]

I n 1995, France was tired with socialism. But more than anything, French voters were fed up with the constant corruption scandals of the Mitterrand era. For years, the press had been writing about the reckless racketeering of Socialist political barons across France, who extorted companies to use fake invoices and bogus consulting contracts to disguise hidden payments to support their personal lifestyles and their political campaigns; yet despite the exposure and, more recently, attention from French investigative magistrates, the fraud continued. Even Mitterrand's own adviser and close personal friend François de Grossouvre had grown weary of the corruption of the president's inner circle. When journalist Jean Montaldo told him the title of his forthcoming book on the scandals (*Mitterrand and the Forty Thieves . . .*), de Grossouvre grimly joked: "Only forty thieves?" Three months later, at the age of seventy-six, de Grossouvre committed suicide in the presidential palace, apparently disgusted that the president was going to drag him down into the mud. (De Grossouvre's name appeared on the deed of the farmhouse in Gordes, near Avignon, that Mitterrand had asked him to purchase and renovate for his mistress.)[11]

Chirac's victory in May 1995 against Socialist candidate Lionel Jospin was supposed to herald a new beginning. Instead, almost as soon as the accordions from the election night celebrations went silent, the new president and his prime minister, Alain Juppé, had to face familiar but less pleasant music.

The bad news initially surfaced where it often does in France, in the satiric left-wing weekly *Le Canard Enchainé*. In an article that appeared on June 28, 1995, *Le Canard* published a letter signed by Juppé to the head of the public housing office in Paris two years earlier, asking him to lower his son's rent. But Juppé's son was not living in a housing project: he had a luxury apartment on the rue Jacob, one of the most exclusive areas of the Left Bank. As the story developed, it turned out that Juppé himself lived in taxpayer-subsidized public housing and that his daughter, his half-brother, and his former wife had all been given apartments by the public housing office of the city of Paris—at a time when some sixty thousand Parisians were on the waiting list for low-income housing, some of them for more than a decade.

Arnaud Montebourg, then a lawyer working with a nonprofit tax-payers group (L'Association pour la défense des contribuables parisiens), wrote to the public prosecutor demanding a criminal investigation. Juppé called Montebourg's action "an operation of political destabilization" and insisted that he had "not benefited from any favor, nor committed any irregularity. I have a lease."[12]

Chirac stepped in and publicly supported his embattled prime minister, and the state-appointed district attorney set aside prosecution on condition that Juppé leave his apartment by the end of the year (he moved his family into the prime minister's palace on the avenue Matignon instead).[13] But the public housing scandal was a big deal, because it opened a window onto potential criminal activity by the French president during the eighteen years he had ruled Paris with an iron fist and a velvet purse. And it was just the beginning.

As Juppé's popularity plummeted, Dominique de Villepin, Chirac's chief of staff at the Élysée, saw the judicial sharks circling ever closer to his boss and felt the best way to cut them off was to hold new elections. Although Chirac wasn't required to hold parliamentary elections before the spring of 1998 when the five-year mandate of the sitting Parliament expired, at Villepin's suggestion he called snap elections on April 21, 1997. Villepin "had dreamed of a blitzkrieg [but] the Right finished the campaign with its back to the wall," Chirac's biographers noted. For his arrogance and his questionable relationship to reality in calling for early elections, Mrs. Chirac would refer to Villepin thereafter as "Nero."[14] In May 1997, the Socialists were back in power, with Lionel Jospin leading a new round of cohabitation as prime minister. This time, Chirac was president and the Socialists controlled the day-to-day affairs of government.

Christine Deviers-Joncour says she was tipped off in early November 1997 by an article in Le Parisien two days before four policemen and a policewoman burst into her Paris apartment at six A.M. and placed her under arrest. For four hours, without lawyers present, they searched her personal effects, carting off letters, bills, paychecks, and photographs in front of her two wide-eyed children. But nothing could prepare her for the ordeal she was about to endure. "You're taking me with you, I know," she said. "But where?"

For the next forty-eight hours, virtually nonstop, she was interrogated by teams of financial investigators on her employment with the French oil giant Elf Aquitaine and her amorous relationship to French foreign minister Roland Dumas. When she was finally allowed to see her lawyer, it was eight o'clock in the evening of the second day, and Judge Eva Joly ordered her locked up indefinitely. In France, such treatment is called "preventive detention." Christine Deviers-Joncour was not a dangerous criminal, nor was she suspected of treason, espionage, murder, or any other capital crime. Instead, as one editorialist would write, she was considered to be "the whore of the Republic." After five months in jail, where she was held virtually incommunicado, she found the sobriquet fitting and took it as the title of her memoir on the Elf Aquitaine scandal.[15]

*L'Affaire Elf,* as it was known in French, was just one of many corruption scandals then under investigation by a new generation of investigative magistrates in France—magistrates willing, for the first time in the Fifth Republic, to directly challenge the nation's top politicians for their promiscuous relationship to money and power. It began when Thomson-CSF, which had signed a $2.7 billion contract to sell six frigates to the Taiwan navy, encountered problems in securing the necessary political approval for the deal from the French government. According to Deviers-Joncour, Thomson turned to her boss at Elf, Alfred Sirven, who turned to her.

"It all began with a trip to Geneva with Alfred Sirven," Deviers-Joncour recalls. "In the Elf Aquitaine Falcon jet was another man, very discreet, whom I didn't know." After meetings at the Elf office in Geneva, the three of them drove to Lausanne, where Sirven went into a bank. The other man, whom Deviers-Joncour refuses to identify, told her that he worked for Thomson and needed her help in getting government approval to sell the frigates to Taiwan.

A few days later, she was taken to Thomson-CSF headquarters high above La Défense, with its magnificent view of the Arc de Triomphe and the Seine. After lunch, one of the Thomson men made the pitch she had been brought to hear. "We must convince [Foreign Minister] Roland Dumas to authorize the sale of these bloody ships to the Taiwanese. . . . We know your relationship to Roland Dumas. Do you think you could do something?" Later, she was promised 45 million francs ($9 million) as commission if she could convince her lover, Dumas, to lift his veto on the sale.

Despite repeated efforts during private dinners and evenings at the opera to convince Dumas to change his mind, Deviers-Joncour failed. Dumas was afraid Communist China would break diplomatic relations with France if the French started selling arms to Taiwan, she says. But Sirven, Elf, and Thomson-CSF had too much money at stake to let go and pressed Deviers-Joncour to renew her efforts with Dumas. She was so insistent that it became a joke between them if she forgot to bring up the subject when they met. "Well, well, my Mata Hari, what about your frigates?"[16]

Deviers-Joncour was still in prison in March 1998 when Roland Dumas was finally indicted for his role in the affair. Shortly before appearing before a judge, Dumas told *Le Figaro* on March 9, 1998, that Thomson-CSF had paid $500 million in "retrocommissions" on the frigate deal with Taiwan, including large payments to French political parties, from left to right. The man most frequently mentioned as the head of Elf's political support network on the Right was Charles Pasqua, a top Chirac ally at the time the frigate deal occurred.

Elf president Lok Le Floch-Prigent says Sirven was told by Chirac's chief of staff, Dominique de Villepin, that he should ignore the summons to testify he had received. "What's preferable is for you to flee the country, and we will protect you," Le Floch-Prigent claims Villepin said (Chirac's legal counsel, Francis Szpiner, denied this claim). Le Floch-Prigent said that in his own conversations with Chirac, the French president shrugged off the scandal by saying, "It won't get back to City Hall."[17] Only later, writes Le Floch-Prigent, did he understand that by "City Hall" Chirac meant himself.

Readers in America will find the events that follow hard to believe. But they are critical to understanding the virtual monarchy that the Fifth Republic has become, as well as the man who could be its last president. The corruption scandals that grew in intensity and ultimately threatened to land Chirac in jail provide an essential backdrop to the Iraq crisis of 2002–2003 and the French president's conscious decision to sacrifice a 225-year-old alliance with America on the altar of political expediency.

For starters, Roland Dumas was not just any former foreign minister. At the time he was indicted, he was chief justice of the French Supreme Court, the Conseil Constitutionnel. (His appointment to that job in 1995 was one of President Mitterrand's last official acts. Such appointments in

France are not subject to approval by Parliament.) When Dumas was summoned by Judges Laurence Vichnievsky and Eva Joly to testify on the Elf scandal on March 18, 1998, he knew it was time to call in his chips.

Dumas's first stop was the Élysée Palace, where he met with President Chirac. Nothing has filtered officially from this discreet meeting, but Arnaud Montebourg—who was elected to Parliament as a Socialist in 1997—remains convinced that the two struck a deal. "On July 14, a statement was released by the president's office: 'The president of the Republic [Chirac] considers that the president of the Constitutional Court [Dumas], just as any citizen, has the right to be presumed innocent even if he is indicted but not convicted.' " Chirac's public statement of support relieved the pressure on Dumas to step down as head of the Supreme Court. Pro-Chirac deputies in Parliament, "whose hatred and viciousness usually emerge with customary violence in such circumstances, kept a courteous silence," Montebourg observed.[18]

Dumas's next step was to phone friends in the press, to whom he explained that he hadn't realized Christine Deviers-Joncour had bought a pair of $2,000 Berluti shoes for him with an Elf Aquitaine credit card, but that at any rate, he had paid her back. As for the $600,000 in cash he had deposited in his personal account, it came from the judicious sale of artwork and from legal fees. Then he hinted that if questioned by the judges, he would have to reveal all he knew about the huge commissions paid on the frigate deal, which he claimed "had been approved with the authorization of the Ministry of Finance and the presidency. . . . That decision is recorded, but I will not publicly reveal the beneficiaries," he said darkly. French writer Airy Routier observed that the relentless pursuit of the investigative magistrates in the Elf scandal showed "a conflict between two cultures—French power play and raison d'état, and a new approach, a more Anglo-Saxon one, which values transparency and openness and a much diminished economic role for the state."[19]

At the same time the noose was tightening around Dumas's neck, investigative magistrates in the Paris suburbs of Créteil, Nanterre, and Evry were getting closer and closer to the president himself. For eighteen years—from virtually the moment he left the Matignon Palace in 1977 after his first stint as prime minister, until May 1995, when he took office as president—Chirac used his position as mayor of Paris to build a national political party, a reputation as a hard-nosed scrapper, and a solid source of off-books cash he could dip into whenever he wanted to dispense political favors.

Hervé Liffran of *Le Canard Enchaîné* reported that Chirac kept a special safe in his office toilet in the Paris City Hall for this money. " 'One day, Chirac opened it in front of me to show me a confidential document, and there were stacks of 500 franc notes this high,' recalls [ . . . ], a former Paris city councilman, who—still struck by the sight—indicated a stack a foot high. . . . 'Before turning the combination of the safe, [Chirac] flushed the toilet so no one could hear the number of clicks,' another of his old companions said."[20]

Now the cozy schemes carried out in Chirac's name—extortion and racketeering in public housing, political campaign workers and party employees placed full-time on the municipal payroll, huge sums for nonexisting consulting jobs paid to political cronies, and cash slush funds he personally managed—were coming to light. Some of these cases were "set aside" by public prosecutors, who remained loyal to the politicians who appointed them. Albin Chalandon, who served as Chirac's Minister of Justice from 1986 to 1988, remarked on the surreal character of the French justice system: "One day we need to get beyond the point where the justice minister's role, as far as the political class is concerned, comes down to getting his friends out of trouble and plunging his enemies into it."[21] But other cases just wouldn't go away.

When Lionel Jospin took over as prime minister in June 1997, he pledged sweeping judicial reforms to prohibit intervention by the government in cases before the courts or cases being developed by investigative magistrates. (Yes, in France the justice minister can simply call up a prosecutor and order him to set aside a case he is working on, although it is usually done with slightly more finesse through subordinates who "suggest" that "reasons of state" make it imperative that the case be dropped.)[22] Chirac initially went along with the idea of the reform, which required the French National Assembly and the Senate to pass separate laws, then meet together to amend the constitution. Just twenty-four hours before the constitutional convention at the Palace of Versailles was scheduled to begin, he pulled the plug.

"The annulation of this convention was received as a divine benediction by part of the political class who, in judicial matters, have Napoleonic manners," wrote Chirac critic Arnaud Montebourg. "They only like judges who are muzzled and kept on the leash."[23] He traced the corrupt relationship between France's political masters and the courts to Napoleon, who set the example when he was First Consul in prosecuting the Duke d'Enghein on allegations of fomenting a monarchist plot against him:

> The brother-in-law of the First Consul named the members of the court who judged the accused without mercy. His grave was dug even before the sentence. The judges, chosen for their lack of education and their servility, pronounced the death sentence in a written order that left blank the relevant law, which they ignored. But their sentence stipulated that the execution should take place "immediately." The First Consul, once he became Emperor, later said: "It was a sacrifice necessary for my security and my grandeur."[24]

Montebourg regularly invokes the despotism of Napoleon when criticizing the Fifth Republic and the monarchic powers of its presidency. This has earned him the ire of Villepin, who has vowed a cult of devotion to the emperor that I will examine in more detail in the final chapter of this book. "Montebourg and the Montebourgeois" was how he maliciously referred to the Socialist lawyer and taxpayer advocate. The trope may be more apt than Villepin had intended. Students of French history recall that the French Revolution of 1789 began as a revolt of the bourgeoisie, fed up with the corruption and exclusive rule of the Bourbon monarchs who refused to share power with an elected assembly, as British kings had done since the Glorious Revolution a century earlier. When I asked Montebourg about Villepin's neologism, he just smiled. "Actually, where I come from, people are called Montebourgiens."

In a country where each village prided itself on declining the name of its inhabitants in masculine and feminine forms, Montebourg's correction was the ultimate slight. Villepin had made a grammatical error.[25]

F or Socialist justice minister Elisabeth Guigou, a fiercely partisan animal, it was time to turn up the heat. With Roland Dumas in the dock, the entire "Mitterrand generation" was under indictment. "As any Frenchman, the president of the Republic can be prosecuted by the courts if he has committed a crime," she told a national radio interviewer, inserting herself into the hottest debate of the decade. "I don't see why we should have a special system for the president of the Republic, once it has been clearly established that there is no difference when it comes to the criminal statutes" between the president and an ordinary citizen.[26] The Socialists were rubbing their hands together at the thought of Chirac being forced to appear before a judge for alleged crimes of corruption committed while he was mayor of Paris. Chirac risked being called as a material witness in at least three separate corruption cases then under way.

The Élysée responded initially much as the Clinton White House—by stalling. When a Chirac adviser suggested at one point that he "lance the boil" and voluntarily agree to testify, Dominique Galouzeau de Villepin turned up his aristocratic nose. "You just can't get any stupider than that," he scoffed. "We might as well give them everything all wrapped up in a vegetable basket."[27]

At issue was a question of constitutional law, similar to the debate then raging in the United States over the Paula Jones case. Was a sitting president criminally liable for crimes committed before he took office? Article 68 of the French Constitution states that the president of the Republic is immune from prosecution for acts committed while in office that relate to his official functions, with one exception: high treason. In that one case, the president can be tried before a special "high court" composed of the members of the National Assembly and the Senate, similar to an impeachment trial in the United States. But for everything else—including crimes committed while in office that *don't* relate to his official functions—the constitution says nothing.

Montebourg and Justice Minister Elisabeth Guigou argued that this silence in the constitution did not constitute legal immunity. "The constitution protects the exercise of official functions, but not a criminal who might be sitting in the Élysée Palace. Imagine that a president of the Republic one day commits a serious crime, such as a rape or a murder," Montebourg wrote. "Obviously, it is not part of his official functions to rape or murder. That is why the constitution did not intend to protect such acts. . . . The constitution is not made to allow criminals to find a convenient refuge by installing themselves at the summit of State."[28]

As this debate was raging, Roland Dumas's plight had become almost comic. Despite the indictment weighing against him, Dumas refused to resign as head of the French Supreme Court. One day he appeared before an investigative magistrate to answer questions about allegations that he had taken bribes from the state-owned oil company Elf Aquitaine. The next day he donned his judicial robes and wielded the gavel as the nation's highest legal authority, the ultimate arbiter of presidents and of Constitutional law. It was a situation without precedent in France.

On January 22, 1999, Dumas's critics say, it became apparent why he had hung on for so long. He had been waiting for a particular case to come before his court, in which he inserted language that paralleled a legal argument prepared long before by Chirac advisers.[29]

The Rome treaty that created the international criminal court, signed on July 8, 1998, by the French government, contained provisions that required review because of an apparent conflict with the constitution of the Fifth Republic. According to the original language, the new court had authority to try anyone for war crimes or crimes against humanity "without any distinction based on their official position." Even Chirac's critics agreed this was not compatible with Article 68 of the French Constitution, which gives special protection to the president and his cabinet for actions taken in the exercise of their official functions. But in the French Supreme Court decision released on January 22, 1999, Dumas went well beyond that distinction. Dumas spelled out what amounted to blanket immunity, stating that "for the duration of his office, [the president] cannot be brought before any court other than the High Court of Justice, whose sole authority was to conduct trials for treason." For Montebourg and his Socialist colleagues, Dumas's ruling was "highly suspect" and amounted to "changing a simple privilege of being judged elsewhere into total criminal irresponsibility, a hallmark of royalty rather than a republican principle."[30]

It was a breathtaking new interpretation of the constitution and had nothing to do with the case at hand. Montebourg claims that Dumas added the phrase protecting the president as his part of a deal with Chirac. Both the Élysée and Dumas have vigorously denied such connivance.

Thierry Bréhier, writing in Le Monde four days later, provided details Montebourg used to support his claim: "The question had obviously been prepared in great detail during preparatory sessions before Friday. When the nine justices received their binders, the litigious phrase was already in the proposed language of the judgment. In presiding the discussion, Roland Dumas made sure that the debate focused on what went before and what went after, without this insertion being debated or even submitted to a special vote."[31]

For Montebourg, Roland Dumas had just "rendered a service to a president of the Republic besieged by judicial inquiries." As a form of "recompense," he said later, Chirac made sure that Dumas's legal assistant, a doctrinaire Socialist named Noëlle Lenoir, was brought into the center-right government of Jean-Pierre Raffarin in 2002, where she became a minister of state for European affairs under Foreign Affairs Minister Dominique de Villepin.[32] Dumas was ultimately sentenced on corruption-related charges to six months in prison on May 2, 2001, but his conviction was overturned on appeal in November 2002 after the French government called for an end to "political prosecutions."

When I asked Arnaud Montebourg whether Chirac could have run for a second term of office in April 2002 without Dumas's help, he was categorical. "Absolutely not," he said. "The judges would have been all over him. Already, Judge Halphen wanted to call him as a witness. We were heading straight for a constitutional crisis. Chirac supported Dumas when Dumas was in trouble, in exchange for a favor. To me, that is absolutely clear."[33]

I n mid-April 1999, General Wesley K. Clark got a taste of what NATO military operations could be like if the French, as Chirac seemed to be suggesting, actually agreed to rejoin the integrated military command.

It was the third week of Operation Allied Force, the NATO air campaign in Kosovo. France had agreed to join the air war against Serbian dictator Slobodan Milošević, despite having backed Serbia in its earlier campaigns against Croatia. More than one hundred French warplanes took part in the bombing campaign as part of the NATO air armada by the time it was done. It was the first time NATO had ever carried out a war of aggression, unprovoked, against another nation; it was also the first time France had participated in NATO military operations since de Gaulle withdrew from the integrated military command in 1966. Chirac threw himself into the war in Kosovo with a frenzy. It was a welcome escape from his problems at home.

Allied intelligence had already picked up signs that the Serbian military was moving helicopters and fighter jets into underground bunkers at an air base near Podgorica, the capital of Montenegro. At the morning intelligence briefing in mid-April, Clark was informed that Milošević had now gone one step further. Not only was he trying to use Montenegro's neutrality as a shield to protect his military assets, he was now shelling northern Albania from positions in Montenegro. Clark agreed it was time to teach the Serbian leader a lesson, by destroying the Podgorica air base. That's when his staff reminded him that French president Chirac, as a condition to joining the NATO campaign, had demanded a veto on any air strikes against Montenegro.

" 'Forget the French!' Clark thundered, according to participants. 'No, no, no, wait! Hold off on that,' he said. 'I'll get French permission. I'll get it.' "[34] It took a full day of phone calls back and forth between Secretary of State Madeline Albright, National Security Adviser Sandy Berger, Secretary of Defense William Cohen, and their French counterparts, but the next morning Clark had the political approval for the strike. This and similar anecdotes of political "vetos" toward particular targets during the Kosovo campaign were widely reported in the United States and led to charges that President Clinton was allowing NATO to run a military campaign "by committee."

For Chirac, the Kosovo campaign was a godsend. It allowed him to appear "presidential," despite the cohabitation with Socialist premier Lionel Jospin, who acquiesced to his handling of the war. He solemnly addressed the French people in nationally televised "updates" on the military operations and briefed reporters in small groups at the Élysée Palace.[35] He also used France's contribution to the war effort as leverage to exert a high price for France's eventual reintegration into the NATO integrated command, threatening to walk out of the fiftieth-anniversary NATO summit in Washington, D.C., that began on April 21 if the United States did not agree to allow France to take command of NATO's southern flank. (The United States did not agree, and Chirac stayed, after President Clinton phoned him to say that his early departure from the summit "would have been perceived as disunity and would encourage Milošević," according to administration notes of the call.)[36] Chirac ultimately concluded that he didn't need to rejoin the NATO military command to obtain all the advantages membership afforded. As defense analyst Jean Guisnel wrote, to rejoin or not to rejoin was a bit like "a discussion of the sex of angels." France was already the leading European component in the NATO war in Kosovo, having contributed the second-largest force after the United States.[37]

Chirac displayed his true priorities after meeting with Russian president Boris Yeltsin in Moscow on the Kosovo crisis on May 13, 1999. "The world, which is gradually becoming multipolar, is beginning to need international law, which would be based on the UN and the Security Council.

Both Russia and France share this point of view," he told reporters.[38] Despite those words, Chirac never raised the issue of seeking United Nations approval for the Kosovo war, as he later did in Iraq. Once France had agreed to commit its military, the French considered United Nations approval to be irrelevant. "That's what was interesting," says Alain Madelin, the leader of the French neoconservative movement and a former minister in Chirac's government. "You had a consensus among democracies, a Euro-Atlantic consensus outside of the UN, that should have led us to construct something new on the basis of Kosovo. This was a big missed opportunity."[39]

In fact, the French have rarely turned to the United Nations when they have felt their national (or partisan) interests were at stake. French leaders including Chirac repeatedly have sent troops to the Ivory Coast, Chad, and the two Congos without so much as a whisper to the UN.

In October 1998, for instance, Chirac helped orchestrate a coup d'état in the Republic of Congo (Brazzaville) that successfully restored to power former military strongman General Denis Sassou-Nguesso. With French help, Sassou-Nguesso tossed out democratically elected president Pascal Lissouba, murdering thousands of his fellow countrymen in the process. Why did the French conspire with the former and current dictator of the Congo? "They said it was an unfriendly act" to offer oil-drilling contracts to the Exxon Corporation instead of to the French national oil company Elf Aquitaine, Lissouba told Ben Barber of the *Washington Times*.[40] The former president of Elf, Lok Le Floch-Prigent, explained in his memoir that Elf considered Sassou-Nguesso their man, despite his flirtation at the peak of the cold war with the Soviet Union. The Congo "for a time became Marxist," he wrote dismissively, "but was always under Elf control." Such control was worth the blood of thousands of African citizens in the eyes of *La Maison France.*

And the Congo is just one example. The French government under former Chirac ally Édouard Balladur arranged for an arms shipment worth $500 million to the government of Angola in 1993–1994, in violation of a United Nations arms embargo. President José Eduardo Dos Santos needed the weaponry to combat the UNITA guerrillas, who for more than a decade had been backed by the United States as part of the global battle with the Soviet Union and its proxies. What was the overwhelming national or humanitarian interest for the French? A top aide to then interior minister

Charles Pasqua was indicted on charges of funneling kickbacks from the scheme into Gaullist political coffers.

France claims that its objections to the war in Iraq were based on logic and consistency. If so, the logic and consistency focused on the role of France—not the United Nations—in determining world affairs.

I n the end, it was a dead man who sprang the trap on Jacques Chirac. Jean-Claude Méry was a real estate promoter in the Paris region who became a Central Committee member of Chirac's RPR party and a top fund-raiser. In 1994, Méry—whose last name was pronounced almost identically to *mairie,* or municipality—went to jail for five months for illegal fund-raising and racketeering. He was the bagman for the Chirac shakedowns, the one who personally brought the cash to Chirac's office at the Mairie de Paris, the Paris City Hall. Before he died in June 1999, his ties to Chirac had become so notorious that he was known as "Méry de Paris."

Jean-Claude Méry never got over going to jail on Chirac's behalf, and in 1996 he recorded a three-hour videotape in which he explained the inner workings of the illegal fund-raising apparatus, with names, dates, and amounts.

Following the example of Marcel Dassault, who was always careful to share the spoils with his political enemies, Jean-Claude Méry set up a system to "ventilate" the kickbacks paid on school construction and maintenance contracts to the various political parties, including the Socialists and the Communists, according to their relative political strengths. In one case, reported in detail in a transcript of the "Cassette Méry," as his videotaped confession came to be known, *Le Monde* quoted him describing a 10-million-franc bribe (then worth around $1.7 million). "I split it between myself—with 5 million francs for [Chirac's party] the RPR . . . 1 million francs for the Communist Party; 3.5 million francs for the Socialists, with the rest going in commissions paid to the Left and the Right to make sure the work got done correctly."[41]

Méry was also put in charge of hitting up the companies responsible for heating the vast number of lower-income apartments owned by the Paris Bureau of Public Housing, the HLM. "These contracts represented on average 1.2 billion francs per company" over a twelve-year period—between $200 million and $250 million. Commissions paid on these contracts "were paid directly to . . . Mr. Chirac," Méry alleged.[42]

Méry's posthumous testimony hit the presidential palace like a nuclear blast. Chirac's first reaction, when Villepin told him of the story about to appear in *Le Monde*, was to reassure his staff: "This doesn't concern me." But once the transcript appeared, Chirac went on the offensive. "Everything that is in this pseudomessage is for me without foundation, lies, calumnies, and manipulation," he said. "A man who has been dead for more than a year is made to speak about unbelievable events that happened more than fourteen years ago." Even Chirac's biographers, who generally sympathize with his plight, said his "ambiguous formula sounded to many like an avowal."[43]

As reporters jumped on the story, more details came out. "Tens of millions of francs had been paid into an account opened with the Union de Banques Suisse in Geneva in the name of a Panamanian company called Farco Enterprise," *Le Monde* reported. "We knew it was part of the RPR [fund-raising] apparatus," one of the Swiss administrators told French government investigators.[44]

On December 1, 2000, Chirac's former chief of staff, Michel Roussin, was jailed for five days. Members of the RPR campaign finance staff were questioned. On March 28, 2001, despite the Supreme Court decision that the president of the Republic was immune from prosecution for as long as he remained in office, Chirac was summoned as a witness by Judge Halphen. Later, Chirac's own wife and daughter were summoned to testify on overseas vacations they had taken while Chirac was mayor of Paris, when millions of francs were spent on the First Family's behalf by aides peeling off bills from thick wads of 500-franc notes. It was all over the press, and Chirac seemed doomed.

Ironically, it was the September 11 attacks on America that saved the presidency of Jacques Chirac.

Chirac had no particular love for President George W. Bush. In December 2000, during a visit to Washington, D.C., he was the first Western leader to meet with the president-elect. He later told reporters that he found him "intelligent, open, lacking experience, but apt to acquire it rapidly." He was favorably impressed with Colin Powell but found the Bush team "incredibly reactionary." It was a term that came frequently to the French president's lips. Although they claimed to be Gaullist conservatives, Chirac and his advisers found it hard to believe in the sincerity of a national leader who placed moral values at the core of his administration.[45]

Chirac was scheduled to give a speech in Rennes on unemployment when the news of the September 11 attacks hit the wires. Canceling the speech, he issued an immediate statement of solidarity with the American people and rushed back to Paris to meet with Socialist premier Lionel Jospin and his cabinet. That evening, he gave a nationwide address on prime-time television. What happened in the United States "concerns all of us," he said. "France knows it is only possible to fight effectively against terrorism through determined, collective action." Behind the scenes, however, both Chirac and the Jospin government would see to it that French counterterrorism judge Jean-Louis Bruguière could not present evidence in a U.S. court that would help convict suspected 9/11 conspirator Zacarias Moussaoui as long as he could be subject to the death penalty.

On September 18, Chirac made sure French camera crews were present when he emerged from meeting George W. Bush in the Oval Office and reaffirmed France's support to America in its time of peril. But he insisted that France would not give the United States "a blank check" for any military response. "Military cooperation, of course, can be envisaged, but only if we have been consulted ahead of time on the targets and the means to be used," he said. Sounding a theme that comforted Islamic fundamentalist groups in the United States and their supporters, Chirac said he had warned Bush not to transform the war on terror into a "clash of civilizations" or a war on Islam. Seven months away from the presidential elections in France, Chirac's advisers were hoping he could exploit the terrorist attacks to "widen the gap with [Jospin]," who as prime minister was stuck with managing the day-to-day affairs of government. "You can count on [Chirac] to exploit this event shamelessly," a Chirac adviser told journalists Marie-Bénédicte Allaire and Philippe Goulliaud. "He does that very well. He is totally cynical, while at the same time he feels a real sympathy."[46]

Once the United States began military operations in Afghanistan, Chirac took advantage of his role as commander in chief to announce that French troops were en route to help the United States secure the airport in Mazar-e Sharif. Although limited, it would have been useful support had not Chirac's premature announcement tipped off Uzbekistan authorities, who held up the French for nearly two weeks.

If Chirac displayed the "lack of experience" in international affairs he had imputed to George W. Bush, his domestic political instincts were

acute. When Socialist prime minister Lionel Jospin announced his intention to attend the France-Algeria soccer match on October 6, 2001, at the
Stade de France in a predominantly Arab suburb of Paris, Chirac wisely
declined the invitation to join him. It was the first time the two national
teams had played against each other since France acquiesced to Algeria's
independence in 1962 after a long and bitter war.

The stadium was packed and fell into a "religious silence" when the
loudspeakers blared out the anthem of Algeria's National Liberation Front,
proud victor in France's last colonial war. But jeers, catcalls, and whistles
drowned out "La Marseillaise" when it came time to play the French national anthem. At the second half-time, with the French team leading the
Algerians 4–1, Algerian immigrants went wild. "Water bottles and cell
phone batteries were flying in every direction," one of them landing on the
head of Justice Minister Elisabeth Guigou. Jospin didn't know what to do
and ducked out of the stadium without a word. The match was called off
after seventy-five minutes. Jospin was humiliated.[47]

Malek Boutih, president of SOS-Racisme, a leftist group that was attempting to better integrate France's North African immigrants, did what
he could to help Jospin. "Paradoxically," he told *Le Figaro,* the behavior of
the soccer spectators "is a sign that they feel French. If they had been Algerians, they never would have dared to treat a host country this way."[48]

For Chirac, the incident was sent by heaven. The outrageous behavior
at the soccer stadium not only made Jospin look bad, it set off a backlash
of anti-immigrant feeling that ultimately benefited Chirac at the polls.

At the same time, Jospin and his government failed to respond to a
wave of anti-Semitic attacks across France that shocked Jews worldwide.
Synagogues were fire-bombed and Torah scrolls destroyed for the "first
time since the Middle Ages," Jewish community leader Michel Mimouni
told me in the Paris suburb of Trappes. Contrary to Mitterrand, who immediately denounced the desecration of a Jewish cemetery in Carpentras
in 1982, Chirac kept silent as the attacks increased in number and violence.
While Jospin alienated Jewish constituents by his laxity in the face of these
attacks and by the rabid pro-Palestinian statements of Foreign Minister
Hubert Védrine and other Socialist Party leaders, Chirac roused the Right
by denouncing petty crime in the predominantly Arab immigrant suburbs.
(Later, he would sharply accuse American Jewish groups who dared criti-
cize France for failing to crack down on anti-Semitic violence of engaging

in "an anti-French campaign" on orders from Israel.) On March 27, less than one month before the elections, far-left candidate Arlette Laguiller led a "march against racism and anti-Semitism." Arab immigrant counter-demonstrators tagged the procession, screaming, *"Allahu Akbar"* ("God is Great"), and nearly came to blows with the demonstrators. On April 7, more than fifty thousand French Jews gathered in Paris to protest the anti-Semitic attacks. The only presidential candidate who showed up was free market conservative Alain Madelin. In the words of a senior Israeli diplomat, who attempted in vain to get the French to crack down on the worst anti-Jewish violence in centuries, "it is not just who commits these acts. There are those in the French government who permit them to occur, who create an atmosphere of tolerance toward anti-Semitic acts."[49]

This volatile mix transformed what initially had appeared as a dull rematch of the 1995 presidential election between Chirac and a lackluster Lionel Jospin into a historic upset. As election results from the first round started coming in on the evening of April 21, 2002, it became clear that support for Chirac was so thin within his own political family that he wouldn't manage to win even 20 percent of the vote. But the Left was even more divided and dispirited, with front-runner Jospin winning just 16.1 percent. Creeping in between them came far-right candidate Jean-Marie Le Pen, who with 16.8 percent would automatically face Chirac in the runoff.[50]

"Be prepared for surprises," French television anchors warned as the polls were about to close. When they announced the results, the French were stunned. Le Pen had been around for years and was generally dismissed as a buffoon known for his bad taste and dubious associations. A former French Foreign Legionnaire, Le Pen proudly evoked his military service during the Algerian war, when the French openly tortured proindependence guerrillas (known as *fellaga*), leaving wounds that have never fully healed. In a television appearance in 1987, Le Pen called the Nazi gas chambers "a detail of the Second World War." One year later, he dismissed a political opponent named Durafour in a play on words ("Durafour-crematoire") that compared his name to the Nazi crematoria ("four" means "oven"). When he was condemned by a French court for that racist slur, Le Pen turned around and used the case as further evidence that France was controlled by the Jews.

But Le Pen's appeal was genuine among ordinary Frenchmen and -women, who were fed up with the politicians, the scandals, and the abandon of French national sovereignty to supranational organizations such as the European Union and the UN. Taking Joan of Arc as his hero, Le Pen skillfully painted France as a victim of an international conspiracy of Jews, Freemasons, and American interests who sought to destroy the French national identity through immigration and globalization.

Once the shock of election night subsided, the entire French political class united behind Chirac. Massive street demonstrations "against racism" were held in cities across France that allowed the Socialists to mobilize their troops against Le Pen. French Jews and Muslims momentarily set aside their differences and marched together. "Le Pen made both Jews and Arabs afraid, so they joined together to fight a common enemy," says Thierry Keller of SOS-Racisme.[51] Even the Communists called their voters to support Chirac in the runoff. Chirac suddenly became a hero, the very incarnation of the permanent values of *La France.* In his own election rallies and television appearances, Chirac painted Le Pen as an enemy of the nation and of French values and called on leftist voters "who might feel orphaned from the democratic debate" to unify behind "humanist values" and the respect for human rights that he now incarnated in the name of France.[52] The press joined Chirac in painting the runoff election as a turning point in French history and called on French voters to reject the "racism" and "xenophobia" they claimed Le Pen represented.

The results were better than even Chirac had expected. The president who had been preparing his prison reading just months earlier was re-elected on May 5, 2002, to a second term with 82.21 percent of the vote. Demogoguing Le Pen was easy, and it worked. Parliamentary elections just weeks later gave Chirac a crushing majority and a mandate to rule France as he wished. Jacques Chirac's moment to make history had finally arrived.

# 12

# Saving Saddam

A nn Clwyd was not surprised when the *Daily Telegraph* correspondent telephoned her in London in late April 2003 from Baghdad to tell her about the documents he had found in the ruins of the Iraqi Foreign Ministry in Baghdad. Chairman of Indict, a nonprofit organization partially funded by the U.S. Congress under the Iraq Liberation Act of 1998, Ann Clwyd was also a British Labour Party member of Parliament. The organization she chaired was established to gather evidence for the prosecution of Saddam Hussein and his top henchmen in an international tribunal for war crimes and crimes against humanity.[1]

In April 2000, Indict had organized an international conference in Paris to raise awareness in the French media of the horrendous human rights record of Saddam's regime. They brought in victims of torture, who described in detail the methods used by Saddam's eldest son, Uday, and the security services to punish suspected enemies. (One of Uday's favorites was to plunge his victim into a vat of acid and listen to him scream as the acid burned off his skin.) Indict had gathered testimony from survivors of the poison gas attacks on Kurdish villages and had interviewed parents who had been forced to watch as their children were raped before their eyes. They had videotape from Baath Party files that was seized during the

1991 uprising, showing Saddam's cousin Ali Hassan al-Majid personally interrogating prisoners who were forced to their knees in front of him, hands tied behind their back, then kicking them in the face and shooting them in the head. Known as "Chemical Ali" because of his role in the gassing of the Kurds, Ali Hassan al-Majid had been appointed "governor of Kuwait" by Saddam in 1991. (In the deck of cards given to U.S. soldiers to help them identify top regime officials, Ali Hassan al-Majid was the king of spades.) The litany of horrors uncovered by Indict, compiled into evidence books against some two dozen top Baath Party members, was overwhelming. And it was systematically ignored by most of the French press.

Daniel Mitterrand, the widow of the former French president, showed up to open the conference on April 14, 2000, at the Hotel Concorde Lafayette, just down the street from the Arc de Triomphe and the Champs-Élysées. Mrs. Mitterrand was well-known as a supporter of Iraq's Kurdish population and regularly had denounced the crimes of the Iraqi regime even as her own husband was approving additional arms sales to Baghdad.

When she arrived at the hotel that April morning, she was greeted by a crowd of angry hecklers, who jostled her and shouted out obscene comments. "At the time, the Iraqis who were working for us told us the picketers were Iraqis who were being paid by the regime," Ann Clwyd told me. "So when I heard about the documents, I was not surprised at all."

One of the picketers managed to acquire fake credentials to the conference and showed up inside. "We noticed that he was filming victims of the regime who were making witness statements about how they had been tortured. This was quite sensitive stuff. We called on the French police to get him to stop and to return his film," Clwyd recalled. "When they finally did catch up to him, he presented identity papers showing that he was an Iraqi diplomat accredited to the Moroccan embassy in Paris"—where the Iraqis had an interests section. "The police told us that since he had diplomatic status, they couldn't touch him."

Later that same afternoon, someone phoned in a bomb threat, forcing Indict to evacuate the conference hall for several hours. "After that, we had a telephone threat to the Indict office in London," Clwyd said, warning them to call off the conference. "We were very angry, particularly because of the filming, since everyone who testified had relatives inside Iraq and understandably didn't want to be identified."

At the time, Clwyd told me, she blamed the French for their "total inaction." Two Indict researchers went to the French police and gave statements about the behavior of the hecklers and the Iraqi diplomat, but nothing happened. "The people who were doing the picketing were being paid, it was very clear. They were all Iraqis." At the time, Clwyd says, she suspected the French were refusing to do anything about the harassment "because France was still doing business with Iraq."

Already, at the reception they had held the night before the official conference opening, one of Clwyd's Iraqi staff told her that Saddam's people had gotten inside. When she asked how that could have happened, she was told that he had managed to get hold of an official invitation despite the tightly controlled invitation list. The documents found by the *Daily Telegraph* reporter "only confirmed what I had already suspected, given the French police behavior."

Among the documents was a six-page letter dated February 1998 from Saddam Hussein to Jacques Chirac, "welcoming the French president's support in the campaign against sanctions and assuring him that Iraq did not have weapons of mass destruction," the *Daily Telegraph* reported. The "most damning" document that revealed the direct role played by the French authorities in harassing participants in the Indict conference was a March 28, 2000, memo to Saddam Hussein's presidential office from the head of Iraqi intelligence, the Mukhabarat, Tahir Jalil al-Habbush (the jack of diamonds among most wanted Iraqi war criminals). In the letter, al-Habbush states that "one of our sources" met the "deputy spokesman" of the French Foreign Ministry, "with whom he has good relations." The letter went on to claim that French Justice and Interior Ministry officials were working on finding a "legal way" of preventing the Indict meeting. Among other steps the French government pledged to take was to deny visas to Iraqi opposition leaders who wanted to come to France. At the time, day-to-day affairs of government, including the Justice and Interior Ministries, were run by Socialist premier Lionel Jospin, while President Chirac dominated defense and foreign affairs.

Although the French failed to find a legal way of preventing the Indict conference, they turned a blind eye to the strong-arm tactics Iraqi government agents operating virtually openly in France used to intimidate Indict. A follow-on memo, dated April 18, 2000, showed how grateful the Iraqi government was to the French for their help. Headed "The Failed Enemy Conference in Paris," it noted that Iraq's efforts to frustrate the conference goal of generating publicity to its efforts to indict Saddam and his cronies for war crimes had succeeded brilliantly, since the French media "ignored the event." That memo was signed by Foreign Minister Mohammad Said al-Sahaf, the same Iraqi official who, wearing a French beret, became known as "Comical Ali" during the war for the surrealistic briefings he gave as information minister.

The day the story appeared in the *Daily Telegraph,* Ann Clwyd asked British foreign secretary Jack Straw to investigate. She also demanded a formal apology from the French. Neither has been forthcoming. Instead, she says, the French embassy in London issued an immediate denial and sent a threatening letter "demanding" a meeting with her. "It was clear they were trying to put pressure on me," Ann Clwyd says. "The whole tone of the letter was outrageous. It's absolutely clear that they were in cahoots with Iraqi intelligence. I have no doubt about that whatsoever."

There was one other document in the package cited by the *Daily Telegraph.* One month after the successful operation against Indict in Paris, Saddam's personal office sent a memorandum to the Finance Ministry authorizing them to pay $383,439 to undisclosed beneficiaries in France. The subject line read "Role of Southern France," without further explanation. Some of President Chirac's most trusted operatives, known for handling delicate matters with his friends in the Arab world, lived and operated in the golden triangle in the south of France, although none was mentioned in the document. Their stomping ground ranged from Grasse—where I met Bernard Guillet and legendary arms brokers Samir Traboulsi, Walid Khoraitem, and many others—to the hills above St. Tropez, where Chirac crony Rafic Hariri, a billionaire wheeler-dealer who became Lebanon's prime minister, maintained a vast vacation residence. The point of the triangle jutted out into the Mediterranean at Cap d'Antibes, a wild promontory known for megabuck estates where uniformed private security guards patrolled the coast with automatic weapons at the ready. Chirac favored the Hotel Eden Roc, an exclusive resort that dominated the rugged coastline between the last estate on the Cap (home of Russian oligarch Boris Berezovsky) and the after-midnight disco town of Juan-les-Pins.

One of the more discreet part-time residents of Cap d'Antibes in the mid-1990s was Patrick Maugein, a Chirac family friend from Corrèze in the salami-and-cheese central mountains of France. An oil trader and intermediary who got his start with Marc Rich, the renegade American ultimately pardoned by President Clinton on his last day in office, Maugein had managed to keep his name out of the press until 1998, when he became embroiled in a very public battle over the ownership of the fabulously rich Yanacocha gold mine in Peru. Presenting himself as an adviser to the French government, Maugein told participants that the imbroglio was considered "an affair of State at the highest level in France" since it involved the sale of a 24.7 percent stake in the holding company that owned the mine held by the French state mining conglomerate, BRGM (Bureau de Recherches Géologiques et Minières).[2]

In his youth, Maugein had wanted to become a matador, although he now says that reporters have "slightly embellished" his story. ("Patrick was no more of a bullfighter than was Hemingway," his personal assistant, Alan Crossley, tells me. "But he did study bullfighting and speaks with great authority on the subject.")[3] The *International Herald Tribune* called him "a swashbuckling, secretive French business figure."

In addition to close ties to Chirac, Maugein helped set up a nonprofit association of opera lovers with former Socialist foreign minister, Roland Dumas, that put Dumas's mistress, Christine Deviers-Joncour, on the payroll. Later, he agreed to become the association's president, and flew Dumas to Vienna on board his private Falcon jet to hear the celebrated tenor Placido Domingo perform *Lohengrin*. It was just another discreet way of helping his friends. "Patrick is fairly apolitical," Crossley explained, and had friends across the political spectrum. "He is not even a card-carrying member of the RPR," Chirac's political party at the time.

Maugein says he first became close to Chirac in 1978, when he gave Chirac the idea of promoting Paris by bestowing honors on opera stars, starting with Domingo. "Soon Mr. Maugein was operating as a freelance diplomatic agent, he says, using his business network to feed information to Mr. Chirac and delivering messages from him."[4] That relationship reportedly continued after Chirac became president in 1995, although Crossley claims "it is friendly as opposed to the more sinister implications that one sees in the French press, that portray [Maugein] as some kind of grey eminence or advisor on international affairs. They are friendly people, who enjoy a chat, but that's all there is to it." I first heard Maugein's name in 1988, when he served on the board of the French government's prestigious Institut du Monde Arabe in Paris.

Maugein's close ties to Chirac were also well-known to Lok Le Floch-Prigent, president and CEO of French state-owned oil company Elf Aquitaine, who was jailed in 1995 and again in 2002 on corruption charges. In his often bitter and self-exculpatory memoir, *Affaire Elf: Affaire d'État*, Le Floch-Prigent claims that Maugein played a role in several commercial projects in which Elf was accused by investigative magistrate Renaud Van Ruymbeke of distributing kickbacks to French political parties and their leaders.

One of those deals—the purchase of the Spanish oil refinery Ertoil in 1990—was the handiwork of an Iraqi businessman named Nadhmi Auchi, who later became a target of the worldwide hunt for Saddam Hussein's hidden assets that was spearheaded by Wall Street investigator Jules Kroll. Auchi's main venture was a Luxembourg-based holding company called General Mediterranean Holdings (GMH). He was named in a June 16, 1988, Italian parliament investigation as one of two intermediaries who helped broker a $1.6 billion deal for Cantieri Navali Riuniti of Italy to sell six "Lupo" class frigates to Iraq in 1980, an activity that generated a $23 million payment to Auchi's Dowal Corporation, according to company documents discovered by the Italian Guardia di Finanza. Neither the Italian parliament or the Kroll investigation established that Auchi had violated existing laws or that he was sheltering Iraqi government assets, despite alleged ties to Saddam Hussein's half-brother Barzan Ibrahim al-Tikriti, a former Iraqi intelligence chief (Auchi today denies he had any relationship to Barzan). GMH bought the Ertoil refinery on Elf's behalf in late 1990 and resold it to Elf a few months later at a profit of at least 300 million French francs. French prosecutors were investigating claims that some of that money had been distributed to French political parties.[5]

"Everyone knows there were strong ties, longstanding ties, between expatriate Iraqis and the RPR," Le Floch-Prigent explained. "That party has a president, whose name is Jacques Chirac. Chirac knows Saddam Hussein, who knows Auchi." If you wanted to understand the ties among Chirac, Auchi, Iraq, and Elf, Le Floch-Prigent said, the man to see was Patrick Maugein, whose name was "inseparable from that of Chirac." Maugein "was very much involved in oil, from Iraq to Africa. Today he heads a British oil company, SOCO." Asked by coauthor Éric Decouty whether he was implying that Auchi had financed Chirac's political activities through Maugein, Le Floch-Prigent replied evasively: "I'm saying that the subject of investigation is the following: Trace the links from the Iraqis—both abroad, and inside Iraq—to the RPR. Nadhmi Auchi is part of the Iraqi diaspora. . . . If the prosecutors want to really investigate the money Auchi is said to have distributed, they may find the RPR which Chirac headed.[6]

But Maugein insists that he never knew Auchi, was never involved in fund-raising on Chirac's behalf, and "had never met or ever sought to meet Saddam." Auchi also denies any involvement in the alleged fund-raising scheme. Crossley noted, correctly, that Le Floch-Prigent never pursued the more startling "revelations" contained in his book when he took the witness stand during his public trial. Maugein freely admits that he traveled often to Baghdad in the 1980s, when Iraq was a major economic partner of France. Even after the first Gulf War, he told *Le Canard Enchaîné*, he went to Baghdad "more than once as an emissary for Chirac," who was then mayor of Paris.

Maugein has never sought to hide his friendly relationship with Tariq Aziz and the top management of Iraq's oil ministry or that he considers Iraq "part of [his] business," Crossley says. During the UN embargo, Maugein sent a shipment of free medicine to Iraq, "because there was a humanitarian problem there." He also introduced Tariq Aziz, whom he knew because of his oil contacts in Iraq, to Le Floch-Prigent when he became president of Elf, "because there was a dispute over fields the Iraqis wanted to take away from the French and give to the Russians." Maugein's intercession appears to have been successful, since the Iraqis announced in January 1999 that they had signed a production-sharing agreement with Elf Aquitaine for the Majnoon oil fields that was nearly as generous as the $40 billion to $60 billion deal negotiated earlier with Total for Nahr Umar.[7] "Patrick maintained these contacts during the embargo in the belief that when the embargo was lifted it would be useful to his London-based oil company, in which American interests were also represented," Crossley says.

After Le Floch-Prigent got caught up in the corruption scandals and was jailed, Elf officials claimed in 1998 that Maugein had helped negotiate a black market oil deal with Iraq through a British-Dutch trading company named Trafigura Beheer BV. Maugein called the allegation "pure fantasy." Iraq had become "a dangerous country, explosive, full of killers," and he was now avoiding it, he said.[8] According to a close confidant of Tariq Aziz I interviewed in Europe, who had personal knowledge of Saddam's secret overseas procurement network, Maugein may have served as an occasional intermediary between Chirac and Iraqi officials in the mid-1990s, but if he did, those relations soured by 1997–1998. "Chirac wanted to get rid of Saddam and get out from the shadow that relationship had cast upon him," this intermediary told me.

If the men from Elf Aquitaine had mistakenly identified Maugein as involved in the illicit traffic with Iraq, they were right to identify Trafigura. But it would take almost three full years for the United Nations to figure out what was going on right under the noses of its own monitors, who were paid to verify every single shipment of Iraqi oil leaving under the UN oil-for-food program. Those were three very lucrative years for Saddam and his friends in France.

Claude Dauphin and Eric de Turkheim had known Maugein when they worked together as oil traders at Glencore, the Marc Rich company based in Zug, Switzerland, far from the eyes of prying financial investigators. Like Maugein, they had "graduated" from the Marc Rich school of wheeling and dealing and in 1993 set up their own trading company, Trafigura. From Marc Rich, they learned the ins and outs of the offshore banking world and did their business through the Bahamas and the Virgin Islands, while setting up their front offices in London, Los Angeles, Beijing, and other major cities.

Nobody knew how long Trafigura had been engaged in a traffic that violated the United Nations sanctions on Iraq when the scheme finally came to light in November 2001, although the men from Elf Aquitaine first talked about it in February 1998. Trafigura's lawyers claimed the company had been duped by unscrupulous middlemen and "had no way of knowing" what was really going on.[9] But by all accounts, the trade had been a lucrative one—until the U.S. Treasury Department got on their case.

Ambassador Valery P. Kuchinsky of Ukraine says the UN sanctions committee became aware of the scheme when they received a letter from Theofanis Chiladakis, the captain of the *Essex*, a Liberian-registered "turbine tanker" that had UN approval to load Iraqi crude at Iraq's main export terminal at Mina al-Bakr. The problem, the captain wrote, was that after the UN monitors had signed off on his cargo, the Iraqis held him back at the port so they could "top off" his tanks with an extra 272,000 barrels. And it wasn't just a onetime affair. The *Essex* was twice topped off in Iraq under his command, on May 13 and August 27, 2001, Chiladakis wrote. On both occasions, the *Essex* had been chartered by Trafigura Beheer BV. Its smuggled oil netted $11.7 million at then market prices, money that reportedly "ended up in bank accounts controlled by the Iraqi government."[10]

As Ambassador Kuchinsky began to dig, he discovered that Trafigura was not alone in the scheme. After requesting assistance from the British and Dutch governments, where Trafigura operated, Kuchinsky discovered that a Trafigura subsidiary called Roundhead Inc. had bought the oil from a subsidiary of the French oil trader Ibex Energy, located in the British Virgin Islands, a well-known safe haven for offshore business. As part of the arrangement, Trafigura claimed it paid Ibex a "premium" of 40 cents a barrel over the official UN selling price, a condition frequently imposed by Iraq's state oil marketing organization as a means of freeing up additional cash for Iraq for other purposes, outside of UN control.[11]

The intelligence officers at the U.S. embassy in Athens who had interviewed Chiladakis also sent his information to CIA headquarters in Langley, where it was promptly forwarded to the Pentagon. Just days later, in early October 2001, U.S. warships quietly intercepted the *Essex* off the coast of the Caribbean nation of Curaçao before it could offload its illegal cargo. For four months the ship circled the island, unable to dock, as the U.S. Treasury Department negotiated with the company's attorneys. The incident wound up costing Trafigura more than $5 million in additional shipping costs and led them to sue Ibex in a London court for having misled them. Trafigura's lawyers claimed "there would have been no way to know that Ibex lifted oil outside the oil-for-food programme."[12] But Ibex managing director Jean-Paul Cayre claimed in an affidavit that Trafigura had cooked up the scheme to "make up for an earlier loss on an Iraqi oil deal that fell through in 1999." He also acknowledged paying SOMO $3.7 million via a Lebanese bank account, a clear violation of UN rules.[13]

The *Essex* case was just the tip of the iceberg. Diplomats detailed to the UN sanctions committee believed that this particular form of smuggling, by topping off vessels, had been going on for years. "It was by pure coincidence that we found out, and only because the captain of the ship alerted the UN," one diplomat said.[14] This particular scheme netted Iraq around $300 million per year, U.S. and UN officials believed, while Iraq's overall revenues from illegal oil trading brought in as much as $2.5 billion a year, which Saddam was using "to develop weapons of mass destruction and consolidate his power."[15] The incident clearly embarrassed the French government, which had certified Ibex Energy to the UN authorities as a legitimate trader. The French government suspended Ibex from the UN-approved oil-for-food program on November 9, "until French authorities completed investigations of its activities," particularly its alleged involvement in the *Essex* case.[16]

The oil-for-food program, enshrined in UN Security Council resolution 986 in 1995, had become a farce by the time the *Essex* was intercepted off the coast of Curaçao. For starters, the resolution itself was misnamed: the UN had never banned Iraq from importing food and paying for it with oil, even at the height of the embargo that was imposed to punish Saddam for his August 1990 invasion of Kuwait. Indeed, Security Council resolution 661 of August 1990 established a UN sanctions committee to monitor Iraqi purchases of food, medicine, and humanitarian goods. Known as the "661 Committee," that same UN group supervised the expanded trade arrangements agreed to in 1995 that allowed Iraq to sell crude oil worth several billion dollars per year. Under the "oil for food" resolution, Iraq was supposed to use the money to rebuild its oil industry, water purification plants, electrical power grid, and basic infrastructure. Thirty percent of the total was held in reserve by the UN compensation commission for war reparations to Kuwait and other victims of Iraqi aggression. Iraq could spend the rest to buy industrial equipment that had been approved by the sanctions committee on a case-by-case basis.

From the very start, Saddam violated even these generous UN restrictions. He began with the money: Saddam insisted the UN use the Banque Nationale de Paris (BNP) as the sole repository of Iraqi funds, perhaps hoping that his friends in France would look the other way so he could dip into the account for other purposes. When that didn't happen, the deposits built up—until more than $13 billion in unspent cash had accumulated in the BNP account in New York. "The BNP sent the UN an embarrassed letter," says former World Bank economist and Middle East specialist Patrick Clawson, "asking them to reduce the Iraq escrow account by spreading it across several different banks." The Iraq account had become the single-largest cash account on the BNP books and "had become a problem with their regulators," Clawson told me.[17]

Next, Saddam turned to fooling export-licensing authorities, using techniques that had been tested and proven by Hussein Kamil al-Majid, Amir Rashid al-Ubaydi, Amir Hamoodi al-Saadi, Safa al-Habobi, and others during the 1980s. Under the guise of "civilian" projects, he imported dual-use equipment that was intended for biological weapons labs, chemical weapons plants, ballistic missile production, or his clandestine nuclear weapons development program. Throughout the seven years of the oil-for-food program, oil sales worth more than $50 billion were approved by the UN's Office of the Iraq Program.[18] "The holes in the sanctions were big enough to drive a missile launcher through," a former congressional staffer who tracked the trade told me.

Under the UN procedures, companies seeking to sell equipment to Iraq first sought authorization from their own governments, which were responsible for vetting their bona fides. Once that vetting turned up no red flags—it seldom did—their governments would then submit the license request through their UN mission. In theory, the 661 Committee would review the contracts to make sure they included no military equipment. The UN's licensing procedure clearly indicates which mission submitted each contract and includes the mission's own reference number for the contract.

In a database I compiled of 2,858 separate export requests submitted to the 661 Committee, 1,646 were put on hold because of objections by one of the permanent members of the UN Security Council. In most cases, the holds were accompanied by requests for additional information from the exporter on the type of equipment involved; at times, they were motivated by the inherent military use of the equipment. In several cases, Britain notified the committee that it could not approve particular sales for as long as Iraq continued to deny UN arms inspectors free access to industrial sites around the country, since the proposed exports all presented "significant BW concern." In not one single case—not one!—was the hold placed on an export at the request of France. The French simply didn't consider Iraqi weapons of mass destruction a threat. It was an attitude that I would hear repeated again and again by French officials and politicians from all sides of the political debate. "Even if Saddam has these weapons, so what?" was the refrain. "He has never threatened France."

Saddam's intentions were transparent from the start. During the early phases of the oil-for-food program, he turned to front companies in three Arab countries: the United Arab Emirates, Egypt, and Jordan. It was clear that none of these countries actually produced the equipment their governments had approved for export to Iraq. They were transit countries—fronts for large industrial concerns in the United States, France, the United Kingdom, Germany, and Russia. The United States and Britain blocked hundreds of requests from all three, especially from the UAE, where Saddam's own sons were controlling the trade through cronies and cutouts.

Saddam also turned in a big way to Communist China, whose government routinely forwarded for UN approval contracts with its top arms exporters. Why would China North Industries Corp. (aka NORINCO), a company described by U.S. China experts as "*the* arms manufacturer of the People's Liberation Army," be selected by Iraq as its privileged supplier of "adult milk"? Yet China North received UN approval for five such sales, worth $22.4 million, in December 2000. Another major Chinese arms exporter, the China Aero-Technology Import-Export Company (CATIC), received additional contracts for the same product, worth $4.8 million. Perfectly innocuous? Perhaps. But despite repeated calls to the UN sanctions committee and to U.S. diplomats who had approved those particular sales, no one could tell me what "adult milk" actually was. NORINCO's primary product line was main battle tanks, field guns, and rocket launchers.

Much worse, from the U.S. point of view, were sales by Chinese manufacturers of fiber optics gear from Iraq. CATIC won approval from the UN in July 2000 to sell $2 million worth of "cables," which U.S. officials believe was fiber optic cable used for secure data and communications links between national command and control centers, long-range search radar, targeting radar, and missile launch units. China National Electric Wire & Cable sold $6,104,000 worth of unspecified "communications equipment/supplies," while another $15.5 million worth of goods came from the China National Technical Import Telecommunications Equipment Company, revealed in UN records made available to me by confidential sources.

German firms were doing the same thing. Companies such as Karl

Kolb—identified by UN arms inspectors as a key supplier of Saddam's chemical weapons plants—were back in Iraq, doing business fully authorized by the German government and the UN. Karl Kolb received twelve separate approvals for shipments to Iraq from its German parent company and another six approvals for shipments from its Austrian subsidiary, worth a total of $7,641,103.61, according to my database of oil-for-food contracts. Another five contracts, worth $1,135,332.87, were put on hold by the U.S. For many Iraqis—especially Iraqi Kurds who had borne the brunt of Saddam's chemical weapons assaults—having Karl Kolb do business in Iraq was akin to having the makers of Zyklon B gas, used to murder the Jews in Nazi crematoria, rebuild the German chemical industry after World War II. Words harsh enough to describe such an outrage are hard to find.

As for the Russians, in many cases they didn't even bother with the UN. In documents made available to me by an Iraqi businessman who was secretly cooperating with the Iraqi opposition, the former head of Russia's state-owned arms export monopoly, General Sergey Karaoglanov, proposed his own trading company, Kompomash, as an intermediary for purchases from the arms industry of the Russian Federation. One set of documents, dated October 27, 2000, is addressed to Mr. Ahmed Saeed al-Naboodah, managing director of Gulf Technical Trading and Services LLC in Dubai, after that company's earlier requests to ship goods through the UN program had been put on hold by the United States. Later, the Russians sold the weapons directly, including upgrade kits for Iraq's T-72 tanks and BMP troop transport vehicles, Russian-built Stingers, advanced gun-launched missiles, and other equipment.[19]

The French saw what was going on and didn't want to be left out. Saddam had once again become a $10 billion–per-year market, despite the UN sanctions. While that was less than half the pre–1991 Gulf War total, Saddam's Iraq was once again a land of opportunity for French exporters. Starting in 1998, they began to exploit the UN system shamelessly. By the time of the second Gulf War in March 2003, the French had become the largest single supplier of Saddam's regime, according to the CIA's *World Factbook*. My own conversations with export officials at a broad cross section of French companies, from telecommunications giant Alcatel to small, unknown manufacturers of agricultural equipment, showed clearly that the French government was backing the trade in a big way. They helped exporters get "accredited" as approved partners in the UN Oil for Food program—including shady dealers such as Ibex Energy, which had offered its services to procure over $11 million of industrial equipment Iraq was seeking to purchase on the international market, the UN data base shows. And the French pushed hard to get such contracts approved by the sanctions committee at the UN. Alcatel alone had signed contracts worth $100 million to upgrade Iraq's communications infrastructure with fiber optics equipment, which U.S. intelligence agencies complained made Iraq military communications more difficult to monitor. Just weeks after his inauguration in January 2001, President George W. Bush ordered U.S. fighter-bombers to strike Iraqi air defense sites that had been enhanced with newly imported fiber optics gear.[20]

Agricultural equipment suppliers Irrifrance, Ceva Sante Animale SA, EnviroTech Pumpsystems, Action Chimique et Thérapeutique, Alldos, and many others supplied equipment that the United States feared could be used for Iraq's biological weapons program. Other French companies were supplying specialized pumps of potential use for Iraq's centrifuge uranium enrichment programs. In all these cases, the French government not only approved: it pushed for UN authorization of the sales.

French automakers Renault and Peugeot had large outstanding contracts to supply military trucks, including tractor-trailers that could be modified for use as SCUD launchers. DOW Agrosciences, a French subsidiary of Dow Chemicals, had signed contracts to supply pesticides. A $40 million contract with the French subsidiary of Siemens to supply unspecified "engineering services" was put on hold by the U.S. mission at the UN, because of the potential benefit to Iraq's proscribed weapons programs. The United States and the United Kingdom placed "holds" on 271 French applications, worth more than $365 million, the UN records showed, often because of potential weapons use.

The single most important thing President Chirac did after his reelection in May 2002 was to push hard at the UN to "streamline" the procedures for getting exports to Iraq approved—in essence, gutting the export control process. "It used to take us twelve to eighteen months to get our contracts approved," the head of Middle East sales at agricultural equipment manufacturer Irrifrance told me. "The United States has blocked lots of our contracts. . . . But since mid-July [2002], there's been a 'revolution' in the procedure, thanks to the efforts of the French government. Now the

UN has only two ten-day periods to review the requests. Failure to meet that deadline means automatic approval," he told me.[21] In other words, thanks to the French, the UN controls over Saddam Hussein's imports effectively had been lifted. This was a major, unpublicized element that contributed to the U.S. sense of urgency in moving against Saddam later that year. The Bush administration knew full well that it was only a matter of time before Saddam managed to acquire all the equipment he needed to fill the gaps in his weapons programs. Thanks to the French, the floodgates had been lifted.

"Ahmad" is a former lieutenant colonel with Saddam Hussein's Special Security Organization (SSO), the outfit that orchestrated the incredible shell game with UN weapons inspectors, loading weapons production gear and biological weapons materials onto eighteen-wheel tractor-trailers and hauling it from one end of Iraq to the other, just ahead of the inspectors' visits. "Ahmad" ran a procurement company in the United Arab Emirates for the SSO for five years and knew all the ins and outs of the clandestine trade in weapons and dual-use gear.

In 1998, he was arrested and brutally tortured, on suspicion that he was cooperating with the Iraqi opposition (he was). The last thing he remembers from his months in prison was being severely beaten, then given a shot and dragged out into a car. When he came to his senses, he was lying in a Baghdad street, bleeding from his mouth and his nose. Half-conscious and in incredible pain, he managed to rendezvous with a contact from the opposition Iraqi National Congress, who operated a rat line to spirit defectors out of Baghdad to the Kurdish-controlled areas in the north, where they could eventually escape to Turkey. When he was examined several days later by human rights workers, they found that "Ahmad" was also bleeding internally. The Iraqis had injected him with thallium (rat poison) and dumped him on the street, thinking he would die. It was a favorite technique of Saddam's Mukhabarat.

I met "Ahmad" in the London office of Dr. Ahmad Chalabi, the leader of the Iraqi National Congress, six months before the war. He explained that the clandestine Iraqi procurement networks were split between Saddam's two sons Qusay and Uday. "For instance, Alia is a company with offices in the Gardens district of Amman," he said. "It is legally registered as a Jordanian company, but it is controlled by Uday via share ownership and cutouts. Alia tells companies who want to sell to Iraq that they must use their services to get Iraqi government contracts. They add 10 percent onto the contract as a kickback for the family."

French exporters I interviewed were aware of Alia and its French operation, known as Sofrag Alia Development, and said they tried to avoid them—when they could. But if Alia found out they were going behind its back, all of a sudden the doors at the ministry where they had been received gladly the day before would close. "It never failed," one exporter told me. "They clearly had tremendous power." Dozens of French companies used Alia's services.

The French government had approved a contract from Sofrag Alia Development France to provide $1 million worth of oil well–logging equipment to Iraq, ostensibly to help rebuild Iraqi oil fields. The French UN mission submitted the contract for UN authorization on May 2, 2001. Such equipment was particularly sensitive because it contained neutron generators, which UN weapons inspectors discovered were key components in the crude gun implosion nuclear device Iraq had designed and tested before the 1991 Gulf War. The French knew this—indeed, their nuclear experts working with UN arms inspectors were among the best. And yet, they let such sales go through, giving them the full backing of their UN delegation. One can only wonder what their motives could have been.

There was another scheme Saddam used to cheat the UN, "Ahmad" said: "They are so desperate for cash to use for other purposes, such as building up their weapons, that they signed fake contracts with suppliers just to unblock funds from the UN escrow account," he claimed. In exchange for this complicity, the Iraqis paid the company up to 40 percent of the face value of the contract, just for their services in faking contracts submitted to their governments and the UN. "They let the company keep 40 percent without shipping any goods, so they can get the other 60 percent from the UN account in cash," he said.

There was a whole underworld of fly-by-night trading companies and shady middlemen representing major French companies doing business with Iraq. Saddam Hussein and his sons knew they could trust the French government not to blow the whistle on the kickback schemes, since the French were also getting their cut.

Just how much was that cut? Lebanese lawyer Elias Firzli has been dealing with Iraq for nearly forty years and says that he first met Saddam Hussein, Tariq Aziz, and other top Iraqi Baath Party leaders in 1962 when he was the publisher of the Beirut daily newspaper *Al-Sayyat.* As an unofficial adviser to the Iraqi government, he saw many of those brokers vying for their piece of the pie. "In 1994, it was like the gold rush. Everybody wanted to get there first. They even set up companies in Paris to facilitate trips and visas to Iraq," he told me.

But by the time the war broke out in March 2003, Firzli claims that most of that activity had fallen off. "Saddam thought Chirac was still his friend and sent him a telegram of congratulations for his election in 1995," he recalls. "But Chirac was afraid of being publicly tied to Saddam Hussein, and so he never answered. Saddam had the telegram published in the Iraqi press, and Chirac was furious. It was all downhill from there," Firzli claims. This was one reason why Chirac told UN chief arms inspector Rolf Ekeus that he was "angry" with Saddam when he met with Ekeus privately in New York that autumn.*

There may have been another reason for Chirac's "anger" with Saddam, Firzli hinted. "Someone running for president in France would expect tens of millions of dollars, not hundreds of thousands, which is the most anybody would have been getting on the oil deals" under the UN embargo. Chirac cronies were still receiving oil contracts from Iraq at the time of Chirac's election, "but it was small stuff. They would get two million barrels, three million barrels. Say they earned 10 percent. That's a few hundred thousand dollars. In the 1980s, the contracts were in the tens of billions of dollars, so the commissions were on a very different scale."[22] Chirac's reaction is reminiscent of Barzini's, the Mafia don in *The Godfather* who turned against the aging Don Corleone because he was no longer sharing the wealth. "[H]e has to let us draw water from the well," Barzini says in the movie, explaining his revolt to his fellow crooks.

But if the trade was relatively small, the French industrial lobby saw it taking off like a rocket once the sanctions were lifted; and if Chirac represented anyone, it was the industrial lobby. French conglomerate Vivendi, for instance, was negotiating a billion-dollar deal to rebuild the Iraqi water purification system shortly before the 2003 war broke out that would have kept it busy in Iraq for a decade. And that was just one example.

---

*See chapter 10.

"Deep in the soul of Jacques Chirac, he believes that Saddam Hussein is preferable to the alternative that is likely to emerge when Iraq is liberated," Richard Perle said prophetically in February 2003.[23] And he was right. Chirac knew that France would never get the same kinds of deals from a free Iraqi government, established under U.S. supervision, that operated transparently and awarded contracts according to merit and price, not political favoritism, kickbacks, and bribes. And that is one reason the French insisted the United States turn Iraq into a United Nations protectorate, in the hope they could reassert their corrupt and corrupting influence after the liberation, far from the light of day. When that idea fell flat, the French insisted on rushing full sovereignty onto a new Iraqi government in the belief it would be crippled by factionalism and, thus, easy for France to manipulate to its benefit. There was no logical connection between these two diametrically opposed positions, other than the bold assertion of French commercial interest. French commentators, for all their slavish devotion to Cartesian logic, have universally failed to pick up on the fundamental absurdity of this policy about-face by their government.

"French diplomacy today continues to consider Iraq as a cake to be divided and not as a democracy to be constructed," former Chirac ally Alain Madelin told me. "One of the demands of France [at the UN] is that there be an [Iraqi] authority not under American control over Iraq's economy, in charge of contracts."[24] Top on the list of French priorities were the Total and Elf production-sharing contracts, which combined in the now privatized TotalFinaElf conglomerate would be worth well over $100 billion over seven years, if the new Iraqi government could be coerced into accepting their blatantly disadvantageous terms.

Whenever I evoke those contracts with French officials, I hear sighs and the cracking of knuckles. "It was not illegal to negotiate those contracts, but we wouldn't let Total sign," a top adviser to Foreign Minister Dominique Galouzeau de Villepin told me. "We get all the blame, but not the signature! We are still kicking ourselves for that. We pass for a country that is cynical and immoral," he complained, "without getting the business such an attitude is presumed to bring."[25]

*Quel scandale* indeed! I thought.

# 13

# The Quest for Glory

Not a day goes by that I don't inhale the
perfume of the discreet violet.
—DOMINIQUE DE VILLEPIN

W ell after the fall of Baghdad on April 8, 2003, embedded French reporters with U.S. and British troops continued to file doom-and-
gloom stories back home. Like Comical Ali, who insisted that U.S.
tanks would "never, ever" enter Baghdad as they were visible to television
viewers just behind him, France could never quite believe that the United
States had vanquished Saddam Hussein and his bloodthirsty regime after
just three weeks of fighting. They continued to refer to Iraq's liberators as
the "Anglo-American forces," a phrase that has particular resonance with
the French, since it was how the Vichy collaborationist government referred to the Allies who were landing on the Normandy beaches to liberate
France from the Nazi occupation in 1944. After a Radio France Internationale editorial reminded French reporters of that unfortunate association, some headline writers switched to an almost comic alternative: *les
forces coalisés*. The formula was as awkward in French as it was in translation ("the coalesced forces") and made the coalition of nearly forty countries that contributed troops and equipment sound like a mayonnaise
whipped up by President Bush and Secretary of Defense Rumsfeld. When
it became impossible even for the French to deny the obvious, they interviewed supporters of Saddam Hussein in hiding who claimed they would

"never, ever" accept defeat—even after Saddam's capture on December 13, 2003!

Middle East specialist Gilles Kepel, normally a sane and interesting commentator, gave a hilarious interview to *Le Figaro* explaining in all seriousness why the Americans absolutely needed French "expertise" to understand tribal society of Iraq, as if the feuding of Hatfields and of McCoys was something beyond the intelligence of the American military officers who were dealing with Iraqi tribal leaders on a day-to-day basis, rebuilding schools and bridges, opening factories, staffing hospitals, providing jobs, training policemen and a new army, and taking part in school graduation ceremonies in the presence of the entire population of rural towns as welcome guests, protectors, role models, and heroes.[1] When reality so starkly contradicted everything they had been told by the government and were repeating to the French people, the French media simply denied reality. Reading the French press reporting on Iraq or the United States is like falling down a rabbit hole and waking up in Wonderland.

The very public clash with America hit a responsive chord with the French media elite. Latent anti-Semitism on the Left and Far Right combined with fears of American power and preeminence to unleash a hurricane of anti-American invective that began well before the war and lasted well afterward. Fanciful conspiracy theories were brandished by otherwise reputable people. In one of the most scurrilous, the Washington, D.C., correspondent of the French daily *Le Monde* argued that Bush administration neocons were actually secret Israeli citizens, pushing the administration to do Israel's bidding.[2]

French foreign minister Dominique Galouzeau de Villepin appeared to agree with those sentiments. In a closed-door session with members of the French Parliament shortly before Baghdad fell, he reportedly claimed that the "hawks" in the U.S. administration were "in the hands of [Israeli prime minister Ariel] Sharon." The war in Iraq was being led by a "pro-Zionist" lobby that included Deputy Defense Secretary Paul Wolfowitz, White House staffer Elliot Abrams, and Pentagon adviser Richard Perle, all of them Jews.[3] In my interviews with a broad cross section of French government officials, it was clear that France's leaders had failed to understand the determination of the American president and the American people after 9/11 and had failed even to game out the possible consequences of their actions. But for Villepin, it was all a Jewish conspiracy.

While the French never let up in their criticism of the United States during the war, they rushed to demand their "share" of reconstruction contracts once the fighting stopped, under the pretext of turning over control of the occupation to the United Nations. Now that the war was won, they argued, the United States should step aside so international bureaucrats could divvy up Iraq's economy—and future oil production—treating them as the spoils of war. But Colin Powell wasn't having any of it. When asked by U.S. television interviewer Charlie Rose on April 23 if there would be consequences for having opposed the United States, Powell said, "Yes. . . . We have to look at all aspects of our relationship with France in light of this."

The bitterness was palpable on both sides of the Atlantic. Two days after Powell's remarks, a surreal exchange took place in the packed press room at the otherwise elegant Quai d'Orsay, where Villepin's sweating spokesman did his best to sweep aside direct questions from reporters with the haughtiness others used to reprimand foolish schoolchildren.

**Journalist:** How would you characterize the Franco-American relationship?

**Spokesman:** We have already addressed this point on many occasions, and I have nothing new to add today. I would refer you to the statements by the French authorities and by the American authorities, since you have to be two to have a relationship.

**Journalist:** What is France's reaction to the U.S. intention to resort increasingly to the NATO planning committee [which does not include France] instead of the Atlantic Council?

**Spokesman:** That is a hypothetical question.*

**Journalist:** Is it true that French diplomats are not welcome when they visit their American counterparts during official visits to the United States?

**Spokesman:** I have no comment, but I would suggest that you interest yourself in things that are less anecdotal than the rumors you find in the press.

**Journalist:** How can we accept statements, such as that made by Mr. Bush yesterday, when he said we shouldn't expect him to invite President Chirac to his ranch?

---

*No, it wasn't. The United States had gone to the planning committee in March to seek approval to dispatch defensive equipment to Turkey at its request, after the French and the Germans blocked the request in the council.

**Spokesman:** No comment.

**Journalist:** Have you gotten a sense that there's an American willingness to downgrade French participation in international meetings?

**Spokesman:** No comment.

**Journalist:** Two days ago, you described the conversation between Mr. Villepin and Colin Powell as "very cordial." Could you tell us more?

**Spokesman:** No.[4]

Condoleezza Rice told reporters famously after the war that the Bush administration intended to "pardon Russia, isolate Germany, and punish France." The administration began manifesting its displeasure through small gestures, many of which never made news. In April, a French request to extend the tour of duty of the French military officer assigned to the U.S. Air Force global-positioning system (GPS) program office in Los Angeles was denied. The space-based navigational system provides coordinates worldwide for everything from pleasure boats to cruise missiles. Without GPS data, French combat jets can't fly. Defense Secretary Donald Rumsfeld himself banned the armed forces from sending military aircraft to the upcoming Paris air show, as in 1993, and encouraged U.S. defense contractors to boycott the show, with mixed results. He also banned military attachés around the world and Pentagon officials in Washington from attending any social functions hosted by the French diplomatic corps, a top Rumsfeld adviser told me.[5]

And that was just for starters. In early May, the Pentagon called the French military attaché in Washington to inform him that France would not be getting its usual slots at the March 2004 Red Flag exercise, NATO's premier live flying war game. The United States traditionally invited its best allies to participate in the exercise at Nellis Air Force Base in Nevada, and the French had been regular and avid guests. Later that same month, Homeland Security officials at Los Angeles International Airport detained and expelled six French journalists who had come to cover a video game trade show, because they didn't have visas. The U.S. visa waiver program applies to French tourists and business travelers but specifically exempts working journalists, who are required to apply for visas. The six French reporters were handcuffed and taken to a detention facility until they could be put on the next flight home.[6] Later, a request from the French chief of staff to visit CENTCOM headquarters in Tampa, Florida, was blocked by President Bush in person.

Colin Powell traveled to Paris on May 23 for a breakfast session with Dominique de Villepin—the first one-on-one meeting between the two since Villepin ambushed him at the UN months earlier. By all accounts, the coffee was cold. Powell told reporters they still had to "work out any remaining sharp edges . . . that are still there as a result of this disagreement." Among the topics on the agenda was the Middle East "road map" the Europeans had co-sponsored with Russia and the United States, in an effort to move Israelis and Palestinians further from violence and closer to negotiations. Powell knew that Villepin was planning a trip to the region and specifically asked that he not undermine the road map by meeting with Yasser Arafat, who was refusing to hand over responsibility for his security forces to newly appointed prime minister Mahmoud Abbas (Abu Mazen). The United States was encouraging Abbas to crack down on elements in Arafat's security forces who were aiding terrorist groups, but he was getting nowhere because of Arafat's interference. Powell argued that it was critical to sideline Arafat if Abbas was to succeed.

Just one week after the icy espresso with Powell, Villepin traveled to the Middle East and pointedly made a very public pilgrimage to Ramallah, where Arafat had been confined by the Israelis. But it was much more than just a quiet courtesy call: it was a direct slap in the face to Powell. Villepin came bearing a "message of encouragement" from President Chirac, he told reporters. When questioned later, he praised Arafat as the "legitimate elected president of the Palestinian Authority." As with Saddam Hussein, Arafat was a leader the French could deal with, because they had invested so much in propping up his corrupt regime and had received so much in return.

Clearly the climate in U.S.-French relations was not improving; the memories of Chirac and Villepin's bald-faced lies to the president and to Powell were just too fresh. With the annual G-8 economic summit scheduled to be held at the fairy-tale lakeside resort at Evian in early June, there were suggestions that President Bush might forgo the event entirely or at the very least refuse to spend the night on French soil. (Excellent hotels were just a short boat trip across the Lac Leman in Lausanne, Switzerland.) He didn't, and he even met—however briefly—with Chirac before the working lunch. But the president's advance team orchestrated the diplomatic ballet in such a way as to deliver an unmistakable snub. According to protocol and past practice, Bush should have flown directly from Andrews Air Force Base to France, to highlight the primacy of ties to an old ally. Instead, he first stopped off in Poland, where he challenged the "new Europe" to join as partners with America in fighting terrorism, proliferation, and famine. Seated at the long formal head table, waiting to address a press conference with his fellow leaders, the president pointedly refused a waiter's effort to serve him from a bottle of the town's famous mineral water, jokingly beckoning to American reporters to ask if they could get him a coffee instead.[7] But when Chirac insisted on the need for a "multipolar" world, the fur began to fly. "We have an alliance," White House spokesman Ari Fleischer told reporters. "Allies treat each other as partners without regard to poles. It's not a matter of a multipolar relationship. There's no need for somebody to be between the United States and anybody else."[8] Bush made sure he headed out—to a summit in Aqaba, Jordan—before the final banquet. Canadian prime minister Jean Chrétien told reporters after it was all over that the meetings had gone well. Why did he say that? they asked. It took him a while, but finally it dawned on him: "Because it could have been a disaster."

French philosopher and columnist André Glucksmann mocked the French president's willingness to "stand up" to America by allying himself with Russian leader Vladimir Putin. "Down with the 'cowboy' and his adventurism! Long live the despot and his war in the Caucasus!" Putin's troops, Glucksmann wrote, bound Chechen civilians together like bundles of sticks, blew them up with explosives, and threw their remains into the ditch. But despite this barbaric behavior, and despite the murder of an estimated one hundred thousand civilians during the Chechen war, for French president Chirac, "Russia fascinates, its immense riches sharpen the appetite, its brute, disproportionate use of force inspires respect."[9]

If Chirac was ever troubled by the contradictions inherent in his new faith or the brutal behavior of his new "partner," he never let on. Like demagogues before him, he was too caught up in the thrill of the fast-charging stallion beneath him to see that he was riding France headlong back to the nineteenth century, when Europe was divided into opposing armed camps, each poised at the other's throat. Writes Glucksmann, "The new 'multipolar' world is nothing but a carbon copy of the old model of the European balance that held sway from 1648 until 1914."[10]

There were many reasons the French opposed the United States on Iraq. Money was certainly one of them. To appreciate the importance of the

THE FRENCH BETRAYAL OF AMERICA

cozy oil deals the French had negotiated with Saddam, multiply the $100 billion TotalFinaElf hoped to earn by five (the relative size of the U.S. economy) and you get half a trillion dollars—clearly no trifling benefit for remaining loyal to Saddam Hussein. All of those deals were likely to include generous backdoor payments to French political parties, from left to right. (Despite new laws that provided generous public financing for political campaigns, the appetite for cash remains unabated.)

For Alain Madelin, the role of money in forging Jacques Chirac's determination to oppose the United States and Britain on Iraq was absolutely clear: "You can't have billions and billions in arms deals or large construction projects when you know that the kickbacks on those contracts was often greater than 5 or 10 percent. Huge sums of money were put into circulation as a result of these pro-Arab policies. That is the hidden face of these policies. We'll know the extent of it one day, perhaps."

But not everyone in France agreed with Chirac on the benefits of supporting Saddam Hussein. Indeed, a group of twenty top French business leaders flocked to the Élysée in February 2003 as France was threatening to veto the latest United Nations war resolution, in a last-ditch effort to convince Chirac to drop his opposition to the U.S.-led war effort. "They understood that Chirac's attitude could have a long-lasting impact on French business in the United States," a knowledgeable U.S. official told me.[11] By that time, however, Chirac had concluded that saving Saddam Hussein had become synonymous with saving Chirac. He had gone too far to turn back without losing face.

Although he was no longer threatened with going to jail, at least for as long as he remained in the Élysée, Chirac was widely considered by friends and foes alike as a lightweight, a *guignol* (puppet), a poor imitation of de Gaulle. Without a grand international victory that put France back on the map, Chirac would be remembered as an *affairist*, a scandal-plagued president who relied on black money and corruption for the source of his power because he could never muster any real depth of popular support or even respect. Opposing America and saving Saddam was going to be Chirac's ticket to history's hall of fame. Chirac was determined to make France a world power once again, after sixty years of betrayal, mediocrity, and decline.

Chirac "believed diplomacy was a zero sum game," the U.S. official said. "For France to go up" in prestige and world esteem, "the United

States had to go down." Despite efforts to convince him otherwise, and despite a personal offer from President George W. Bush during the Evian summit to "work together in partnership" after war, Chirac responded without any real conviction. "You could tell he didn't really believe it," the official said.

French politicians and policy commentators I interviewed from left to right agreed that a number of factors motivated Chirac's willingness to cast aside the 225-year-old alliance with America in favor of a tinpot dictator from a mud-and-wattle village on the outskirts of Tikrit whose ability to survive was cast in doubt. "Opposing the United States was a form of consensus politics," said a member of Chirac's ruling coalition. "There was broad support for the policy for domestic political reasons." The French Socialists liked to remind Chirac that he was reelected to the presidency with their votes, so he had been careful to do nothing to antagonize them. And the Socialists were dead set against the war. "It was leaders in Chirac's own party who were uncomfortable with his policy toward the war, not us," left-wing Socialist Party leader Arnaud Montebourg told me. "We supported him 100 percent because we felt this was an illegitimate, imperial war."[12] In October 2003, five months after President Bush declared the end of major hostilities in Iraq, public opinion polls in France continued to show that more than 80 percent of those surveyed in France still supported Chirac's decision to keep France out of the war. It was a wildly popular position that stemmed from a deep underlying identity crisis that had seized Europe with the end of the cold war. To affirm its difference from America the victor, Europe had to wage a "war against war."

For Guy Millière, a professor at the University of Paris and a Bank of France economist, Chirac had "five million reasons" for supporting Saddam: the five million–plus Muslim residents of France, now 10 percent of its total population, many of them living in suburban housing projects that had become virtually off-limits to the police. France's Arab population supported Saddam overwhelmingly, with a passion verging on frenzy. For them, Saddam Hussein was the embodiment of Arab dignity, of Arab independence. Not themselves subject to the Iraqi leader's brutal repression, they could indulge the romantic image Saddam created for himself as a modern-day Saladin, come to liberate the Arab and Muslim world from foreign occupation. "French leaders . . . will never take a decision that could make young radical Muslims angry," Millière noted. If the French had supported the U.S.-led war, "the results would have been riots in the suburbs."[13]

Millière and others have claimed that under Chirac, France behaves more and more as if it is the "leader of the Arab world," not a liberal Western democracy.[14] A member of Chirac's own party told me that Chirac is known in Gaullist circles as "the Sukarno of the northern hemisphere," after the former leader of Indonesia who aspired to be the leader of the developing world in the 1960s. "That's not to say that Chirac is an advocate of the third world: he is not," this politician confided. "But it gives you an indication of how low he has come in seeking to curry favor on the international scene, and how bad his relations with Washington have become."

Up until January 2003, members of Chirac's own party believed he would back down, agree to a U.S. resolution at the UN that specifically endorsed the use of force against Saddam, and send French troops to the battlefield as part of the coalition. But even here it turned out that there were practical problems. "Militarily, we simply didn't have the means to effectively join the coalition," says François d'Aubert, a former cabinet minister in the ill-fated government of Chirac protégé Alain Juppé. "For six years the army was in a shambles, with no financial resources. Our aircraft service rates were abysmal. Because we already have so many troops overseas in peacekeeping operations, we simply didn't have the forces ready to deploy."[15]

And then there was oil. Since the 1973 oil crisis, d'Aubert pointed out, "France has been plagued by the fear that we could actually lose access to energy supplies, or at least have them become so expensive that they would destroy our economy. That's what happened in 1973. The French economy has never fully recovered from the 1973 oil shock, and it still haunts us today." That was why the French liked to enter long-term supply contracts and were certainly counting on Saddam for future supplies, just as they had relied on him in the past. "Oil is absolutely critical to understanding French foreign policy," d'Aubert said. "In France, we feel that when our national oil companies are present, we have a physical guarantee of oil supplies. It may also help to reduce the price." Perhaps. But by signing such contracts with less than democratic regimes in places such as Gabon, Nigeria, and Iraq (instead of Norway or Britain, which were closer by), the French also were able to capitalize on "special relations" with the leaders of those countries, which often included kickbacks and special discounts.

But underlying it all was an unbridled quest for glory.

A lain Madelin fell silent for nearly a minute when I asked him what he thought had pushed Chirac and Villepin to actively undermine the U.S. effort to build an international coalition at the United Nations and at NATO. Finally he gave a sigh:

"You've got to understand that a good part of this is the personal saga of Dominique de Villepin. If you read his book *Le Cri de la gargouille* [*The Gargoyle's Cry*], you understand everything. His heroes are Machiavelli and Napoleon. He explains that the French people have been disenchanted by their Prince and need to fall in love with him again through a grand, flamboyant, international epic."

I read Villepin's book, as well as his five-hundred-page account of Napoleon's three-month return to power in 1815, and Madelin is right. They provide extraordinary insight into the thinking and character of Chirac's top foreign policy aid. Written in a rhapsodic prose that at times would embarrass a college sophomore for its self-indulgence, Villepin argues that France today stands at a crossroads. Destiny calls her forward to continue the "great epic" of French history, "from Clovis to Louis XIV, from the Revolution to Napoleon, from Clemenceau to General de Gaulle!" But France also risks irrelevance. "Will France become an island swept away by her fantasies, justifying the critics who evoke her vain arrogance? Or will she be faithful to herself and find the strength and imagination to surprise yet again?"[16]

Villepin's political essay is driven by a deep fear that France will be unable to adapt to the post–cold war world or compete in the global marketplace, where the advantages and subsidies granted by the state to French companies would be subjected to international scrutiny and possibly banned. In August 2003, for instance, when the French government went into overdrive to craft a support package of 3 billion euros ($3.6 billion) to protect heavy industry giant Alsthom from bankruptcy, the European Commission considered retaliation, a move unheard of just a few years earlier. France fears "the sun of new realities," Villepin writes. (p. 17) The real struggle in today's world, he believes, is not between freedom and tyranny, but between the French religion of the all-powerful state and the Anglo-American system of transparency, checks and balances, which he reminds his readers "inspired only contempt" when the original generation of

French revolutionaries looked across the Atlantic for support in 1793. (p. 33) I think he is right—for France. Americans need to understand that our values and our model pose a challenge for the French, who have consistently favored authoritarian regimes over democracy, not just in the third world but also in Europe, where they still are attempting to force an autocratic constitution for the European Union down the throats of the newly liberated nations of the former Soviet bloc despite an outright rejection of their model by a European summit on December 14, 2003.

Villepin's answer for France's ills is to revive the "French model" of government from the top down, as opposed to the American model of government from the bottom up. "Long ago, power had an aura that no one would dispute. You kneeled before the powerful because a single gesture, a word spoken slightly more loudly than another, a sign of satisfaction or irritation, would be decisive, announcing an act modifying the order of the world." Today, the French believe that "power has abandoned them," Villepin writes with apparent regret. "What is power that can do nothing?" (pp. 15–16) Faced with the challenge from America, its overwhelming economic success, its "unbridled domination" (p. 49), the frightening mobility of a classless society where social norms must be reinvented with each generation, "how could some of us not feel tempted by nostalgia for a time when France was ruled by an all-powerful state, that had only to appear to be obeyed? France is obsessed with power; it is a national illness come from the depths of the ages." (p. 17) First among Frenchmen who share that obsession are Dominique Galouzeau de Villepin and his "Prince," Jacques Chirac.

Today's France has been unable to adapt to the loss of its previous aura of power and prestige, Villepin believes. "The French model, just yesterday the incarnation of modernity, has not aged well in these new times. . . . The face of progress has ceased to be friendly [to France]." (p. 66) For government to re-enchant the people, Villepin says it "must restore its sense of mission, circumscribe uncertainty, impose limits, establish its authority without hesitation, provoke without limit. . . ." (p. 80) France as a country "doubts and is bored," he writes with all the haughty certainty of a Left Bank coffee shop intellectual. "Here is a country that had the vocation of inspiring princes and kings, that sent its philosophers to the Courts of Europe whose elites spoke our language, that built new ideas in the hope of spreading them around her, that criticized, judged, appreciated, and distilled the lightning bolt of reason from the chaos of history. Today hardly anyone listens to her any longer and the universe moves on without her, when it doesn't judge her with contempt or commiseration." (p. 88) Poor France!

Villepin's solution is an authoritarian state—the "republican monarchy" established by de Gaulle, ruled by a charismatic leader who, like Napoleon, will "vanquish or die" in pursuit of glory. France has "a rendezvous with destiny," he says, exhibiting his trademark originality. (p. 214) "Rich with their assets, [the French] intend to revive the epic of the great collective adventures." (p. 212) Such adventures, Villepin makes clear, are those of the "great" leaders, from Napoleon, who subdued the entire European continent only to lose it—and the lives of millions of soldiers and civilians—when the rest of Europe had had enough, to de Gaulle, who proclaimed France a great nation after its debacle of collaboration with the Nazi enemy.

"Not a day goes by that, seized by doubt, I don't meditate on these voices from the past," he writes in the preface to his hymn to Napoleon, *The Hundred Days*. (p. 9) "Not a day goes by that I don't inhale the perfume of the discreet violet," which he hastens to explain is the "symbol of loyalty to Napoleon." (p. 10)

Such words and sentiments, penned by a mature individual at the summit of power in a major state, bespeak a dangerous delusion and a penchant for authoritarianism. With little regard for the realities of the world after the fall of the Berlin Wall and the collapse of communism, de Villepin merrily turns back the clock to March 1815—his favorite period of French history.

And Jacques Chirac—the president who nearly wound up in jail—actually believed the late-night fantasies of his aristocratic foreign minister, taking them for achievable reality. France has always defined itself in opposition; Chirac hoped to find glory in opposing U.S. "hegemony." Indeed, Chirac likes to boast that he now represents 80 percent of world opinion—not just the French—in leading the opposition to the United States and the increasing globalization of the world economy. "After he won reelection with over 80 percent of the vote, the figure of 80 percent seemed to stick in his head," French journalist Anne-Elisabeth Moutet told me. "He keeps repeating it at every occasion."[17]

Villepin went to London not long after the Iraq war began, claiming he sought to smooth ruffled feathers in the transatlantic dispute. Instead, his speech before the International Institute for Strategic Studies was a ringing indictment of U.S. policy, which he accused of having "shattered" the world order. Asked by a reporter which side he wanted to win the war, he replied testily: "I'm not going to answer. You have not been listening carefully to what I said before. You already have the answer." But reporters present did not agree, and headlined Villepin's studied ambiguity the next day, saying that his refusal suggested sympathy for Saddam at the very moment U.S. and British forces were engaged in combat. The French foreign ministry said it was "indignant" at the reports.[18]

Villepin's strutting and delusions of grandeur at times turned France into an object of ridicule. After the war, at an international meeting in Versailles, Villepin solemnly proclaimed that he and the Pope—and they alone—had saved the West from a clash of civilizations with Islam. "There was an audible gasp in the room," one participant said. "People couldn't believe what they were hearing. They were visibly stunned." Within hours, Villepin's comments were being whispered in Parisian salons as if they were the stuff of divine revelation. I heard them repeated by government officials without the slightest hint of irony.

Such pretensions would be pathetic—if they weren't coming from France, a country bound to America through generations of a love-hate relationship and a country that still has much to offer.

Major Andrzej Wiatrowski, a spokesman in Iraq for Polish troops who had joined the coalition, was excited. During an inspection of a former military factory near al-Hillah south of Baghdad on September 29, 2003, Polish peacekeepers had come across an ammunition depot that contained four French-made Roland air defense missiles. The crates containing the missiles were stamped "KND 2003," leading Wiatrowski to announce— erroneously, as it turned out—that the missiles had been manufactured and delivered that same year to Iraq. Photographs of the missiles and the date stamp were broadcast on television networks around the globe. French president Chirac was furious and cornered Polish prime minister Leszek Miller twice during a European summit meeting that weekend in Rome, to protest the way the Polish Defense Ministry had handled the revelation. Production of the Roland missile had ceased fifteen years earlier,

Chirac said. The last time the French government had issued a munitions license for arms shipments to Iraq was in late July 1990—just days before Saddam invaded Kuwait. "Polish soldiers confused things," Chirac told reporters covering the Rome summit. "I told . . . Miller so frankly." A French Foreign Ministry spokeswoman condescendingly told reporters that "it was unlikely that the missiles could be used seventeen to eighteen years after their delivery."

But the French denials were inaccurate and incomplete. The Roland 3, using an upgraded launcher that looks similar to those Iraq purchased in the 1980s, was still in production at the end of 2003. And the production line for the Roland 2—the model the Iraqis purchased—didn't shut down until 1993. During the 1980s, Iraq was the best customer of Roland manufacturer Euromissile, a joint venture between Aérospatiale-Matra (France) and DaimlerChrysler Aerospace, now known as MBDA. After many rounds of consolidation in the European defense industry, MBDA is now owned by BAE Systems PLC of Britain, the European Aeronautic Defence and Space Company NV (the old Euromissile partners plus much more), and Finmeccanica spA of Italy. Today the parent companies have all become partners with Boeing Co. in building America's national missile defense, the most sophisticated, complex, and expensive military program in the history of the world. Among them are the very units that built and sold the Roland to Iraq. What guarantees do we have that they will not share the secrets they have gained from working with the United States on missile defense with America's enemies around the world?

The Polish discovery was not the first time a Roland missile had been found by coalition forces in Iraq. Indeed, troops of the 101st Airborne first stumbled on Roland shelters hidden near a school in Karbala as they were advancing toward Baghdad in early April, Central Command spokesman General Vince Brooks told reporters on April 9, 2003. Many more were found at Baghdad International Airport and protecting other strategic sites. The United States believes the Iraqis succeeded in downing at least one A-10 "Warthog" ground attack jet with a French-made Roland, and possibly a F-15E Strike Eagle.[19] U.S. military sources reported that among the Rolands captured at Baghdad Airport was a charred Roland 3 launcher, complete with its radar and fire control system. The French reaction? *Impossible!*

The "KND 2003" date stamp on the missile crate found by the Poles turned out to be an inspection stamp. Similar markings were found on other missiles, which had been inspected in 2002. It remains unclear who continued to inspect the Iraqi missiles, but documents that came to light during an Italian court case suggest that French defense companies concluded fresh contracts to supply maintenance and spare parts with Iraq in 1994, in direct violation of the United Nations embargo.[20] The French government—and the companies—have denied that any parts were delivered. However, Iraqi opposition sources told me on the eve of the war that thanks to deliveries of French spare parts, Iraq's fleet of Mirage F1 fighter-bombers was flying once again, after years of being grounded because of the UN embargo.

Unlike U.S. aerospace manufacturers, which used standardized parts that could be outsourced and bid competitively, aircraft manufacturer Dassault was notorious for having designed aircraft that required Dassault-made tools and Dassault parts. Brokers for Dassault parts exist, and middlemen could have purchased parts from other countries—such as Libya—that had bought Mirage jet fighters. But if the French government had felt any concern over a spare parts conduit not under Dassault's strict control, it could have made inquiries with Dassault to determine potential sources. No such inquiries were ever made, just as the French never objected at the United Nations to a single proposed sale of dual-use technology to Saddam Hussein, despite clear evidence that some of that equipment was winding up in Iraqi weapons plants.

Coalition intelligence teams discovered extensive evidence of French treachery after the fall of Baghdad that went far beyond the well-documented love affair between Saddam Hussein and Jacques Chirac that began in 1975. Half of the remote-controlled rockets used in the attack that targeted the Rashid Hotel in Baghdad while Deputy Defense Secretary Paul Wolfowitz was visiting on October 25, 2003 (and killed a U.S. colonel and wounded seventeen others) were French and had been built to equip Iraq's French-built helicopters. According to coalition sources in Baghdad, they had been delivered to Iraq "recently."

In addition to French weaponry and remnants of equipment the French had provided by ramming extensive industrial contracts through the UN sanctions committee during the five years before the war, covert assistance and an extensive intelligence relationship were uncovered. Documents discovered in the ruins of the Iraqi Foreign Ministry and in other government buildings in late April 2003 revealed that top French diplomats were regularly briefing the Iraqi government on what they had learned about the U.S. war on terror and were providing detailed "read-outs" of closed-door UN Security Council sessions with the United States during the lead-up to the war. The French briefings "kept Saddam abreast of every development in American planning and may have helped him to prepare for war."[21]

One report, found in a file labeled "France 2001," warned the Iraqis that the Bush administration was planning to allege an Iraqi involvement with terrorism as "cover for an attack on Iraq." Another report, sent by Iraqi foreign minister Naji Sabri on September 25, 2001, to Saddam's palace, provided an extraordinarily detailed account of Chirac's private talks with President George W. Bush in Washington, D.C. Sabri wrote that his information was "based on a briefing from the French ambassador in Baghdad" and indicated that diplomats at the French embassy in Washington, D.C., were also funneling information to the Iraqis.

Suspicions ran high that the French were providing active intelligence assistance to Saddam's regime during the fighting. Bill Gertz of the *Washington Times* reported in early May 2003 that the United States believed French diplomats in Syria had provided senior Iraqi officials with European Union passports after the fall of Baghdad, allowing them to escape to Europe undetected. "It's like Raoul Wallenberg in reverse," Gertz quoted an unnamed Bush administration official as saying, a reference to the Swedish diplomat who handed out Swedish passports to Jews as they were boarding trains to escape Nazi Germany.[22] Within hours, President Chirac indignantly declared that he had done a "thorough investigation" and determined that the reports were "without foundation." When his words did not stop the presses, he instructed the French embassy in Washington, D.C., to issue a "fact sheet" claiming that France had become the target of a "disinformation campaign aimed at sullying France's image and misleading the public."[23]

The reports of missing French passports spurred an aide to Iraqi National Congress leader Ahmad Chalabi into action in Baghdad. "I grabbed a gun and two bodyguards and drove over to the French Cultural Center in Baghdad," he told me a few weeks later. He had received a tip that fresh French passports, numbered sequentially, had been stashed in the center and that they might have been of the same series as those allegedly issued to fleeing Baath Party members. "The door was locked, so we blew the lock off, only to find the caretaker inside with the keys," he said. Despite the caretaker's presence, the place had been ransacked. If once there had been passports, they were now gone. "We gave the caretaker $50 to repair the lock and left empty-handed," the aide told me.[24] Later, former DGSE officers reportedly admitted that they had issued European Union passports to Iraqi "sources" so they could leave Baghdad before it fell to U.S. forces on April 8, 2003.[25]

Among the most prominent Iraqis who fled Iraq during the final hours of Saddam's reign were Saddam's own sons, Uday and Qusay, who escaped to Syria along with Iraqi vice president Taha Yassin Ramadan. Others fled to Amman, Jordan, including Saddam's two daughters and the son of Deputy Premier (and former foreign minister) Tariq Aziz. Uday and Qusay were sent back to Iraq after Colin Powell personally pressured Syrian leader Bashar al-Assad during a trip to Damascus in June. They were ultimately killed on July 22, 2003, during a firefight with soldiers from the 101st Airborne in Mosul, a predominantly Kurdish city near the Syrian border, where they had sought refuge with Baath Party loyalists. Ramadan was also sent back and was captured peacefully. But Saddam's daughters remain in Amman, Jordan, where they have told reporters that their father was "betrayed" by his closest aides during the final days of the regime. Also on the loose and apparently still trying to do business is Ziad Tariq Aziz. I know this because a business partner of his in Paris telephoned him in front of me in October 2003 to inquire about an Iraqi front man who had done business for the previous regime.

Also coming to light, I can reveal here for the first time, was the extensive assistance the French provided to Iraq's long-range ballistic missile program. These were weapons that formed the core of Iraq's strategic strike force, which UN arms inspectors believed the Iraqis were upgrading during the 1990s so they could accommodate larger, heavier warheads consistent with the nuclear warhead design Iraqi engineers had devised.

Starting in 1996, after UN weapons inspectors had partially digested the half-million pages of documents that came to light following the defection to Jordan of Saddam's son-in-law and nephew, Lieutenant General Hussein Kamil al-Majid, the Iraqi government became more forthcoming in providing UNSCOM with details on their far-flung overseas procurement network. They did this not out of altruism, but because they knew that Hussein Kamil, who had been in charge of that network, had leaked information to the UN.

Shortly before Saddam expelled the weapons inspectors two years later, the Iraqi government provided the UN with a substantially upgraded "Full Final and Complete Disclosure" document on a set of CD-ROMs, which included for the first time detailed information on their foreign suppliers. Among them were many French companies—including the state-owned Société Nationale des Poudres et Explosifs (SNPE)—which had not been considered to be suppliers of Iraq's weapons of mass destruction programs before the Iraqi disclosure.

I was able to obtain a copy of that report through an intermediary who received it directly from Deputy Prime Minister Tariq Aziz. It included much information the French government has never admitted, since they claim to have tightly controlled the sale of nuclear and missile technologies to Iraq.

For example, a major stumbling block to building long-range solid-fuel rockets was the fuel itself. For years, Iraq had been attempting to acquire the technology to build an ammonium perchlorate (APC) production line from manufacturers in Italy and the United States. Only a handful of companies in the world made APC or had mastered the production processes of this essential—and highly volatile—ingredient for solid rocket fuel. According to the Iraqi disclosure, French state-owned explosives manufacturer SNPE submitted an offer in 1987 to build an APC plant in Iraq through Iraq's German-based procurement agency, TECO, valued at 20.5 million DM (approximately $12.5 million). The Iraqis claimed the plant was "not developed" and listed no delivery date or letter of credit. But in other cases where deals had not gone through, the Iraqis provided details, including letters of credit, meeting dates, contact persons, and other supporting information. Several cases include the notation "Did not arrive because of embargo." The Iraqis provided no further information on SNPE, which had been a major supplier of conventional explosives during the Iran-Iraq war.

Another key technology for making long-range missiles effective was the inertial navigation system (INS) that guided them to their targets. I had reported in the early 1990s that French manufacturer SAGEM had supplied INS gear to Iraq, which SAGEM vigorously denied. But Iraq's Full

Final Complete Disclosure states that Iraq invited SAGEM to send a delegation to Baghdad at the end of 1989 to discuss a major order for their missile research development center. During two meetings held in Baghdad, "the company submitted an offer for manufacturing ULISS 21 and ULISS 47 and an offer to supply ULISS 30 units"—precisely the type of INS equipment that was suitable for missile programs. The Iraqis concluded: "The aim of the discussions was to establish a factory provided with modern and sophisticated technology" to assembly SAGEM INS units. So much for those SAGEM denials.

Many of the previously undisclosed French exports were sent to the State Establishment of Electrical Industries under the cover of Project 144/54, the code name used by the Iraqis to designate the indigenous SCUD missile launchers they were building.[26]

Others were earmarked for Project 1728, Iraq's al-Hossein missile. The French government has always denied that French companies helped Iraq build the missiles that killed more than 130 Americans during the first Gulf War and terrorized Israel. But the Iraqi documents I have obtained show that French participation was extensive and consistently covered up by the French government. This is the first time this information has been made public.

Servimetal, for instance, provided a wide variety of heat-resistant brazing materials used for welding the turbo-pump impellers in the liquid fuel engine for the Iraqi SCUDs, with one contract signed less than two months before Saddam invaded Kuwait. ECM Company contracted on July 24, 1989, and again on May 20, 1990, to ship vacuum furnaces and heat treatment equipment to make the engine combustion chamber. Crylor signed up to provide special oxygen supply systems for flow-forming machines that were used to make engine parts, while Capel contracted to build an electro-chemical coating plant that would integrate much of this equipment. A plant to build special corrosive-resistant piping for the SCUD engines was to be supplied by Calorstate. UGINE contracted to provide specialty steels for corrugated engine rings.

The Iraqis also disclosed that French companies had been essential partners of their clandestine nuclear weapons program, assistance the French government has always denied that I can reveal here for the first time. Almost immediately after Israel destroyed the core of the Tammuz-I reactor near Toulon in 1980—and before the French repaired the reactor and shipped it to Iraq—the French government decided to give Iraq access to gaseous diffusion technology similar to that developed by the EURODIF consortium, so they could acquire weapons-grade fuel without having to build a reactor. "Work started in 1982 and was directed towards the understanding of the main scientific and technical aspects of the program through many studies and experiments and research," the Iraqi declaration states. Between 1985 and 1989, Iraq established twenty-two separate projects in connection with its gaseous diffusion program to enrich uranium, all located at Tuwaitha or Rashdiya.

And that was not all. In a separate effort, in 1980 the French government offered to provide AVILIS (Atomic Vapor Isotope by Laser) enrichment technology for yet another clandestine uranium enrichment program that eluded UN inspectors for years. Initially, the Iraqis turned down the French offer "because of lack of interest at the time and the high cost suggested for the program." But the Iraqis changed their mind and established a laser isotope R&D program in 1988, and planned to build a pilot AVILIS plant at the Tuwaitha nuclear research center south of Baghdad with the help of French companies. "Items ordered from France for this pilot plant were not delivered due to the sanctions imposed on Iraq in August 1990," the declaration states. But other equipment the Iraqis subsequently admitted they used for their nuclear research programs was supplied by French companies before UN sanctions went into effect. Among these suppliers, according to the Iraqi declaration, were Robatel-France, Corning-France, Thomson-CSF, Télemechanique, Alcatel, Rousselet, Europhysical Accoustic, Creusot-Loire, and Carbonne-Lorraine. CAMECA provided a special electronic microscope the Iraqis said they used in the banned nuclear programs, while Riber SA provided test and analytical equipment. Technicians from Assistance Industriel Dauphinoise commissioned some of this equipment in Iraq in 1989, the Iraqi declaration states. Iraqi defectors I interviewed in 1999 for *Reader's Digest* provided me with drawings of AVILIS equipment, which I provided to baffled IAEA analysts in Vienna, who insisted Iraq's program had been shut down in 1987—before, in fact, it had even begun. "If Iraq had an AVILIS program for ten years, I can walk on water," the head of the Iraq inspection unit told me. Here again, as in so many other areas of its WMD programs, Iraq pulled off an incredible deception scheme, right under the noses of international weapons inspectors. Had the French wanted, they could have lifted all ambiguity in this area years ago by providing a full accounting of their nuclear exports to Iraq to the UN. Instead, they chose to maintain the cover-up.

Even more astonishing was the revelation that Air Liquide, one of the world's largest suppliers of industrial gases and cryogenic fuels, had contracted on May 30, 1988, to build a production plant for liquid nitrogen that would feed the huge electromagnetic uranium enrichment plant at Tarmiyah. Known as Project 7307 (al-Amil), the Air Liquide plant went into service at the beginning of 1990 and stayed on-line until November 1991, when UN weapons inspectors finally realized its purpose. Iraq needed a steady supply of liquid nitrogen to cool the giant diffusion pumps of the enrichment accelerators and to lower the heat emissions from the plant, making it harder to detect by U.S. or Israeli satellites. (The liquid nitrogen produced at the plant could also be used in liquid rocket fuels.) Air Liquide's previously undisclosed role in Iraq's secret bomb program, never acknowledged by the French, was absolutely critical to its success.

W hen Jacques Chirac came to New York on September 23, 2003, it wasn't to issue apologies.

"No one can act alone in the name of all, and no one can accept the anarchy of a lawless society," Chirac told the opening session of the UN General Assembly. "There is no alternative to the United Nations." Although Chirac never cited anyone by name, French diplomats were quick to point out to reporters that the French president had aimed his remarks squarely at George W. Bush, who had called on the world body to strengthen international cooperation in the fight against terrorism and the proliferation of weapons of mass destruction. The "lawless society," they added, was the United States.

It was another Alice-in-Wonderland presentation from "Mr. Eighty Percent," the man who truly believed he represented the conscience and the dreams of the overwhelming majority of the world's people. CHIRAC DEFENDS THE UN AGAINST BUSH, ran the headline in the "gray lady" of French journalism, Le Monde. Here was George Bush, "the man who started a war without the UN," who had the nerve to appear in the same time slot as "three advocates of multilateralism"—Kofi Annan, Brazilian president Luis Inacio Lula da Silva, and Jacques Chirac. Cheeky indeed. Le Figaro subsequently headlined a meeting between Chirac, Russian president Putin, and German chancellor Schroeder: THE "PEACE CAMP" MEETS

RIGHT UNDER BUSH'S NOSE![27] A source close to Chirac told the paper that the French president considered Bush and his administration "the most reactionary administration" he had ever seen—*plus réac, tu meurs!* in the gutter-chic slang of Foreign Minister Villepin.

There was comic relief in the wretched reporting, such as this gem from a backgrounder in *Le Figaro:* "Not long after the election of Bush the father, Jacques Chirac was the first French leader to meet him—even before [French] President Mitterrand—during a trip to the United States in May 1989. A trip during which the former French Prime Minister [Chirac], who had just been beaten in the presidential election, met everyone who counted for anything in American society at the time: from the president of Disney, Michael Eisner, to film stars Gregory Peck, Jane Fonda, Sarah [*sic*] Fawcett and Sidney Poitier." The French, who pride themselves on their sophisticated worldview, still have a hard time seeing beyond Hollywood and Disney World.

As the months wore on and the terrorist campaign against U.S. forces and international aid agencies in Iraq intensified, some governments that once had sided with France began to grow weary of Gallic hubris. At the international donors conference in Madrid that was organized in late October 2003 to raise money for the reconstruction of Iraq after thirty years of devastation by Saddam Hussein, the French didn't even deign to send Foreign Minister Villepin, despite open criticism from the French press. "Does the level of French participation reflect the level of France's financial contribution?" one reporter asked a typically irascible Quai d'Orsay spokeswoman. "I don't see how a minister's title can define the level of financial contribution," she said, referring to the government's envoy to the conference, a junior minister for cooperation. France was "preoccupied with the reconstruction of Iraq" and planned to make a generous contribution. How generous? "You know that the European Union has already announced it would contribute 200 million Euros, and France contributes 18 percent to the EU budget."[28] Do the math: French generosity for the Iraqi people, whose dictator they had armed, aided, and abetted for a quarter century, amounted to just over $40 million—less than 1 percent of the profits the French had earned from Saddam.* And that's without counting

---

*From 1975 to 1990, French arms exports to Iraq amounted to $20 billion at a bare minimum, while the French earned another $20 billion minimum from large-scale civilian contracts.

the $100 billion they had hoped to earn from oil. The United States pledged $20 billion but had already spent much more.

At the conference itself, even French ally Belgium expressed exasperation with the French. "I find it a shame that France and Germany have stuck to their positions," said Belgian cooperation minister Marc Verwilghen. "I deplore the fact that certain countries have come here to restate their position [against the war]. Iraqis are confronted with immediate needs. Such an attitude does nothing for the Iraqi people," he said.[29]

Hoshyar Zebari, Foreign Minister of Iraq's postwar Governing Council, shamed the French—the world's lone "counter-power"—for continuing to play the spoiler's role in Iraq. In a dramatic speech before the UN Security Council on December 16, 2003, he exhorted Security Council members to stop "settling scores with the U.S.-led coalition" and to get to work at bringing real stability to Iraq. "One year ago, this Security Council was divided between those who wanted to appease Saddam Hussein and those who wanted to hold him accountable," he said. "The United Nations as an organization failed to help rescue the Iraqi people from a murderous tyranny that lasted over thirty-five years and today we are unearthing thousands of victims in horrifying testament to that failure." Instead of trying to sideline a Governing Council they could not control, as the French were trying to do, Zebari reminded the UN that the "Governing Council is the most representative and democratic governing body . . . in a region well known for its authoritarian rule."

In an underground vault beneath the French Atomic Energy Commission computer center in the Paris suburb of Bruyères-le-Chatel, a gigantic Hewlett-Packard/Compaq supercomputer hums away as French nuclear weapons designers use its 2,560 processors to simulate the extraordinarily complex events that occur in just a few millionths of a second during a nuclear blast. When it was delivered in 2001, the U.S.-built Tera machine was the fourth most powerful supercomputer in the world. (Today it ranks seventh.) Just to house the guts of the 170-rack machine requires a space that is bigger than half a football field, sixty meters by sixty meters. The French boast that the Tera machine can perform five thousand billion floating operations per second (5,000 gigaflops), boosting the computing power available to the weapons designers of the Direction des Applications Militaires one-hundred-fold.[30] Without it, the French would be unable to remain confident in the reliability and safety of their nuclear weapons arsenal without violating the Comprehensive Test Ban Treaty they signed after their final round of underground nuclear tests in 1996. That's how critical it is.

The French eventually will use Tera or machines like it to exploit data gathered from fusion experiments conducted in the $2 billion megajoule laser fusion center they are building south of Bordeaux with U.S. assistance. The giant laser, scheduled to go on-line in 2008, is modeled on the National Ignition Facility (NIF) operated at Lawrence Livermore National Laboratory in California, one of America's three nuclear weapons labs. Like the computer simulation center on the outskirts of Paris, the megajoule laser couldn't have been built without extensive help from the United States. Both projects, and much more, were the subject of a top-secret nuclear cooperation agreement the United States concluded with France on June 4, 1996. Signing for the Clinton administration were Assistant Secretary of Energy Victor Reis and Assistant Defense Secretary Harold Smith. The names of their French counterparts have remained secret to this day—as does the very existence of the agreement itself, which the French government has never acknowledged in any public document or report. But interviews with current and former U.S. officials, as well as conversations with French nuclear weapons designers in France and others who attended classified seminars in November and December 2003 at the Lawrence Livermore National Laboratory, made it clear that the 1996 pact laid the framework for a new security relationship with France that continues today, despite the rabid anti-American onslaught of President Chirac and his Napoleonic briefcase bearer, Dominique Galouzeau de Villepin.

"The French nuclear weapons program is basically the U.S. program divided by seven—like the Franc used to be to the dollar," says Victor Reis, now a Beltway security consultant. "They spend seven times less money, they have seven times fewer people, and seven times fewer weapons. But otherwise, it tracks pretty closely with our own." At the time it was signed, the Clinton administration felt the agreement was a "clear benefit for the United States," he says. "I never saw any downside to it, even today. By cooperating with France, we actually cut our costs."[31]

As part of the 1996 pact, the United States agreed to transfer to France key technologies for the National Ignition Facility, including an exotic new form of "laser glass" that forms the core of the largest laser system ever built. (The French contributed to development costs.) The NIF uses 3,072 plates of laser glass, each weighing one hundred pounds and measuring eighty centimeters long by forty-five centimeters wide and four centimeters thick. Altogether, these laser generators weigh 150 tons and, placed end to end, would extend some two miles. The 192 separate laser beams they generate race through tubes that resemble a giant erector set construction in the seven-hundred-foot-long building, gathering in strength and intensity until they simultaneously bombard a capsule of tritium or deuterium the size of a grain of rice for a fraction of a second with nearly two megajoules of energy. The tremendous impact creates a burst of nuclear fusion energy identical to the explosion of a hydrogen bomb. Designing such a facility— described to me by a senior official at Livermore as "probably the only big science being done today in the United States"—was so expensive and so complex that it is doubtful the French could have done it on their own. (Britain had planned to build a copy, but gave up after concluding that the tremendous cost was not politically acceptable.) Livermore allowed the French to test their own variants of the NIF design at an experimental facility they had set up to prove the NIF concept.[32]

Analyzing what the weapons designers call "thermonuclear burn" is key to understanding the workings of nuclear weapons. This is why the Department of Energy considers the NIF to be the cornerstone of their stockpile stewardship program, an effort launched by the Clinton administration to maintain the U.S. nuclear weapons stockpile in working order without underground nuclear tests. While some unclassified science experiments will also be performed at the NIF, it was built primarily to conduct highly classified research. Using Department of Energy supercomputers to compare experimental data obtained from the NIF against a database of over one thousand actual nuclear weapons tests, U.S. nuclear weapons scientists believe they can identify potential problems as the warheads age and correct them or, if the problem is too severe, withdraw defective weapons from the arsenal and replace them with new, reliable warheads.[33]

Under the still secret 1996 agreement, the United States also gave France access to our entire data base of nuclear weapons tests, in exchange for their own. This is just about the most sensitive and most highly classified information available to nuclear weapons designers, short of the actual weapons designs themselves. While the French obviously had built their own knowledge base with information from the 210 live nuclear tests they had carried out in northern Africa and the Pacific, their data was less extensive and less useful in managing their nuclear stockpile under a test ban, weapons designers familiar with the exchanges told me. In addition, explained Roger Baléras, former head of the French nuclear weapons program, their nuclear weapons "have not been planned for long stockpile life. Even if the lifetime of the weapon system was twenty years, we have built shorter-life nuclear weapons; then, instead of testing the old one, we have replaced it with a more modern, but not very different one."[34] The French absolutely needed to build an equivalent to the National Ignition Facility, to prevent their entire nuclear weapons arsenal from going "off-line" in less than a decade. Without ongoing U.S. assistance, the French nuclear program would grind to a halt because of prohibitive costs and technological hurdles. With it, the French can design entire new warheads without testing, should they so choose—although "live testing remains the simplest method."[35]

Not only do the U.S. supercomputers and data base give the French the ability to design and maintain their own new weapons without testing; they could export that capability or simply rent it to would be proliferators, should they chose. Just one example: Iran. It's no secret that the U.S. and France disagree over how to deal with the ruling clerics in Iran, with the French government encouraging French companies to flaunt the U.S. embargo in order to expand French exports. Is it unreasonable to worry that a day could come when France would again discover a national interest in proliferating nuclear weapons technology, as a means of "countering" U.S. power?

How will the French ultimately respond to the emergence of a new, democratic (and most likely, pro-American) Iraq? Could national interest—or spite—lead certain parties in France to quietly help Iraq's enemies to design a workable nuclear weapon by using the fancy new simulation gear and U.S. warhead data base they have now acquired? With access to these instruments, Iran could design simple, robust nuclear weapons and have 100 percent confidence that they would work—all without tipping its hand. Iran is already much closer to a nuclear capability than most people realize. Even the IAEA was forced to conclude in November 2003 that Iran had deceived the international nuclear "watchdog" agency for eighteen years by building a host of secret facilities designed to produce missile material. U.S. Undersecretary of State John Bolton and his top deputy

Steven Rademaker said the "massive and covert effort" by Iran "only makes sense as part of a bomb program." Adding to those fears were reports I first heard from former UN chief weapons inspector Ambassador Rolf Ekeus that Iran had also prohibited IAEA inspectors access to the two seismic listening stations in Iran that had been installed to monitor Iran's compliance with the Nuclear Nonproliferation Treaty. Taking such a dramatic step suggests that Iran wants to conduct some form of test, possibly a low-yield explosion of non-nuclear components of a nuclear weapon.[36] When the U.S. sought to bring Iran's NPT violations before the UN Security Council on November 20, 2003, France was among those members of the IAEA Board of Governors that objected vigorously.

Should the United States be sharing nuclear weapons secrets with a country that in many ways has declared itself an enemy? That question generated a great deal of gnashing of teeth when I asked people who are involved in the cooperation or who are advising the Department of Energy and the Pentagon on these matters. Astonishingly, their answer was almost uniformly yes. And it was based on hard facts and an assessment of just how much the French already know.

"The French are among the biggest players in the nuclear field, so it's an area where we want to have their cooperation," declared a top member of the Defense Science Board who advises Secretary of Defense Rumsfeld. "If they prove to become villainous in the nuclear business, we'd have a real problem. We want to keep them inside the tent on nuclear matters." Besides, this adviser told me, "maintaining ties with the French military is a good idea, because they are the only folks in the French decision-making process who are pro-American, apart from the business community." That was an opinion I heard on both sides of the Atlantic. However, there was less agreement on whether the United States should continue to subsidize the French nuclear program, as we are doing as a result of the 1996 agreement and by sharing the secrets of the NIF. "France should be made to pay the full cost of their nuclear weapons program," says Richard Perle.

The thought of the French returning to their earlier policy of selling nuclear weapons technology to third world dictators, practiced by Jacques Chirac as prime minister in the mid-1970s, sets off shudders—and quick denials—among U.S. officials involved in the nuclear exchanges. "If you declare France as an enemy, the consequences are great," a top official at one of our national nuclear labs told me. "This isn't the 1970s. This isn't the exact same Chirac, who is brushing up on his Arabic in order to coddle Saddam Hussein. But on the other hand, we've got a problem, and we have to be very serious about it. There are lots of things I'm sure the French would love to have, that I don't believe we would ever want to give them."

Beyond a doubt, U.S. assistance to France is helping to ensure that France remains a nuclear weapons state for the next generation. Is that something ultimately that is in the long-term U.S. interest? Beyond the knee-jerk "hate the French" reaction many Americans feel, it is a question that gives serious heartburn to U.S. government officials who are involved in day-to-day interactions with the French.

Consider this: The French are now developing a new generation of breeder reactor, far more advanced than the Osiris reactor they sold Saddam Hussein in the 1970s. They now propose to sell this technology throughout the developing world. Clearly, U.S. supercomputers and advanced lasers they acquired as part of the Clinton-era nuclear cooperation agreement that continues today are helping the French prove the concept of the new reactor design much more quickly than they could do otherwise, by avoiding the lengthy and costly trial and error of building actual prototypes and observing how they behave over time. They claim the new breeder consumes as much plutonium as it produces, because of limits they have placed on the reactor. But to some U.S. officials knowledgeable of the French plans, it sounds like they want to sell the Devil a Ferrari while claiming to limit its speed to thirty miles per hour: any third world mechanic worth his salt would have those speed locks off quicker than you could say "Kill the Jews."

And the French are not merely proposing to relaunch nuclear exports to the third world; they have also won contracts in the United States to produce a new form of reactor fuel from U.S. weapons-grade plutonium currently stockpiled at the Savannah River Plant near Aiken, South Carolina. The Department of Energy awarded the contract to COGEMA Inc., the U.S. subsidiary of the state-owned Compagnie Générale des Matières Nucléaires (COGEMA), on the basis of the French company's extensive experience in running reprocessing plants. But the Institute for Energy and Environmental Research, a Maryland-based antinuclear group, believes that COGEMA's experience is not quite as positive as the Department of Energy claims. In a report released in May 2002, the group claims that COGEMA has defied a series of lawsuits in France that allege it has repeatedly violated nuclear waste disposal laws. One French judge raided COGEMA offices in 1997 to seize documents relating to allegedly illegal waste storage at the company's main reprocessing plant at The Hague. COGEMA's behavior in the case prompted South Carolina State senator Phil P. Leventis (D-District 35) to write U.S. senator Strom Thurmond in 1999: "Do we want a company operating in our state whose culture includes defying the law?"[37] In France, Socialist member of Parliament Christian Bataille, a strong supporter of the nuclear industry and the author of France's nuclear waste law, told the center-left daily *Libération* that COGEMA behaved in a manner suggesting that it "considers itself above the law."[38] At issue was extensive legal wrangling over whether radiation levels of hundreds of millions of liters of liquid waste it had dumped into the English Channel from The Hague reprocessing plant qualified as "low-level radioactive waste" and thus required further purification before their release. The residents of the South Carolina Lowcountry and nearby Savannah, Georgia, have a clear interest in knowing whether COGEMA will be held to U.S. standards in operating the new fuel plant.[39] In addition, nonproliferation analysts worry that the MOX fuel itself could readily be broken down into its components by determined proliferators without great difficulty, thus making this ostensibly civilian fuel a ready source of bomb-grade material. "In fact, every 100 kg of MOX contains 6 kgs—one bomb's worth—of weapons usable plutonium," former deputy assistant secretary of defense Henry Sokolski tells me. "It is a simple chemical matter to get at this plutonium—far, far easier a process than reprocessing spent fuel."[40]

C an we trust the French?
   The dramatic video simulation for their battlefield management system shows how early warning radar and air defense missiles thwart an attack on a major city by incoming aircraft. The attackers bear the distinct V tail fin of the F/A-18 Hornet. That is clearly a capability that would have been of interest to Saddam Hussein. It remains of interest to many authoritarian regimes around the globe.

   The company selling this state-of-the-art equipment is ThalesRaytheon-Systems (TRS). It boasts of being the "first transatlantic joint venture between two major global defense companies." Raytheon is well-known in America as the manufacturer of the Patriot antimissile systems used with mixed success against Iraq. Thales is the successor of Thomson-CSF, the company that helped arm Saddam Hussein. The companies began working together in 1996 as a way of expanding their business into the heavily protected defense markets of their respective countries, France and the United States. In 2001, they established their joint venture, and since then they have bid successfully on major air defense and defense electronic contracts in France and the United States and at NATO. Now TRS is serving as the conduit for bringing French companies into the massive U.S. National Missile Defense (NMD) program.

"Industry is ignoring the transatlantic tensions," a senior Pentagon official who is working to attract European participation in NMD told me. "Industry's view is to make business where and how you can. Most of the leading aerospace firms now have arrangements with European companies for missile defense." Boeing has the lead on National Missile Defense and also leads in attracting the Europeans. Boeing CEO Phil Condit (who has since resigned) announced a number of cooperation agreements with European firms on missile defense during the Farnborough air show in July 2002, just as the U.S.-French tensions over Iraq were beginning to heat up. Ironically, Boeing's largest partner was the European Aeronautic Defence and Space Company, parent of Airbus Industries, Boeing's biggest rival in the civilian airliner industry and allegedly a recipient of favors from French government intelligence agents working for the DGSE.

Boeing's action was neither casual nor spontaneous: it was part of a successful strategy put in place by the White House and by Defense Secretary Donald Rumsfeld to get European governments to drop their opposition to National Missile Defense. Rumsfeld called former U.S. ambassador to Paris Evan Galbraith out of retirement and sent him to NATO headquarters in Brussels just before 9/11 as his personal representative. Galbraith's mission was to get European companies to sign on as industrial partners to NMD. His working assumption was that once the companies came on board, their governments would eventually follow.

But such cooperation, if it developed, was extremely sensitive. For instance, one deal under discussion with MBDA to sell ramjet technology from the Aster missile, "would bring the French right into the middle of the missile defense business," a U.S. official following the talks told me. Other deals were discussed at Top Secret briefings between the Pentagon's Missile Defense Agency (MDA) and French weapons designers at a series of "conferences" held far from prying eyes at Livermore, California, in November and December 2003. When I called one of the French participants, who turned out to be a top manager at the CEA's Military applications division, I asked him why a delegation of French nuclear weapons designers would travel to California to discuss missile defense with MDA, when its headquarters was located at the Pentagon in Washington, D.C. "The weather is better in California," he joked. The meetings were so close hold that neither side would divulge the names of a single participant, other than to confirm that the meetings did indeed take place. Does the United States want to depend on France for its defense in the event of a nuclear missile strike from a rogue nation? What is to keep the French from threatening to "veto" our efforts to defend our interests—this time not at the United Nations, but on American soil? Or to forbid their companies from delivering critical spare parts to us when we are at war, as the Swiss government did during the liberation of Iraq?

"France is a country that has to define itself by what it is not, rather than what it is," a former Reagan administration official who works on joint U.S.-French strategic projects suggested. "France is not the United States. And they just can't seem to get over it. It's almost a dysfunctional psychological mental state, and you wonder: Why are we doing this?"

France has always loved to play the spoiler's role. "Most of the time it has been worth the price to placate the French, to keep them from leaving their turds in the punch bowl," said one former senior U.S. official. Secretary of State Colin Powell has had to face intense criticism from his subordinates and from administration colleagues because he soft-pedaled the French during the Iraq crisis, throwing them bone after bone in hopes they would come around. "France loves the UN not out of some 'Kumbaya' one-world federalism, but because they have a veto," one administration official acknowledged. "They love the Security Council not because it can do things, but because they can keep it from doing things."

Well after the end of the war to liberate Iraq, Chirac's refusal to join the U.S.-led war effort still commanded overwhelming support from the French in public opinion polls, and Chirac continued to promote France as an "alternative" to the United States in ways that were "very dangerous," U.S. officials say. As I sat with French officials in late August 2003 in Paris going through Chirac's annual pep talk to the French diplomatic corps, they rolled their eyes with embarrassment when he exhorted his ambassadors to deploy every effort to guarantee a "multipolar" future. "There he goes again with that multipolar nonsense," one of them said. Part of the French problem, of course, was the failure of the French state-driven economy to recover as quickly as the United States from the global slowdown that followed the September 11 attacks. America bashing was convenient for Chirac, since it placated the ultranationalists of the Far Right, while satisfying the Left who voted for him against Le Pen, as he attempted to ram through economic reforms unpopular to both.

I asked Hoover Institution scholar and Nobel Prize–winning free market economist Milton Friedman if he thought the French Socialist economy could survive in a competitive international marketplace, once the United States deprived France of subsidized markets (such as Saddam Hussein's Iraq) for its goods. "Sure, but at the cost of a lower standard of living," he told me. "This is because a large part of economic resources are used for nonproductive purposes. So you have fewer workers, lower production, and a large part of their product goes to financing the welfare state."

Professor Friedman agreed that there was a direct link, as I have seen firsthand in France, between corruption and government ownership. "The essence of government ownership is that everyone is spending someone else's money. And when that happens, no one has any incentive to worry about the bottom line. So there is a lot of temptation" for officials at all levels to dip into the trough. "But in some cases, corruption can be a good thing," he said. "Take Russia under the Soviet Union, with a centrally controlled system of allocating resources. The only way anything ever got done was by corruption. It was very tempting and indeed desirable to make under-the-counter deals, to redistribute raw materials more efficiently." Anyone who has done business in France or in other tax-intensive European countries today knows just how much they depend on a "cash" economy.

In the end, Professor Friedman believes, the French will be able to maintain their corrupt Socialist system for as long as French workers accept the lower standard of living it brings with it. "Clearly if they had a free and fair market, they would have a larger income and would be better off. Who's paying for the social welfare system? It's the workers."[41]

Gerald Hillman, a political economist, investment manager, and member of the Defense Policy Board, agrees that the French insistence on maintaining the social welfare state has bred resentment that has contributed to the rupture with America. "Socialist policies make it difficult for high-tech and skilled labor to move quickly between one situation and another or to live through the boom and bust cycles of the economy," he told me. Because of the high social welfare taxes imposed on employers, high-tech companies simply go out of business when the economy goes south, "and this dampens their ability to raise new venture capital money" when the rebound begins. "That's why France's growth rate is nowhere. It's not growing new sectors or new industries. If you ask an investor, Is the talent there? he'll say yes. But if you ask him, Are you ready to invest? he'll say no—please take me to Belgium or to Poland."[42]

France is growing away from America in important ways. Our security interests no longer converge, and our economic systems increasingly appear to be at loggerheads. The French haven't understood the changes in America since September 11 or the determination and bravery of the American people in facing up to the historic challenge that has been laid on our doorstep. The French still believe they can do business as usual with dictators around the globe, without having to pay any serious price. September 11 showed Americans this was not so.

Are the historic and cultural ties that bind us together stronger than the forces that are pushing us apart? I believe they are. But without a new Tocqueville, who can succeed in interpreting the American character to the French as his ancestor did in the 1830s, the France of Jacques Chirac and Dominique Galouzeau de Villepin and what commentator Tod Lindberg calls "the overheated salons of the Parisian left"[43] risks simply becoming irrelevant. Given the French character, that could be the worst punishment of all.

# NOTES

## 1 Le Divorce

1 *United States of America v. Zacarias Moussaoui,* United States District Court, Eastern District of Virginia, December 2001.
2 Kenneth R. Timmerman, "Codes, Clues, and Confessions," *Reader's Digest,* March 2002.
3 Senior French official, interview with the author, August 27, 2003.
4 Jean-Louis Bruguière, interview with the author, August 28, 2003.
5 French Foreign Ministry official, interview with the author, August 2003.
6 Jean-Louis Bruguière, interviews with the author, October 2001; December 2001; August 2003.
7 "Moussaoui Making Use of Court-Appointed Defense Lawyers He Despises," Court TV, August 23, 2002. See www.courttv.com/trials/moussaoui/082302_ap.html.
8 Quentin Peel, Robert Graham, James Harding, and Judy Dempsey, "War in Iraq: How the Die Was Cast Before Transatlantic Diplomacy Failed," *Financial Times,* May 27, 2003.
9 Interview with a member of the U.S. delegation to the United Nations who was present at the special session, August 4, 2003.
10 "Réunion du Conseil de Sécurité au niveau ministériel sur la lutte contre le terrorism; discours et conférence de presse de M. Dominique de Villepin, ministre des affaires étrangères, 20 janvier 2003." Official transcript provided by the French Foreign Ministry.
11 Confidential source, interview with the author, October 2003.
12 Ibid., August 4, 2003.
13 Glenn Kessler and Colum Lynch, "France Vows to Block Resolution on Iraq War," *Washington Post,* January 21, 2003.
14 Fischer quote: ibid. Blix told the Security Council on January 27 that Iraq was failing to make weapons scientists available and was not providing documents he had requested.
15 Confidential sources, interviews with the author.
16 Condoleezza Rice, "Why We Know Iraq Is Lying," *New York Times,* January 23, 2003.
17 "Deputy Secretary Wolfowitz Speech on Iraq Disarmament," policy address at the Council on Foreign Relations in New York City, January 23, 2003; Department of Defense transcript. See www.defenselink.mil/news/Jan2003/t01232003_t0123cfr.html.
18 Senior French official, interview with the author, August 27, 2003.
19 Stephen F. Hayes, "Case Closed: The U.S. government's secret memo detailing cooperation between Saddam Hussein and Osama bin Laden," *Weekly Standard,* Nov. 24, 2003.
20 Mark Landler and Alan Cowell, "Powell, in Europe, Nearly Dismisses UN's Iraq Report," *New York Times,* January 26, 2003.
21 Senior French official, interview with the author, August 27, 2003.
22 Ibid., August 28, 2003.
23 U.S. diplomat, interview with the author, October 1, 2003.
24 "Pentagon Adviser Says France Only Interested in Iraqi Oil," Agence France-Presse, January 26, 2003, quoting *FOX News Sunday.*

25 "Does French Business Interest Effect UN Voting?" Fox Special Report with Brit Hume, January 23, 2003, transcript #012301cb.254.

26 "United We Stand: Eight European Leaders Are as One with President Bush," *Wall Street Journal Europe*, January 30, 2003.

27 Member of the U.S. delegation to the United Nations who was present at the special session, interview with the author, August 4, 2003.

28 Author's notes, Seminar on Iraq, organized by Benador Associates, February 4, 2003, Willard Hotel, Washington, D.C.

29 Member of the Defense Science Board, interview with the author, July 2003. Powell quote: UN Security Council transcript, S/PV.4701, February 5, 2003.

30 "Discours du ministre des affaires étrangères, M. Dominique de Villepin, lors de la r'únion du Conseil de Sécurité au niveau ministériel," February 5, 2003; official text from the French Ministry of Foreign Affairs.

31 Kenneth R. Timmerman, "What the IAEA Hasn't Found in Iraq," *Wall Street Journal Europe*, January 28, 1993; see also Timmerman, "Does Iraq Have the Bomb?" *Middle East Defense News (Mednews)* 6, no. 8 (January 25, 1993).

32 Thomas L. Friedman, "Vote France off the Island," *New York Times*, February 9, 2003.

33 Jean de Belot, "Irak: La Ligne de Paris," lead editorial, *Le Figaro*, February 10, 2003.

34 Peter Finn, "U.S.-Europe Rifts Widen over Iraq," *Washington Post*, February 11, 2003.

35 "Standing with Saddam," *Washington Post*, February 11, 2003, page A20.

36 Nicholas Kralev, "NATION 'Breaking Up' as Iraq Action Nears," *Washington Times*, February 12, 2003.

37 U.S. diplomat, interview with the author, August 4, 2003.

38 John Chalmers, "EU Candidates Endorse Latest Warning to Iraq," *Washington Times*/Reuters, February 19, 2003.

39 Ibid.

40 Senior French diplomat, interview with the author, Paris, August 2003.

41 Jean-Louis Turlin, "La France demane une nouvelle r'únion du Conseil de Sécurité le 14 mars après le rapports des inspecteurs devant le Conseil de Sécurité," *Le Figaro*, February 16, 2003.

42 Elaine Sciolino, "France's Most Vocal War Foe Proves Tireless," *New York Times*, March 9, 2003.

43 "Cheney Defends Iraq Mission," Associated Press, July 24, 2003.

44 Remarks by Richard Perle, February 13, 2003. Transcript courtesy of Benador Associates.

45 This and following quotes from Robert Kagan, "Power and Weakness," *Policy Review* 113 (June 2002), Hoover Institution, Stanford University.

46 Bernard E. Brown, "Are Americans from Mars, Europeans from Venus?," *American Foreign Policy Interests* 24 (2002): 481–89 (published by the National Council on American Foreign Policy in New York).

47 "La Longue marche ver l'armée nouvelle," *Le Figaro*, July 14, 2003; quoted by Andrew Borowiec, " 'Long March Toward a New Army,' " *Washington Times*, July 20, 2003.

48 Alain Frachon, "Paris-Washington: UN Conflit multiforme," *Le Monde*, February 26, 2003. Lellouche made this comment in a *New York Times* op-ed.

49 William Schneider, interview with the author, July 30, 2003.

50 Bistrot owner Jacques Melac, in conversation with the author, October 2003.

51 Donald Rumsfeld, interview in Munich with Charles Lambroschini, *Le Figaro*, February 10, 2003.

52 Jean-Marie Le Pen, "Vivre l'Irak, messieurs," March 31, 2003. See www.frontnational.com/lesdiscours.php?id_inter=4.

53 Jean-Pierre Chevènement, *Le Monde*, April 7, 2003.

54 Kenneth R. Timmerman, "What's Wrong with France?" *Insight* magazine, February 18, 2003.

55 Senior adviser to Foreign Minister Dominique de Villepin, interview with the author, August 27, 2003.

56 Ondine Millot and Stéphanie Platat, "Après les tensions diplomatiques sur la guerre en Ikra, les Americains ne débarquent plus en France," *Libération*, July 28, 2003.

## 2 Second Marriage

1 *New York Times Magazine,* May 12, 1968.

2 Robert S. Norris et al., *The Nuclear Weapons Databook,* vol. V: *British, French, and Chinese Nuclear Weapons,* Westview (Boulder: 1994), table 4.5, "French Nuclear Warheads, 1964–2000," p. 214. Despite the small numbers, de Gaulle ceremoniously declared the French strategic nuclear force operational in 1968.

3 Norris notes (p. 236) that qualification launches of the preproduction S2 missiles continued through March 1973, while tests of operational missiles continued until 1977. In 1971, when the missile base was declared operational, only nine warheads had been delivered to the Plateau d'Albion.

4 This was Frédéric Joliot Curie, a son-in-law of Marie Curie who adopted her name after marrying her daughter, Irène. Peter Pringle and James Spigelman, *The Nuclear Barons,* Avon Books (New York: 1981), p. 128.

5 Norris et al., *Nuclear Weapons Databook,* p. 192.

6 Charles de Gaulle, *Mémoires d'espoir,* cited in Dominique Lorentz, *Affaires atomiques,* Les Arenes (Paris, 2001), p. 88.

7 Norris et al., *Nuclear Weapons Databook,* p. 188.

8 Henry Kissinger, *Diplomacy,* Simon and Schuster (New York: 1994), p. 604.

9 Richard H. Ullman, "The Covert Connection," *Foreign Policy* 75 (Summer 1989): p. 9. Ullman says he conducted over one hundred interviews with top U.S. and French officials who were personally involved in the cooperative nuclear programs, who agreed to speak to him on background about what was arguably "the best-kept secret" in the United States or French governments.

10 Ibid., p. 10.

11 The new M20 missile was introduced in 1977 with the launch of France's fourth ballistic missile submarine, *L'Indomptable,* and was the first missile that carried a two-stage thermonuclear device, the TN60 warhead (Norris et al., p. 252).

12 Ullman, "Covert Connection," p. 11.

13 Norris et al., *Nuclear Weapons Databook,* p. 190.

14 Stanford Research Institute (SRI), Wynfred Joshua, New Perspectives in U.S.-French Nuclear Relations, partially declassified and released under the Freedom of Information Act, Research Memorandum SSC-RM-8974-2, August 1972, p. 52; quoted in Norris et al., *Nuclear Weapons Databook,* p. 190.

15 SRI report, pp. 78–79, cited in Norris et al., *Nuclear Weapons Databook,* p. 191.

16 Fred Charles Ikle, interview with the author, July 25, 2003.

17 Norris et al., *Nuclear Weapons Databook,* p. 192.

18 Department of Energy (J. D. McBridge, Office of Military Application), "International Atomic Defense Cooperation," October 27, 1978, 0–1; cited in Norris et al., *Nuclear Weapons Databook,* p. 191.

19 Norris et al., *Nuclear Weapons Databook,* pp. 192–93. The secret agreement was signed in 1978, and the first Cray 12 machine was installed in the CEA's main weapons design lab at Limeil-Valenton in August 1982.

20 Ullman, "Covert Connection," p. 11.

21 Randy Rydell, interview with the author, July 22, 2003. Rydell worked under Senator John Glenn (D-Ohio), a strong proponent of the NPT and a leading voice for tighter control on the export of nuclear technology, especially to aspiring nuclear powers and to undeclared nuclear states, such as Israel and South Africa.

22 Ullman, "Covert Connection," p. 13.

23 Ibid., p. 14.

24 General Pierre-Marie Gallois, interview with the author, March 5, 1985. The phrase "de tous azimuth's" was actually coined by General Ailleret in 1967, but has long been associated with De Gaulle.

25 Interview with former senior DOE official, July 21, 2003.

## 3 Dangerous Liaisons

1 *Le Monde*, September 9, 1975.

2 Quoted by Dominique Lorentz, *Affairs atomiques*, Les Arenes (Paris: 2001), p. 256.

3 United Nations Special Commission, Inspection Report, UNSCOM 15-Mission Inspection Report, 20 September–3 October, 1991 (unpublished; author's collection).

4 Jean-François Dubos, *Ventes d'armes: Une Politique*, Gallimard (Paris: 1974), pp. 60, 63. Published as a doctoral thesis, Dubos's study is one of the clearest expressions of French policy in the area that exists. Dubos went on to become a senior aide to Socialist defense minister Charles Hernu, who continued French arms sales to Iraq. He was later accused by the French newsweekly *L'Express* of having authorized clandestine arms sales to Iran by French defense manufacturer Luchaire in 1984–1985.

5 For instance, after an official trip to India on January 27, 1976, Chirac stopped off in Baghdad for a three-day "private" visit on his way back home, where he was Saddam's personal guest. Chirac announced to the press that he just wanted to pay his respects to his "personal friend," Saddam Hussein. But in fact, Saddam treated Chirac to all the honors of a full state reception.

6 Douglas Porch, *The French Secret Services: From the Dreyfus Affair to the Gulf War*, Farrar, Straus and Giroux (New York: 1995), p. 448.

7 Sarkis Soghanalian, interview with the author, September 15, 2003.

8 The photo, distributed by the official French Press Agency, Agence France-Presse, can be viewed on-line at www.boston.com/news/packages/iraq/globe_stories/030203_chirac.htm.

9 Senior official at the Commissariat à l'Energie Atomique, interview with the author, September 18, 1992.

10 Five-page confidential memo, Office Générale de l'Air, March 19, 1975; author's collection.

11 "Entente cordiale entre Paris et Baghdad," *Le Monde*, September 9, 1975.

12 Eric Laurent, "Depuis trente ans, l'Irak essaie de fabriquer la bombe A," *Le Figaro*, September 3, 1990.

13 Senior CEA official, comments made during my tour of the original Osiris reactor in Saclay in October 1990.

14 Senior CEA official, October 1990.

15 Kenneth R. Timmerman, "French Arms Sales Compared," *Middle East Defense News (Mednews)* 3, no. 17 (June 11, 1990).

16 André Glucksmann, *Ouest contre Ouest*, Editions Plon (Paris: 2003), p. 128.

17 Caramel: Jérome Dumoulin, "L'Irak et la bombe," *L'Express*, July 19–25, 1980.

18 I interviewed scores of French arms salesmen in Baghdad and at their homes in France between 1984 and 1993, and they told me stories such as these on strict conditions of confidentiality. The stories were too good not to share, most of them felt. But if they were ever exposed as the source, they risked their jobs and, in Baghdad, their lives.

19 Hamdani was a member of the three-man strategic planning committee in charge of secret procurement. The other two members were Saddam himself and his cousin and defense minister Adnan Khairallah. I wrote extensively about the strategic planning committee in *The Death Lobby: How the West Armed Iraq*, Houghton Mifflin (Boston: 1991).

20 Ullman, "Covert Connection," p. 21.

21 Ibid., p. 23.

22 Ibid., p. 18.

23 Ibid.

24 The Daily Diary of President Jimmy Carter, January 4, 1979; Carter Presidential Library, Plains, Georgia. Carter's movements over the next five days were tracked minute by minute in the White House logs.

25 Interview with Parviz Shahnavaz, Radio Sedaye Iran, July 16, 1998. See "In Guadeloupe, Carter Announced That Shah Must Go: VGE," Iran Press Service, October 6, 1998.

26 President Jimmy Carter, White House press conference, December 12, 1978.

27  Former French intelligence officer, interview with the author, August 14, 2003.

28  Alexandre de Marenches with Christine Ochrent, *Dans le Secret des Princes*, Editions Stock (Paris: 1986), p. 270; author's translation.

29  I tell the story of the Nogeh coup in much greater detail in *The Death Lobby: How the West Armed Iraq*, chapter 5.

## 4 Communists in the Cabinet

1  Interview with the author, January 19, 1989.

2  Kenneth Timmerman, "Iran-Iraq: La Guerre des villes. L'Armée de Baghdad ne sait pas exploiter la puissance des armements livrés par la France," *Le Monde*, March 17–18, 1985.

3  Sarkis Soghanalian, interview with the author, September 15, 2003.

4  While dismissing Richter's charges, the IAEA acknowledged that Osirak/Tammuz I would be capable of producing around ten kilograms of plutonium per year, or enough "for about one or two significant quantities [that is, weapons] a year" once production began. Cf. H. Gruemm, "Safeguards and Tammuz: Setting the Record Straight," *IAEA Bulletin* 23, no. 4 (December 1981).

5  Communication with Rabbi Abraham Cooper, associate dean, Simon Wiesenthal Center, Los Angeles. Cooper commissioned the report in May 1981. The report was conducted by Georges Amsel, Jean-Pierre Pharabod, and Raymond Sarre of the French National Research Center (CNRS) and is also mentioned in Pierre Paen, *Les Deux bombes*, Fayard (Paris: 1982), p. 172.

6  Amos Perlmutter, Michael Handel, and Uri Bar-Joseph, *Two Minutes over Baghdad*, Vallentine Mitchell & Company (London: 1982), pp. 69–70. See also Pierre Paen, *Les Deux bombes*, p. 172.

7  Eyewitness reports: See Richard Wilson, "A Visit to the Bombed Nuclear Reactor at Tuwaitha, Iraq," *Nature* 302 (March 31, 1983); precision-guided munitions: "Iraq's Nuclear Programme in Limbo," *Defence* (London), August 1985.

8  Pierre Paen, *Les Deux bombes*, pp. 88–89.

9  Captain Paul Barril, interviews with the author, 1990. Barril was former deputy commander of the GIGN commandos (the French equivalent of the Delta Force) and second in command of presidential security for Mitterrand.

10  Cheney made this statement in a speech I attended at the Israeli embassy in Washington, D.C., in late April 2001, to commemorate Israel's independence day.

11  Fred Charles Ikle, interview with the author, July 25, 2003.

12  Richard Perle, interview with the author, July 12, 2003.

13  Henri Conze, interview with the author, August 29, 2003.

14  Kenneth R. Timmerman, *La Grande fauche*, Editions Plon (Paris: 1989), chapter 5.

15  Pierre Marion, *La Mission impossible*, Calmann-Lévy (Paris: 1991), p. 36.

16  Ibid., p. 38.

17  Thierry Wolton, *Le KGB en France*, Bernard Grasset (Paris: 1986), p. 241.

18  Dr. Stephen Bryen, interview with the author, July 10, 2003.

19  Wolton, *KGB en France*, p. 249.

20  Gus W. Weiss, "Duping the Soviets: The Farewell Dossier," *Studies in Intelligence*, 39, no. 5, 1996 Central Intelligence Agency.

21  Marcel Chalet and Thierry Wolton, *Les Visiteurs de l'ombre*, Bernard Grasset (Paris: 1990). Chalet's account, told as a series of interviews with investigative reporter Thierry Wolton, traces Farewell's career before and after he agreed to spy for France. "Friendly gesture," p. 160; "Dostoievski," p. 185. A subsequent account, based on detailed interviews with Chalet's second in command, Raymond Nart, provides additional names and details. Eric Merlen and Frédéric Plonquin, *Carnets intimes de la DST*, Fayard (Paris: 2003), chapter 2.

22  Ibid., p. 174. Raymond Nart identifies "Maxime" as Major Patrick Ferrand, the French military attaché posted to Moscow since 1979. As an official intelligence officer working in Moscow, the KGB apparently considered Ferrand "too obvious" to be given the task of running an illegal agent and so never placed him under close surveillance. See Merlen and Plonquin, *Carnets intimes*, p. 33.

23 Chalet and Wolton, op. cit., p. 175.

24 Kenneth R. Timmerman, *La Grande Fauche*, chapter 2.

25 Chalet and Wolton, p. 181.

26 Merlen and Plonquin, *Carnets intimes*, p. 44.

27 I was given a copy of this 1982 report by a French official a few years later.

28 Gus Weiss, "Duping the Soviets."

29 Former senior French official, interview with the author, 2003. The French began providing documents from the Farewell file to the CIA in April or May 1981, well before Mitterrand revealed the existence of an agent-in-place to Reagan at Ottawa. In those exchanges, however, this official and former Reagan administration officials told me, the French never revealed the source of the information.

30 Chalet and Wolton, p. 185.

31 Ibid., p. 187.

32 *Soviet Acquisition of Militarily Significant Western Technology: An Update*, Washington, D.C., September 1985 (CIA white paper). One such organization used by the KGB collectors was the International Institute for Applied Systems Analysis (IIASA) in Vienna, Austria, created initially with money from the Ford Foundation to foster East-West détente. Through the 1970s and early 1980s, it was run by Djermen Gvichiani, son-in-law of Soviet president Kosygin, a KGB general and top technology collector. Among other things, Gvichiani used IIASA to tap into hundreds of aeronautics and space file servers run by Lockheed, NASA, the European Space Agency, and others.

33 Chalet and Wolton, p. 183.

## 5 Honeymoon

1 Henri Conze, interview with the author, August 29, 2003. Nixon gave a glowing account of his June 1963 lunch with de Gaulle at the Élysée Palace in *RN: The Memoirs of Richard Nixon*, Grosset and Dunlap (New York: 1978), p. 248.

2 *RN*, ibid, pp. 479–80.

3 William Schneider, interview with the author, July 30, 2003.

4 Interview with Mark Broman, colonel, United States, director of the Office of Defense Cooperation, U.S. embassy, Paris, September 30, 1982.

5 The following quotes are from my interview notes with Conze, January 21, 1983. See also Kenneth R. Timmerman, "France Committed to Nuke Weapons, a Strong Defense," *USA Today*, February 8, 1983.

6 Former senior Reagan administration official, interview with the author, 2003.

7 Peter Schweizer, *Victory: The Reagan Administration's Secret Strategy That Hastened the Collapse of the Soviet Union*, Atlantic Monthly Press (New York: 1994), p. 82.

8 Ibid., p. 83.

9 Ibid., p. 107.

10 Ibid., p. 111. George P. Shultz, *Turmoil and Triumph: My Years as Secretary of State*, Charles Scribner's Sons (New York: 1993), pp. 138–41.

11 Schweizer, *Victory*, p. 111. In a speech to the House of Commons, she responded immediately only to the June 18, 1982, decision to impose sanctions. "The question is whether one very powerful nation can prevent existing contracts being fulfilled; I think it is wrong to do that." Shultz, *Turmoil and Triumph*, p. 136.

12 Richard Perle, interview with the author, July 22, 2003.

13 According to the DST report, the twelve components of the VPK were the Ministries of Aviation (which handled civilian and military jets), Machine Building (which did projectiles and explosives), Defense Industry (armor and electro-optics), General Machine Building (strategic missiles and space), Communications Equipment, Radio (radar and large-scale computers), Medium Machine Building (nuclear weapons and high-energy lasers), Shipbuilding, Electronics, Chemicals, Electronic Equipment, and Oil.

14 Kenneth R. Timmerman, *La Grande Fauche*, op. cit., chapter 5.

15 Fred Charles Ikle, interview with the author, July 25, 2003.

16 Shultz, *Turmoil and Triumph*, p. 144. Under the deal, the United States agreed to lift sanctions on existing contracts to the pipeline, while the French agreed to examine alternative energy sources, to limit export credits to the USSR, and to stronger CoCom controls.

17 Stephen D. Bryen, interview with the author, July 10, 2003.

18 Interview with CIT-Alcatel officials J. P. Chapon, J. P. Durand, and M. Fonseca, April 13, 1989.

19 Richard Perle, "Keeping Western Technology Western," *Wall Street Journal Europe*, July 23, 1987.

20 "Soviet Ballistic Missile Defense," National Intelligence Estimate, NIE 11-13-82, October 13, 1982. Secret—declassified and released in 1996 under the CIA Historical Review Program. This and subsequent NIEs I consulted that relate to Soviet strategic weapons and missile defense are available to researchers at the National Archives in College Park, Maryland. I am grateful to retired Defense Intelligence Agency analyst William T. Lee for bringing them to my attention. Cf. Kenneth R. Timmerman, "Missile Defense Deployed in Russia," *Insight* magazine, April 30, 2001. Eventually, the United States was able to document Soviet violations of the ABM treaty (deployment of thousands of SA-5 launchers, illegal phased array radar at Krasnoyarsk, and "henhouse" battle management radar). This added to President Reagan's growing conviction that he had a duty to the American people to launch the Strategic Defense Initiative.

21 Romulo Fajardo, "Mass Peace Rallies Across the Country," *Daily World*, June 15, 1982. Cited in Kenneth R. Timmerman, *Shakedown: Exposing the Real Jesse Jackson*, Regnery (Washington, D.C.: 2002), p. 140.

22 Shultz, *Turmoil and Triumph*, p. 349.

23 "Discours prononcé par M. François Mitterrand, président de la République Française, devant le Bundestag à l'occasion du 20ème anniversaire du Traité franco—allemand de coopération, Bonn, jeudi 20 janvier 1983," official text as released by the Élysée Palace.

24 Kenneth R. Timmerman, "French Split on American Missile Protests," *Atlanta Journal-Constitution*, October 30, 1983, p. 41-A.

25 Richard Perle, interview with the author, July 12, 2003.

26 In his 1980 political manifesto, *Ici et maintenant*, Fayard (Paris: 1980), Mitterrand wrote: "I admit that the Pershings are unbearable [insupportable] for the Russians. I am still waiting for the Russians—and for the leaders of the French Communist Party—to understand that the SS-20s are unbearable for France." (p. 235)

27 The NSA intercepted a message from Iranian intelligence in Tehran to their embassy in Damascus four weeks before the bombing, ordering them to attack the Marines. The existence of that intercept only became public twenty years later. Cf. Kenneth R. Timmerman, "An Invitation to September 11," *Insight* magazine, January 6, 2004.

28 Ullman, "Covert Connection," pp. 22–23.

29 Brigadier Keith Crosser, interview with the author, June 27, 1985.

30 U.S. diplomat, interview with the author, November 1984.

31 Colonel Mark Broman, interview with the author, March 1984. Ford confirmed the story in a separate interview.

32 "We realized we couldn't sell a purely French system to the United States," Fernand Grange, the RITA program manager at Thomson-CSF told me at the time. "It's better to get part of something than 100 percent of nothing."

33 Cf. Kenneth R. Timmerman, "France Wants to Swap Phones for AWACS," *Atlanta Journal-Constitution*, December 23, 1984, the biggest ticket Boeing purchased from France was CFM-56 jet engines produced by a U.S.-French consortium for AWACS, KC135 tankers, and other aircraft in the U.S. fleet.

## 6  Bonanza in the Gulf

1 Samir al-Khalil, *Republic of Fear*, p. 17.

2 According to former French counterespionage director Yves Bonnet, Madame Chevènement was an Egyptian Jewess. Yves Bonnet, *De Qui se moquent-ils?*, Flammarion (Paris: 2001), p. 309.

3 Vibrachoc paid François Mitterrand 293,000 francs in unspecified "fees" from 1972 to 1980 and paid Gilbert Mitterrand, his son, 579,429.92 francs between 1981 and 1989, the year of Pelat's death. Jean Montaldo, *Mitterrand et les 40 voleurs . . .*, Albin Michel (Paris: 1994), pp. 220–21. French intelligence officials told me in interviews of the Vibrachoc commission on the Exocet deals in Iraq in the late 1980s.

4 Richard Murphy, interview with the author, March 7, 1991. But Iraq's support was raised in a "private" meeting between Secretary of State George Shultz and Tariq Aziz in Paris on May 10, 1983, as I reported in *The Death Lobby*. Shultz told Aziz that if Iraq wanted to improve relations with the United States, it could start by getting rid of Abu Nidal. Before the end of that year, Baghdad complied, paving the way for the resumption of diplomatic ties in early 1984.

5 Fred Charles Ikle, interview with the author, July 25, 2003. For all of the rumors to the contrary, the Reagan administration never approved U.S. arms sales to Saddam, although it facilitated the transfer of weapons-production gear and provided billions of dollars in agricultural credits, which the Iraqis used to purchase dual-use equipment worldwide. See chapter 8.

6 Confidential sources.

7 Henri Conze, interview with the author, August 29, 2003.

8 Jacques Attali, *Verbatim I*, Fayard/Livres de Poche (Paris: 1993), p. 779. The Mirage arrived in Baghdad on October 8, 1983.

9 Henri Conze, interview with the author, August 29, 2003.

10 Department of State cable E.O. 12356, dated December 21, 1983, from Donald Rumsfeld to Secretary of State George Shultz via U.S. Embassy/London. "I made clear that our efforts to assist [in mediating an end to the 1980–1988 Iran-Iraq war] were inhibited by certain things that made it difficult for us, citing the use of chemical weapons, possible escalation in the Gulf, and human rights," Rumsfeld wrote in his reporting cable.

11 *Global Spread of Chemical and Biological Weapons*, hearings before the Committee on Governmental Affairs and Its Permanent Subcommittee on Investigations, United States Senate, May 2, 1989, pp. 166–67.

12 According to a 1982 agreement, renewed yearly through 1986, Iraq sold France 122,000 bpd, of which 80,000 bpd, worth slightly more than $5.2 billion, went for arms.

13 Stephen D. Bryen, interview with the author, July 10, 2003.

14 The troop withdrawal agreement negotiated by Cheysson was signed on September 17, 1984. Cf. Kenneth R. Timmerman, "Mitterrand's Dealings with Khadafy Create Uproar," *Atlanta Journal-Constitution*, November 25, 1984.

15 Dumas was the lead attorney representing Colonel Dakhil Moufta and the Libyan Central Military Agency in Paris, in a complaint filed on November 26, 1977, against arms broker Georges Starckmann for night-vision devices known as "startrons."

16 Henri Martre, interview with the author, December 1984.

17 The French Aerospace Industry Association, GIFAS, released the following figures in 1988 for military sales as a percentage of total aerospace exports: 1980: 74 percent; 1981: 67 percent; 1982: 60 percent; 1983: 68 percent; 1984: 64 percent; 1985: 63 percent; 1986: 64 percent; 1987: 51 percent. Source: Groupement des Industries Françaises Aéronautiques et Spatiales, Conférence de Presse du Président, Paris, February 24, 1988; author's collection.

18 Interviews with Daniel Burroni, July 16, 1989, and October 23, 1989.

19 The former Libyan mole went on to become a Socialist member of Parliament. My calls to his office asking for comment on this story in 1989 were never returned.

20 Jacques Attali, *Verbatim II*, Fayard/Livres de Poche (Paris: 1995), p. 57.

21 Jacques Attali, *Verbatim*, Fayard/Livres de Poche (Paris): vol. I, covering the years 1981–1986, appeared in 1993; vol. II, covering 1986–1988, appeared in 1995; vol. III, covering 1988–1991, appeared in 1996; hereafter, *Verbatim I, Verbatim II, Verbatim III*.

22 Attali, *Verbatim II*, p. 26.

23 Ibid., p. 27.

24 Ibid., pp. 29–30.

25  Ibid., p. 35.

26  Ibid., p. 25.

27  Abu Iyad, *Palestinien sans Patrie,* Fayolle (Paris: 1978), p. 163.

28  "Imad Mugniyah: The Real Story," *Middle East Defense News (Mednews)* 1, no. 15 (May 2, 1988).
     For more on Mugniyah, see Kenneth R. Timmerman, "Likely Mastermind of Tower Attacks,"
     *Insight* magazine, December 31, 2001.

29  Attali, *Verbatim II,* p. 38.

30  Ibid., p. 56.

31  Ibid., pp. 58–59.

32  Caspar Weinberger, *Fighting for Peace,* Warner Books (New York: 1990), p. 192.

33  Shultz, *Turmoil and Triumph,* p. 684.

34  Ibid., p. 63.

35  April 24, 1986, *Heure de vérité;* cited in Attali, *Verbatim II,* p. 70.

## 7  Techno-tensions

 1  Michel Lopoukhine, interviews with the author, April and May 1989.

 2  For a complete biography, see *Le Monde,* April 23, 1988.

 3  "Des fraiseuses françaises auraient servi à la fabrication de MiG," *Le Monde,* August 27, 1988,
     and author's sources. A French Foreign Ministry source told me in April 1989 that the Soviets
     were seeking to return the machines because a subsequent French government embargo on in-
     stallation, maintenance, and spare parts had rendered them "unusable."

 4  Lopoukhine scoffed at the technology transfer agreement he had signed with the Soviets in June
     1987. "Only the Russians would buy machines like that," he said. "If one head broke, nine oth-
     ers stopped working."

 5  French Foreign Ministry official, interview with the author, October 1987.

 6  Nungesser gave the award on October 6, 1986, as president of the Franco-Soviet Chamber of
     Commerce.

 7  Ministry of Foreign Affairs official, interview with the author, 1989.

 8  General Bernard Retat (Director of Foreign Military Sales, Délégation Générale pour l'Arme-
     ment), interview with the author, June 1988.

 9  Montaldo, *Mitterrand et les 40 voleurs . . . ,* pp. 180–98.

10  François d'Aubert, interview with the author, November 28, 1991.

11  Jacques Attali, *Verbatim II,* p. 487.

12  Fred Charles Ikle, interview with the author, July 25, 2003.

13  Jacques Attali, *Verbatim II,* p. 462.

14  Ibid., p. 470. Chirac's call to Mitterrand took place on September 5, 1987.

15  "Russian Pilot and Navigator Shot Down by French over Chad," *Middle East Defense News
     (Mednews)* 1, no. 1 (September 28, 1987).

16  Habré's troops captured an extensive arsenal of Soviet weapons from the Libyans that fall. In
     addition to SA-13 missiles and launchers, they appropriated 125 T-55/T-62 tanks, 10 Lohr/
     Oshkosh tank transporters, 39 BM-21 Katyusha rocket launchers, and 12 complete batteries of
     SA-6 air defense missiles. (Source: "Chad Expects New Libyan Attack," *Middle East Defense
     News [Mednews]* 1, no. 5 [November 30, 1987].)

17  General Pierre-Marie Gallois, interview with the author, March 1988.

18  Stephen Bryen, interview with the author, July 10, 2003. Bryen told me virtually the same thing
     at the time of Mitterrand's trip to Moscow.

19  Accompanying Mitterrand were Foreign Minister Roland Dumas, Finance Minister Pierre Béré-
     govoy, Industry Minister Roger Fauroux, Agricultural Minister Henri Nallet, Minister for PTT,
     Communications, and Space Paul Quilès, Foreign Trade Minister Jean-Marie Rausch, and a
     handful of presidential advisers. Also accompanying him were longtime confidant Edgar
     Pisani; Roland Nungesser, president of the Franco-Soviet Chamber of Commerce; Jacques Ral-
     lite, former Communist Party minister of health; Frederic d'Allest, president of Arianespace

and a director of the French National Space Agency, CNES; Nicolas Beypout, publisher of the economic daily *Les Echoes;* building trade and television magnate Francis Bouygues; fashion designer Pierre Cardin; Michel Doumeng, president of Interagra and son of the late "Red Baron," Jean-Baptiste Doumeng, the French answer to Armand Hammer; Jean Gandois, president of aluminum giant Pechiney; Jean-Yves Abraire, president of Crédit Lyonnais; Jean-Claude Leny, director of the French nuclear energy monopoly, Framatome; Jean-Louis Lyons, president of the CNES; and Michel Pecquer, president of Elf Aquitaine.

20 Quoted in *The Soviet Space Challenge,* Department of Defense, Washington, D.C., November 1987.

21 Document made available to the author by French government sources, 1988.

## 8 Gulf War One

1 French defense industry executive, interview with the author, April 1989. Fadel Khaddum became a director of the Iraqi-owned, Britain-based Matrix Churchill, which supplied many of the machine tools the Iraqis used to manufacture chemical weapons and equipment for their clandestine nuclear weapons program. He was also a key interlocutor for BNL Atlanta. See "The BNL Blunder: A Mednews Special Report," *Middle East Defense News (Mednews)* 4, no. 7 (January 7, 1991).

2 Gerald Bull, who was assassinated just one year after the Baghdad arms fair, presumably by an Israeli hit team, had set up shop at the stand of Astra Holdings, a British financial group that had just bought out the Belgian munitions maker PRB.

3 British export control records, which became part of the Scott Inquiry into British exports to Iraq and were turned over to the United Nations arms inspection effort, UNSCOM, showed that between 1987 and 1989, the British government approved the sale to Iraq by Matrix Churchill of 176 advanced machine tools. All 176 machine tools went into Iraqi weapons plants, many of which were manufacturing equipment for Iraq's clandestine nuclear weapons program. There were no records I am aware of that show how many Matrix Churchill machines the Iraqis managed to assemble in Iraq.

4 William Schneider, interview with the author, July 31, 2003.

5 French assistance to the Iraqi missile program was indirect and handled through a cooperation agreement with Brazil. In early 1987 the Iraqis shipped half a dozen SCUD-Bs to Brazil, where they were stripped apart in special hangars off the military airstrip at São José dos Campos by Iraqi and Brazilian engineers, under the watchful eyes of a team of French missile experts. Together they came up with the solution that extended the range from 300 km to roughly 800 km, bringing Tehran—and later Israel—into range (*The Death Lobby,* pp. 247–49). The actual transformation of the SCUD-Bs into al-Hussein missiles was done in Iraq.

6 I had written extensively about the Iraqi missile programs at the time of the "war of the cities" in February 1988, explaining how Iraq had cut up three SCUDs, then welded them back together to build two al-Husseins. My account, which appeared in French defense magazines and elsewhere, was greeted with skepticism by military "experts," who insisted that what the Iraqis claimed to have done was impossible. But it was duly noted in Baghdad and, according to this engineer, had been made required reading by Amir Rashid al-Ubaydi. His suggestion about the cryogenic fuel was probably just a boast, although the Saab-Scania launch vehicles the Iraqis displayed for the al-Hussein were large enough to contain the necessary refrigeration equipment. UN inspectors later found a liquid nitrogen plant at al-Amil, but it was believed to be dedicated to the nearby Tarmiyah uranium enrichment plant, which needed liquid nitrogen to cool its electromagnetic isotope separation devices, known as calutrons. (See chapter 13 for more.)

7 I am grateful to Associated Press bureau chief Harry Dunphy and my colleagues at the Anglo-American Press Association, who personally met with three government ministers to protest the actions of Defense Minister Pierre Joxe against me. Thanks to their efforts, my accreditation was restored. Without accreditation, I could not continue to work as a legitimate journalist in France. It is an old cliché but a true one, that the only difference between a journalist and a spy is that the journalist makes public all that he finds.

8  "Thomson-CSF White Paper in Support of Non-Intervention by the Committee on Foreign Investment in the United States in the Thomson-CSF/LTV Missiles Division Acquisition."

9  Thomson never contacted my publishers—either in France or in the United States—asking them for corrections. Nor had they contacted editors at *Le Monde,* or the French defense magazines where I first wrote about Thomson's Iraq contracts starting in 1985, demanding corrections.

10  See also "Thomson-CSF and the Iraqi electronics industry," *Middle East Defense News (Mednews),* 4, no. 10 (February 18, 1991). Thomson-CSF was a paying subscriber to my newsletter, but never called to protest or question that article or indeed, any other article that reported on their business in Iraq. The Thomson-CSF White Paper insists that "Thomson-CSF was never involved in the development or construction of the AWACS prototype. Thomson-CSF did provide the ground-based Tiger-G radar, which even *The Death Lobby* concedes was never designed for use in an AWACS-like format." Indeed, part of the inventiveness of the Iraqis was to adapt weapons—often, with stunning success—to missions for which they had not been designed, such as their frequent marrying of Soviet and French systems.

11  Thomson-CSF also claimed that they had "never dealt with Banca Nazionale del Levoro in Atlanta, contrary to *The Death Lobby.*" In the hundreds of BNL letters of credit I obtained from the House Banking Committee, which was investigating the BNL scandal in 1991 and 1992, I found that Thomson-CSF had received three payments from BNL Atlanta, totaling over $5.5 million, for unspecified "electronic components." In the BNL gray books, they were logged for payment on April 19, June 27, and July 17, 1989.

12  Of that amount, $491 million involved a sale of GM trucks (that never materialized) by a company called Gateway International.

13  Richard Murphy, interview with the author, March 7, 1991.

14  "Chevènement to Baghdad," *Middle East Defense News (Mednews)* 3, no. 9 (February 19, 1990).

15  Senior French Finance Ministry official, interview with the author, February 16, 1990.

16  Jacques Attali, *Verbatim III,* p. 692.

17  Ibid., pp. 705–10.

18  Ibid., p. 724.

19  Ibid., p. 895.

20  "Desert Storm Total Coalition Combat Losses by Cause," from Eliot A. Cohen et al., *Gulf War Air Power Survey* vol. V, U.S. Government Printing Office, 1993, p. 641. The United States alone flew more than sixty thousand combat sorties (p. 651). Tables of U.S. air power from vol. I, p. 35.

## 9  Spies and Bribes

1  Peter Schweizer, *Friendly Spies,* Atlantic Monthly Press (New York: 1993), pp. 120–21.

2  "Newsmakers," *Los Angeles Times,* June 6, 1991, p. E1.

3  "Corporate Spying May Not Be for Us," *Washington Post,* June 27, 1993, p. C-2.

4  Schweizer, *Friendly Spies,* p. 99.

5  "Air France Denies Spying on Travelers," *International Herald Tribune,* September 14–15, 1991.

6  William M. Carley, "A Chip Comes in from the Cold: Tales of High-Tech Spying," *Wall Street Journal,* January 19, 1995, p. A-13.

7  Schweizer, *Friendly Spies,* p. 115.

8  Silberzahn interview: Vincent Jauvert, "Espionnage: Nos succès et nos échecs," *Nouvel Observateur* no. 1586 (March 30, 1995).

9  Vincent Jauvert, "Quand nos espions font la guerre economique," *Nouvel Observateur* no. 1635 (March 7, 1996).

10  *Brief of Texas Instruments in Bull CP8 v. Texas Instruments Inc.,* U.S. District Court for the Northern District of Texas, Dallas Division, civil action no. 3:93-CV-2517T, cited in John Fialka, *War by Other Means,* W. W. Norton & Co (New York: 1997), p. 94.

11  James Adams, "France Steps Up Spying on Both Friends and Foes," *Sunday Times* (London), April 5, 1992.

12 "The Mitterrand Plan," *Middle East Defense News (Mednews)* 4, no. 18 (June 10, 1991). Boucheron subsequently fled France for Brazil, when he was sought by a French judge on corruption charges.

13 "Arms Control for the Middle East: Words, or Deeds?" *Middle East Defense News (Mednews)* 4, no. 18 (June 10, 1991).

14 Cited in Vincent Jauvert, "Les Espions VRP de la CIA," *Nouvel Observateur*, December 12, 1995, p. 30. Taiwan went on to purchase *both* the American and the French planes.

15 Fialka, *War by Other Means*, p. 95.

16 Ibid., p. 95. Original source: "Current and Projected National Security Threats to the United States and Its Interests Abroad," Senate Select Intelligence Committee hearing, January 25, 1994, p. 81.

17 Ibid., p. 97. Original sources: Woolsey, "The Future of Intelligence on the Global Frontier," speech to the Executive Club of Chicago, November 19, 1993; and "Current and Projected National Security Threats to the United States and Its Interests Abroad," testimony before the Senate Select Committee on Intelligence, January 25, 1994, p. 21.

18 R. James Woolsey, conversation with the author, July 2003. I refer to Woolsey's op-ed on economic espionage, "Why We Spy on Our Allies," below.

19 A copy of the draft contract, which a French source gave to me two months before it was announced, broke down the contract as follows: 388 main battle tanks, two driver-training tanks, forty-six recovery vehicles (virtually identical to the tanks), 400,000 1,200-mm tank rounds, including depleted uranium armor penetrators, third-echelon maintenance workshops, two years of training, technical assistance, and 142 simulators, for a total of 21.6 billion francs. Cf. "France to Sell Leclerc to UAE," *Middle East Defense News (Mednews)* 6, no. 6 (December 12, 1992).

20 Pierre Chiquet, interview with the author, Abu Dhabi, February 14, 1993.

21 "French Tanks to UAE," *Middle East Defense News (Mednews)* 6, nos. 10–11 (March 1, 1993).

22 Pierre Chiquet, *La Gabegie*, Albin Michel (Paris: 1997), p. 103.

23 Colonel Pierre Lethier later wrote a memoir about the secret payoffs and his involvement in the oil for arms networks. Cf. Pierre Lethier, *Argent secret: L'Espion dans l'affaire Elf parle*, Albin Michel (Paris: 2001).

24 Chiquet, *La Gabegie*, p. 111.

25 "La France suspend ses livraisons de chars aux Emirats Arabes Unis," *Le Monde*, January 19, 2001.

26 Jacques Isnard, "La Cour des comptes épingle le coût du char Leclerc," *Le Monde*, October 27, 2001; Chiquet's claim appears on p. 59 of his book, cited earlier.

27 Francois-Xavier Verschave, *Noir Chirac*, Les Arenes (Paris: 2002), p. 145. Concluded under the Socialists, the tank deal was not signed until the center-right government of Édouard Balladur came to power in March 1993. From numerous judicial investigations, including the high-profile failed prosecution of former Socialist foreign minister Roland Dumas for allegedly taking illegal payments from state-owned oil company Elf Aquitaine, it became clear that major export contracts included payments to political parties on the Left and the Right.

28 Chiquet, *La Gabegie*, p. 119.

29 R. James Woolsey, "Why We Spy on Our Allies," *Wall Street Journal*, March 17, 2000.

30 Greve's story, accompanied with lists of the U.S. companies that were targeted, appeared in Knight Ridder newspapers such as the *Miami Herald* on April 18, 1993. The entire document was reproduced in the *Congressional Record*, April 28, 1993, pp. H2105–2107.

31 Jauvert, "Espionnage: Nos succès et nos échecs."

32 Senior French defense official, conversation with the author, June 1993. My interviews with French and U.S. aerospace executives and government officials at the 1993 Paris air show were conducted as part of a staff delegation from the House Committee on Foreign Affairs and remain confidential.

33 Jauvert, "Les Espions VRP de la CIA."

34 William Drozdiak, "French Resent U.S. Coups in New Espionage," *Washington Post*, February 26, 1995.
35 Cited in Jauvert, "Les Espions VRP de la CIA."
36 Cited in Jauvert, "Espionnage: Nos succès et nos échecs."
37 William Drozdiak, "Resentment over U.S.-French Spy Flap Could Last Years," *Washington Post*, March 7, 1995.

## 10  Old Lovers

1 William Drozdiak, *Washington Post*, January 24, 1994.
2 Rolf Ekeus, interview with the author, November 1, 1995. I spoke to Ekeus repeatedly, almost from the day he was appointed in 1991 until he left UNSCOM in 1998. I also spoke and exchanged information with countless senior members of his staff as well as biological, chemical, and missile specialists detailed to UNSCOM by Security Council member states, including France. In most instances, they asked to remain anonymous in the stories I wrote based on their information.
3 In 1991 alone, the Security Council passed three separate resolutions with specific requirements concerning Iraq's weapons establishments: 687 (the cease-fire resolution of April 3, 1991, establishing UNSCOM) required the total destruction of Iraq's weapons of mass destruction; 707 (August 15, 1991) required Iraq provide a "full, final, and complete disclosure" of its weapons capabilities, including suppliers; 715 (October 11, 1991) established long-term monitoring of Iraq's industrial establishments with the view of prohibiting the manufacture of WMD components.
4 These 603 machines, cataloged during IAEA inspection 11 and IAEA 12, were only part of the story. In my own scouring of export licensing records in Britain, Germany, Italy, and the United States, I found that approximately two thousand machine tools had been sold to Iraq by those countries in the 1980s. Because export controls on machine tools were being relaxed at the same time, and because certain governments were seeking to expand their machine-tool exports to Iraq by decontrolling items that normally would have been controlled, it was impossible to estimate how many more machine tools were actually delivered to Iraq without individually validated licenses. The U.S. Department of Commerce licensed only a handful of machine tools; much production equipment was shipped without licenses, such as thirty-foot-long boring machines intended for making long-range artillery tubes. Of the 603 nuclear-relevant machine tools found in Iraq, the IAEA database showed that 502 were not licensed by exporting authorities. In the case of Great Britain, 49 of the 83 machine tools found by the IAEA were subject to export licensing restrictions. However, British export licensing records, made available to Parliament as part of its inquiry into British arms sales to Iraq, and which I incorporated into my databases, revealed that the Department of Trade and Industry had licensed 313 machine tools to Iraq from 1987 to 1989—and, by all accounts, only a fraction of what was actually shipped. By the most conservative estimate, therefore, at least 264 British tools were never found by the UN inspectors. It is unlikely they were destroyed by allied bombings during the first Gulf War, since Hussein Kamil ordered factory directors to evacuate production equipment, computers, records, and materials two months before the bombings began. U.S. spy satellites photographed this activity only days before the air war began, but the underground storage sites never became high-priority targets during the war.
5 Rolf Ekeus, author's notes. I included this quote from Ekeus in an extensive report I wrote in March 1993 at the request of the House Foreign Affairs Committee. Cf. *Iraq Rebuilds Its Military Industries*, staff report for the Subcommittee on International Security, International Organizations, and Human Rights of the House Foreign Affairs Committee; U.S. Government Printing Office, October 1993.
6 *Iraq Rebuilds Its Military Industries.*
7 In a similar case that became public, U.S. and Saudi officials boarded a German-registered ship on December 28, 1993, as it steamed past a Saudi port en route to Beirut. On board they seized

two containers full of ammonium perchlorate, an essential ingredient for solid rocket fuel. Although the ostensible destination for the chemical was Lebanon, my sources at the UN Special Commission were convinced the final destination had always been Iraq. They said that an analysis of the Chinese-origin chemicals showed that "the grain size was suitable for ballistic missiles, such as those Iraq had been making before the Gulf War and has pledged not to make anymore."

8 Cf. *The Death Lobby,* pp. 286–87. I was given copies of many of these letters by House Banking Committee investigators.

9 *Al-Sharq al-Awsat,* editions of October 19 and 24, 1994.

10 For instance, on July 2, 1993, the governor of Iraq's Central Bank, Tariq Tukmaji, was in Paris for two days of talks with the Balladur government, accompanied by Foreign Ministry undersecretary Riyadh al-Qaysi.

11 General Jeannou Lacaze, interview with the author, February 18, 1994.

12 "Oil Talks Begin in Paris," Baghdad Republic of Iraq Radio, March 5, 1994; Foreign Broadcast Information Service, Near East-South Asia, April 28, 1994.

13 Senior State Department official, interview with the author, May 1994. I specifically asked about French rumors that Occidental Petroleum, Boeing, ITT, and Chevron were talking with the Iraqis. "We have heard those rumors and put the question to the companies directly," this official stated. All four responded that they had no ongoing contacts with Iraq. Nevertheless, he added, the State Department "officially discouraged them from all commercial contacts."

14 Senior French government official, interview with the author, August 28, 2003.

15 Reuters, June 18, 1994.

16 Ibid., June 21, 1994.

17 Richard Perle, interview with the author, July 12, 2003.

18 Gerald Hillman, interviews with the author, July 22 and November 24, 2003.

19 Senior Kuwaiti official, interview with the author, May 12, 1994.

20 Hoshyar Zebari, interview with the author, May 13, 1994.

21 Reuters, October 28, 1994.

22 Marie-Bénédicte Allaire and Philippe Goulliaud, *L'Incroyable septennat: Jacques Chirac à l'Élysée, 1995–2002,* Fayard (Paris: 2002), p. 60, note 3; Eric Halphen, *Sept ans de solitude,* Denoel-Folio (Paris 2002) pp. 135–140.

23 Ibid., p. 39.

24 Richard L. Garwin, vice chairman of the Federation of American Scientists, Christopher E. Paine, senior research associate at the Natural Resources Defense Council, and Ray E. Kidder, senior consultant at the Lawrence Livermore National Laboratory, "A Report on Discussions Regarding the Need for Nuclear Test Explosions to Maintain French Nuclear Weapons Under a Comprehensive Test Ban," trip report, Paris, November 2–7, 1994 (published by the Federation of American Scientists and the Natural Resources Defense Council, Washington, D.C., January 1995). Garwin, Kidder, and Paine spoke to the head of nuclear weapons development at the CEA, his predecessor, President Mitterrand's top military aide, as well as political leaders involved in nuclear weapons planning, who were virtually unanimous in recommending the new series of tests.

25 Confidential source, November 1995.

26 Iraq's "Full Final and Complete Disclosure" to the United Nations Special Commission; originally drafted in 1996, revised in 1998. Gary Pitts, a lawyer for veterans afflicted with Gulf War syndrome, obtained the FFCD from Iraq in the fall of 2002 and agreed to share parts of it, including the supplier lists, with the author.

27 Joshua Muravchik, "Unfair and Unbalanced," *Weekly Standard,* September 22, 2003. Muravchik expanded this article into a well-documented monograph, *Covering the Intifada: How the Media Reported the Palestinian Uprising,* Washington Institute for Near East Policy (Washington, D.C.: 2003).

28 Allaire and Goulliaud, *L'Incroyable septennat,* p. 215.

29 Interview with the author, 1986. Delamare was assassinated in April 1981; the Ezbekhieh car bomb went off two months later, when Pierre Marion was head of the DGSE, then known as SDECE.

30 Former Israeli government minister, interview with the author, Jerusalem, October 2002.

31 Allaire and Goulliaud, *L'Incroyable septennat*, pp. 215, 219. This exchange was widely reported by the French Press Agency and other French media at the time.

32 Cited by Allaire and Goulliaud, *L'Incroyable septennat*, p. 221.

33 "France-Iran: The Eurodif Agreement," *Middle East Defense News (Mednews)* 5, no. 7 (January 6, 1992); "Iran-Contra Killing in Switzerland?," *Middle East Defense News (Mednews)* 6, no. 5 (December 7, 1992).

34 Cf. "Iran Threat Spurs UAE Procurement," Iran Brief, Serial 0506, April 3, 1995.

35 Senior UAE official, interview with the author, Abu Dhabi, March 1995.

36 "U.S. Vows to Enforce Iran Sanctions on Total Deal," Reuters, September 29, 1997.

37 Kenneth R. Timmerman, "U.S. Inches Toward Iran," WorldNetDaily.com, September 21, 2000. This was one segment of a seven-part series I wrote on the secret Clinton administration back channel toward Iran for the Western Journalism Center, which appeared in installments on wnd.com.

## 11 The Lady Is a Whore

1 U.S. official, interview with the author, October 1, 2003. See also Allaire and Goulliaud, *L'Incroyable septennat*, p. 17; Franz-Olivier Giesbert, *Jacques Chirac*, Le Seuil paperback (Paris: 1987), p. 67.

2 Giesbert, p. 23.

3 Verschave, *Noir Chirac*, p. 90.

4 Giesbert, p. 26.

5 Pierre-Marie Gallois, *Le Sablier du siècle: L'Age d'homme* (Paris: 1999), cited in Verschave, *Noir Chirac*, p. 92. Marcel Bloch and his wife, Madeleine, abandoned Judaism after the war and were baptized as Roman Catholics.

6 Philippe Madelin, *Les Gaullistes et l'argent: Un Demi-siècle de guerres intestines*, L'Archipel (Paris: 2001), p. 121.

7 Giesbert, p. 61.

8 Verschave, p. 98.

9 Henri Deligny, *Chirac ou la fringale du pouvoir*, Alain Moreau (Paris: 1977), pp. 41–42; cited in Verschave, *Noir Chirac*, p. 98.

10 Verschave, *Noir Chirac*, pp. 105–06.

11 Cf. Montaldo, *Mitterrand et les 40 voleurs . . .*, pp. 252–53.

12 Arnaud Montebourg, *La machine à trahir*, Editions Denoel (Paris: 2002), pp. 85–86; Allaire and Goulliaud, *L'Incroyable septennat*, pp. 57–60.

13 In the fall of 1997, Juppé's former 1,520-square-foot duplex apartment was put on sale by the city of Paris and was bought at auction by Socialist partisan Alain Gomez, the head of Thomson-CSF, for 7.1 million francs (around $1.3 million). Gomez was subsequently outbid by an unknown party, who purchased the apartment for 7.8 million francs. Cf. Allaire and Goulliaud, *L'Incroyable septennat*, p. 60, note 2.

14 Allaire and Goulliaud, *L'Incroyable septennat*. The blitzkrieg comment appears on p. 247, "Nero" on p. 558.

15 Christine Deviers-Joncour, *La putain de la République*, Calmann Levy (Paris: 1998).

16 Ibid., p. 129.

17 Loïk Le Floch-Prigent, *Affair Elf: Affaire d'État*, Editions Cherche-Midi/Folio (Paris: 2001), p. 26.

18 Montebourg, *La machine à trahir*, p. 266. Arnaud Montebourg, interview with the author, October 1, 2003.

19 Julian Corman and Edith Coron, "If the shoe fits . . . ," *The European*, March 16, 1998, p. 8.

20 Hervé Liffran, "Monsieur le maire avait un sacré coffre," *Le Canard Enchaîné*, July 18, 2001 (cited in Verschave, *Noir Chirac*, p. 125).

21 Cited in Montebourg, *La machine à trahir*, p. 23.

22 Montebourg mentions several examples by name, including the case of Alain Juppé, where the

chief of staff of Justice Minister Jacques Toubon, Alexandre Benmakhlouf, "demanded that the prosecutor in charge of the Central Directorate for the Prevention of Corruption not hand in his report." (p. 91) Every year, Montebourg writes, "the 122 prosecutors of France or their substitutes take 753,000 decisions to set aside prosecution for crimes where the authors are well-known. Most of these decisions are never justified, and rarely is the plaintiff or the informant notified. The power to prosecute or not, in other words, to ensure impunity or the application of the law in the same conditions for each citizen of the Republic is exercised beyond appeal and without control." (p. 90)

23  Montebourg, *La machine à trahir*, p. 103.

24  Ibid., p. 79.

25  Arnaud Montebourg, interview with the author, October 1, 2003.

26  Europe 1, May 17, 1998; cited in Allaire and Goulliaud, *L'Incroyable septennat*, p. 343.

27  Allaire and Goulliaud, *L'Incroyable septennat*, p. 342.

28  Montebourg, *La machine à trahir*, pp. 268–69.

29  Allaire and Goulliaud, *L'Incroyable septennat*, p. 341. The language and legal argument Dumas would use in his January 22, 1999, decision were virtually identical to an October 1995 brief, prepared at the request of pro-Chirac justice minister Jacques Toubon, on the possibility of legal action against a sitting president.

30  Montebourg, *La machine à trahir*, p. 269.

31  Thierry Bréhier, *Le Monde*, January 26, 1999; cited in Montebourg, *La machine à trahir*, p. 270.

32  Interview with RTL radio, June 18, 2002.

33  Arnaud Montebourg, interview with the author, October 1, 2003.

34  Dana Priest, "Bombing by Committee; France Balked at NATO Targets," *Washington Post*, September 20, 1999, p. A1.

35  Allaire and Goulliaud, *L'Incroyable septennat*, p. 417.

36  Ibid.

37  Jean Guisnel, *Le Point*, July 9, 1999.

38  ITAR-TASS, May 13, 1999.

39  Alain Madelin, interview with the author, September 17, 2003.

40  Ben Barber, "Congo's Ousted Leader Accuses France of Encouraging Coup," *Washington Times*, October 7, 1998.

41  "Cassette Méry," transcript appearing in *Le Monde*, September 21, 2000.

42  "I remember that Mr. Chirac had just taken over as Prime Minister of the first cohabitation," Méry says on the tape. "I personally took the money to the office of Mr. Michel Roussin, chief of staff of the Prime Minister. The Prime Minister sat down in front of me . . . That day, I put five million francs in cash directly onto the desk of Mr. Roussin in the presence of Mr. Chirac." Ibid.

43  Allaire and Goulliaud, *L'Incroyable septennat*, p. 519.

44  "J-C Méry: Les Secrets du compte Farco," *Le Monde*, September 22, 2000.

45  Chirac used a French colloquialism during his May 2, 2001, interview with reporters—*plus réac, tu meurs*—that became a refrain French officials liked to repeat whenever they referred to the Bush administration. A "French adviser"—possibly Villepin—used similar terms to dismiss Bush's address to the UN General Assembly on September 23, 2003 (Anne Fulda, "Avec les Bush, une complicité perdue," *Le Figaro*, September 24, 2003, p. 3). The French couldn't understand why the U.S. president raised the issue of female sexual slavery instead of endorsing a French proposal to "transform" the United Nations.

46  Allaire and Goulliaud, *L'Incroyable septennat*, pp. 620–22.

47  Ibid., pp. 631–33.

48  *Le Figaro*, October 25, 2001, quoted in Allaire and Goulliaud, *L'Incroyable septennat*, p. 633.

49  Senior Israeli diplomat, interview with the author, June 13, 2002. I reported on the rise of a "new" anti-Semitism in France and elsewhere in Europe in *Preachers of Hate: Islam and the War on America*, chap. 9.

50 Combined with the 2.35 percent of National Front dissident Bruno Megret, Le Pen's movement won 19.1 percent of the vote—nearly as much as Chirac.

51 Thierry Keller, interview with the author, July 10, 2002.

52 Allaire and Goulliaud, *L'Incroyable septennat*, p. 702, citing Chirac's address to an April 23, 2002, election rally in Rennes.

## 12  Saving Saddam

1 Ann Clwyd, interview with the author, August 2, 2003. The documents she refers to were revealed in Alex Spillius and Andrew Sparrow, "French Helped Iraq to Stifle Dissent," *Daily Telegraph*, April 28, 2003. The description of them below is drawn from the *Daily Telegraph* account and independent translations of the Arabic-language documents they published on their Web sites.

2 "It happens that the president knows [Maugein] well, because he also comes from Corrèze," Dominique de Villepin told investigative reporter Jean Montaldo in 1998, when Villepin was still Chirac's chief of staff at the Élysée. Cf. Jean Montaldo, *Les voyous de la République*, Albin Michel/Pocket Books (Paris: 2001), p. 218. Maugein's name first surfaced in conjunction with the mining story in Nicolas Beau, "Un Homme d'affaires en or dans l'ombre de Chirac," *Le Canard Enchaîné*, February 18, 1998. The Maugein quote is from minutes of a July 2, 1997, meeting in which Maugein took part reproduced in Montaldo, p. 322.

3 Alan Crossley, interview with the author, November 25, 2003. Crossley answered my questions at Maugein's request.

4 Joseph Fitchett, "French Connection: Power, Politics and Gold," *International Herald Tribune*, March 2, 2001.

5 Le Floch-Prigent, *Affaire Elf: Affaire d'État*, p. 208. Le Floch-Prigent says it was "only logical that the risk [Auchi] took be remunerated" by the increased price. Elf could not buy the refinery directly at first because of European regulations on monopolies.

6 Ibid., pp. 213–14.

7 "Iraq Oil Rush Looms as France Seeks End to Embargo," Reuters, January 14, 1999; The Elf and Total deals figure separately on a list compiled by the vice president's Energy Task Force, "Foreign Suitors for Iraqi Oilfield Contracts," dated March 5, 2001, that was obtained by Judicial Watch through its Freedom of Information Act lawsuit against the White House.

8 Beau, "Un Homme d'affaires en or dans l'ombre de Chirac."

9 Carola Hoyos, "Oil Smugglers Keep Cash Flowing Back to Saddam," *Financial Times*, January 16, 2002.

10 David Nissman, "Iraqi Oil Smuggling Examined," Iraq report, Radio Free Europe/Radio Liberty, November 2, 2001.

11 Alix M. Freedman and Steve Stecklow, "Illegal Surcharges Let Saddam Profit from Oil-for-Food," *Wall Street Journal*, May 2, 2002, p. A1.

12 Hoyos, "Oil Smugglers Keep Cash Flowing Back to Saddam."

13 Alix M. Freedman and Steve Stecklow, "The Oil 'Top-Off': Another Way Iraq Cheats U.N.," *Wall Street Journal*, May 2, 2002, p. A10.

14 Nissman, "Iraqi Oil Smuggling Examined." Actually, Chiladakis had "walked in" to the U.S. embassy in Athens in late September.

15 Freedman and Stecklow, "Illegal Surcharges Let Saddam Profit from Oil-for-Food."

16 Report by Ambassador Kuchinsky under UNSC Resolution 661, dated December 31, 2001, UN Security Council document S/2001/1341.

17 Patrick Clawson, interview with the author, February 12, 2003.

18 United Nations Office of the Iraq Program, Weekly Update, January 15, 2002. Iraq's oil revenue since December 10, 1996, when the oil-for-food program officially got under way, was broken down into U.S. dollar and Euro accounts, $38.6 billion and 13.6 billion Euros (then worth $11.8 billion), for combined exports of 2.85 billion barrels of oil.

19 Documents in the author's possession.

20 I exposed this issue in greater detail in "Rogues Lending a Hand to Saddam," *Insight* magazine, February 8, 2002.

21 Export official, Irrifrance, interview with the author, September 11, 2002.

22 Elias Firzli, interview with the author, October 8, 2003.

23 Perle made those comments at a conference on Iraq in Washington, D.C., sponsored by Benador Associates on February 4, 2003.

24 Alain Madelin, interview with the author, September 17, 2003.

25 French Foreign Ministry official, August 27, 2003.

## 13 The Quest for Glory

1 Marie-Laure Germon, "Gilles Kepel: 'Washington aura besoin de l'expertise française,' " *Le Figaro*, August 27, 2003, p. 12. Some of Kepel's thoughts betrayed a deeper prejudice. The "greater part of their knowledge [of the region] today comes either from the Israelis or the Turks," he said. Later, he opined that the United States made a great error in "conducting an offensive that minimized collateral damage, in itself a good thing, because the United States did not appear as the feared victor in the eyes of the Iraqi population."

2 Patrick Jarreau, "Enquête sur les faucons de Bush," *Le Monde*, October 3, 2002.

3 See Michael Gonzales, "Lest We Forget," *Wall Street Journal Europe*, April 10, 2003, p. A10.

4 Quai d'Orsay, "Réponses du porte-parole aux questions du point de presse," April 25, 2003.

5 Interview with the author, July 30, 2003.

6 Karen DeYoung and Vernon Loeb, "Still Angry over War, Pentagon Limits Contacts with France," *Washington Post*, May 22, 2003, p. A29.

7 "How the Evian Summit Turned Water into Words," Reuters, June 3, 2003.

8 Joseph Curl, "Bush Sets Pace on Terrorism, AIDS," *Washington Times*, June 2, 2003, p. A1.

9 André Glucksmann, *Ouest contre ouest*, Editions Plon (Paris: 2003), p. 154. Glucksmann takes the Chechnya anecdote from *Newsweek*, October 14, 2002.

10 Ibid., p. 22.

11 Administration official, interview with the author, October 1, 2003.

12 Arnaud Montebourg, interview with the author, October 1, 2003.

13 Guy Millière, "A New Muslim Country," FrontPageMagazine.com, May 12, 2003.

14 Jamie Glazov, "The Death of France," a FrontPageMagazine.com symposium with Guy Millière, Alain Madelin, Jean-François Revel, and others, Frontpagemag.com, June 9, 2003. My thanks to Michael Gonzales, editorial page editor of *The Wall Street Journal Europe*, for pointing out this particular aspect of the French-Iraq nexis to me. See his excellent article, "Five Million Reasons France Opposed the War," *Wall Street Journal Europe*, July 2, 2003.

15 François d'Aubert, interview with the author, October 1, 2003.

16 Dominique de Villepin, *Le Cri de la gargouille*, Albin Michel (Paris: 2002), p. 9.

17 Anne-Elisabeth Moutet, conversation with the author, October 25, 2003.

18 Anton La Guardia, "Villepin Refuses to Say Which Side He Supports," *Daily Telegraph*, March 28, 2003, and Philip Delves Brought and David Rennie, "Indignant French Deny Opposing a U.S. Victory," *Daily Telegraph*, March 29, 2003.

19 Charles R. Smith, "No U.S. Military Jets at Paris Air Show," *Newsmax*, April 30, 2003.

20 Cf. Stephen Grey, "Banker Who Hid Saddam's Millions," *Sunday Times—Insight*, April 13, 2003.

21 "Dossier Reveals France Briefed Iraq on U.S. Plans," *Sunday Times* (London), April 28, 2003.

22 Bill Gertz, "France Gave Passports to Help Iraqis Escape," *Washington Times*, May 6, 2003.

23 "Letter from Jean-David Levitte, Ambassador of France to the U.S., to the Congressmen, Administration Officials and Media Representatives," May 15, 2003, distributed by the French embassy in Washington, D.C.

24 Aide to Ahmad Chalabi, interview with the author, June 12, 2003.

25 Private communication with the author.

26  Suppliers included Francelco, which delivered "special connectors" for the launcher, in the first half of 1989 and the first half of 1990 that the Iraqis claimed were destroyed by UN arms inspectors with the launchers in mid 1991, and Carbone Lorraine, which sold 900 blocks of carbon black. Iraq declared it intended to use them to make "missile graphite vanes." That particular contract was made via Avions Marcel Dassault (AMD Co.) in Amman, Jordan, the Iraqi declaration states, during the second half of 1990.

27  Luc de Barochez, *Le Figaro*, September 25, 2003.

28  "Irak/Conference de Madrid," French Foreign Ministry spokesman, daily press briefing, October 21 and 23, 2003.

29  "France Criticizes U.S. Iraq Plan," *Washington Times*, October 25, 2003.

30  "Simuler le fonctionnement d'une arme nucléaire," briefing document prepared by the French Atomic Energy Agency, *Les Défis du CEA*, June–August 2003, p. 4.

31  Victor Reis, interview with the author, Nov. 13, 2003.

32  LLNL press release, August 1, 1998: "Beamlet Laser to Leave Livermore Lab for New Life at Sandia Lab." See www.llnl.gov/llnl/06news/NewsReleases/1998/NR-98-08-01.html.

33  For more information, as well as a technical overview of the processes involved in building the gigantic lasers of the NIF, see National Ignition Facility Fact Sheet, Lawrence Livermore National Laboratory. See www.llnl.gov/nif.

34  R. L. Garwin, R. E. Kidder, and C. E. Paine, "A Report on Discussions Regarding the Need for Nuclear Test Explosions to Maintain French Nuclear Weapons Under a Comprehensive Test Ban," Federation of American Scientists/Natural Resources Defense Council, Washington, D.C., January 1994, p. 14.

35  Senior CEA official, *Direction des applications militaires*, interview with the author, Dec. 12, 2003.

36  Ambassador Rolf Ekeus, communication with the author, Nov. 17, 2003.

37  Letter from S.C. State senator Phil P. Leventis to U.S. senator Strom Thurmond, November 4, 1999, made available to the author by Arjun Makhijani of IEER.

38  Matthiew Ecoiffier, "La Mise en examen de la Cogema, un juge dans l'antre du nucléaire," *Libération*, July 13, 1999.

39  Annie Makhijani, Linda Gunter, and Arjun Makhijani, "COGEMA: Above the Law?" Report available from the Institute for Energy and Environmental Research or on-line at www.ieer.org.

40  Henry Sokolski, communication with the author, November 17, 2003. Sokolski directs the Nonproliferation Policy Education Center. Much of his work is available at www.npec-web.org.

41  Professor Milton Friedman, interview with the author, July 24, 2003.

42  Gerald Hillman, interview with the author, July 22, 2003.

43  Tod Lindberg, "C'est la vie: The Future of U.S.-French Relations," *Washington Times*, December 16, 2003.

# ACKNOWLEDGMENTS

T his book could not have been written without the assistance of many old
friends and trusted sources I have come to know from more than twenty
years of reporting on France and the Middle East. In many cases, as I have
indicated in the endnotes, I was a personal witness to the historical events
I have described. In these instances, I have used my original notes and,
where possible, re-interviewed the participants. For added context, I also
have turned to published memoirs of key players such as George Schultz,
Henry Kissinger, Richard Nixon, Pierre Marion, and Jacques Attali, the un-
tiring diarist of the Mitterrand presidency.

Special thanks goes to John Haydon at the *Washington Times*, who has
responded tirelessly to my requests for research materials; to my brother,
William A. Timmerman, for his encyclopedic knowledge of French history,
and with whom I have an ongoing debate over the underlying forces behind the French Revolution of 1789; to Gary Pitts, a lawyer for veterans afflicted with Gulf War syndrome, who obtained Iraq's Full Final Complete
Disclosure of its WMD programs to the United Nations and agreed to
share parts of it; to Ambassador Rolf Ekeus, the former Executive Chairman of the UN Special Commission for the Disarmament of Iraq
(UNSCOM) and to several of his former associates at the International
Atomic Energy Agency (IAEA) in Vienna, including Michael Kelly, David
Kay, and Maurizio Zifferero, for allowing me to probe their memories and
insights into Iraq's weapons programs; to Ronald Lehman, director of the
Center for Global Security Research at Lawrence Livermore National Nuclear Laboratory, whose excellent conference, Atoms for Peace After 50
Years, provided insight into the whole question of nuclear cooperation between the United States and France. Many current and former lab officials,
some of whom were directly engaged in the nuclear cooperation effort
with France, agreed to share their impressions and experiences with me, on

condition I not attribute specific comments to them by name. Thanks also to Craig Wuest and Bob Hirschfield at Livermore, who explained the arcana of laser glass, growing giant crystals, and confined inertial fusion to me as we walked through the National Ignition Facility, surely one of the most breathtaking achievements of modern science.

In Paris, I received assistance from Henri Conze, Thérèse Delpech, François d'Aubert, Elias Firzli, and Judge Jean-Louis Bruguière that goes way beyond the comments attributed to them in the book. A special nod goes to Marie Masdupuy of the French Foreign Ministry's press service, who put up with my questions and helped set up background interviews with senior officials; and to Georges LeGuelte, the CEA official who first took me on a guided tour of the original Osiris nuclear research reactor at Saclay, France, in 1990.

Of the scores of French defense contractors I have spoken to over the years about Iraq, few stand out as vividly as Hugues de l'Estoile and his equally brilliant nephew, Olivier de l'Estoile, both of whom worked for Dassault. But others also regularly shared information and insight, including Patrick Mercillon, Francis Gigot, Jean-Louis Espès, Gen. Paul Baujard and Jean-Claude Salvinien at Aérospatiale; Gen. Bernard Rétat, Yves Robbin, Christine Mougin and Gen. Pierre Pacalon at Dassault; the since deceased Paul Tannous, Jean Legeay, Roland Sanguinetti, and Frédéric Aragon at Matra; Daniel Thuillier, François Baudouin, and Gen. Georges Béreste of GIAT; Monique Navarra, Col. Jacques Masson-Regnault, and Jean-Claude Sompeyrac of SOFRESA; Daniel Jolivet and Yves Cuénnot at TRT; Jean-Pierre Ruland, Gen. Patrick Henin, Gen. Pierre Audigier, Alain Niox-Chateau, Patrick Sandouly, Christophe Robin, Dominique Lamoureux, René Anastaze and Serge de Klebnikoff of Thomson-CSF; Raymond Bartczak, of Acmat; and Juan Carlos Dubois of the Spanish aerospace conglomerate, CASA. Many of you I can name here for the first time, now that the tyrant—or at least his regime—is dead.

Many officials currently serving in the Defense Intelligence Agency, the White House, the Department of Defense, and the State Department—both in the United States and abroad—provided candid assessments of U.S.–French relations on the condition they not be named. Former officials who helped my research or provided guidance, including Allan Gerson, Rich Williamson, Fred Charles Ikle, Richard Perle, Stephen Bryen, Victor Reis, and William Schneider. Gerald Hillman and Prof. Milton Friedman were both generous of their time in explaining how an inefficient Socialist economy can continue to compete in an open, fair marketplace (short answer: it can't).

In London, Stephen Grey of the *Sunday Times* was kind enough to share some of the banking documents his team of investigators turned up, as did Jules Kroll, whose investigation into Saddam's hidden billions in the early 1990s first took the wraps over the elaborate financial support system propping up the Iraqi dictator. In Madrid, Alan Crossley gave generously of his time so I could put French–Iraqi oil deals in better context. Maurice Botbol, publisher of *Intelligence Newsletter*, helped me navigate the shoals of the French corruption scandals. And special thanks to the friends and neighbors with whom I debated many of the points in this book.

Finally, I am honored to call Dr. Ahmad Chalabi a friend of many years, as are many of his colleagues on the Iraqi Governing Council. When you were in opposition, you risked your lives so Iraq could be free; today, you are on the way to realizing that dream. I wish you God's speed.

KENNETH R. TIMMERMAN
Hjortsberg Gård, Ste. Maxime,
Washington, D.C.

# INDEX

# ABOUT THE AUTHOR

KENNETH R. TIMMERMAN, an investigative reporter who lived in France for almost two decades, is the author of the *New York Times* bestseller *Shakedown: Exposing the Real Jesse Jackson, The Death Lobby: How the West Armed Iraq,* and *Preachers of Hate: Islam and the War on America.* He has written for *Time, Newsweek,* the *Wall Street Journal, Insight* magazine, and *Reader's Digest.*